Freudian Fadeout

# Freudian Fadeout

*The Failings of Psychoanalysis in Film Criticism*

ARIJ OUWENEEL

McFarland & Company, Inc., Publishers
*Jefferson, North Carolina, and London*

LIBRARY OF CONGRESS CATALOGUING-IN-PUBLICATION DATA

Ouweneel, Arij, 1957–
　　Freudian fadeout : the failings of psychoanalysis in film criticism / by Arij Ouweneel.
　　　　p.　　cm.
　　Includes bibliographical references and index.

　　**ISBN 978-0-7864-6893-5**
　　softcover : acid free paper ∞

　　1. Film criticism.　2. Psychoanalysis.　3. Motion pictures — Psychological aspects.　I. Title.
PN1995.O89　2012
791.4301'9 — dc23　　　　　　　　　　　　2012009402

BRITISH LIBRARY CATALOGUING DATA ARE AVAILABLE

© 2012 Arij Ouweneel. All rights reserved

*No part of this book may be reproduced or transmitted in any form or by any means, electronic or mechanical, including photocopying or recording, or by any information storage and retrieval system, without permission in writing from the publisher.*

On the cover: Natalie Portman in *Black Swan*, 2010 (Fox Searchlight Pictures/Photofest); background © 2012 Shutterstock

Manufactured in the United States of America

*McFarland & Company, Inc., Publishers*
　*Box 611, Jefferson, North Carolina 28640*
　　*www.mcfarlandpub.com*

# Table of Contents

*Preface*   1

*Introduction: Into the Deep*   7

1. Bertie's Stammer   29
   Hysteria in *The King's Speech* (2010);
   Tom Hooper (director), David Seidler (writer)

2. Agnostic Bella   52
   The Deep in *The Rite* (2011) and *The Twilight Saga: New Moon* (2009); Mikael Håfström (director), Michael Petroni (writer); and Chris Weitz (director), Melissa Rosenberg (writer)

3. Carol's Predicament   80
   The Body in *[SAFE]* (1995) and *Jennifer's Body* (2009); Todd Haynes (writer and director); and Karyn Kusama (director), Diablo Cody (writer)

4. Alex's Decision   104
   Gender Choice in *XXY* (2007) and *Chloe* (2009); Lucía Puenzo (writer and director); and Atom Egoyan (director), Erin C. Wilson (writer)

5. Wendy's Advice   125
   Nightmares in *Mysterious Skin* (2004) and *Dioses* (2008); Gregg Araki (writer and director); and Josué Méndez (writer and director)

6. Clementine's Whisper  151
Consciousness in *Eternal Sunshine of the Spotless Mind* (2004) and *Drama* (2010); Michel Gondry (director), Charlie Kaufman (writer); and Matías Lira (writer and director)

7. Melinda's Silence  175
Conceptual Metaphor in *Speak* (2004) and *Cosas insignificantes* (2008); Jessica Sharzer (writer and director); and Andrea Martínez (writer and director)

8. Nina's Double  197
The Illusion in *Black Swan* (2010) and *The Virgin Suicides* (1999); Darren Aronofsky (director), Mark Heyman, Andrés Heinz, and John McLaughlin (writers); and Sofia Coppola (writer and director)

Afterword
Out of the Deep  226

*Chapter Notes*  241
*Bibliography*  261
*Index*  285

*I've read some news in scientific magazines that targeted memories can be wiped out ... on mice. I wonder if mice experience painful break-ups? So far, technology has only succeeded in making us forget everything ... except the things we don't want to remember.*

— Michel Gondry,
director of *Eternal Sunshine
of the Spotless Mind* (2004)


*"Do you dream often?"*
*"Sometimes," replied the colonel, ashamed of having fallen asleep. "Almost always I dream that I'm getting tangled up in spider webs."*
*"I have nightmares every night," the woman said. "Now I've got it in my head to find out who those unknown people are whom one meets in one's dreams."*
*She plugged in the fan. "Last week a woman appeared at the head of my bed," she said. "I managed to ask her who she was and she replied, 'I am the woman who died in this room twelve years ago.'"*
*"But the house was built barely two years ago," the colonel said.*
*"That's right," the woman said. "That means that even the dead make mistakes."*

— Gabriel García Márquez,
*No One Writes to the Colonel*, New York 1968,
translation of *El coronel no tiene quién le escriba*
(1961) by J.S. Bernstein, p. 44.

# *Preface*

In film studies, and perhaps in cultural studies in general, two main theoretical currents seem to be in debate: cognitive sciences versus psychoanalysis. This book lines up with cognitive science by arguing what is wrong with specific psychoanalytical concepts in comparison to cognitive concepts. Studying film and film criticism over the past few years, I found that psychoanalysis was still taken too seriously as another partner in debate. From cognitive science I learned about simulation theory, which means that narratives "learned" from films could work in human minds as simulations for finding solutions to particular problems. Fiction, says Keith Oatley, is the mind's flight simulator.[1] If these simulations would include psychoanalysis, we are obviously on the wrong track. Evolutionary and cognitive science inspired critics argue for a different way of film critique — and perhaps of "narrative critique" in general. The topic of narrative simulation in the mind is new in cultural studies and also in film studies. The book asks for more research into this field. The discussion is based on the criticism of a small corpus of recent feature films from North and South America.

The idea of the mind's flight simulator is not difficult to grasp. Gaining insights into the human condition requires what literary scientists and cognitive psychologists call mindreading. This is the ability to interpret behavior of others in terms of their assumed states of mind. The system that invokes our mindreading ability is not only active in real life, but also when reading fiction or watching fiction television and feature films. The system makes use of the so-called mirror neurons in our brain. It does so constantly, even when seeing photographs of abstract figures. In general the information obtained is not forgotten but checked for usefulness by the brain and then stored as memory. The brain can use the information at any moment rather freely, for instance to run simulations about situations that seem at hand, or to get a grip on complex realities. Economists, meteorologists, or linguists do exactly the same. Sometimes, in fantasizing about events and situations, or dreaming about them, the simulations can be useful as exercises of future behavior and a test of the emotions involved. For convenience of comparison, the simulations work with a limited number of variables. Complexities can be more conveniently arranged this way. Perhaps we should regard all our thinking as simulative, because we seem to run simulations in the split seconds before behavior is set in motion. For that reason, scholars argue, we build up as many simulations we can in order to be prepared for "correct" behavior. Apart from real life experiences, this includes stories we tell each other about real life experiences of others and fiction. As simulations, fictions serve us well because they are not direct copies of reality and condense complex information — regarding interactions between multiple autonomous and intentional agents — without substantial discarding of key elements, while simultaneously revealing the principal underlying chords of the social world. The social reality is ineffably too complicated and too detailed to do otherwise. Therefore, we need to regard narrative worlds as such simulations of social behavior.

On leaving the cinema, any moviegoer will recognize the experience of having been transported to the narrative world of the film. In general, human beings share openness to the image screened, a readiness to interpret the life of others, even from the past or the future, and the ability to observe, to conjecture, to experience, and to be carried away with emotions. In giving substance to the psychological lives of characters, the moviegoer must use his or her own experiences. These are encoded in what we call *mental schemas,* to bridge gaps in narratives, including facts and emotions to bear on them. On the basis of such acquired mental schemas and personal temperament, the moviegoer uses the space provided by these individual differences to form various interpretations of performances. One of the main products of such performances is an inference to bridge gaps of various sizes in the narratives. Because we continually draw inferences and exhibit participatory responses in everyday life, we may look at our reality as constructed as much as any narrative world. Knowledge outside the narrative is often critical to the adequate construction of a so-called narrative world. Whenever we attend a movie, we are actively supplementing the narrative. The narrative psychologist Richard Gerrig writes that although we cannot see her lower torso, "we are quite willing to infer that Mona Lisa has legs."[2] Even when we interact with what seems to be a complete photograph or film, we show a systematic bias toward expanding its boundaries and toward imagining a continuation outside the diegesis, our mind hard at work filling in around the edges. This filling in includes the psychology of the characters in the movie.

The mental schemas for doing so may come from any source, but seem to be dominated by popular psychology, which provides answers — right or wrong — about motivations of family members, friends, lovers, colleagues, and strangers. It gives us tools to seemingly understand romantic relations, friendships, memory lapses, emotional outbursts, performances, and the like. As a theory, popular psychology leads us to interpret the common senses, intuitions, and first impressions. Nevertheless, it is a mythological theory, *psychomythology*. It helps us to fit the experiences into a story we understand and preferably also like to hear. Simulations of social worlds through abstraction, simplification, and compression is not only to simulate varieties of behavior but also to prepare us to better understand situations we encounter. The abstractions serve to disconnect them from specific circumstances or persons. Stories from real life or fiction include a timeline, characters, and a stage. These are the "variables" of our simulations. Fiction is perhaps as important as non-fiction, for as the title of an article by Raymond Mar and Keith Oatley runs: "The Function of Fiction Is the Abstraction and Simulation of Social Experience."[3]

Starting with a key scene from *The Killer Inside Me* (2010), the introduction discusses key points for reading the book, including the so-called Freudian Excuse Trope and the nurture assumption, as articulated to folk psychology and simulation theory. Freud made use of a series of ideas and beliefs from European popular psychology. It is a vicious circle, because thanks to its early 20th-century popularity in the United States and Europe, Western popular culture has adopted a series of Freudian beliefs in turn. We need to understand Freudian psychomythology as originating in the Romantic mind. In Western culture, psychoanalysis has guided popular psychology for almost a century, but is on the retreat now. Better equipped with proven results and theories that work, cognitive and evolutionary psychology has driven psychoanalysis out of the spotlight. In fact, the Freudian Edifice is already in ruins. Serious psychology and psychiatry ceased working with Freudian concepts like neuroses, repression, regression, or the Oedipus Complex in the 1980s, when all psychoanalytical concepts were deleted from the most important psychiatry manuals. New theories explain the ensemble of emotions and behavior much better. Only in some humanities in the academic world, including literary studies, history, anthropology, and cultural and film studies, do scholars and critics still have faith in Sigmund Freud's writings. They believe that his work, and that of his followers, including Jacques Lacan (1901–81), the "French Freud," is unavoidable in gaining insights into the human condition. Many authors of criticism published in magazines and newspapers share this view. Nevertheless, cognitive and neuropsychology are rapidly winning territory. They are triumphant in their own fields, where hardly anyone refers to Freud or his followers at all, but also in the more popular sectors victory seems at hand. This means that by now, and increasingly, many scholars in cultural and film studies, the literary sciences, history, and anthropology are lagging behind. This book serves to indicate why this is the case, by showing how the Freudian Excuse is used in films or film studies — including reviews — and why this is not in line with insights into the human condition.

The interest of this book lies in the anchoring of the films in Freudian psychomythology, in order to argue that it is *avoidable* in gaining insights into the human condition — perhaps that it should be avoided. I will treat the films under study as possible simulations of a social and personal reality and evaluate where the simulations work or would not work for real life. Therefore, the choice of films is not entirely random. Viewing a series of recent films, I recognized some Freudian Excuses and found them highly unlikely because they did not improve the message of the films at all — on the contrary. This was the reason to start investigating their contexts. What was wrong here? The argument needed to be anchored in specific theories and even a wider vision of historical development because all my studying of Freud, Lacan, and others confirmed the serious conservative and authoritarian views of psychoanalysis are not progressively "liberating" at all, as some in cultural studies think them to be. Psychoanalysis resembles more Romantic ideas than modern Darwinistic views. We will recognize this as a political issue.

Discussing the Academy Award–winning British film *The King's Speech* (2010), directed by Tom Hooper, the first chapter seeks to make the reader aware of how the Freudian Excuse works in the hands of both filmmakers and film critics. It concludes that the Freudian Excuse is unnecessary and unwished-for. Following the model set for each case, the chapter recapitulates modern psychological research into the stammerer's problems to demonstrate that the Freudian Excuse in fact opens doors to discrimination, in this case against the stammerer. But it also shows that Freud himself, the inventor of the theory, had no idea what he was doing. Viewing *The Rite* (2011), directed by Swedish Mikael Håfström, and *The Twilight Saga: New Moon* (2009), directed by Chris Weitz after work by Melissa Rosenberg, the second chapter ventures into the Romantic underpinnings of Western intellectual culture, by sketching one of its so-called master narratives (which are not "dead" yet, as the postmodernists proclaimed): the "deep." For over two centuries, filmmakers, writers, and folk psychologists used to look for something "deep" in explaining specific human features. This goes back to 16th-century witchhunters and their struggle for faith. It gave Western intellectual culture the "exorcist" and the "exorcist paradigm," both, in fact, acknowledged and followed by Freud. However, contemporary films with witches and werewolves seem to ignore the exorcist paradigm, opening up to cognitive folk psychological views of humanity. In Western narrative, psychological problems must be "exorcized" out of the "deep." The "deep" in Freud's time circled around the hysteric; not so long ago it was fatigue or unspecified illnesses — in the 1980s, some thought it also included AIDS. An overview of the psychomythology articulated to Todd Haynes's second major feature *[SAFE]* (1995) and Diablo Cody's *Jennifer's Body* (2009), directed by Karyn Kusama, shows that psychoanalysis cannot define the hysteric at all any longer, or any other "disorder." The references to "fatigue," and indeed AIDS, are vague and unspecified. Next to exorcism, the loss of a Freudian foothold is a key here. It offers the opportunity to go into some fundamental questions: Where did the concept of hysteria come from? Why was it rooted in such Romantic, almost reactionary convictions? What is the subconscious? And, what does the "hysteric" mean today, as a contemporary Freudian Excuse? Discussing *[SAFE]*, it is clear that misinformation can be damaging. Understanding the psyche using modern insights gives better results. Interestingly, modern filmmakers, working with updated folk psychology, usually recognize this, as is the case of hallucinations in *Jennifer's Body*.

In the next chapters of the book, the assumptions of the Freudian Excuse and contemporary non–Freudian criticism are addressed. Discussing the Argentine film *XXY* (2007) by Lucía Puenzo and Canadian Atom Egoyan's *Chloe* (2009) offers opportunities for a critical look at contemporary feminist scholarship based on the work of Judith Butler, which works with the awkward and erroneous Freudian concept of the innate bisexuality of humankind. Interestingly, supported by contemporary psychology and biology, queer and transgender theorists disagree with the notion of innate bisexuality. A new vision of gender performance is inevitable. Gregg Araki's *Mysterious Skin* (2004) and Peruvian Josué Méndez's *Dioses* (2008) can be discussed as contesting the traditional idea that films are like dreams. As an example of an emerging new folk psychology, with "theories" of dreaming that are more in line with scholarly writings, *Dioses*, especially, offers a more accurate view of dreaming and remembering. The Freudian idea of repression suggests that parts of the "subconscious" cannot be brought to "consciousness," unless assisted by the therapist. Films like *Eternal Sunshine of the Spotless Mind* (2004) by Michel Gondry and Charlie Kaufman, the Chilean film *Drama* (2010) by Matías Lira, Jessica Sharzer's *Speak* (2004), and the Mexican feature *Cosas insignificantes* (2008) by Andrea Martínez, however, show the opposite, and are therefore in line with recent results in consciousness studies: the mind is fully open to all thought; there is no "dustbin" for repressed thoughts. These films are also used to discuss the importance of conceptual metaphor theory and the cognitive insights of the embodiment of the mind. As in all other chapters, attention is given both to the films and to theory, in order to suggest a new kind of criticism. Behavior in these films reflects these theories. Finally, viewing Darren Aronofsky's *Black Swan* (2010) and Sofia Coppola's *The Virgin Suicides* (1999), the illusion can be addressed, articulated to a popular theme in cultural studies, the so-called "Uncanny." In this chapter, it is argued that fears and illusions are fed by different things than the "Uncanny" assumes. It shows that all memory is contemporary and that the juxtapositioning of Good and Evil has been given a much more contemporary content of social and political choices, devoid of the old Christian/Romantic. This vision is in line with the cognitive-evolutionary way of thinking that is gaining ground in our time, feeding a new folk psychology. In the end, I think the camera performs a role similar to the brain's left hemisphere interpreter. Coined as such by neuroscientist Michael Gazzaniga,[4] this "interpreter" could be a new instrument for modern film criticism and leave the ruined Freudian Edifice as a relic of the past.

In *Understanding Cinema* (2003), film theorist Per Persson describes how cinema spectators make use of popular psychology when viewing and making sense of film. Mental processes involve perception, comprehension, interpretation, evaluation, judgment, inference making, and emotion. From an individual perspective, Persson says, these are the processes by which the phenomenal world emerges in our consciousness. Thus, preceding the phenomenal world is a complex and multilayered web of processes that takes cues or signs from the physical, social, and cultural environment, but also transforms, adds to, and makes richer those cues or signs. People who believe in psychoanalysis try to experience the meaningfulness and coherence Freud sought to include into his Edifice. A theory contains principles or rules that are used to explain how something works. Because it is used to explain mental states, popular psychology, then, should be understood as a theory — but a mythological theory or *psychomythology*. Psychomyths of popular psychology are typically stable and strongly held beliefs about human nature, influencing how the believers understand the world, despite the fact that they are contradicted by well-established evidence. True, it is armchair psychology about what makes our family members, friends, lovers, colleagues, and strangers tick, but it gives us tools to seemingly understand romantic relations, friendships, memory lapses, emotional outbursts, performances, and the like. As a theory, popular psychology jibes with the common senses, with the gut hunches, intuitions, and first impressions.[3]

Why pursue this kind of endeavor in a book like this? Because myths matter. "Those of us who believe erroneously that people typically repress the memories of painful experiences may spend much of our lives in a fruitless attempt to dredge up memories of childhood traumatic events that never happened," Lilienfeld et al. write in *50 Great Myths*. The function of psychomyths is clear: they attempt to explain the otherwise inexplicable of seemingly perennial mysteries. The belief that dreams have been shown to possess symbolic meaning is an effort to grapple with the underlying significance of the nighttime mental worlds. The error of psychomythology comes to us through word-of-mouth, through a desire for easy answers and quick fixes, through selective perception and memory, through too easily inferring causation from correlation, through superficial resemblance, through the exaggeration of a kernel of truth, through terminological confusion, and, Lilienfeld et al. stress, through inaccurate portrayal in the entertainment and news media. The myths must be corrected: "In our view, mythbusting should be an essential component of psychology education, because deeply entrenched beliefs in psychological misconceptions can impede students' understanding of human nature." The same can be said for other students of human nature: in the literary sciences, anthropology, history, and cultural and film studies.[4]

The idea that we can make "unwise decisions" after viewing or reading fiction only makes sense if we follow the hypothesis of psychologists Raymond Mar and Keith Oatley: "The function of fiction is the abstraction and simulation of social experience." Fiction stories are not direct copies of reality, because reality is ineffably complicated and detailed. By entering a so-called "narrative world," readers and viewers of works of fiction run a simulation of a social world via abstraction, simplification, and compression. The narrative simulates, or models, basically through abstraction. This abstraction, Mar and Oatley write, "condenses complex information regarding interactions between multiple autonomous and intentional agents without substantial discarding of key elements, while simultaneously revealing the principal underlying chords of the social world."[5] Simulations provide information by offering models when access cannot be direct. Think of predicting the weather, they say, which is based on simulations that include a series of variables like barometric pressure, humidity, winds, and temperatures. In fiction, characters are perhaps precisely such variables of narrative worlds that allow people to infer other people's mental states to which direct access is difficult.

Narrative worlds, or *storyworlds,* writes David Herman, "can be defined as the worlds evoked by narratives, and narratives can be defined in turn as blueprints for world-creation." These "blueprints" or simulations are clusters of mental schemas, as laid down in the expressive resources of spoken language, but also in the written word and its typographical formats, the disposition of space on the printed page, diagrams, sketches, and illustrations. Furthermore, it includes theatrical scenes and the diegesis of a film. In order to better understand, generalize to other circumstances, and act upon, a narrative world functions to abstract social and personal information about human behavior. Interlocutors in contexts of face-to-face storytelling, Herman continues, viewers of films, and participants in computer-mediated modes of storytelling use a variety of cues to decode what has been offered. They need to construct a timeline for events, a broader temporal and spatial environment in which those events occur, an inventory of the characters involved, and a working model of what it must have been like for these characters to experience these events. The narrative world as a simulation of human behavior and its underlying cognitions and motivations — of specific stages during specific moments and events — achieves a form of learning through experience by facilitating the communication and understanding of social information and making it more compelling. "Although narrative is entertaining, its function is not of mere entertainment." This is why mythbusting serves the viewers in their personal and social performance.[6]

Mar, Oatley, and Maja Djikic empirically tested the idea that reading and watching fiction has psychological and social benefits. For example, they found that children's use of terms for mental states and their abilities for mind-reading were related both to the amount of reading parents did with them, and to the number of mental-state terms that parents used. The key was for children to imagine such mental states. As compared with those who read a nonfiction essay about women's rights in Algeria — this is another investigation they referred to — the students reading a chapter from a novel about the life of an Algerian woman reported that they would be less likely to accept current norms for relationships between men and women in the country. The students came from a Western country. In yet another study, comparing the effects of a fiction story and a nonfiction journalism piece, they found that the readers of the fiction did better on a test of social reasoning, though not on a test of analytical reading, than those who read the nonfiction. Other researchers found that readers of a fictional (love) story changed their personality in small but measurable ways, and in idiosyncratic directions. These changes were mediated by the changes in emotion that readers experienced in the course of reading. In a further study, student readers who were asked to project themselves mentally into the situation of the story showed decreased tolerance for current norms compared to readers who were invited to concentrate on the structure of the story.[7]

Simulations are used to prepare for unknown situations. In his book *Stumbling on Happiness* (2006), Daniel Gilbert shows that people have problems using their imagination to simulate the future and seem to take the wrong things into account in their simulations. One way to learn to improve, Oatley says, is to talk with others. This we do abundantly — even more so, now that we have portable cell phones. "In its explorations of the what-ifs of social life, fiction offers more experience and more consultations than we could otherwise have." Filmmaker Krysztof Kieslowski has explained that in making the ten one-hour films of *The Decalogue* (1989) his purpose was explicitly to depict ordinary characters in moral dilemmas that would enable viewers to think about them. Finding solutions to the problems posed in films constitutes a major part of the entertainment of films. Perhaps we will go along with Lou Ford and try to find out in our minds, by going through all our schemas and running simulations while we watch, why he kills the women he loves. But the filmmaker gives us a character that is heavily disturbed. This book will continue to argue that "deep" roots of mischief and disorder usually cannot be found. Curiously, even the creators of *The Killer Inside Me* are not satisfied with this outcome. They introduce the Freudian Excuse to help the viewers out, although a good viewer will recognize the de-rootedness of Lou's actions.[8]

Simulations are also designed to use theories about the world. It is the process by which we come to "have a world," forming the basis for our physical, cultural, social, and ethical behavior in the world. It connotes processes of perception and cognition as well as processes of emotions and feelings — continuously on the move. That theories are rooted in experience and experiments, and also in education, debates, and other forms of the exchange of ideas, means that as an empirical theory, the common sense psychology of understanding is susceptible to replacement by a better theory with radically different conceptual resources if experience asks for it, or when specific scientific theories are severely discredited. Just as other folk theories have been overthrown by scientific theories — like folk biology — it is to be expected that older forms of popular psychology will be overthrown by more recent forms. These include recently formulated basic theories and notions of scientific psychology or neuroscience. Eventually, in our modern globalizing world people will transform their popular psychology — as the theory behind their simulations — with increasingly more notions, concepts, and theories of contemporary cognitive psychology and neuroscience, at the expense of psychoanalysis.

# 3

Tropes are generally anchored in psychomythology. Although by definition myth is not true, we have learned that, in general, evidence for defining truth is contextual. In the social sciences, data or evidence supports a hypothesis or theory to the extent that every hypothesis or theory remains provisional, subject to change whenever new evidence becomes available. In real life, evidence may give different degrees of proof. Because the establishment of fact will be based on statements by the people around us and contradictory statements in the media — including voices of direct witnesses and of experts — we do something very commonsensical: we *believe* some of these statements — are *convinced* that they are true — no matter how vague, incomplete, suspect, contradictory, or even mistaken they appear. The decision to believe is made on the basis of beliefs about the likeliness of some accounts, about the vulnerability of the people involved, and the supposed reasons to lie or tell the truth. This includes determining the plausibility of the stories heard. The theory of anchored narratives says that we, as triers of fact, reach our decisions on the basis of two judgments. First, we make an assessment of the plausibility of the accounts of what happened and why. Second, we consider whether this narrative account can be anchored by way of evidence to common sense beliefs that are generally accepted as true most of the time. In the end, evidence derives its meaning from a story context. It is anchored in this context.[9]

Thus, all stories we hear, including films and novels, need "evidence," true or false but believable by anyone involved, thus anchoring in a "ground" of generally accepted common sense rules and values accepted by some culture or group of people at a specific time. This "ground" is the "obvious" for a group of people; it is the group's culture and needs to meet the group's logic. To be believed and to be of sound logic, in almost all cases of storytelling, the anchoring of any specific narrative is in the "obvious."[10] Anchoring can be deceptive if people think a statement, hypothesis, or theory is accepted as true because everyone thinks it is. For this reason, popular psychologies like psychoanalysis can be convincing, when they succeed in anchoring their "facts," "evidence," and "notions" in a widely experienced common sense "ground." Colleagues from critical theory identified a part of the "ground" as consisting of master- and metanarratives. A metanarrative is seen as an abstract idea that is thought to be a comprehensive ordering and explanation of historical experience or knowledge. The "meta" refers to "about": a metanarrative is generally a rarely told or made conscious story about stories, justifying a culture's power structures, encompassing and explaining other "little stories" within totalizing schemes — as Nationalism, Marxism, or Christianity were thought to have been. They tend to be reinforced by these other more specific narratives told within the culture, without being told outright. A master narrative is defined as a coherent system of interrelated and sequentially organized stories that share a common rhetorical desire to resolve a conflict by establishing audience expectations according to the known trajectories of its literary and rhetorical form. A master narrative is a theory to run mental simulations. Over the past century, theorists have disseminated the idea of the death of metanarratives. However, built around certain key ideas, most of them are still very much alive. The idea of exorcism is one of them, needed to legitimate the androcentric or male-centered turn in the late Middle Ages.

A large part of the "ground" of psychomythology is androcentric — Freud theorized the "male," while *othering* the "female" at the same time — and theorizes the potent man with his exorcizing powers. Curiously, as we shall see, Freud also theorized that the "male," as part of his "normal development," had to make a gender choice, thereby defeating the woman in himself. This is the Oedipus Complex, an automatic supposedly biological procedure that exorcizes the Devil Within — the "female." Reading through the literature, the roots of this exorcist narrative can be found in the problem of consciousness: If we are thinking, who does the thinking? All around the world, people have come to the intuitive conclusion that there is a "someone" in our body, who is guiding us. The cockpit must be somewhere in our brain, in the unconscious. Most of the people around the world call it the *soul,* given us by God, representing Good. But God is fighting Satan, fighting Evil. The world is full of evil. That cannot be God's work. Perhaps, Satan has taken over some or a very large sum of the souls and turned them into Evil. In the end, so says the Bible, God will win his war with Satan. During the war, however, the forces of Good may win back lost souls by driving out Evil. This is a difficult and dangerous job, which can better be left to specialists who know the right words and correct rites and rituals. Exorcism needs true men, powerful men of God, fighting the weak and effeminate powers of the Devil — and anyone they defined as demon lovers. Thus, one of the key metanarratives of Western culture presents us with the othering of women by inventing and reestablishing as inevitable the exorcist powers in men.

Anchoring the great myths of popular psychology is vital not only for future behavior — avoiding making unwise decisions. To look at the future is to look at the past. The answer to the question: *Who are we?* is found in the future: *Where are we going?* and in the past: *Where do we come from?* This is because of our mind-reading abilities. Recently, these insights have entered the field of literary criticism. In her *Why We Read Fiction* (2006), Lisa Zunshine demonstrates that mind-reading is the key to answering the question in the title of her book. "Attributing states of mind is the default way by which we construct and navigate our social environment, incorrect though our attributions frequently are." One type of mindreading is done if we observe other people around us, or on the television or cinema screen, or when we read about their behavior. We are mostly successful in assuming, guessing, and deducing what the other(s) might think, because most of the people around us share the same culture — they "run" the same mental schemas for that moment in that space — and the same education, learned or inherited. The actions we observe of the people around us may be called representations of their minds and we include in the observations the three basic points of any action: present, past, and future. All animals have this evolved cognitive ability to keep track of sources of these representations and of our own. Therefore, we are metarepresenting them: *meta* in the sense of source-tracking. Any mind-reading, including any reading of fictional narratives in print or on screen, will "rely on, manipulate, and titillate our tendency to keep track of *who* thought, wanted, and felt what and *when*."[11] This is important for our judgment of accurate behavior and correct information. If the source is doubtful or incorrect, we may do or think the wrong way — wrong in the cultural sense. In this book, the source, the mind behind the psychomythology discussed, is mostly Freud, but also a series of psychological works. By metarepresenting a series of behaviors and motivations from films, we can assess if they are correct or not, in this case correct for our insights into human nature.

# 4

The wider background of the history of this context can be found in a large period between, say, the 18th century and the present. Most current psychomythology seems to be anchored in the so-called Romantic Order. Following Dutch philosopher Maarten Doorman, such an Order is a composite narrative world; it is the subject, conscious or not, of the majority of authors in a limited period.[12] The Romantic Order had been conceived in Europe around 1800 and gave birth to a predilection for the past, idolizing local and national cultures, a preference for nature and the exotic, a reverence for brilliance and authenticity, a focus on the fate of the individual, striving for high ideals — which typically remain unattainable — and the like. Within the Romantic Order, the idea of the individual with his own personality became hegemonic, including his imagination, his emotions, and his desires, which, by the way, classically remained unfulfilled — lovesick in vain, deception and despair, *Paradise Lost*. In 1776, it was revolutionary that the American Declaration of Independence proclaimed the pursuit of happiness. In the coming chapters, we will get to know Freud also as a representative of this Romantic Order. As the successor to the Enlightened Order, the Romantic Order did not fully replace it. Remnants of the former are still at work in our time, while the characteristics of the latter may nowadays be understood as hegemonic. Probably, interpreting the signs of our times, a new Order is slowly intruding on this hegemony: the Cognitive-Evolutionary Order (see the discussion throughout this book on Conceptual Metaphor Theory and Schema Theory). This is no distant future; its formation can be observed around us today. Even television broadcasts scientific results to inform the audience. Populations inherit traits from generation to generation that were selected for survival of the human race. Cognitive science nowadays operates according to lines set out by evolutionary thoughts.

A speculative argument like this might benefit from a little refinement. One of the major arenas for the Romantic Order to revolutionize European culture was the attitude toward nature, landscape, and forests. Europeans began walking through the woods for recreation but also to find their "inner selves": the forest as a mirror of the soul. The Romantics witnessed a radical transformation. The Enlightened Order stood for citizenship and the social contract, reason, codification of rights, controlling nature, the universal rights of man, civilization, the nation state, the collective, citizenship, objectivity, analysis, and analyzing hard data. The Enlightened were looking for Man, for universal principles, the laws of nature, orders for good conduct — society and civilization could be built under full control. In the struggle for survival, nature was to be exploited as fully as deemed necessary. The Romantics, however, began departing from the image of an organized humanity, structured and collectively embedded in an ordered community. They began departing from the idea that man has to identify with a functional role, to find an attitude, to present his external, and began looking for the *self*-image of *being* someone — or better: *becoming* someone — meaning his so-called inner, authentic inward-looking self. The collective opened to the individual, the group to the person, and the universal to the private. The Romantics preferred feeling above thinking, subjective above objective, ironic above explicit, synthesis above analysis, qualitative above quantitative, art above science, the organic above the mechanical, spiritual above material, the hybrid and ambiguous above division and partition, suggestion above contours, difference above blending, dark above light, night above day, absence above presence, the concealed above the exposed, the unconscious above the conscious, and man as above nature and not part of nature. It transformed, for example, marriage arrangements: from the public interests of families and communities to love and personal happiness. The Romantic Order brought alienation: of happiness, of being, of health, of nature, of the past, of memory, perhaps even of culture itself. For most of us, this is still our daily discourse.[13]

As suggested, the Enlightened Order has a lot in common with functionalist thinking. Functionalists regard societies as coherent, bounded, and fundamentally relational constructs that function like an organism in which many parts operate together to maintain and reproduce the "organism" and thus to sustain the whole. Its various parts are assumed to work in an unconscious, quasi-automatic fashion toward the maintenance of the overall social equilibrium by stability and internal cohesion to ensure its continued existence over time. The social and cultural phenomena are effectively deemed to have a "life" of their own and are understood in terms of this function they play. Individuals are significant in terms of their status and their roles and behavior associated with it. This means that the social structure is the network of statuses connected by associated roles. Hence the idea of the Functionalist-Enlightened Order. Its counterpart, the Romantic Order, has a lot in common with structuralist thinking. This is produced and reproduced through various practices, phenomena and activities that serve as systems of underlying, learned structures of collective signification and cultural meaning; sometimes based on natural taxonomies and survival strategies, sometimes on pairs of binary oppositions such as hot/cold, male/female, culture/nature, cooked/raw, or marriageable versus tabooed women. The popularity of identity as something *deeply* felt as part of their personality by the people involved is typically Romantic but does also mirror structuralist thinking: the Structuralist-Romantic Order.[14]

The difference between the Enlightened and Romantic orders can also be illustrated by comparing the 18th-century French novel *Les liaisons dangereuses* (*Dangerous Liaisons*) (1782) by Pierre Ambroise François Choderlos de Laclos (1741–1803) and Stephen Frears's film *Dangerous Liaisons* (1988), written by Christopher Hampton, and based on his play adapted from the French novel. Doorman demonstrates that the French novel is basically interested in the functionality of the public characters, their staged performances, whereas Frears's film focuses on the affectionate relationships, love and jealousy. Interestingly, Frears's film does give us a glance of the original in the opening scene: the Marquise de Merteuil is dressed by her staff in careful detail. At the same time, the attendants of her opponent, the Vicomte de Valmont, are powdering his hair. They are preparing for their roles at a party. In that era, people not only played a persona but regarded this public presence as their factual being on that spot at that moment. Someone's individuality was not important, as in Frears's film, but how he or she acted in public.* In his recent study, *The Culture Wars of the Late Renaissance* (2007), historian Edward Muir confirms views on Renaissance selfhood as a difficult negotiation between inner promptings and outer social roles — typical for the Functionalist-Enlightened Order. By looking both inward for emotional sustenance and outward for social assurance, says Muir, Renaissance individuals seemed to have developed a fragmented self-image. Hence, psychological distress became an issue for debate, including the contents of the new concept of human psychology — a term coined in this period — and the ensuing question of the relationship between body and soul. In the widely read publications of the philosophers of the Venetian University of Padua, for instance, reason soon became dethroned and passions given a higher value. From then on, 16th-century writers could and would speculate about the heart as a greater force than the mind in determining human conduct. "When the body itself slipped out of its long-despised position," Muir added, "the sexual drives of the lower body were liberated and thinkers were allowed to consider sex, independent of its role in reproduction, a worthy manifestation of nature."[15] The influence of the Renaissance lingered on well into the 18th century. What was crucial in Frears's Romantic approach, that the defeat of the Marquise de Merteuil is rooted in her denial of her inner feelings of love, plays no role whatsoever in the Enlightened novel.

Problematic, schematic, and simplistic though this juxtaposition of Functionalist-Enlightened versus Structuralist-Romantic may be, it can be used to look at two different attitudes toward the work of a scholar. Doorman presents the theory of colors as a key example. The British researcher Isaac Newton (1642–1727), in a way an ambassador of the Enlightened Order, not only designed a theory of gravity but in 1669 he also had the luminous idea to use a prism to study the light of the sun. White light came through the prism and was projected on a wall. Newton registered that this white light was built up by red, red-orange, yellow, green, blue-green, and violet. This insight was not only confirmed many times later using modern devices, it is also a theory that works in painting, drawing, fashion, and such, both by hand or using electronic equipment. The theory can be effectively used in daily practice — including the construction of lightbulbs, movies and film, photography, television, computer screens, and so forth. However, German Romantic writer, philosopher, and scholar Johann Wolfgang von Goethe

---

*A note about a problem in the politics of gender in scholarly writing. As a male writer I use "he" or "him" where one can read "she/he" or "him/her" as a gender impartial indication. I follow a suggestion by feminist writer Gayatri Chakravorty Spivak, who consistently uses "she" in such cases; see her *A Critique of Postcolonial Reason* (1999). Here we have a nice and workable gender division of labor.

(1749–1832) designed a theory of colors on a different basis. During many visits to museums on his first Italian journey (1768–88), Goethe decided to look at a wall *through* a prism like a looking glass — hence no projections. Of course, Goethe observed something completely different from Newton: the white wall in the center of the prism and the colors in circles toward the edge. The colors seemed to correspond to the dark side of the room, as if they formed a shadow world. Goethe responded with the axiom that colors were liminal, a kind of tension within light, and that he had found out the "deep" of colors. Erroneously, Goethe thought that Newton's theory must be too superficial.[16] We regard Newton's theory as *true* because it *works* in real life. Goethe's observations, on the other hand, cannot be replicated. His axiom cannot be used for the construction of lightbulbs, movies, or anything like it. It does not work. One may only experience individually a similar "depth" of colors as Goethe and share his poetic feelings.

At the time, the period of nascent evolutionary thinking had a much faster impact than we may infer from the slowness of these almost epistemic movements. For example, H. Porter Abbott describes how the work of Charles Darwin (1809–82) caused a crisis in storytelling in 19th-century English literature. Writers became convinced that the developments they narrated in their fictional work could not be sudden and overnight any longer. Before, for example, in the work of Charles Dickens (1812–70), the character Scrooge, after a single night, could rise up the next morning a transformed man. This was impossible after Darwin had introduced, with his almost geological vision, the slow pace of change of "infinitesimally small inherited modification." Abbott calls this the Darwinian gradualist model. Modern evolutionists, including geologists, do not agree with this model. They stress the frequency of sudden changes of mutation. The 19th-century Darwinians, however, worked with this image of processes so slow as to be almost invisible. Darwin's success, writes Abbott, confirmed the gradualist template well beyond biology and geology as the implicit standard of credibility for almost all representations of the way things change. Writers began portraying biographies from this gradualist stance, painting the gradual self-unfolding of their characters. They founded the principle that to know someone is to see that person narrativized with a persuasive sufficiency of detail stretched out over a long period. There was left only one way of dealing with exceptions like sudden conversions: these must have been in the making for a very long time. Any conversion could not have been but a gradual awakening — "a flow of unconscious life rising now and then into conscious will," a writer wrote at the time. On general, seemingly instantaneous events began to be understood as "natural" products of "subconscious incubation." For these writers, the "subconscious" functioned as a "womb" in which the narratable process of incubation would naturally lead to the event of the conversion. Being "born again" was nothing but the culmination of a gradual series of hidden events unfolding in narratable order. With his writing, Freud mined the Darwinian cause-and-effect paradigm of submerged narratable action and he became the next in line to anchor his work in the need to preserve the explanatory power of linear narrative. From the outset, psychoanalysis was written according to the emerging laws of gradualist literary narrative.[17]

## 5

Thanks to these developments, the power of unconscious thinking was well established in Freud's time. It is no wonder that his work, shortly after its publication, received "a great many signs of recognition and extraordinary respect." The unconscious in itself had been explored for a very long time indeed. Writers theorizing the differences between conscious rearing and unconscious forces, sometimes even thinking about a kind of catharsis to release unconscious constraints, include, among many, Aristotle (384–322 B.C.), Augustinus (354–430), Dante Alighieri (1265–1321), William Shakespeare (1564–1616), Blaise Pascal (1623–62), Baruch or Benedictus de Spinoza (1632–77), Gottfried Wilhelm Leibniz (1646–1716), and Johann Herbart (1776–1841), from the latter even in *Lehrbuch zur Psychologie* (*Psychology Textbook*, 1834). The uncle of Freud's future spouse, Jacob Bernays (1824–81), a philosopher, had written about catharsis, as had Alfred Freiherr von Berger (1853–1912) and Goethe in his play *Iphigenie auf Tauris* (1779). Catharsis, of course, is also known from a practice recognized by the Roman Catholic Church as the institution of confession. At the beginning of the Victorian Era in England (stretching through the reign of Queen Victoria, 1837–1901), a diarist recorded his conviction that a young woman's dismay at the prospect of ending her platonic association with an older man "was sexual though she did not know it." Another writer thought that sexual desire in absence of a specific object, "when it does not yet understand itself, or has been sacrificed to some other interest," bursts out in various directions, "like religious devotion, zealous anthropy," the fondling of pet animals, and the love of nature and art.[18]

Freud historian Frank Cioffi found in Daniel Hack Tuke's *Dictionary of Psychological Medicine,* published in London in 1892, thus three years *before* the birth of psychoanalysis, the following remark by a certain H.R. Donkin, under "hysteria": "Among the activities artificially repressed in girls, it must be recognized that the sexual plays an important part and, indeed, the frequent evidence given of dammed up sexual emotions [...] have led many to regard unsatisfied sexual desire as one of the leading causes of hysteria [...]; forced abstinence from the gratification of any of the inherent and primitive desires must have untoward results." From 1864 onwards, the Viennese physician

Moritz Benedikt (1835–1920) had published about the causes of "hysteria" and other illnesses in "painful secrets," mostly pertaining to sexual life; as had Jerome Gaub (1705–80) in the 18th century and Pierre Janet (1859–1947) in France during the 1880s. When Freud began to publish his ideas about the existence of unconscious mental processes, he did not meet by any means widely with denial and incomprehension, as he himself wanted his readers to believe. The cultural climate of the Structuralist-Romantic Order had already opened its doors for discussion of someone's complexes fed by sexuality. No wonder, one reviewer could write that psychoanalysis was "nothing but the kind of psychology used by poets"; thus, ordinary knowledge poetically well-uttered and therefore more Goethe than Newton. Another reviewer said that it was "interesting to note a *return*, in part at least, to the old theory of the origin of hysteria in sexual disorders."[19]

Despite his self-representation as a radical and his admiration for the work of Darwin, Freud preferred the writings of one of Darwin's predecessors, the French naturalist Jean-Baptiste Pierre Antoine de Monet, Chevalier de Lamarck (1744–1829). Lamarck and Darwin both wrote about plants and animals, including humans, changing over time from one form into another. Darwin suggested, correctly, we know now, that evolution follows no grand plan, no drive toward perfection, and no inheritance of acquired characteristics. Evolution privileges diversity because in any given population, individuals are not exactly alike and they vary from each other. Evolution follows also the principle of natural selection of individuals who, in their differences and adaptations, are the most suited to the habitat in which they live. Lamarck thought evolution follows entirely different principles. He proposed, among other things, that organisms have a built-in drive toward perfection. Furthermore, he thought that acquired characteristics can be passed on to offspring instantly, and argued first, that, life is driven toward always more complex forms by contact with the outside world, and, second, that therefore evolution is fueled by the inheritance of acquired characteristics. This current in evolutionary thought has been proven wrong. Freud had put all his eggs in the wrong basket by holding on to Lamarck's theory and not Darwin's — the choice of a Romantic.[20]

If we believe Slavoj Žižek's book *In Defense of Lost Causes* (2008), the attraction of psychoanalysis is politically progressive. He notes a congruency of psychoanalysis and Marxism as the two ideologies of liberation. Since Paris May 1968, as we will see, psychoanalysis promised the liberation of repressed thoughts from the mind.[21] However, in Freud, the Romantic prevailed. Historian Bruce Mazlish analyzed Freud's reading lists. The publications Freud cited with consent reveal a reader who must have been politically conservative, anti-materialistic, and perhaps even reactionary. His essay on "Thoughts for the Times on War and Death" ("Zeitgemässes über Krieg und

Tod," 1915, translated in 1916) was received in the United States as a justification of the Prussian theory of the supremacy of the State over morals and ethics and "a subtle apology for the central powers"—"an admirable essay in propaganda teutonica." Of course, as a Jew in Vienna, Freud understandably worried about his future, above all after the electoral victory of the anti-Semite Karl Lüger in 1895. He admired French writer Émile Zola (1840–1902), the novelist who, in 1898, championed Alfred Dreyfus (1859–1935) for his fight against anti-Semitism in France. But in *The Interpretation of Dreams* (1900), his magnum opus of the first phase of psychoanalysis, Freud wrote with approval and appreciation about the Roman colonization of the Mediterranean and the foundation of the British Empire in India and Africa. He referred with consent the novels *She* (1887) and *Heart of the World* (1896) by the British colonialist author Henry Rider Haggard (1856–1925), in part also because of his esteem for restricted Victorian morals. Haggard, Mazlish continues, "perambulates on the border where life and death seem to meet, where daily activity and dreams merge, and where the humdrum world is transmogrified by fantasy." In *She,* the reader confronts a seemingly chaotic dark world of love, sex, death, and the male search for the female—*La belle dame sans merci,* Mario Praz (1896–1982) would call her. In a way, Rider Haggard voiced the "civilizing mission" of the British Empire in the non–European world. His novels thus served some of the authoritarian ideological and psychological needs of British imperialism. Confirming Freud's love for authoritarian politics, French philosopher Michel Onfray published one of the most effective dismantlings of Freud's philosophy I have read over the past few years; *Le crépuscule d'une idole: L'affabulation freudienne* (2010): Freud preferred the inventor of Austrian Austrofascism Engelbert Dollfuss (1892–1934) to the social-democrats or other leftist groups, and he admired Italian Benito Mussolini (1883–1945) as protector of Austria and a "cultural hero." Both were fascist dictators of their countries.[22]

In good Romantic tradition, Freud wanted to be recognized as a *brilliant* scientist. Curiously, he succeeded eventually above all in the United States where his work was well-received almost directly after translation. By 1916 there were some 500 self-styled psychoanalysts practicing in New York. In addition, Freud's method had become an amusing game for the city's elite in women's clubs. A character in F. Scott Fitzgerald's *This Side of Paradise* (1920) described herself as "hipped on Freud and all that." In 1923, D.H. Lawrence (1885–1930) referred to the Oedipus Complex as "a household word [...] a commonplace of tea table chat." A tea table chat—this was hardly what Freud had strived for. No wonder he was not particularly fond of his American success. He told his Welsh biographer Ernest Jones (1879–1958) that "America is a mistake; a gigantic mistake." In part, Freud's dislike for America came from the general European feeling at the time that America could serve as a convenient scapegoat to protect conservative European traditions from what they regarded as American "ahistoricism," its "wild and experimental culture," its "optimism," and its "vulgar commercialism." Curiously, however, Freud above all disliked America because Americans did not acknowledge psychoanalysis as a grand meta-psychological theory. In short, Freud feared that the modern "savagery" of American culture might invalidate his findings. Todd Dufresne, author of *Killing Freud* (2003), concludes: "Consequently, when he wasn't too low on filthy American lucre, Freud could afford to dismiss Americans — as when he refused to continue treatment of an American patient, ironically claiming that *he had no unconscious.*"[23] He believed that the patients must have a capacity for suffering as an ennobling aspect of existence and that this was characteristically absent in, for example, the New York City's women's clubs' psychoanalysis without tears.

Among many at the time, the German physician and painter Carl Gustav Carus (1789–1869) wrote in 1846 (Freud was ten years old then) in his book *Psyche, Zur Entwicklungsgeschichte der Seele* that the "key of knowledge" of conscious life should be found in the "realm of the unconscious." He believed it nearly impossible to access that realm, but if there ever was a chance to "descend into this deep," the researcher should not hesitate.[24] In *The Origins of Concepts in Human Behavior* (1977), Mark Altschue writes: "It is difficult — or perhaps impossible — to find a 19th-century psychologist or medical psychologist who did not recognize unconscious cerebration as not only real but of the highest importance."[25] Note the value of this insight; the existence of unconscious thinking was a very popular theme of the *fin de siècle* of the late 19th century and the first decades of the 20th. In fact, the unconscious as the Dark Continent of the Mind had been standard knowledge for centuries, perhaps millennia. Furthermore, Freud's time saw the Golden Age of the (visual) art movement called Symbolism, a term to indicate the systematic use of symbols or pictorial conventions to express an allegorical meaning. The movement began early in the 1880s and was of Belgian and French origins, but soon gained many followers in England, Germany, Austria, and Russia. Freud's Vienna was one of its centers. The movement began as a reaction against naturalism and realism in art, which painted the humble and the ordinary. It was also a reaction against urbanization, materialism, and other effects of the Industrial Revolution, allowing liberation from nature as a model. The Symbolists were Romantic idealists and painted spirituality, imagination, and dreams.[26]

In general, the Symbolist painters believed that art should aim to capture *deeper* thoughts, usually referred to as the Ideal. This could only be accessed through indirect methods using symbolic imagery. In the French daily *Le Figaro* of September 18, 1886, Jean Moréas published a Symbolist Manifesto, in which it was said that scenes from nature, human activities, and all other real world phenomena would not be painted or depicted for their own sake but as "perceptible surfaces created to represent their esoteric affinities with the primordial Ideals." Consequently, the painters mined Greek and Roman mythology, Christian mysticism and imagery from Ancient Egypt and Medieval Europe, as well as from dreams, for a visual language of the inner world, seeking evocative paintings that would bring to mind the "deep" world of the psyche. What they unearthed were fears of death, debauchery, perversion, and eroticism. In fact, the painters prominently figured a sense of the malign power of sexuality, promoting the theme of the *femme fatale*—*La belle dame sans merci*. Freud, looking at their visual language of the inner world, must truly have felt at home among them, he could freely borrow their ideas and themes. His followers like to repeat what he wrote about himself and his Edifice: "Psychoanalysis can never become the dominant or received perspective from which to view ourselves," wrote South African psychoanalyst Gavin Ivey, for example, a few years ago, "precisely because the truths it presents us with are so perturbing." Over much of the 19th century, the "truths" Ivey speaks about were not perturbing in art, literature, and psychology at all but almost mainstream. Psychoanalysis had become a "dominant or received perspective" in 20th-century popular psychology.[27]

# 6

Romantic popular psychology postulates the deep. For Freudians, what comes out of the deep of the unconscious usually expresses repressed thoughts like wishes and traumatic memories. It must be exorcized, in "normal development" by the boy himself during the Oedipus Complex, or by the psychoanalyst during therapy. The popularity of identity and ethnicity as something "deeply" felt as part of their personality by the people involved is typically Romantic but does also mirror Structuralist thinking. Being transported into this "deep" narrative world is the privilege of the analyst; he has the theory. The patients do not need to go "into the deep." They cannot — due to their "neuroses." The analyst does, and he thereby has an active role to play in constructing the memories of their narrative worlds. But in the very beginning Freud found out that this theory did not work. For example, he first argued that the origins of hysteria were based on repressed memories of sexual abuse in childhood. He could find no evidence. Then he argued that the origins of hysteria must be found in *imagined* memories of sexual abuse or even of repressed thoughts of sexual desires, not on accurate remembrance. Again, he found no evidence, simply because the patients could not have memories of this. And so descending the staircase of hypothesis, in the end he assumed that, for example, a speech impediment could have been the wish of a mouth full of semen after fellatio, and disagreement with the analyst became resistance to his theory. Trying to correct his own fallacies, Freud moved further away, step by step, from the academic standard of testable hypotheses — publicly lying to his readers, deceiving himself.[28] Freud very well knew the unfortunate fate of his patients. For example, he told writer Stephan Zweig (1881–1942) about it as well as Ernest Jones, his biographer, and mentioned it to several people in his letters. None of the concepts Freud introduced can escape these hurtful roots; every concept, every notion goes back to this personal fiction of its founding father.

Reading the literature, everyone can recognize Freud's fallacies and his own disappointment. For example, Dutch historian Han Israëls read some 300 letters Freud wrote to his fiancée Martha Bernays (1861–1951) during their engagement and he concluded that if anything characterized psychoanalysis, it was fiasco, deceit, fraud, and fiction, not science, not an academic attitude. Although the point was made by others before him, Israëls leaves it beyond any doubt that Freud fabricated his "research results" and lied about previous results — or better, the lack of results — during this crucial phase of psychoanalysis. Israëls demonstrates that especially in his famous cases, on which psychoanalysis built its authority including the formulation of concepts and assumptions, Freud stepped from one lie or invention to the next. French philosopher Mikkel Borch-Jacobsen, now working in the United States, recently wrote: "The defenders of psychoanalysis are indignant and speak of gutter-press journalism, of paranoia, of 'Freud bashing,' but they are obviously on the defensive."[29] The "critics" were not Freud-bashers but Freud-historians who studied Freud's methods carefully. Titles of these Freud historians include: Henri Ellenberger, *The Discovery of the Unconscious* (1970); Albrecht Hirschmüller, *Physiologie und Psychoanalyse* (1978); Elizabeth Thornton, *Freud and Cocaine* (1983); Janet Malcolm, *Psychoanalysis* (1988); Malcolm Macmillan, *Freud Evaluated* (1991); Allen Esterson, *Seductive Mirage* (1993); Han Israëls, *Het geval Freud* (1993; *The Freud Case*) and *De Weense kwakzalver* (1999; *The Viennese Quack*); Frederick Crews, *The Memory Wars* (1995); Richard Webster, *Why Freud Was Wrong* (1996) and his *Freud* (2003); Mikkel Borch-Jacobsen, *Lacan* (1991) and *Remembering Anna O* (1996); Edward Erwin, *A Final Accounting* (1996); Frank Cioffi, *Freud and the Question of Pseudoscience* (1998); Todd Dufresne, *Tales from the Freudian Crypt* (2000) and *Killing Freud* (2003); Jacques Bénesteau, *Mensonges freudiens* (2002); Mikkel Borch-Jacobsen, et al., *Libro negro del psicoanálisis* (2007 [2005]); Borch-Jacobsen and Sonu Shamdasani, *Le dossier Freud* (2006); and Michel Onfray, *Le crépuscule d'une idole* (2010). The list is much longer, and growing by the year.

In psychiatry, Freud fell from grace in the 1980s. First psychologists and then psychiatrists judged the Freudian Edifice to be non-scientific. The third edition of the foremost psychiatry manual *Diagnostic and Statistical Manual of Mental Disorders,* or *DSM-III* (published by the American Psychiatric Association in Washington, D.C., 1980) dropped the psychoanalytic neurotic conditions from its guide of psychiatric disorders and they have been absent in the psychology of disorders ever since. Later editions, from the *DSM-IV* (1994) onwards, provided even more radical rejection. The reason: Freud's concepts could not be used for any serious and practical diagnosis — they did not work. Regardless of its enormous success in the decades after World War II, Richard Webster concludes, psychoanalysis "has failed to do the only thing we ultimately have a right to demand of explanatory theories — it has failed to explain." Richard Haslam stated: "Although Freudian concepts and terminology have attained virtual ubiquity in Western popular culture, their knowledge claims have in recent years been increasingly and convincingly questioned." And Christian Perring, less courteously, has said that psychoanalysis "has been so thoroughly discredited as a scientific theory that it is hard for some to see why it is any longer worth some attention." Indeed, there were insufficient results, and other theories and medication proved to be better. Until the 1960s, few had hopes that quality treatment could be offered for severe psychiatric illnesses. Patients were confined to mental hospitals, where they were given alternating hot and cold baths, electroshocks, or psychoanalysis. Nothing was successful until drugs from the pharmaceutical industry suddenly had results. Since then much progress has been made — even in understanding why the drugs were successful in the first place. The cognitive revolution in psychology, including the flowering of neuroscience, is one of its main academic results. Of course, the pharmaceutical industry has an interest in selling as much of its products as possible but they can only expose their interest so much because of the fact that drugs work. Medication succeeded where Freud and his followers failed. The neurological focus of modern psychiatry is the direct consequence of its scholarly, scientific, and therapeutical accomplishment.[30]

Although today, many writing in anthropology, history, and the study of literature, film, or other cultural sciences, nevertheless keep on believing in psychoanalysis as a bona fide theory of human behavior. For anthropologist Mary Weismantel, for example, in her *Cholas and Pishtacos* (2001), a turn to the work of Freud should be welcomed because it "can be read both for the *insights into human psychology* and as a historical record of the emotional lives of the Victorian bourgeoisie." In all, many scholars tend to agree with statements like this one by British psychoanalyst Andrea Sabbadini, that where Freud originally intended his theory to underscore a form of therapy for the neuroses — which means that they believe that people have neuroses — psychoanalysis soon became a more ambitious project: "a general psychology for the investigation of mental functioning."[31] It makes the true believers react to any kind of criticism by either denying the problems with their trait or neglecting that critical studies have been published. Others simply react by scolding and cursing, like historian Paul Robinson. As an echo of Freud's own

Romantic criticism on the Enlightenment, Robinson tried to expose that the critics were conservatives who aimed at the reconstitution of 18th-century humanism and the image of rational man. Moreover, he believes that these neo-positivist "violent apostates," who underscored some "broad-scale revolt against the culture of modernism," belonged to the political camp of neo-liberal reactionaries who registered "a profound discomfort with the fundamental intellectual transformation of the 20th century," invoking a "backlash," "lending it a curious resonance with the politics of the 1980s." Most often, Freud's critics are said to suffer from "repression" and fear of the passions, the motives from the unconscious, and above all the darker realm of sexuality. The critic cannot cope with his motives, and should be diagnosed as being tormented by a disorder in his psychic structure. In his *Sex, Death, and the Superego* (2003), one-time president of the British Psychoanalytical Society Ronald Britton consoles his readers: psychoanalysis is not dead; there still are many patients in treatment; and there is no need to respond to the critics. Writer, therapist, and philosopher François Roustang has a simple solution: the number of analysts must grow, for if there are only psychoanalysts left, criticism will grow silent. In his 1989 sympathetic article on psychoanalytical writing, Roland Littlewood concluded that if "psychoanalysis becomes increasingly congenial to anthropologists then this might merely mean we are all psychoanalysts now; everyday psychology reproduces psychoanalysis."[32]

Because of the medical, therapeutic failure of psychoanalysis, analysts have moved to the hermeneutics of popular psychology — left as the single alternative for triumph. Freud himself would not have agreed. Indeed, *his* psychoanalysis was not meant to be "simply" a narrative, or merely a hermeneutic tool. Freud explicitly declared that his theory could not be reduced to a philosophical system. He regarded his theory as *clinical*. It had to produce an integral theoretical structure. Psychoanalysis was meant to serve in the mental hospital, to cure people. Still most psychoanalysts see themselves indisputably as medical doctors of the unconscious. Freud's methods and models were about "existing diseases," explicitly not about hermeneutics. The issue is significant indeed: if psychoanalysis does aspire to the status of a *science* of the unconscious, then the old problem of its clinical and experimental validity re-emerges. This is even recognized by the hermeneutic psychoanalysts, who all try to find implications for their "clinical work." Nevertheless, will some hermeneutic turn be rewarding? In *On Flirtation* (1994) psychoanalyst Adam Phillips relays without criticism a proposal made by French writer and Freudian Julia Kristeva for dealing with patients who are severely depressed: vowels, consonants, or syllables may be extracted from the signifying sequence of the depressed patient's language and construed by the psychoanalyst "treating" the patient in the service of constructing new meanings according to the lines of some Freudian theory. Critic Richard Webster, who frequently signals such unfeasible curiosities, not only concludes that this would turn psychoanalysis into a kind of higher anagram-making, but found it also shocking that a practicing child psychoanalyst like Phillips seems actually prepared to play such games at the expense of emotionally vulnerable people, who may very well be suicidally depressed. In his book, Phillips qualifies Kristeva's work on depression and melancholia as one of the very best in its field. Webster then responds: "That such a judgment should be passed at all is disturbing. That the psychoanalyst who makes such a judgment should be widely regarded as a profound and skeptical writer and praised as 'one of our greater contemporary psychoanalytic thinkers' is a depressing sign of just how deep is the intellectual trouble we are in."[33]

Until recently, many scholars in film studies were also Freudian fellow travelers. However, present-day film scholars increasingly criticize the use of Freudian and Lacanian semiotics in film studies. In 1995, philosopher Gregory Currie published his influential *Image and Mind*, demonstrating that Lacanian theories about thinking as a language or the illusory character of film are utterly wrong. In his *Emotion and the Structure of Narrative Film* (1996), psychologist Ed Tan writes that the concepts borrowed from Lacan have met "with scathing scientific criticism and rightly so." The ontological status of the concepts is unclear, Tan continues, "the logical consistency of ideas leaves something to be desired, and the frugality requirement appears to have been reversed." In their introduction to the collection of essays on *Narration and Spectatorship in Moving Images* (2007), editors Joseph and Barbara Anderson note a new vitality in the arts and humanities, "a new spirit of enquiry, a new level of confidence in the future," as a result of the recent resurrection of the old idea to conduct fruitful scientific investigations of "non-rational or perhaps even irrational areas of human experience such as art, music, and motion pictures." They see this current clashing with one that was dominant through most of the 20th century, called Grand Theory, a reference to psychoanalysis. Nevertheless, in *Making Meaning* (1989), and *Moving Pictures* (1997), the otherwise critical cognitive film theorists David Bordwell and Torben Grodal take psychoanalytical authors still too seriously, which they would probably not have done with, for instance, critics inspired by astrology. In a more recent essay, published in the collection *Post-Theory: Reconstructing Film Studies* (1996), Bordwell suggests, perhaps too optimistically, that the main influence of Lacan in film studies remained limited to the 1970s and 1980s — although, for example, Laura Mulvey's very popular essay, Lacanian-inspired "Visual Pleasure and Narrative Cinema," published in *Screen* (1975), is still taken seriously at universities and in important scholarly publications. In several studies on film, the work of Lacanian author Christian Metz (1931–93) is discussed without realizing the problematic origins of his work. In 2007, Todd McGowan published his *The Real Gaze*. But it is thanks to Bordwell,

Grodal, and others that cognitive science not only entered the terrain that seemed to have been reserved for psychoanalysis, but also came up with much better explanations. Nowadays, works of art like novels, paintings, and feature films, or indeed all moving images on television and the Internet, can be discussed as a representation of the innovative movement of the cognitive sciences. The cognitive revolution in psychology and the flowering of neuroscience can be traced back in many recent feature films.[34]

# 7

The Freudian Excuse is not just a trope in literature and the art film. On the contrary, some serious scholarship works with the trope as well. In part, this is because the gradualist narrative triumph spread into journalism, the arts, and academia. Following the by now more than 150-year-old paradigm, to reach the truth about a person's or a group's development the analyst feels he must descend into the deep. Inevitably, artists and authors think, events in a person's life and his personal character must be articulated to a force hidden *deeply* in a "subconscious," originating, for example, in some childhood trauma — the major Freudian Excuse. Due to the social character of our thinking, many Westerners also believe in a society with a "deep," the so-called "collective subconscious." Therefore, throughout the book several Freudian arguments are discussed, but especially the erroneous idea of the Freudian haunting unconscious that needs to be exorcized requires attention. It continues a life as a popular psychological tool to design mental simulations that invoke a sharing of fear, hope, pleasure, pain, anxiety, desires, beliefs, and such with the audience. The idea is rooted in late 18th-century and 19th-century Romantic thinking, flowering around the decades of World War I, and surviving into the 20th century in works of art like novels and films. If anything characterizes psychoanalysis in our time, it is its fadeout. Do people really care for the childhood abuse of Lou Ford in *The Killer Inside Me?* In fact, is it important for the argument of the film? When critics saw the film, they noted that audience members started to laugh when they recognized Freud's name passing by. The mental simulation of the film was designed wrongly. A good film does not need a Freudian Excuse at all, especially not now that the audience is leaving the Freudian Edifice and exorcism seems increasingly anachronistic.

# 1

## *Bertie's Stammer*

### Hysteria in *The King's Speech* (2010)
Tom Hooper (director), David Seidler (writer)

1

Some 20 minutes after the opening scenes, Mrs. Johnson introduces the film's main characters to each other. At an earlier visit, she had to reveal herself as the Duchess of York, Elizabeth Bowes-Lyon (1900–2002, played by Helena Bonham Carter; later Queen Elizabeth and the Queen Mother). The scene takes place in an old building somewhere in the poorer parts of early 20th-century London. It is the house and the practice of Lionel Logue (1880–1953; played by Geoffrey Rush), an unqualified Australian speech therapist who had success helping shell-shocked World War I (1914–18) veterans regain their voices. By then, the viewers of the film are informed about Logue's background as an actor in Australia. Obviously, Mr. Johnson is embarrassed because the visit means conceding a defeat: he is a stammerer. Mr. Johnson, of course, is Prince Albert (1895–1952; reigning as King George VI, 1936–52, called Bertie among family), Duke of York (played by Colin Firth), the second son of King George V (1865–1936; reign 1910–36). The acquaintance is not proceeding smoothly. Logue invites the Prince to take a seat on a couch — not the Freudian way, Logue is not a psychiatrist — and he himself takes a seat on a chair in front of the Prince, at a distance of nearly ten feet. It is not only a difficult conversation because of the Prince's embarrassment, but also because Logue insists on being on equal terms. He wishes that they address each other by their Christian names. This is a breach of royal etiquette, teasing the relationship of monarchs to citizens and Britain's natives to their Australian kin — and, furthermore, he forbids the Prince to smoke. Logue explains: "My castle, my rules." Next he starts his treatment (the ellipses below are used to indicate the Prince's stammering):

> LL: What was your earliest memory?

The Prince cannot believe the question:

> PA: What? ... On earth, do you mean?
> LL: Your first recollection.
> PA: I'm not ... here to discuss my personal matters.
> LL: Why are you here, then?
> PA: Because I bloody well stammer! (The Prince is angry. Logue answers imperturbably:)
> LL: You have a bit of a temper?
> PA: One of my many faults.
> LL: When did the defect start?
> PA: I've always been this way!

Here starts the crucial part:

> LL: I doubt that.
> PA: Don't ... tell me! It's my stammer!
> LL: It's my field and I can assure you, that no infant starts to speak with a stammer. When did yours start?
> PA: ... four or five.
> LL: That's typical.
> PA: So I've been told. I can't remember not doing it.
> LL: I can believe that. Do you hesitate when you think?
> PA: Don't be ridiculous.
> LL: How about when you talk to yourself? Everyone natters occasionally, Bertie.
> PA: Stop calling me that!
> LL: I'm not going to call you anything else.
> PA: Then we shan't speak!

Logue stands up, to pour out a cup of tea, but he lets the tea brew a bit longer:

> PA: Are you charging for this, Doctor?
> LL: A fortune. So, when you talk to yourself, do you stammer?
> PA: Of course not!
> LL: Well, that proves your impediment isn't a permanent part of you. What do you think was the cause?
> PA: I don't know. I don't care! I stammer! And ... no one can fix it.

Logue convinces Prince Albert to read Hamlet's "To be, or not to be" soliloquy. At the same time he invites the Prince to listen to Mozart on headphones. In a fit of temper, convinced that he has stammered throughout, the

Prince leaves without listening to the record. Logue gives him the recording anyway. It is clear that the Prince has no expectations of Logue's method and shows him little respect.

## 2

This five-minute scene is the key to *The King's Speech* (2010), the Oscar-winning English movie directed by Tom Hooper and written by David Seidler, now in his seventies. The latter wrote from experience; he had a stuttering problem as a child. Early in his career he wanted to write a screenplay about the king's struggle to overcome his stuttering problem. Dutifully asked for permission, the Queen Mother agreed, but told Seidler "not in my lifetime." As we can deduce from her age, it was a long wait. The film is also a story about a man who is psychologically scarred and trapped in a situation from which he could have no escape and facing it with courage. The first scenes transport us to the close of the 1925 British Empire Exhibition at Wembley Stadium. Accompanied by his wife Elizabeth to offer the closing speech, the anxious prince approaches the microphone like a condemned man walking his last mile. Facing the excited crowd, the prince opens his mouth and chokes on every unruly vowel and rebellious consonant. He hears the echo of his words in the outdoor stadium. He looks desperately unhappy as the audience watches with expressions ranging from sympathy to impatience. All this is enough to thwart his efforts. He looks frustrated and timid, low in self-confidence, but warm-hearted nevertheless. Later we learn that he also occasionally loses his temper. To be cured from his horror, the prince tries several treatments, until the duchess persuades him to see Logue. The film's script was based in part on Logue's diaries.[1]

The prince learns from his father King George V (Michael Gambon), the importance of radio broadcasting for the modern monarchy. Later, Prince Albert returns to Logue. He had run back the Hamlet recording and then noticed an unbroken recitation of the Shakespearean passage in his own voice. The sessions at Logue's — no house calls, even for royalty — are filled with pathos and humor. An unlikely friendship begins between two men from vastly different worlds — Logue insists on equality, calling the prince "Bertie." Logue believes that stammering results from traumatic childhood experiences. The prince scoffs at this assertion. Logue believes that no infant begins talking in a stammer. Viewers see hilarious scenes with the prince dancing, rolling across the floor, waggling his jowls, singing his thoughts to the tune of "Swanee River," blurting out eruptions of uproarious profanity, and plain cursing — the only time the prince does not stammer. The two men work together on physical exercises and breathing exercises. Although these must have contributed to the cure of the problem, Logue simultaneously tried to probe a psychological root of the stammer. When the prince reveals some of the pressures of his childhood, the door to a psychoanalytical excuse is opened. There are, in fact, several such excuses. First, the prince is shown dominated by the perpetual negative reinforcement from a very strict father. Second, the prince suffers from the repression of his natural left-handedness and a painful treatment with metal splints for his knock-knees. Third, the nanny favored his elder brother — Prince of Wales David (1894–1972, King Edward VIII during 11 months in 1936; played by Guy Pearce), deliberately pinching Prince Albert, so he would cry during the daily visits to their parents. It seems the parents did not want to receive him while he was crying. Finally, the prince remembers with intense sadness the early death of Prince John in 1919, his little brother. In the film we see that when the Prince and his family listen to Adolf Hitler giving a speech, one of the princesses asks him what the German chancellor is saying. "I don't know," the prince replies worriedly. "But he seems to be saying it rather well."

King Edward VIII accedes to the throne on January 20, 1936. However, the new king wants to marry Wallis Simpson (1896–1986; played by Eve Best). The marriage to this American divorcée socialite would provoke a constitutional crisis. The contrast between George and Edward VIII surfaces the opposition between duty and hedonism, between the Romantic fulfillment of one's personal quest for happiness versus the once Enlightened overcoming of one's worst fears on behalf of the people and country. Prince Edward is shown as a spoiled, selfish boor. At a party in Balmoral Castle, Prince Albert points out to his brother that marriage to a divorced woman makes it impossible to access the throne. In reaction, Prince Edward leaves his brother tongue-tied venturing a medieval-style plot: Were Albert's speech lessons not an attempt to ready himself for the throne? Was he not usurping the throne? And Prince Edward snarls: "B-B-Bertie." In truth, the viewer learns that Prince Albert dreads becoming King as he breaks down in tears when he realizes his fear is about to become reality. Eventually, when King Edward indeed abdicates to marry, Prince Albert is reluctantly thrust unto the throne and into the spotlight. Inevitably, as King George VI, he needs Logue's help. In fact, during the coronation in Westminster Abbey Logue is invited to take a seat in the king's box.

The most important radio broadcasting challenge for the new king came in September 1939, after the declaration of war with Germany. Albert summons Logue to the palace to prepare him for the occasion. He must not only deliver a faultless speech, but also one that would bring comfort to the country. When the king, with Logue as his sole companion, moves to the improvised palace studio, he meets Winston Churchill (1874-1965; played by Timothy Spall). The politician reveals that he too suffered once from speech impediment but used it to his advantage ever since. Intensely coached by Logue, the king delivers his speech as practiced many times over again — as if to Logue. Afterward, the kings enters the palace balcony with his family to be received by the people. The thousands gathered there applaud him enthusiastically. It seems the film earned much applause as well at this same moment at the Roy Thomson premiere. A final title card explains that Logue had been present during each and every speech King George VI gave during the War. Also that "King George VI made Lionel Logue a Commander of the Royal Victorian Order in 1944." "What fascinates me about this story," said actor Geoffrey Rush, who played Logue, "is that you have the most unlikely meeting of two people, an imperial figure and a colonial nobody. And they find common ground. We started calling it a bromance about halfway through."

# 3

The critics called *The King's Speech* a sturdy entertainment — a dazzling example of a buddy film rendered as art — an uplifting period piece, achieving its dramatic potential without sacrificing historical accuracy. Previously, director Tom Hooper had been hailed for his skill at hauling historical icons out from their textbook confines and presenting them as flesh-and-blood, warts-and-all human beings. Therefore, one critic found it intriguing that the director veered away from the sumptuousness expected in a film about royals: many of the film's most essential scenes take place in Logue's rather shabby London flat. Critic Roger Ebert, well-known for his film review column in the *Chicago Sun-Times* (since 1967, and later online), agrees: "Director Tom Hooper makes an interesting decision with his sets and visuals. The movie is largely shot in interiors, and most of those spaces are long and narrow. That's unusual in historical dramas, which emphasize sweep and majesty and so on." Reviewer David Edelstein expresses that "[W]ith his pursed lips and edgy rectitude, Colin Firth is ideally cast as an uptight fellow in serious need of therapy [...]." He adds that Firth must have felt that despite his reserved demeanor, there is real pain when the Prince tries, and fails, to speak. For reviewer Ann Hornaday of the *Washington Post*, the actor "has mastered what may be the most crucial ineffable element of acting: withholding everything from viewers save that tiniest, most crucial sliver of humanity to which they can completely relate."[2]

In general, critics recognized the film's Freudian Excuse. Reviewer Colin Covert of the Minneapolis-based *Star Tribune* pointed at Logue's therapeutic model as a sort of stealth psychotherapy. The script, he continues, delves into the dynamics of the royally screwed-up royal family that stifled the prince's "authentic" voice. In an interview with *USA Today*, Hooper offered a popular psychological explanation as to why his film connected with audiences so well: "We all have blocks that inhibit us from being our best selves with other people. Whether shyness or insecurity, we have those blocks. This is about liberating someone's blocks." In *Salon*, Andrew O'Hehir said: "For all the pomp and privilege of his upbringing, Bertie was essentially an abused child, tormented by nannies, plagued by childhood ailments and raised in isolation from the outside world. [...] But [Logue's] then-radical idea that stuttering was as much a psychological problem as a physiological one, and that its roots lay in childhood, is exactly the medicine the future king required." On the other hand, Chris Vognar of the *Dallas News* countered: "I could do without the heavy-handed exposition of the king's childhood traumas, crucial plot elements too often conveyed with a maudlin touch. With its rich source material shaped from real-life events, *The King's Speech* doesn't need to overplay its hand — especially not with a king waiting in the hole." Although Logue's method in the film truly is indebted to the Freudian, Nick Schager in *Slant Magazine* believes: "Yet despite such simplistic psychologizing, *The King's Speech* barely buys what it's selling," for "no sooner are these explanations introduced than they are discarded."[3]

Several critics seem regular visitors of the Freudian Edifice. In *New York Magazine*, David Edelstein, for example, noted that "Logue is Australian, but it's easy to imagine that he's Austrian — Freud-trained and Jewish — and here to administer an emotional enema." Anthony Lane in the *New Yorker* noted: "Born left-handed, in 1895, the Prince was forced to become right-handed. As a knock-kneed child, he wore corrective splints on his legs. None of this put the boy at ease in his own body, or anywhere else. No wonder he stammered." Lane continued: "Make no mistake: when patient and therapist are alone, in Logue's shabby rooms, we are watching not a slice of 'Masterpiece Theatre' but a case study — like Frau Emmy, the woman who went to Sigmund Freud, in 1889, and whose efforts to speak were convulsed by what he called 'clackings.' Freud diagnosed a series of underlying traumas, and that is what Logue does, too, pointing not just to the friendless marooning of anyone, of any sensitivity, who is raised in a ruling tribe but to all that is clenched and misted-over in the English character." In his turn, *NPR* critic Bob Mondello believes that Logue's notions about unlocking tongues with psychology were decidedly out of step with the era's conventional elocution theories. We may doubt this, because psychoanalysis was much less unconventional than Freud wanted us to believe. In several critiques, the movie has been criticized for historical inaccuracies. However, on this point the film depicted what was more or less believed at the time. Logue was certainly not unique in trying to "draw patients out on the traumas that might have led" them to function in society. "A more elaborate Freudian explanation," writes J. Hoberman in the *Village Voice*, "might link Bertie's retentive-expulsive speech patterns to his unconscious equation of words with feces."[4]

Unconsciously linking words with feces? In a *Wall Street Journal* blog on January 24, 2011, science journalist Jonah Lehrer posted a warning against possible misunderstandings. He is an insider: "I'm a stutterer. Although I've mostly outgrown the affliction, it took several years of speech therapy before I stopped dreading sentences that began with certain vowel sounds. I can still recall the terror of having to read aloud in class, staring [at] a text that was filled with phonetic speed bumps and stop signs." Lehrer admires the phenomenal acting: "Firth's stammer feels so sincere that I had to close my eyes for many of the scenes — it was simply too distressing to watch someone else re-enact my vocal shortcomings." But: "My main problem with the film was its depiction of stuttering as a by-product of emotional repression and abuse. In the neat narrative presented in the movie, the King's stutter is largely caused by his unloving parents and abusive nanny." For that reason, the filmmakers wrote a vital scene. Urged by Logue the King had to confront his supposed childhood demons. The Freudian Excuse used here is that he has been holding back memories. "This is a view of stuttering first popularized by Sigmund Freud, most notably in his case study of Frau Emmy von N., a 'hysteric' woman with a terrible stutter. After treating the patient, Freud concluded that the cause of her speech impediment was emotional repression. In fact, these memories were so deeply repressed that they could only be revealed when Frau Emmy was hypnotized." Freud collected the following "evidence" of Frau Emmy's reported origins of "repression": "When I was five, my brothers and sisters threw dead animals at me.... Then, when I was seven I saw my sister in her coffin; then, at the age of eight, my brother was forever frightening me by dressing up in white sheets as a ghost." This is not altogether different from Lou Ford's (*The Killer Inside Me*) childhood memories. True, for Freud, the stutterer could not speak because she was trying to hold everything in; stuttering was a symptom of neurosis, "caused by displacement upward of conflicts over excremental functions."[5]

# 4

However, the roots of Freud's idea go deeper: to his erroneous theory of developmental stages. To demonstrate the "deep" of the error of Freud's thinking, his method and conclusions about the hysteric and the developmental stages must be addressed, if only to encourage future critics to abandon references to psychoanalysis. One major question, then, is: Seen from psychoanalytical evidence, can hysteria be diagnosed credibly? To answer this is to dive into psychoanalytical history. In the early 1880s Freud started cooperating with physician Josef Breuer (1842–1925). This was the first phase of psychoanalysis. Somewhere between 1885 and 1900, with the help of Breuer, Freud set up a practice in neuropsychiatry and began theorizing about psychoanalysis.

They worked together with the first "psychoanalyzed" patient, Bertha Pappenheim (1859–1936), alias Anna O., diagnosed as suffering from hysteria. During the second phase of the founding of psychoanalysis, Freud cooperated with the German otolaryngologist Wilhelm Fliess (1858–1928), who resided in Berlin. The phase lasted from 1887 to about 1902. Over a significant period, the two men wrote each other sometimes every ten days, and they frequently exchanged manuscripts and papers. These letters show that Freud sought approval of his work by Fliess, as previously by Breuer, and therefore he regularly confirmed the ideas Fliess developed. Both phases have some overlap, because Freud was busy creating distance from Breuer, while making the contacts with Fliess more intensive. The third one was the "literary phase," beginning before the outbreak of World War I. This phase marked the corrosion of the friendship with Fliess. Both friendships were dependent. Breuer and Fliess both acted as a sort of patron.

Note how hysteria was diagnosed at the time.[6] When she entered into treatment with Breuer, Bertha/Anna was an attractive 21-year-old girl. Between December 1880 and June 1882, she was analyzed two hours a day. Her complaints included an enduring obstinate cough, paralyses, a convergent squint, lapses of consciousness or "absences" developing into hallucinations, and disturbances in her vision and hearing. In addition, she could not swallow liquids anymore and lost the ability to speak German — she started speaking in English. Moreover, she had developed a kind of split personality. Interestingly, every problem disappeared during therapy. Breuer said he did so by "entering" the unconscious through hypnosis. He argued that the girl blamed herself for her father's death. As some kind of unconscious punishment, he continued, the girl ceased to use the arm she had used cradling her dying father with. Anna had said nothing in this direction; it was the therapist's interpretation. At first, Breuer said his hypnosis worked: his patient improved considerably. But if Breuer was unable to attend, Anna fell back into her problematic state. Breuer could not verify the origins of these collapses. He had consulted psychiatrist Richard Freiherr von Krafft-Ebing (1840–1902), known today from a book on sexual desires, *Psychopathia Sexualis* (1886) — *before* Freud. Breuer included a piece on Anna's therapy over a decade later in the *Studien über Hysterie* (1895), jointly compiled by him and Freud. Freud included chapters on three cases: on Fräulein Lucie R., Fräulein Elisabeth v. R., and Frau Emmy v. N. (the "hysteric" woman with the stutter, mentioned previously). Because the *Studien* marked the birth of psychoanalysis, the Anna O. case is still passionately discussed in our times, comparing the case with a series of letters and other documents written by the persons involved, including the correspondence between Freud and Fliess.[7]

All information indicates that Freud wanted to become a famous physician, a discoverer without predecessors. Probably, this idea originates in Freud's passionate cocaine use. In our own cocainized era we know that cocaine is a stimulant of the central nervous system. Users experience increased energy and a euphoric sense of happiness. Observers note a delusion of grandeur among users. In 1884, Freud felt that cocaine would work as a cure-all for many disorders. Because he wanted to prove that cocaine was a beneficial product for humanity, he chose an experiment with the muscle power to do so. He invited test subjects to perform experiments but he failed to obtain any result. Normally, this is a sign for a scholar to abandon the experiment and its hypothesis — not for Freud under this delusion of grandeur. He blamed his testees for the failure and decided to work with the only testee that he could fully control: *himself*. And indeed, by March 1885 he presented his "results" during two lectures at scientific associations in Vienna. The method of first trying with "patients" and next getting only results with himself as "patient" became Freud's trademark. In the published text, he did not mention that he had been his own subject. Freud loved the scholarly style of writing and presented lectures to a scientific audience but did not play by the rules at all. We cannot call this fraud, but in the view of our times it comes close. After this "success," Freud recommended cocaine to many of his close family and friends. Using cocaine, Ernst von Fleischl-Marxow (1846–91) hoped to overcome a morphine addiction he had acquired while treating a disease of the nervous system. Thanks to Freud's prescriptions, Fleischl-Marxow developed an acute case of "cocaine psychosis." Devastated by pain and disease, he died on October 22, 1891; he was 45 years old. Freud felt great regret but hardly changed his opinion.[8] Freud's delusion inspired him to write that after Galileo's discovery (Galileo Galilei, 1564–1642) of humans not being the center of the universe, and Darwin's of humans not being the crown of creation, the third great humiliation in human history was his own "discovery" that humans are not in control of their own mind. Probably he was not himself, for cocaine made him write like a madman, convincing himself that he could find solutions to all known mental health problems. As could be expected, after such a period he felt depressed and disillusioned.

It is important to realize that Freud and Breuer were not psychologists but neuro-physicians — Freud was a biological neurologist — investigating the pathology of the psyche, as they would have it. Freud would label the illnesses he thought he had found "neuroses." The patients of the two men came to them with *physical* symptoms that were then diagnosed as originating in some neurological and thus physical deficit in the brain — diseases of the brain were considered as psychosomatic. They had no instruments to investigate neurological problems from inside the skull. In an age devoid of brain-mapping techniques like electroencephalogram (EEG), magnetic resonance imaging (MRI), and functional magnetic resonance imaging (fMRI), neurologists inhabited a world of almost complete diagnostic darkness and depended genuinely on poor medical knowledge (which included the failure to make accurate medical diagnoses) and philosophy (which included the ideas that physical symptoms must reflect mental origins). Freud acknowledged that psychology would eventually be underscored by chemical psychology: "We must recollect that all of our provisional ideas in psychology will presumably one day be based on an organic substrate." But this idea was accepted only to a limited degree because the "exclusive sexual interest felt by men for women [...] is not a self-evident fact based upon an attraction that is ultimately of a chemical nature." Heterosexuality was a choice, he argued, not a chemical or bodily process.[9]

A few years later, in his letters to Fliess, Freud made clear what he meant when he diagnosed patients' "illnesses" from the sole source of sexual aberration. On October 6, 1893, for example, Freud informed Fliess about four new cases "whose etiology, according to the chronology, could only be coitus interruptus": a woman (41) with agoraphobia and anxiety attacks; a man (42) with anxiety attacks and heart failure — or, as we would call it nowadays, hyperventilation — because, Freud thought, of coitus interruptus tolerated for ten years; a man (24) with "senile melancholia" because of moderate masturbation, moderate sexual intercourse, and the use of a condom for two and a half years for fear of infection, and a first anxiety attack because of coitus; a woman (24) with attacks of pain because of insomnia, "Coitus interruptus and great fear of having children [even if she already had two]. Hysteria, therefore"; and a man (34) with intestinal problems because of coitus interruptus owing to his wife's illness.[10] Thus, when people masturbate, use a condom during intercourse, or practice coitus interruptus they were vulnerable to neuroses.

Although Freud's sofa is world-famous now, it is a misunderstanding that he was just listening to his patients. In fact, his method was as physical as one could get; as a kind of contra-psychosomatism it consisted mainly of what he called a "pressure technique." This "technique" resided in applying pressure to his patients' foreheads with his hands and instructing them to report whatever came up in their minds. And if it did not bring up images and stories Freud wanted to hear, he increased the pressure mentally by being severe or even by shouting. The pressure was derived from a theory by the German anatomist Franz Joseph Gall (1758–1828): cranioscopy, a method to determine the personality and development of mental and moral faculties by looking ("*scopos*") at the external shape of the skull ("*cranium*"). His follower Johann Spurzheim (1776–1832) later renamed the method phrenology ("*phrenos*" or mind, "*logos*" or knowledge). Gall did make some important discoveries by studying brains of dead people, like the existence of grey and white matter, the cerebral cortex and the origins of the nerves in the grey matter. His theory also stipulated, rather erroneously, that all human mental powers consisted of separate faculties located in definite regions of the surface of the brain. As a chamber deep in his Edifice, Freud's "unconscious" would later appear as one of these "organs." By putting pressure on the skull, Freud hoped to defeat haunting — "repressed" — thoughts. This sounds like exorcism, and it was. Here, Freud differed from Gall, whose phrenology grew to be very popular in the 19th century, although it was unmasked as a pseudo-science before the 20th century began: Gall and his followers had made dubious inferences between the bumps of the skull and people's personalities and used scientific language to write about it.[11]

Although the *Studien* included Breuer's Anna O., the version of events Breuer published left no doubt about the aspirations of the two authors. What made the *Studien* exceptional at the time was not the traditional exorcism it described but, as Webster pointed out, "the extreme and quite unjustifiable claims which it put forward."[12] When Freud had persuaded Breuer to include the case, the two authors claimed Anna *had been cured* by Breuer's treatment — they declared to have produced evidence that psychoanalysis worked. Anna was at last "free from the innumerable disturbances she had previously exhibited. [She] traveled for a while; but it was a considerable time before she regained her mental balance entirely. Since then she has enjoyed complete health." This was not true. All the time, Breuer and Freud have had no idea about the causes and characteristics of Anna's disease and eventually had to send her away — not cured at all. Worse, between July and October 1882, the doctors of a psychiatric hospital had to bring her off an addiction to morphine and choral hydrate. They diagnosed Anna with hallucinations and psychosis. Furthermore, she was treated in the Swiss Sanatorium Bellevue in Kreuzlingen. After discharge from the sanatorium, she left Germany to stay with relatives for a few months. She did a nursing course at the Union Clinic in Karlsruhe. However, her problems returned. For three long periods between 1883 and 1888 she went to Inzerdorf Sanatorium outside Vienna. Eventually, without any assistance of Breuer or Freud, she recovered and moved back to Germany. In Frankfurt she began her impressive public career as a feminist social worker. At the end of her life in 1935, she returned to Vienna where she observed the tragedy that awaited European Jewry. She died of cancer on May 28, 1936. In 1963, her biographer Dora Edinger wrote that Pappenheim always spoke with vitriolic sarcasm about psychoanalysis, although she apparently never mentioned her own illness. Her doctors at Bellevue Sanatorium, however, remembered how she ventured "disparaging judgements against the ineffectiveness of science in regard to her sufferings." In later years, she exclaimed: "As long as I live, psychoanalysis will never penetrate my establishments." For some time, however, Freud's fiancée Martha Bernays kept in contact with her and wrote in a letter that the girl had kept her hallucinations at night.[13]

It is interesting that in February 1880 — a few months before Anna O.

was diagnosed with hysteria — a Danish stage hypnotist by the name of Carl Hansen drew full houses in Austria. Many in the Viennese elite and middle class witnessed the shows; others had heard or read about them, including Pappenheim. Borch-Jacobsen felt that it could be no coincidence that Anna O. performed exactly as Hansen's hypnotized subjects on stage. Anna O. must have understood how to stage hysteria. In December 1881, when Breuer grew desperate with the girl, she confessed that she sometimes simulated attacks. She *faked*. Breuer refused to believe her for he was convinced that he had already seen confirmations of his hypotheses. Freud did not mind. Rumors circulated that in France Pierre Janet was writing a major publication on the sexual background of unconscious motives, and Freud wished to publish about this first, before Janet anyway. Nevertheless, we should be careful not to judge the "faking" too easily. Before film and television, theater, beyond offering entertainment, was important for people to learn about correct social behavior through simulation. The Danish hypnotist made a particular kind of hysteric credible. Members of the audience would have felt the need to copy it, especially those who felt in need of contact or psychological assistance and who were not capable of finding a solution on their own.[14]

In the same period Freud's Berlin friend Wilhelm Fliess shared in tracking the road of error. Fliess wrote a book called (in translation): *The Relations Between the Nose and the Female Sexual Organs from the Biological Aspect* (1897). His theory of "nasal reflex neuroses" postulated that the origins of a woman's problems should be found in masturbation — to be believed as an "erroneous canalization" of sexual energy involved in several types of "unnatural" sexual behavior like coitus interruptus or the use of a condom. Fliess thought that the main symptoms were headaches; migraines; cardiac and respiratory irregularities; vertigo; various pains in the stomach, arms, and shoulders; and the like. Women with these symptoms were immediately diagnosed accordingly. In 1893, Fliess had 130 patients with this syndrome. A true epidemic. A treatment was at hand, for the idea was that, because of the relationship between nose and vagina, operating on the nose — removing the turbinate bone — should cure hysteria caused by masturbation or coitus interruptus. His second theory focused upon periodicity, derived from the menstrual cycle whereby the two periods of 28 and 23 days were significant. With various arithmetical calculations using the numbers 23, 28, 51 (their sum), and 5 (their difference), including the squares and cubes, the mystery of human biology could not only be unlocked but also related to the motions of the stars using the formula: $x \times 23 \pm y \times 28$. He would always find confirmation because any two positive integers can be used to produce any positive number that is desired. No wonder Freud underscored this theory of wonders without hesitation, adopting an attitude of reverence and submission and looking for guidance and advice. Interestingly, in their *Dossier Freud* (2006), Borch-Jacobsen and Shamdasani suggest indirectly that — by curiously noticing some spontaneous infantile erections of his young son — Fliess had confirmed Freud's writing in such a way that he could be regarded at least as a co-founder of psychoanalysis.[15]

Such theories could have devastating consequences for therapy. The main known victim was Emma Eckstein (1865–1924). She had come to Freud at the age of 27, seeking treatment for vague symptoms like stomach ailments and slight depression related to menstruation. Freud diagnosed Eckstein as suffering from trauma, which he regarded as secondary to childhood sexual abuse. In addition, he suspected a "nasal reflex neurosis." He invited Fliess to remove a piece of Eckstein's nose. In the weeks following the operation the girl hemorrhaged profusely as infection set in. She almost died. Desperate, Freud consulted with another surgeon in Vienna, who removed a piece of surgical gauze of some 50 centimeters. Freud wrote Fliess in Berlin about it on March 8, 1895: "That this mishap should have happened to you; how you will react to it when you hear about it; what others could make of it; how wrong I was to urge you to operate in a foreign city where you could not follow through on the case; how my intention to do my best for this poor girl was insidiously thwarted and resulted in endangering her life — all this came over me simultaneously."[16] Then, Freud reassured his friend: "Of course, no one is blaming you, nor would I know why they should." In the days following the hemorrhage, Freud's letters seemed to suggest he *did* put the blame on Fliess. March 8: "[The surgeon] is using iodoform wicks instead of gauze." March 13: "It is now about time you forgave yourself the minimal oversight, as Breuer called it." March 28: "I know what you want to hear first: she is tolerably well, complete subsidence, no fever, no hemorrhage." April 20: "[I am] still very miserable, but also offended that you deem it necessary to have a testimonial certificate from [the surgeon who saved Eckstein's life] for your rehabilitation. For me you remain the physician, the type of man into whose hands one confidently put one's life and that of one's family [...]." Embarrassing. With the left side of her face caved in, Eckstein was mutilated forever. Ostensibly, she did not blame Freud, for after years of more talking cured her, she was initialized as a psychoanalyst herself. After the lifesaving operation, she had greeted Freud with: "So this is the strong sex."

To remove Fliess's guilt altogether, Freud thought, was to prove beyond doubt that Eckstein's bleedings followed the rhythm of her menstrual periods — according to the formula $x \times 23 \pm y \times 28$ — although, as indicated by a letter of April 26, 1896, "the woman, out of resistance, has not yet supplied me with the dates" of the menstrual period. Much later, Freud recognized suddenly specific unconscious motives in Eckstein: the bleedings must have been a deliberate instrument to attract Freud to her bed. They were not inflicted by that piece of iodoform gauze, Freud argued, Eckstein had bled like this out of repressed sexual desire from childhood onwards. To deliver the evidence for the Eckstein case without direct proof, it was inevitable to look at Eckstein's imagination.[17] Eckstein's childhood history of early sexual desires was blown up to the history of childhood in general. It meant a crucial change in Freud's thinking and almost certainly the very beginnings of the theory of the Oedipus Complex. Thus, following this route, repression became the basic foundation of psychoanalysis. Fliess was grateful. Finally, Freud included Fliess's theory on bisexuality: humans were born as bisexuals. This theory still belongs to standard teaching — if we believe Phyllis and Robert Tyson's *Psychoanalytic Theories of Development* (1990) — which, of course, is as erroneous as the nasal reflex neurosis theory.[18] Quite a development following Fliess's catastrophic operation on Emma's nose.

Around 1900, Freud accepted Ida Bauer (1882–1945) as a patient. Psychoanalysts know her as Dora. At first, Freud told the girl that her problems were of organic, thus physical, origins resulting from a father who had syphilis before her conception. However, as soon as she had recounted her symptoms, Freud saw Dora as psychosomatic neurotic and without further physical examination he began his analysis. Although during her childhood at least two doctors had diagnosed appendicitis, Freud disapproved of this diagnosis. Dora's problems, he thought, must have been hysterical. A friend of her father had frequently harassed the girl, Freud speculated, and she had rejected his approaches. Freud wondered why Dora had no sexual desires when she felt the man's erected phallus against her body, and stated that Dora unconsciously desired both the man and his wife (!). Hers was a case of "hysterical pregnancy." In a way, he must have helped to prolong the girl's unhappiness by postulating all kinds of imagined disorders. Feminist journalist Janet Malcolm, who researched in the Freud Archives, became irritated by his notes. She found Freud more like a police inspector interrogating a suspect than like a doctor helping a patient: "'Aha!' Freud would say to poor Dora, a […] girl suffering from a nervous cough, migraine, and a kind of general youthful malaise. 'Aha! I know about you. I know your dirty little secrets. Admit that you were secretly attracted to Herr K. Admit that you masturbated when you were five. Look at what you're doing now as you lie there playing with your reticule — opening it, putting a finger into it, shutting it again!'"[19] Dora denied these desires — masturbating at age five — and after repetitious scenes with Freud, left his analysis. She had suffered three months under this mental harassment. But Freud would write about it as another successful treatment. No doubt it is superfluous to repeat that any scholar with a love for testable observations and respect for the establishment of data should be alarmed by Freud's writing in the Dora case. Not his followers. His well-known pupil Erik Erikson (1902–94), for instance, described Dora's identity as "fragmentary" and her feelings as "snobbish superiority." In fact, Erikson expressed the Dora case as the classical analysis of the structure and genesis of hysteria. Ironically, it is.[20]

In their book, Breuer and Freud, of course, rehearsed the cathartic or exorcist argument that remembering the origins of a certain trauma under hypnosis would remove its poignant consequences for the patient. If there was no result, Freud argued in the book, patients might not "want" to remember — he called this a defense mechanism. Hence, the therapist was always right: the patient had the memories the therapist suggested, consciously by acknowledging or unconsciously by defending. The therapist needed no further data anymore; his theory was sufficient. Freud advised therapeutic hypnotists to press the patient's forehead in order to remove any defenses. Another possibility was to force the patients to remember by actively prompting possibilities. The therapist must deduce the patients' secrets and actively *force* this deduction upon them. Usually, Freud continued, they would give in. Sometimes, it would take much longer. He expressed confidence that his exorcist pressure technique would work. The therapy was successful only when the memories were "full" and "whole" — thus, when a story or a discourse was set up in line with the therapist's theory. Unaware of suggestion, or indifferent to it, Freud supposed an active role for the therapist: he had to formulate a story the patient had to "remember." For sure, this process is extremely suspect: Freud had his answers ready, and his subject needed to be forced — *his* words indeed — to confirm. This was a variant of the "method" he had developed during his cocaine research. In short, the stutter diagnosis of Frau Emmy von N., so important for reviewers writing about *The King's Speech*, found its roots in a period of medical errors and misdiagnosis that is far from a scholarly context.

# 5

All this does not sound very reliable. But many attracted to psychoanalysis believe that Freud had made his observations from studying his patients. This was hardly the case. Freud had invented his theories and wanted his patients to confirm them. Today this counts as a deductive method, but with one basic difference: a deductively working scholar works with hypotheses that can be disproven. Freud, however, had designed his "technique" in such a way that the patients would not dare to contradict. If they did, he recorded their statements as confirmation of his theories anyway, because any contradiction was built in as the "defense mechanism of the subconscious." However, Freud published about only seven fully described case histories: "Anna O.," "Dora," "Fräulein Elisabeth von R.," "Frau Emmy von N.," "Little Hans," the "Rat Man," and the "Wolf Man." The cases of Anna O., Emma Eckstein and Dora have already been discussed; the Wolf Man case will be discussed in one of the following chapters. In addition Freud commented on roughly 35 cases more, including "Cäcilie M.," Emma Eckstein, "H.D." (Hilda Doolittle),

"Fräulein Katharina," "Fräulein Lucy R.," and a man called "E." Few of them had actually terminated the treatment. In a professional life of about 30 years, this means that Freud must have had very few patients per year. To survive economically, he demanded that they have many sessions and he also charged them a lot of money for a consult of one hour; his fee in 1925 was equivalent to about € 400 euros (or some $600) today. Psychoanalysis had no room for poor people; Freud literally said so several times, and he refused to offer consultations free of charge.[21]

Of course, there were periods with more patients. For example, around October 9, 1898, he wrote in a letter to Fliess that things seemed a little better: "The treatments start at nine o'clock — before that two short calls — and last until one-thirty; from three to five a pause for consulting hours, the office being alternately empty or full; from five to nine treatments again. I am definitely expecting another case — ten to eleven psychotherapies a day." A month later, the number of cases was still increasing. Freud explained that he listened to these patients and designed theories about real or imagined sexual seductions, which were in accordance with his recent or his earlier theories. However, as he wrote on January 16, 1899, "two years [of treatment] brought no confirmation of it." This echoes what he wrote on September 21, 1897: "The continual disappointment in my efforts to bring a single analysis to a real conclusion; the running away of people who for a period of time had been most gripped [by analysis]; the absence of the complete successes on which I had counted [...]." In short, he hardly had "results" from his patients. In fact, he found ample time to write his famous "dream book" *The Interpretation of Dreams* (1900) based on the one patient from which he could get a "result," himself.[22]

Next to *The Interpretation of Dreams*, Freud had time enough to write his letters to his friend in Berlin. On October 18, 1893, he reported that the people are "not rushing to consult me," yet he mentioned beautiful cases and recorded that he could make some progress with his thinking. As early as August 1, 1890, he turned down an invitation to visit Fliess in Berlin because he feared he would lose a patient, who "might get well in my absence [...]." The patient did not in fact need him? After noting, in April 1895, that cases of neurosis "are now very rare"— perhaps because people had "proper" sex, abstaining from masturbation, from using the condom or other "improper" ways — and that his time with patients often came to an untimely end, he realized his failures. After Cousin Elise v. G. left his practice he wrote that "it remains to be seen whether it [treatment] was of some use to her." On October 15, 1897, Freud reported once more that his practice "uncannily" left him a great deal of free time. A fortnight later, he admitted that because of the free time, he let himself "be persuaded to take on two cases for treatment without a fee." He also began his self-analysis that year. In December it still was very quiet. "Altogether, this is an abominably bad year." February 9, 1898: "As for the rest, everything is still in a state of latency. My self-analysis is at rest in favor of the dream book. The cases of hysteria are proceeding especially poorly. I shall not finish a single one this year either; and as for the next one, I shall be completely without patient material." On April 13, Freud observed that his "work load has not increased, as it did before Easter." Then, May 25: "Business is in a steady decline [...]; three new contacts have already been broken off; a fourth, of no more value, is about to do the same; I foresee all sorts of difficulties, yet remain in the best of spirits." And: "If in June and July things continue as they are now, with two and a half patients a day, I shall have to write it." Three days later: "The ten analyses are in no hurry [to come]. I now have two and a half! Four prospects did not materialize; otherwise, dead silence. Strangely enough, this leaves me cold. Lately my technique has been near perfect." Soon after this: "For the time being I have almost nothing to do; so I have the leisure to complete it [the book]." The situation was sometimes desperate: "At this time I am just plain stupid; I sleep during my afternoon analyses; absolutely nothing new occurs to me any longer." April 27: "At present my earnings are so bad that I must not stay away a single day except holidays." Soon after this: "I still have nothing to do; that is, two hours [of treatment] instead of ten." January 26, 1900: "Nothing is happening, really. When I remind myself that I have had only one new case since May 1899, one you know, and that again I am to lose four patients between April and May, I am not exactly in a cheerful mood." February 22: "The new patient soon departed again!" And on April 25: "The patient whom I treated for fourteen days and then dismissed as a case of paranoia has since hanged herself in a hotel room." Writing letters could be done during practice hours: "I have just a lady in hypnosis in front of me, so I have time to write you."[23]

No wonder that Freud's writing during these years seems not to have been guided by being a successful therapist, but by becoming a famous scholar. The way to do this was first of all by mimicking the scholarly language in his writing and then by joining in a widely disseminated public debate. He chose the debate about the instrument of hypnosis to cure diseases of the mind and lined up with Jean-Marie Charcot (1825–93) and Janet in opposition to Hippolyte Bernheim (1840–1919). Although it is clear from several letters that Freud had always known that Anna's "prototype of a cathartic cure" was neither a cure nor a catharsis — and that the exorcist method had not worked at all — in his publications he remained silent about this knowledge because he could use the case in this debate. Charcot's argument about the value of hypnosis — replicated in Breuer's writing — originated in the work of another Austrian physician, Franz Anton Mesmer (1734–1815), who later made a career in France. Also Freud's "pressure technique" had links with Mesmer — making him a kind of "mesmerist." In 1774, Mesmer said that he had produced an "artificial tide" in a patient. He made her swallow a preparation containing iron, after which he attached magnets to parts of her body. The patient agreed that she felt streams of some fluid through her body. For several hours, she was relieved of her symptoms. The theory stipulated that because the fluid would flow between two poles, the body functioned like a magnet. If a patient had a psychological problem, an obstacle was thought to impede the free flowing of the fluids. Making use of the poles, the therapist, as a "magnetizer," could attend the patient by removing the obstacle. Inspired by Newton's gravity theory, Mesmer wrote that equally invisible, an extremely thin fluid surrounded and penetrated every living body on earth, which could be blocked in a similar way. To "cure" people, his method was indispensable. Because he could simply use his own hands, he soon stopped using magnets as a part of his treatment. Mesmer used "media," persons called *somnambules*, or magnetic sleepwalkers, to "diagnose" the disease, identify the poles, suggest treatment, and so forth. Historian Robert Darnton calls Mesmer's work and his movement — Mesmer had many followers — "the end of the Enlightenment"— and hence the beginning of Romanticism. He also shows that the "mesmerists" in France were reactionaries who supported the monarchy against the Revolution of 1789 — which is interesting in light of Freud's own choices. In 1784, a scientific committee unmasked mesmerism: it had been nothing but suggestion. In short, the patient performed what the physician suggested. Nothing of the "magnetist" performance originated in the patient's unconscious.[24] Eventually, as a consequence of the fall of Mesmer and Charcot, hysteria would disappear from psychiatry altogether.

Choices like this — defending a lost cause — seem to have been typical for Freud. One rather odd one derived indirectly from the germ theory of chemist Louis Pasteur (1822–95) and physician Robert Koch (1843–1910). Reading their work, Freud grabbed the idea that all genuine diseases had one sole cause. The single key to open all human secrets was sex; not just sex but literally the "healthy coitus." The main purpose of research was to discover the responsible agent. For Freud, the main vehicle that interrupted the "healthy coitus" was the invented world of infantile sexuality. Convinced that this was the sole source for mental illness —*all* mental illnesses, this was the first odd choice — Freud cut off categorically whatever constraints of empirical reality still existed. This belief became the major thread through all the stories and letters about his patients. The second odd choice was to work with the theory of biological evolutionary development by Lamarck's foremost German disciple Ernst Haeckel (1834–1919). Especially catastrophic was Freud's implementation of Haeckel's idea that, first, life is driven toward *always more complex* forms by contact with the outside world, and, second, therefore evolution is fueled by the inheritance of *acquired characteristics*. From this, Haeckel had developed the "biogenetic law" or "recapitulation theory." The theory stipulates that the biological development of an organism —*ontogeny*— replicates the full evolutionary development —*phylogeny*— of a species: as if "ontogeny recapitulates phylogeny." The embryo of an advanced species is thought to recapitulate in the womb the stages the species went through in its evolutionary descent. For the human fetus this would mean re-enacting from a unicellular organism to a fully formed human being, passing through fish-like and mammalian stages.[25]

The human soul, however, if we follow Haeckel, had not stayed on the same pace. He thought that all organisms possessed souls — or consciousness — but that their development could only be initiated by external stimuli, thus, *after* birth. The newly born human baby came into this world with a developed body but only an "embryonic" soul. Consequently, after birth the soul or consciousness of the child had to undergo the same developmental stages as its body had passed in the womb, now by being confronted with the outside world. This was fundamental to Freud. And because for Freud sexual development was its main motor — "sexual" meaning actual intercourse or the wish to engage therein — the Haeckelian development stages were connected to the sexual. It must be said that already at this time, Haeckel was known as a kind of swindler who adapted "facts" to his theory and fabricated a part of his famous embryo-pictures. In modern biology and social studies most of his arguments have been shown to be over-generalizations at best and largely incorrect. No wonder that Haeckel considered himself a Goethe-reincarnate, a faithful disciple of the great German Romantic poet. The Romantic "genius" blended the poet and scholar in one person.

In his *Three Essays on the Theory of Sexuality* (1905), Freud had built on Haeckel's misguided scheme for his own model of developmental stages: the mouth stage of simple organisms, the cloacal stage of reptiles and birds, and so forth. In progressing from having the sexual consciousness of a simple animal to that of a reptile, for Freud each stage of animal sexuality would succumb to necessary automatic organic repression until a fully human sexual consciousness was achieved. Furthermore, Freud suggested that the sexual instinct must be present in newly born children and, to please Fliess, that it started out as *bisexual*. Sexual pleasure was obtained *phylogenetically* by "autoerotic" movements: children stimulated their "erotogenic" zones through sucking (oral), excretion (anal), and masturbation (phallic). The child would mature as these stages were necessarily repressed, and the sexual energy or *libido* would be organized under the primacy of the genitals and be subordinated to the purpose of sexual reproduction. Only the latter was considered normal development, hence Freud's focus on unrepressed masturbation, homosexuality (anal excretion), and oral sucking (fellatio) as causes of neuroses. It is here that the link between retentive-expulsive speech patterns and an unconscious equation of words with feces, so crucial for the stuttering theory, was theorized. Let it be clear that, after much discussion with Fliess, Freud invented the oral, anal, and phallic phases because he transferred the doctrines of Lamarck and Haeckel to his psychoanalysis and not on the basis of the stories he is supposed to have heard from patients.

Considering Freud's own writings and conclusions there is no need to diagnose a stutterer as hysterical. In fact, there is no reason at all to put trust in Freud's writings from this period. Contrary to the usually general character of the tropes of psychoanalytical popular psychology — "disorders today are the consequences of childhood traumas" — the Freudian Edifice is filled with details. Most of these details do not hold in the light of research. Some scholars, like John Bruer, stress the importance of lifelong learning and development against the myth of the first three years. Reviewing a wealth of material, he contradicts the idea of the first three years of life as the most critical developmental period. The brain takes almost two full decades to mature and even after that time modifications occur. Around age ten, children's brains contain more synapses (neural connections) than at any other time in their lives. At this age they have already experienced a few intensive years of life among their peers. Important as this sounds, the brain is not "cooked" by age ten. In fact, it keeps on developing and its structure is continually affected by experience. Neuroscientists believe that even lost neurons can be regenerated. In her meticulously researched book on motherhood and natural selection, *Mother Nature* (1999), primatologist and anthropologist Sarah Hrdy undermined the myth of the first three years further. She argued that also from the mother's side bonding with her child is not as self-evident as popularly thought. Obviously, there is no rejection of the desperate need of babies to be attached to a caretaker or of infants to feel secure. Her argument revolves around the position of the mother: it can be the mother's choice not to turn over her life to meeting the infant's insatiable need for contact. Bruer reassures his readers that despite all difficulties for the young, most children are relatively resilient. They thrive in a variety of environments as they continue to learn throughout their lifetimes.[26]

Because so few patients found their way to his practice, Freud could not have had a very good reputation. The fact that many patients left Freud's practice because they had found no cure might reflect a centuries-old practice of medical support. For centuries, patients had contracted physicians and other medical "professionals" to be cured but if they were not, they had sent the doctor away — usually without pay. Obviously, for centuries, the medical profession was not as successful as today. The line between a physician and a quack was difficult to draw. This means that physicians had little authority yet, perhaps even not as much status as today. The patients made up their own mind about their illness, even about the desired cure, which the physician then had to deliver. Until well into the 19th century, the experience of illness was still substantially defined and controlled by the patients themselves. It was the sick person who first made an attempt at diagnosis and treatment. The intervention of the doctor was auxiliary and subordinate to the invalid's own initiative in identifying the illness and its appropriate cure. Freud's peculiar self-analysis fell into a very old tradition. The doctor-patient relationship in our culture is second and subordinated to the doctor-illness relationship in which the patient is just the carrier or a case. We regard the doctor as an expert in illnesses — and how to cure or at least treat us. This was not the case in the centuries before Freud's time. Doctors were focused on the patients and on ways of helping them. These physicians focused on the treatment of disease rather than on the diagnosis. Their behavior depended largely on the conditions dictated by the patient. In Freud's time, the patient became, as it were, a corpse to anatomize and the basic rules of medical practice were ever more established by peer groups of professional colleagues. From an active participant, the patient had become passive. But, as in any period of transformation, this might have been more part of the doctor's discourses than yet of the patient's practice. Despite the new attitude of the physicians, the patients would still act as if little had changed. In short, Dora — like many of Freud's other patients — might have acted as one of those active patients that the physicians knew very well indeed.[27] Interestingly, the attitude of Prince Albert at Logue's was in line with such historical precedents.

# 6

In 1995, by simply grouping dispersed research together, development psychologist Judith R. Harris liberated a huge amount of data published in the field of traditional nurture-oriented paradigms. With an article in the prestigious *Psychological Review*—"Where Is the Child's Environment?"— she shook the field of socialization research. Later on, she extended the argument to a book, *The Nurture Assumption* (1998). In it, she reminds the attentive reader that (1) genes are a big part of human developmental variation; (2) the effects of diverse parenting practices are restricted to the home and much less outside it; and (3) environmental effects come largely from peer socialization. A wave of criticism was the result, especially from nurture-oriented therapists like the psychoanalysts. Their voices were taken seriously. Understandably, because on their first contact with psychoanalysis, writes Macmillan, "few people escape the feeling that they have been introduced to an extremely powerful explanatory system." Only later, or on closer reading, they may appreciate the paradox on which that conviction rests. Psychoanalytic explanations and interpretations are basically indeterminate, even though they have the appearance of being comprehensive and rigidly deterministic. "Nothing seems to fall outside the explanatory net," says Macmillan, "but one cannot be sure what has been caught." They have been tricked by the skilled writer Freud was. For some, his "dream book" can be read as a novel about a "psychoanalyst" studying himself, in the meantime inventing a theory of the "subconscious." *The Interpretation of Dreams* also has much in common with today's mockumentaries, films or television shows in which fiction is presented in documentary format. As we shall see below, several Freud historians went through key passages of Freud's *Interpretation* to juxtapose them with scholarly results from the cognitive sciences.[28]

In all we realize that too much emphasis is laid on nurture. Stuttering has a genetic component too important to neglect. In his reaction to *The King's Speech*, Lehrer stresses this result from modern research and with good reasons. There are two types of stutterers, writes Ehud Yairi, a well-known speech scholar: those who persist and those who recover. He continues: "Through detailed analyses of the incidence of the disorder within the families of the participating children provided strong evidence not only that stuttering, in general, has strong genetic components, but that the two subsets of children who stutter [...], have different genetic liabilities for stuttering. In other words, the tendency to persist or recover also tends to be heritable." The data suggests, Yiari believes, that parents' personalities or their attitudes can be causally related to stuttering is a belief, a psychomyth no doubt, with no validity. Although scholars still admit that the true cause of stuttering is not known, brain scanning studies have established abnormal circuitry in the basal ganglia combined with an increased activity in the speech involved areas of the brain, suggesting a "traffic-jam" on the neuronal level. Lehrer implies: "It's as if the stammer is triggered by an excess of planning, much like the yips in golf." This, of course, is a mechanical defect, rooted in the functioning of the brain translating thoughts into bodily movements like speech. It has nothing to do with the repression of a deep-seated childhood trauma.[29]

Are the filmmakers to blame? In a way, they are. Lehrer concludes that the antiquated representation of the stutterer and "the way it exaggerated the role of catharsis in fixing the problem" in this film will ruin its good intentions. It has been established that confirmation of a trope underscores its "truthiness." After articulating the prince's stammer with his youth, they screen the problems as ongoing current predicaments for the prince: his father had been harsh with him all the time and his brother still behaves defectively toward him. The viewers will certainly understand these scenes as the confirmation of childhood trauma. Nevertheless, the attitudes of his father and brother rest on fact and Logue, apparently, believed in his theory. This is different from, for example, *The Killer Inside Me*, where it is the filmmaker who explicitly links Lou's murderous mind with his childhood. That is the Freudian Excuse all over. Because of its historicized character, it is somewhat singular in *The King's Speech*. A special editing could have been of some help, however, not linking and stressing the articulation. The best thing the director could have done was to end his film with a screen board about modern views on stammering and pointing at the genetic origins. Lehrer, of course, demands more: "The King didn't get better because he confessed to Logue about his inner pain — he got better because he found, with Logue's help, a way to calm and distract his overexcited brain, practicing his consonants until they became easier to express." To emphasize hysteria as in *The King's Speech* is unfortunate indeed. "Modern science has moved far beyond Freud's description of Frau Emmy, in which the disorder is caused by the repression of early childhood trauma. It is time for Hollywood to move on as well."[30]

# 7

The image left after reading Freud's work, including the Freud-Fliess correspondence, is quite defacing for psychoanalysis. Realizing the potential damage, Freud wished to have had the correspondence destroyed and asked Princess Marie Bonaparte of Greece and Denmark (1882–1962) to take care of it. She did not. The princess was the wealthy great-grandniece of Emperor Napoleon I of France (1769–1821); she inherited her wealth from the principal real estate developer of Monte Carlo — her maternal grandfather — and married Prince George of Greece (1869–1957) in 1907. The princess was less interested in psychoanalysis as a simulation model for social life, as Freud was. Her interest was invoked by lovemaking. She came to Freud in 1925 because of difficulties in achieving sexual fulfillment during missionary position intercourse. Although she apparently saw Freud as a sex therapist, she soon engaged in research of her own on "frigidity." She measured the distance between the clitoris and the vagina in 243 women and concluded that the distance between the two organs was critical for the ability to reach orgasm. Because Freud found orgasm by clitoral stimulation "unhealthy," she regarded vaginal-clitoris combined orgasm with a penis as the only legitimate type. The Princess decided to be operated on in order to surgically move her clitoris closer to the vagina. When it proved unsuccessful in facilitating the sought-after outcome, she ordered a second operation. In her lifelong quest to achieve vaginal orgasm, she invited numerous men to share her bed. Next to her sex-therapy research, she financed several projects of other psychoanalytically inspired researchers, paid Freud's ransom to Nazi Germany, and translated his work into French.[31]

# 2

## *Agnostic Bella*

### The Deep in *The Rite* (2011) and *The Twilight Saga: New Moon* (2009)
Mikael Håfström (director), Michael Petroni (writer); and Chris Weitz (director), Melissa Rosenberg (writer)

### 1

At the tiny courtyard of his home in Rome, young Michael Kovak (Colin O'Donoghue) meets the renowned exorcist Father Lucas Trevant (Anthony Hopkins). "Father Xavier tells me you're troubled," says Father Lucas. Kovak struggles with a lack of faith. "I don't think Father Xavier explained the situation..." Kovak tries to respond, but the Father does not take no for an answer: "He explained it well enough. I have arranged for you to meet someone." This is a girl possessed by a demon. She entered the Father's house with her aunt. Rosaria (Marta Gastini) is a 16-year-old, pregnant by her father. Dressing up, Father Lucas instructs Kovak: "Whatever you do, don't address the girl directly, no matter what she says. And if I ask you to hold her down, it's best you grab her arms from behind and try keeping her in a seated position. The spirit is pretty devious. Hasn't shown itself yet." "Spirit?" Kovak asks. He wants to know how Father Lucas knows about the possession. Father Lucas gives him a plastic bag and asks him to put in something that is his. Kovak gives a dollar bill. Next, Father Lucas absolves him and they go to the next room, where the girl is waiting. "Oh, yes, one other thing. If it does manifest, don't even look into the girl's eyes. Whatever you do, do not address it. Do not speak to it. It's the Devil. Leave that to me. Do you understand?" Father Lucas starts to perform his ritual: lighting candles, talking to the girl. She says the voice in her head keeps talking, even when she sleeps. He asks her to guess what is in the bag. He does so shouting, forcing it out of her: "I'm ordering you to guess! Guess!" She gives the correct answer. How could she know? This was to show Kovak that there is a demon who knows everything. "You see, knowledge of the unknown." For Kovak it could have been just a lucky guess. Father Lucas: "It's the quickest test for possession. The devil is working in and through her right now." The girl is becoming nervous; she starts behaving in an awkward manner. Asked by the Father, Rosaria says she hears these voices in her head, talking about awful things. The Father wants to know the name of the demon. If he knows its name, he can address it directly in the name of God and command it to leave Rosaria's body. The Father looks at the girl's eyes; he takes a Bible and a cross and starts to recite prayers in Latin, while the girl begins to move bizarrely. She scratches viciously at her scalp. Next, the Father touches her forehead, making a cross, and pressing his hand on her head even further. The girl becomes aggressive: "Shut up, priest. You must not touch me. You are disgusting. Keep your dirty hands off me. Shut up! You must not speak. Don't touch me!" She talks in Italian. But the priest hits her on the forehead. Kovak is shocked: a priest hitting someone! Unexpectedly, the girl, now exhausted, appears normal again. Father Lucas is friendly to her as usual. The girl leaves. Father Lucas indicates that the demon had not gone yet. He has won a battle, not the war.

# 2

This scene is from *The Rite* (2011), a feature made by Swedish director Mikael Håfström after a script by Michael Petroni. *The Rite* is not a possession movie — too dull for the horror lovers — and not designed to make the audience scream. It presents itself as a serious film, showing good men of the cloth fighting against the demon Baal. Before opening combat, however, the exorcist has to acknowledge that the demon exists. This is the crucial act. It brands *The Rite* as a film about the crisis of faith that is plaguing our own times. This could also be Freudian, because if a psychoanalyst identifies a repressed thought, the trauma is known and can be handled to disappear. Indeed, Rosaria could be a hysteric like Anna O. or Dora. The "technique" of exorcism as performed by Father Lucas is also quite similar: touching the girl's forehead and shouting violently at the "demon within" to make it identify itself. However, Petroni had no Freudian lenses. Despite the supernatural-looking special effects at the end of the movie, the exorcism scenes are in general considered accurate. Petroni used a manuscript by journalist Matt Baglio, who at the time was finishing his book — *The Rite: The Making of a Modern Exorcist*

(2009)—on the experiences of California priest Father Gary Thomas and his days as a student at the Vatican. Baglio had met him in Rome, at a seminar organized by the Pontifical Athenaeum Regina Apostolorum, run by the right-wing Vatican-sponsored Legionnaires of Christ. As a man living in the age of psychology, the priest acknowledges that most suffering would be due to mental health illness. Therefore, he works in the United States with a team that includes a psychologist. As an exorcist priest, however, Father Gary is also certain about diabolical presence and he saw to it that Baglio and Håfström took exorcism and faith seriously. It could be that the possessed involved in his story found the same way out of their psychological problems as Bertha Pappenheim: by "faking," not the hysterical but the diabolical, as a still legitimate solution in our own time. This skepticism would not convince Baglio, who found his way back to reconnect to the Catholic Church. For *The Rite*, screenwriter Petroni, also a practicing Roman Catholic, coordinated his screenplay with Baglio. Filming the exorcist scenes, Håfström had Father Gary at the set.

The film's focalization switches mostly between Kovak and Father Lucas. The term "focalization" points at a perspectival filter with the camera residing as it were within the storyworld, inviting the viewers to experience from within both minds. This way, the audience learns that Kovak has been grappling with his faith since his mother's death. His father (Rutger Hauer), a mortuary owner, is stubborn, aloof and silent. Kovak finds studying the most obvious way to escape. Without many resources, he decides to enroll in a seminar because the Church offers free degrees. He plans to abdicate his vows upon completion. After four years the moment comes to write his letter of resignation. However, in an attempt to discuss his alleged lack of faith, Father Matthew (Toby Jones), his superior, tries to catch up with him outside the seminary. In the hurry, the Father causes a fatal traffic accident when a biker, a young woman, trying to avoid a collision, hits an oncoming car. Rapidly on the spot, Kovak wants to help the victim. She recognizes him as a priest as he is still wearing his clerical garb and asks for absolution. Kovak knows he cannot refuse and acts out what he has learnt calm and confidently. Father Matthew recognizes the empathy with which Kovak performs the ritual, thereby comforting the young woman visibly. Afterwards, Father Matthew tells Kovak that he is called to be a priest. Furthermore, he invites him to go to the Vatican to attend the seminar on exorcism. Kovak accepts when he knows about the remuneration: the Church would redeem his $100,000 student loan. In addition, Father Matthews cleverly tells him that he could always resign from a position in the Church, even after finishing the seminar in Rome.

At the Vatican, Father Xavier (Ciarán Hinds), one of the teachers, stimulates Kovak into visiting the renowned exorcist Father Lucas. During classes he meets a young woman, Angeline (Alice Braga), who appears to be a reporter covering the course for a newspaper article. With her sense of reality, she functions as the mirror of his modern mind. She wants to interview Father Lucas and asks Kovak to share all the information he gets from the exorcist. However, Kovak, realizing the trap, declines and keeps her away from the exorcist. At his home, Father Lucas is open and direct to Kovak. He wants to show him the indisputable facts of demonic possession and introduces him to one of his "patients," bashing and swearing pregnant teenager Rosaria. This is the scene described above. It appears that the girl was raped by her father. Seeing the girl, Kovak puts into words what the viewers of *The Rite* are supposed to think: the girl should be sent to a psychiatrist. Kovak asks Father Lucas if he thinks these stories about evil supernatural entities are true. "Ah, the truth," the Father counters. "Yeah, certainly..." Critic Andrew O'Hehir appreciates Father Lucas's sarcasm; a demeanor that must be rooted in his matching "with Lucifer's minions on a near-daily basis." The Father's sarcasm includes, says O'Hehir, "discussions of what exactly [Kovak] would like to do with crusading journalist Angeline." But the critic is not convinced. "God knows the Roman Catholic Church needs a new P.R. initiative, with the priesthood advancing in age, declining in numbers and, shall we say, a bit shorn of its traditional prestige." Critic Roger Ebert agrees. He writes that diagnosing whether Satan is involved is above his pay grade, but: "What I must observe is that demonic possession seems very rare, and the Church rejects the majority of such reports." Interestingly, Father Lucas would agree, in fact, for he underscores the possibility of tricks like suddenly speaking English fluently or coughing up three nails. The priests in *The Rite* are not blind believers.[1]

The possession of Rosaria fails to convince the critics, but not Kovak. With empathy she reminds him of the girl biker whom he absolved in the street back home. His visits with Father Lucas to "patients" sow doubt about his disbelief. Near the climax of the film, he receives a phone call from his father, who tells him he is in some kind of danger. Ringing back, Kovak learns that his father has died six hours earlier. Looking at a devotional picture he received from his mother — with her handwriting: "You're not alone, He will be always with you." — he hears strange voices whispering: "Doubter." Looking outside the window, he sees cloven hoofs in the snow. The Devil? He hears a voice of a weeping girl in the corridor. There is no one there, but he does notice a chain on the doorknob. This brings him eventually downstairs, where he meets a mule with blood red eyes. The next moment, everything is normal again. He calls Angeline: Is he losing his mind? He remembers a visit with Father Lucas to a possessed boy and his mother. He thought that the boy knew something about him and he decides to visit him again, this time with Angeline. The boy says he knew about his father's death. How could he know this? Well, the boy says, you know how, you have seen the mule as well. The Devil gets closer and closer. In the meantime, Rosaria has died in a hospital giving birth. Her baby also died. Father Lucas had won battles but not the war with the demon. The girl's death caused him to fall into serious grief. Apparently the demon could make use of his mental weakness because within hours, Father Lucas shows signs of being possessed himself. When Kovak visits him, he asks him to lock him up and look for Father Xavier to exorcise him. Because the Father is out, Kovak decides to perform the ritual himself, assisted by Angeline. Thanks to his regained faith, he succeeds. Successfully, Kovak returns to the United States, starting a new life as a priest. The closing credits tell us that Father Michael Kovak is now working in a Western suburb — which of course is a fib.

# 3

Exorcism is inevitable — this is the Freudian Excuse in *The Rite*. The belief that this must be the case sometimes has been firmly rooted in the Western soul for centuries and has found its way into psychoanalysis, including Freud's "technique." Early in his career Freud recognized the resemblances while reading about witch-hunts, which were set up both to fight the Devil and to accumulate knowledge about his being — and God's, for that matter. A byproduct, perhaps also intended, was the domestication of female sexual potency. This is one of the recurrent themes of mankind, all over the world. For Freud the medieval witch-hunters were unwittingly exorcizing the "demon inside," or, as he would have it: the haunting unconscious. He wrote about it in two letters to Fliess, discussing his "technique" in relation to his "theories." The first letter is from January 17, 1897:

> What would you say, by the way, if I told you that all of my brand-new prehistory of hysteria is already known and was published a hundred times over, though several centuries ago? Do you remember that I always said that the medieval theory of possession held by the ecclesiastical courts was identical with our theory of a foreign body and the splitting of consciousness? But why did the devil who took possession of the poor things invariably abuse them sexually and in a loathsome manner? Why are their confessions under torture so like the communications made by my patients in psychic treatment? Sometime soon I must delve into the literature on this subject. Incidentally, the cruelties make it possible to understand some symptoms of hysteria that until now have been obscure. The pins which make their appearance in the oddest ways; the sewing needles on account of which the poor things let their breasts be mutilated and which are not visible by X-ray, though they can no doubt be found in their seduction stories! Eckstein has a scene [that is, remembers] where the diabolus sticks needles into

her fingers and then places a candy on each drop of blood. [...] Once more, the inquisitors prick with needles to discover the devil's stigmata, and in a similar situation the victims think of the same old cruel story in fictionalized form (helped perhaps by disguises of the seducers). Thus, not only the victims but also the executioners recalled in this their earliest youth.[2]

Apparently, Fliess reacted enthusiastically to the idea of exploring the comparison with the witch-hunts, because a week later, January 24, Freud wrote him the following response:

> The idea of bringing in witches is gaining strength. I think it is also appropriate. Details are beginning to abound. Their "flying" is explained; the broomstick they ride probably is the great Lord Penis. The secret gatherings, with dancing and entertainment, can be seen any day in the streets where children play. [...] If only I knew why the devil's semen is always described as "cold" in the witches' confessions. I have ordered the *Malleus maleficarum,* and now that I have put the final touch on the infantile paralyses I shall study it diligently. The story of the devil, the vocabulary of popular swear-words, the songs and customs of the nursery — all these are now gaining significance for me. Can you *without* trouble recommend to me some good reading from your excellent memory? In connection with the dancing in witches' confessions, remember the dance epidemics in the Middle Ages. E.'s Louise was such a dancing witch; he was first, consistently enough, reminded of her at the ballet. Hence his theater anxiety. Gymnastic feats in the hysterical attacks of boys and the like belong in the category of flying and floating. I am beginning to grasp an idea: it is as though in the perversions, of which hysteria is the negative, we have before us a remnant of a primeval sexual cult, which once was — perhaps still is — a religion in the Semitic East (Moloch, Astarte). Connecting links abound. Another tributary of the stream is derived from the consideration that there is a class of people who to this very day tell stories like those of the witches and of my patients; they are not believed, although their faith in their stories is not to be shaken. As you have guessed, I mean paranoiacs, whose complaints that excrement is put in their food, that they are maltreated at night in the most shameful way sexually, and so on, are pure memory content.[3]

The *Malleus Maleficarum* was a crucial text for Freud — both for the interpretation of his "technique" and the contextualization of the Witches' Sabbath.

The early modern witch-hunters literally crossed over Europe with the *Malleus Maleficarum* or *The Hammer of Witches* at hand. The book was written by Heinrich Kramer (±1430–±1505), a German Dominican monk, who published it under his Latin name Institoris. The book was a vast success during the so-called witch craze (1450–1750), and republished at least 29 times between 1487 and 1669. These were not the so-called Dark Ages or the supposedly superstitious medieval centuries, but the era of the Renaissance, the Reformation, and the early decades of the Scientific Revolution. Inquisitorial and ecclesiastical courts across Europe and North America tried some 110,000 people for the crime of witchcraft, executing around 60,000—mostly women, but in some areas like Finland, Estonia, Iceland, Normandy, and Burgundy the victims were generally male witches. Most witch-hunts took place in Central Europe and Scotland. The *Malleus Maleficarum* served as a guidebook for the Inquisitors and was designed to aid them in the identification, prosecution, and dispatching of witches. It set forth, as well, many of the modern misconceptions and fears concerning witches and the influence of witchcraft. The questions, definitions, and accusations were reinforced by the Inquisition and came to be widely regarded as irrefutable truth. Reading the *Malleus Maleficarum* as almost every historian of witchcraft, historians Stuart Clark in his *Thinking with Demons* (1997), Robert Thurston in his *Witch, Wicce, Mother Goose* (2001), Walter Stephens in his *Demon Lovers* (2002), and Lara Apps and Andrew Gow in their *Male Witches in Early Modern Europe* (2003) point their readers to what may be called the androcentric turn in the late Middle Ages.[4]

Androcentrism works through gender polarization and biological essentialism. Gender polarization does not just mean that women and men are different from one another but that a male/female "divide is superimposed on so many aspects of the social world that a cultural connection is thereby forged between sex and virtually every other aspect of human experience," says feminist psychologist Sandra Lipsitz Bem,[5] like social roles, dress, sexual desire, or the expression of emotion. To expose its roots, we should realize that through biological essentialism, Judaic, Christian, and Islamic peoples from the Middle East, or any other male-dominated society, categorize androcentrism and gender polarization as *natural* and therefore as inevitable consequences of the intrinsic biological natures of the female and the male — which makes crossovers, mixtures, or undefined sexes unquestionably impossible. In our androcentric culture, as the child learns the language, it absorbs the patriarchal androcentric concepts that constitute it. After decades of feminist research we know that androcentric language privileges the male gender by speaking of *man*-kind, of a paternal God, by commonly using "he" as a generic pronoun, and by dividing up the world "into species named by Adam *before* Eve's creation." It is the language of the deeds of men, Jack Solomon writes, "of kings and presidents, warriors and scientists, priests and poets and philosophers." We all know that French author and philosopher Simone de Beauvoir (1908–86) wrote on the role of women as that of "second sex," as minor players and spectators "in a human drama whose leading characters are almost always men and whose script is written in a masculine tongue."[6]

As representations of the exorcist narrative world, it is incorrect to regard witch-hunts primarily as expressions of misogyny. For sure, misogyny has profound roots in European, Jewish, Muslim, and other cultures. Warrior cultures that dominated Southern Europe and the Middle East devaluated women. In our time it is unavoidable to equal the word *feminine* with women. In the witch-hunt era it was not. The feminine and the female were synonymous with the counter polar part of the masculine and the male. The male/female opposition was immanent for the oppositeness of fire and water, earth and air, culture and nature, sacred and profane, good and evil. At a fundamental level, women were associated with the physical body and the senses, while men had associated themselves with the mind and soul. Theorists of the Roman Catholic Church positioned the powers of God, Christ, order, culture, right side, and higher senses like sight, a strong mind, and faith on the male side opposite the powers of the Devil, Anti-Christ, disorder, untamed nature, left side, and lower senses like smell, a weak mind, and heresy on the female side. Taken from ancient European traditions, Clark adds this chain as male: "limit/odd/one/right/square/at rest/straight/light/good"; and as female: "unlimited/even/plurality/left/oblong/moving/curved/darkness/evil." He warns that this "division was not necessarily a malicious devaluing of women, since in the worldview of the period they had to be construed as one of a pair of opposites." A man could be identified as a witch if some of these characteristics were thought to be part of his actions or even of his persona— he had "crossed over," thereby becoming a difference *within* the feminine gender category. Nevertheless, as Clark concludes, what we have here is the symmetry of inversion. When the male factor became dominant and hegemonic, at the end of the Middle Ages, this pair of opposites had led to a kind of eviction: bipolar cosmology faded out, man became *standard* and woman evolved into *non-man*.[7]

By then, the status of women had declined. They were ousted from a number of occupations and from the more lucrative and independent positions within other trades. Marriage had been a key instrument to this; property, above all of land, another. Around the mid–1200s, the Church did celebrate weddings, however not as an active participant and outside of a church building, for instance. Two centuries later, marriage had to be celebrated inside the church, closely monitored by a priest. All around the world, the vast majority of women have always worked—vital work for peasant societies, essential in urban surroundings. In some areas the dowry a woman took with her into her marriage consisted of necessary household items as well as a transfer of wealth from her father's household to her new husband's family. However, until well into the Middle Ages this transfer—or more precisely bride-wealth—had tended to move the other way around, to the woman, and had brought items of value to her family, which could have made her or her family wealthy. Marriageable daughters were a blessing. But little was left of this bride-wealth a few centuries later in large portions of Europe, and due to the new ways of paying dowries, marriageable daughters had become a curse. Land became a limited resource, mostly the eldest son became the focus of inheritance, and competition in urban trades drove women out of them or restricted them to low status positions with little income. In Paris in 1292, women had made up 15 percent of independent taxpayers; by 1313 this percentage had dropped to 10, and by the early 15th century to little more than two. In Barcelona around 1300, women had helped to establish the wool industry as independent traders and entrepreneurs, but two centuries later they had only lower-paying jobs in it. For the dominant men, virginity had become evidence of a loyal attitude and gave the woman the image of a hard-working member of an economic team — a role premarital promiscuous girls could not secure at the time.[8]

The exorcist metanarrative rests on anxiety and the politics of fear. True, there had been "real" enemies attacking Western Europe, particularly the Ottoman Empire until their defeat near Vienna in 1683. It had taken centuries for an effective European counter-warrior elite to develop. Before 1492 Europe was as much the product of a process of conquest and colonization as, after 1492, the initiator of one. Western and Central European states were established by conquest and they peopled liminal areas, like English colonization in the Celtic world, the movement of Germans into Eastern Europe, the Spanish Reconquest, and the Crusaders in the eastern Mediterranean. The expansion began with pushing back frontiers. Members of the leading sectors of society, like nobles, churchmen and merchants, created new political units beyond existing ones. Frankish knights went into an "aristocratic diaspora" from Ireland to Sicily and from Spain to Pomerania to acquire more substantial lordships. As a result, between 950 and 1350 the area under Latin Christendom almost doubled. All the time, military technology was advancing, as were farming, social contracts subordinating peasantries, and the emergence of a novel merchant class. However, in the next century the stronger monarchies reacted by putting a brake on this. They preferred taking territory from each other in order to profit from resources and populations. In their company were priests and monks, diffusing a kind of blueprint including the establishment of religious orders and the dominance of Christianity, the spread of the cults of some saints and the near elimination of others, the town charter, and use of standardized coins and the standardization of names. In short, the European nobility had reorganized itself into two powerful manly warrior units. First, there were groups of trained fighters on horseback; a new military estate or caste. Second, there were the warriors of Christ; delivering ideological support for the warrior estate or caste. The new religious hierarchy relied on affinities of upbringing, shared values and the dedication to combat the invaders from other faiths. During periods of respite and following the schism with the Byzantine Christian or Orthodox Church in 1054, Christianity in Europe would unite into one Roman Catholic Church.[9]

Historians identify the diffusion of a kind of blueprint for the establishment of religious orders and the dominance of Christianity. This included the spread of the cults of particular saints — at the cost of others — and town charters as well as series of standardizations, for example of names and coins. As newcomers moved in, the diffusion of language caused bilingualism, mutual linguistic influencing, and even the death of minor languages. In some areas, native peoples tried to avoid assimilation by conscious efforts to preserve their languages. The same with law, because incomers often brought their law with them to the disadvantage of the conquered. Through weaponry, Christendom, and the law of coercion, took root. This confirms John Hale's well-known *Civilization of Europe in the Renaissance* (1993), in which it was also demonstrated that the concept of Europe as a geographical region with a distinct civilization emerged only in the 15th century, and only in the 16th century did the name *Europe* enter general linguistic usage. And it was largely the work of men, for in Western experience, women have played a small part in the construction and use of coercive organizations.[10]

The women were driven out of this by the men — as were non-white men.[11] Around the year 1000 Western Europe had been a relatively open society with Christians and Jews living near each other and with heresy and sexual deviance like homosexuality considered of little weight. Magicians had been part of society, and evil magic was not as yet seen as a major threat, at least in the eyes of the rulers and the elite. The picture around 1400 was different, writes Thurston: "Jews, now forced to live in ghettos across the continent, had been attacked, tortured and murdered by Christians on many occasions. Heretical movements had appeared, spread, and been the targets of gruesome campaigns of extermination in France and elsewhere. In earlier centuries, lepers had been fastidiously avoided by almost everyone but had not been the object of special persecution; by the 14th century local and royal authorities were rounding up lepers, confining them, stripping them of all civil rights and often murdering them. Homosexuality had been outlawed and made a capital crime in every land. Christian Church and lay authorities had become deeply concerned with how people lived on a day-to-day basis and adopted legislation designed to regulate their behaviour."[12] Through governments and courts, the new persecuting society had been institutionalized, sanctioning violence against inhabitants who practiced "deviant" religions, different ways of life and sexual activities, or were of a different "race." They had been the first "major" minorities. Financed by outside forces, often Muslims, to bring down Christian society, the deviancy of the Jews, heretics, and the lepers purportedly consisted of "disgusting" anti-human practices, of being sexually hyperactive, and being seductive by luring "innocent" people into their ranks, through their sexual prowess.

From within, during the entire period of the making of Europe, bit by bit, the Devil emerged as the major power of evil in the Christian imagination. The Devil had to build an army and, so it was concluded, he must be busy recruiting agents among the Christians. These human assistants came from within, whereas the Islamic warriors came from without. The witches became the principal agents "within." Their task was to seduce as many other witches as they could, guaranteed residents of Hell. This was unique to Europe. "Demons and petty, evil spirits apparently exist in every society," Thurston notes, but "one big devil, almost as powerful as God, or equally powerful in some variants, is largely a western creation [...]." This is not to be confused with the presence of almost equal dualistic powers in other cultures, like light and dark, above and beneath, good and evil, as mostly a dualism of the spirit world versus the earthly. Confirmed by a meticulous reading of the Bible's New Testament, in which the four Gospels tell Jesus' story as a struggle between Jesus and the Devil, in the West, the Devil, who had been originally a minor and innocuous biblical character, could become the singular sovereign of the world of evil spirits. No other religion has invented a Hell as this underground kingdom of doom, represented by dense strata of myth, legend, and religious creed, and with the importance Christianity has given it. No other culture has offered the fighting of the Devil so much prominence. No other worldview has granted exorcism so large a part of its thinking.[13]

The new masculine nation-states had begun exorcizing the Devil within. The Devil's eternal battle with God was one between two male warriors. God's soldiers were priests and monks — "true men." The Church Inquisitors felt right to fight against female adherents of the Devil. At least in the eyes of these elites, at the grassroots there could still be witches, or magicians, fighting at both sides. Historian Carlo Ginzburg discovered that in Northern Italy several groups of witches were fighting at God's side against the Devil and against the witches and devils who were stealing the people's crops. They needed not to be exorcized, because they were *good* witches — *benandanti*, or good-doers. These people told late 16th-century Inquisitors that four times a year they fought the forces of the Devil during nocturnal battles over fertility. In spite of their evident seriousness, their imaginative Sabbath gatherings, as sometimes unreservedly confessed to the Inquisitors, had a kind of festive air about them. However, the Inquisitors, blinded by the exorcist ideal, were preoccupied with identifying the testimonies as *real* experiences. Consequently, they actively challenged the established belief from previous generations of Inquisitors, prelates, and officials that such testimonies were based on dream reports. Also out-of-body-experiences can be understood as dreams, informed by discursive resources that usually go back in time a long way. It is this kind of framing that might have been called "remnants of ancient beliefs." For this reason it is good to stress that in the minds of the peasants, the benandanti gatherings formed an integral part of the non–Christian calendar, or pagan year, along with the Equinoxes and Solstices. We are talking about cosmology, not history.[14] When the prelates of the Inquisition began interpreting the testimonies of this "fertility cult" in negative terms — as if these were inspired by the Devil — the cult eventually resurfaced in the Inquisition's belief as a wicked Witches' Sabbath. The prelates must have realized they stood against a powerful, female enemy.

In sum, following Thurston, between about 1000 and 1400 three developments came together. First, there was the formation of a more coherent Christian cosmology that moved from dominance to hegemony. Second, there was a decline in the status of women — and hence in their worth — in various senses. Third, Westerners believed that Christianity was under attack from without by Islam and invaders from the East *and* from within by heretics and witches — both, perhaps, guided by the same power: the Devil. The concept "witch" had become feminized. The witch had been different from a sorcerer, but by this time had evolved into something with a vastly darker set of associations because of "her" relationship with the Devil, voluntarily and of "her" own free will. Witches carried out evil acts called *maleficia*, or harmful magic, including destroying human and agricultural fertility — their favorite prey as babies. The witch was thought to have had sexual intercourse with the Devil or a lesser demon. Interestingly, intercourse with the Devil was painful. Male and female demons both felt cold like ice. New was also that the witches would fly to great gatherings, where they would celebrate this kind of antimass, which included sex, called a Sabbath. Regardless of his enormous power, the Devil was the weaker side of the cosmic powers and eventually the almighty powers of God would prevail, but it would take a devastating fight. On Earth, the witch who worshipped the Devil was also by definition weak-minded, a trait that had been associated from antiquity with women and the female. Their corporeal frailty had left them susceptible to demonic forces bent on penetrating and polluting their bodies and souls. A trace of this we recognize in *The Rite*, when Father Lucas is penetrated in a very weak moment. Disappointed, in fact depressed, by the death of Rosaria, he had temporarily lost his defenses.[15]

# 4

Curiously, Heinrich Kramer, the writer of the *Malleus Maleficarum*, had much in common with Freud, both in career as in effect. When he wrote the *Malleus Maleficarum*, he was about 56, relatively aged and at the end of his career. The *malleus*, Latin for *hammer*, is a hammer-shaped small bone of the middle ear, which transmits the sound vibrations from the eardrum to the *incus* or anvil. Historian Guido Ruggiero explains this term from a 16th-century Venetian document as a *martello* used to force people to do things by magic. Activated usually by prayer-like language involving Christian imagery to call on God or his heavenly supporters, Ruggiero says it was a widely used form of magic for punishing enemies, as if to hammer them. The second Latin term in the title, from *maleficia*, refers to harmful magic by a magician, sorcerer, or witch. Kramer had put the name of a then well-known but now relatively forgotten Dominican, James Sprenger (1436/38–1494), on the title page of a later reprint, perhaps to give the book more scholarly weight — a trick repeated by Freud with Breuer. It could also have been out of despair, for in early 1486, as Kramer sat down to write the book, he had recently been sentenced to prison for theft of silverware and money in the course of his inquisitorial duties. He had been blocked by other clerics as he tried to convict some 50 recently arrested and promptly tortured women from Brixen, Austria, for witchcraft. Furthermore, he was scorned and threatened by their Bishop. He needed to recoup the respect of the Inquisition and he did so by relying profoundly upon earlier works.[13]

The *Malleus Maleficarum* was divided into three sections. The first section was written to counter critics who hindered witchcraft persecution. The second described forms of witchcraft case by case and its remedies; and, the third was to assist judges confronting and combating witchcraft. The main purpose of the book was to support the Papacy in opposition to the conciliarism of the bishops. To counter skeptics, Kramer systematically refuted arguments that spoke against witchcraft. It was also important to him to prove that witches were mostly female and not male. This characteristic originated in women's supposed mental weakness and intellectual feebleness — although Kramer referred to witches in both masculine and feminine terms. Another goal was to educate magistrates legally on the procedures that could find them out and convict them. Kramer liked to offer his readers a method of conducting a witch trial; from the first steps of initiating a process and accumulating accusations to the interrogation of witnesses. He also provided a guide to the formal charging of the accused. Reading the book closely, however, its argument appears to be more about using the weaknesses of women to make points about correct belief. It was not an assault on women by itself. Nevertheless, for Kramer all witchcraft came from carnal lust, which, he thought, was feminine, and thus in women, insatiable. Next to the "technique" of putting pressure on the victim/patient, this was the motive of the "hidden sexual desire" that so attracted European writers, including Freud, who regarded his "drives" Eros and later Death as the two faces of the Devil Within: Good Within and Evil Within.

And so it appears that the witch-hunts were not about witchcraft after all. They were about belief and evidence. The physical act of sex would prove to the Inquisitors and everyone else in the Christian world that demons and the Devil had a real physical impact on the world. Proving this would mean giving evidence that there really was an "enemy within," and that theories about the Devil did not rest on vague ideas or unfounded fears. Stephens concludes in his *Demon Lovers* (2002) that treatise after treatise written shortly before and during the years of the witch-hunts was written with this argument in mind. Far from being credulous fools or mindless misogynists, Stephens finds that most of the Inquisitors writing about witches were skeptics, rational but reluctant. They tried desperately to resolve contradictions in Christian teachings on God, Hell, the Devil and demons that had bedeviled theologians for centuries. In fact, Western Christian theologians were worrying about demonic presence on earth, demonic anatomy, and physiology for centuries before the first witch trial. Through evidence of intercourse with women the physical existence of demons could be established — and with it the existence of Heaven, Purgatory and Hell, and of course of the truth of the Bible, perhaps of God himself. Writers reviewed every possible objection to demonic reality, both theological and scientific, and then claimed to resolve all the difficulties. Witchcraft theorists like these did not suppose that their theories corresponded with reality: "they were *testing* to discover *whether* a correspondence existed and dreading that it might not." In short, they were looking and searching for proof. Also the *Malleus Maleficarum* might have been written from this stance, including Kramer's instructions to acquire proof of demonic intercourse. The problem of demonic reality was rarely posed explicitly in trials, yet it drove the logic of interrogation in many cases, provided a plausible motivation for otherwise seemingly irrational proceedings.[16]

Read this way, as by Stephens, the treatises on witches reflected a true crisis in belief. The Inquisitors were the first steps on the road of science that led European man through the Functionalist-Enlightenment Order. Although their methods were horrendous — the "evidence" rested sometimes upon torture — the Inquisitors must be regarded, Stephens deduces, as scholars and theorists. The theory they eventually built was about the supremacy of Christianity, about the mystic battle of Christ with the Devil, and the primary function of man on earth. Indeed, of *man*, not of woman, not that weak gender that could easily be seduced by the Devil and work as saboteurs or secret agents against the project of God. The witch-hunters were not demonologists, but theologians. In the slipstream of these theories, the androcentric worldview was formulated and could root hegemonically. Freud formulated his theory in the slipstream of this movement. But did he realize that the witch-hunts were about belief and evidence? It seems he had recognized a few amazing correspondences. First, there was the framing of the Devil Within, dumped from consciousness as repressed thoughts. Next, everything that his patients said during the sessions Freud used as evidence of the existence of repressed thoughts. Third, he identified with the inquisitors to combat the "Devil Within" and "liberate" his patients from their repressed thoughts using an aggressive "technique" that was, if we believe his patients, not unlike torture. Fourth, like the Inquisitors, Freud was convinced that the Devil Within was robustly related to real or imagined sexual activity. And last, Freud turned his modeling into an androcentric way — framing woman as other.

Nevertheless, like Kramer, confronted with a method that did not work with his patients, a theory without confirmation, Freud was constantly torn by doubt. Kramer turned to the Bible for confirmation of his belief, Freud to the ancient Greeks in his library. For *The Interpretation of Dreams* he referred to *Oedipus Rex* (first staged around ca. 425 B.C.), written by the ancient Greek playwright Sophocles (496–406 B.C.). He considered *The Interpretation of Dreams*, designed to develop the Oedipus Complex, his most important work. It was here that he proposed the principles by which he imagined how the unconscious operated — or the "subconscious," as it is labeled in popular psychology. He stated that the interpretation of dreams was "*the via regis to a knowledge of the unconscious element in our psychic life.*" To give credit to this conclusion, he reproduced the familiar psychomythology about the unconscious as our true psychic reality: "In its inner nature it is just as much unknown to us as the reality of the external world, and it is just as imperfectly communicated to us by the data of consciousness as is the external world by the reports of our sense-organs."[17]

The Classics served him to identify the "demons within": "Antiquity has furnished us with legendary matter which corroborates this belief, and the profound and universal validity of the old legends is explicable only by an equally universal validity of the above-mentioned hypothesis of infantile psychology." With "this belief," Freud meant that "falling in love with one parent and hating the other forms part of the permanent stock of the psychic impulses which arise in early childhood, and are of such importance as the material of the subsequent neurosis." Hence his conclusion: "If the *Oedipus Rex* is capable of moving a modern reader or playgoer no less powerfully than it moved the contemporary Greeks, the only possible explanation is that the effect of the Greek tragedy does not depend upon the conflict between fate and human will, but upon the peculiar nature of the material by which this is revealed. There must be a voice within us which is prepared to acknowledge the compelling power of fate in the *Oedipus*, while we are able to condemn the situations occurring in [...] other tragedies of fate as arbitrary inventions."[18] "Antiquity has furnished us with legendary matter..." not the works of his contemporaries. In his eyes, the *Malleus Maleficarum* must also be read as an ageless document. This underscores a particular psychomythological view on human society that seems to have prevailed over the past centuries, that is typically immanent in Christian religion, and is definitively shared by Freud and his followers: over the past centuries, mankind has been essentially the same.

The classic drama *Oedipus Rex* had unprecedented success on German and French stages in the 1880s, 1890s, and early 1900s. According to prophecy, *Oedipus Rex* says, Oedipus, king of Thebes, was doomed to sleep with his mother and kill his father. He attempted to escape his fate but, in the process, unwittingly did the very things he wanted to avoid. Oedipus, confronted with a plague in the city, went to consult the oracles and learned that the plague was caused by the unpunished murder of the former king, Laius. Next, Oedipus vowed to hunt down the criminal. Slowly and by degrees, Oedipus came to realize that he himself had murdered Laius, and that he then had married his own mother, Jocasta. Horrified at the discoveries, Oedipus blinded himself. Jocasta committed suicide. Freud used this story to coin the figuration of a child's relationship to his parent, based on a fantasy that, so he assumed, evolves during the height of the so-called phallic stage of the psychosexual development of the personality, approximately at years three to five. In short, Freud imagined that dreams revealed childhood desires, based on innate so-called "oedipal" wishes to have sex with the mother and replace the father. The Oedipus Complex designates attraction on the part of the child toward the parent of the opposite sex and rivalry and hostility toward the parent of its own. Later it was concluded that women must learn to be desired and men to desire. It was the nuclear complex of the neuroses that constitutes the essential part of their content: "Every new arrival on this planet is faced with the task of mastering the Oedipus Complex; anyone who fails to do so falls a victim to neurosis." Furthermore, we are to believe that the Oedipus Complex marked the triumph of psychoanalysis, because "its recognition has become the shibboleth that distinguishes the adherents of psycho-analysis from its opponents."[19]

Freud saw productions of *Oedipus Rex* in Paris and Vienna, and he immediately believed that the classical play moved modern audiences with as much intensity as it did audiences in ancient Greece because of its universal values. Freud recognized all symbols and signs in it as universal, rooted in the experience of every human being, and that these human beings cannot help attributing certain meanings to those symbols and signs. In the end, psychoanalysts became convinced of the almost deterministic, inborn quality of certain symbolic representations—*inborn*, thus a biological feature of human life. Today, of course, we know that "good" literature, "if we mean by that literature that has endured and still speaks to us today," as Ruggiero reminds us, "often speaks with a different voice today; thus, it is dangerously easy to read apparent continuities or similarities between [the past] and today as real ones [...]."[20] Recently, Richard Armstrong, a reader in modern languages, argues that Freud missed the "Oedipus Mania" that had raged among the European elites at the time. He pointed to the theatrical background to the Oedipus Complex. Surely, in Freud's *Interpretation of Dreams*, Sophocles appears at different moments in the argument as a psychoanalyst *avant la lettre*, but Freud also argued that the Oedipus legend sprang from some "primeval dream-material," simply captured by the ancient Greek author. As usual, Freud was wrong. Instead of engaging in such a theoretical critique of the origins of the Oedipus Complex, Armstrong turns to a more earthly reason for the success of Sophocles's play in the 19th century. He argues that the Oedipus play Freud saw was translated for a modern audience, effective on the modern stage with hefty emendations. Armstrong mentioned the personalities behind the productions at the time, like the companies, the directors, and the actors, who had rewritten the play for and adapted to the tastes of the late 19th-century audience to the point that the text Freud heard in the performance cannot be said to share in a stable identity as *the* text of Sophocles. The late 19th-century *Oedipus Rex* was a *mise en abyme*, with a 19th-century audience looking at their own worldview. Oedipus' success had made Freud think that the play transcended time and place; he was careful not to put the evidentiary weight on the mere antiquity of the story, but rather on its effect on the audience, including himself. It would have been easy for Freud to compare the text that was performed on stage with the original, but he did not bother because he was blinded by essentialism.[21]

# 5

Generations of feminists have correctly fulminated against Western androcentric culture and are effectively reforming it but many of them still feel inspired by the work of Freud or Lacan. What is surprising is that most progressive Liberal or leftist authors defend psychoanalysis, although this "smorgasbord of symbolism" can be comfortably mapped in the politically conservative camp. As said, it is well-known that Freud fulminated against socialists and communists and preferred fascist rulers to social democrats. Furthermore, what to think of the "father" in Freud's pre-war (1914–18) book *Totem and Taboo* (1912–13)? The argument seems to be about universal human psychological features. For Freud, working with the idea that if ontogeny recapitulates phylogeny, every human being, every community, every people, the entire world history could be set in the Oedipus Complex. People must have had a "childhood." Furthermore, myths of ancient societies must have been for a people what dreams were for an individual — hidden messages of the unconscious that contain "repressed" thoughts, wishes, and experiences of a people that are individually, socially, or culturally unwelcome. Mystic religious experiences, Freud later confirmed in "Civilization and Its Discontents" (1930), were nothing more than "regressions" to primary narcissism and thus "infantile helplessness," projections upon the world of a primitive infantile state. It could heal collective stress. These "tribal people" saw their dead ancestors as demons that deserve their hatred, not unlike the neurotic person of his theories, who unconsciously wants at least the father to disappear. The feelings of guilt that come from this are encountered by a projection of negative characteristics onto the vanished person, so that the prior wish seemed justified. Again, he had no undisputed evidence. But should we not agree that *Totem and Taboo* breathes the air of European, Western, white superiority so typical for the first century of the androcentric Structuralist-Romantic Order?[22]

It will help to summarize what Freud says about the role of the "father" in *Totem and Taboo*. He assumed that humankind once consisted of primal herds organized in extended families ruled by primal fathers. The ruling fathers, so Freud's story goes, offered protection in exchange for sex. This excluded the younger men, who planned to kill the hated father and eat his flesh. Cannibalism must have ruled humankind at the time, Freud argued. And indeed, as we understand from popular psychology, jealousy must be just the flipside of love, with which he meant that soon after their meal, the cannibals must have suffered from guilt. What is more, the defeat of the father could not have brought peace and quiet, because the women were now prey for the men, who started fighting among themselves. In the end, full of remorse, the young men rehabilitated the father and "re-built" or "revived" him by making a totem. The totem not only opened the possibility for remembrance and reverence but also reminded them of their bloody deed and their guilt. This was the phallus. Freud presented the "invention" of religion as a product of human needs and desires. It was another method of repression of the basic instincts. Religion would thus be hardly more than the neurosis of humanity, hence, the value of the nature of unconscious processing. According to Freud, the human race realized it was destined to live in childhood forever, in need of the father it had killed. Periodic ritual killing and communal eating of the sacred totem animal — the substitute for the lost father — was not sufficient. The father, says Freud, kept on governing the world through nature and its superior powers. Thanks to the presence of the totem, "incest" among members of the same clan could be prevented. They were exogamous. Although members of such a clan were not related by blood, endogamous relations between them were considered incestuous. This was articulated, Freud believed, with a discussion of a "mother-in-law taboo." He concluded that "uncivilized people" in his days were still haunted by the kind of incestuous wishes that are repressed into the unconscious by civilized people.

This makes the "collective unconscious" androcentric and authoritarian.

One theoretical school explicitly based its work on these ideas, arguing that the "collective unconscious" is filled with archetypes that are not learned but are innate: the school of Freud's pupil and later enemy Carl Gustav Jung (1875–1961). Jung described several archetypes that he deduced from, in general, reading Greek and other European narratives. In two remarkable studies, *The Jung Cult* (1994) and *The Aryan Christ* (1997), clinical psychologist Richard Noll pulled Jung's theories apart. In the first study, Noll argues that the archetypes in Jung's work and such ideas as the "collective unconscious" are rooted in what we may see as the Structuralist-Romantic Order, including late 19th-century occultism, neopaganism, and some Social Darwinist readings. In 1912, Jung broke with Freud, but not to found his own "scientific" psychoanalysis. Instead, he began a kind of religious movement which offered a rebirth by "individuation." He was inspired by ancient mystery cult teachings; Haeckel's monistic teachings; and *Naturphilosophie*, a vitalist school in biology. One of the key components of his cult was a sexual revolution rooted in the notion of polygamy. To get back into the so-called instinctual creative self of our ancestors, the cult advocated the practice of polygamy. By arguing that the monotheistic Judeo-Christian civilization was repressive and harming the soul, Jung could rationalize his personal sexual delight.

Even more than Freud, Jung consciously turned psychoanalysis, formerly the movement of the talking cure, into a personality cult centered on himself. In *The Aryan Christ*, Noll demonstrates that Jung probably believed that he was the manifestation of a lion-headed god. He saw himself as a philandering, self-appointed prophet of a sun-worshipping Aryan cult — a peculiar term to use in the Nazi era — and he actively participated in what we may call his invented rituals. Therefore, he introduced a method to teach people to speak to their dead — or to divine powers if they wanted to. His theory of the archetypes was articulated to his claim that anyone can get racial memories from his ancestors and enter into visionary states and talk to them. Noll also shows that Jung had the cult passed down to the present by a body of priest-analysts extending his charismatic "personal religion" to 21st-century individuals. By now, not much is left of Jung's fame. *The Jung Cult*, especially, acted as a climacteric, effectively changing the agenda of scholarly debate in Jung studies. Readers realized that, like Freud, Jung plagiarized several of his central ideas or based them upon falsified scholarly work.[23] Reason enough to file his work away with other psychoanalytical publications.

Next to the conservative gendering, the Romantic doctrines of Lamarck and Haeckel (ontogeny recapitulates phylogeny) transferred to psychoanalysis (sexual problems arise in childhood but can be overcome) project "human childhood" as traumatic and pathological. Sexual "aberration," or, as the Freudians coined it, "erroneous canalization" of sexual energy including masturbation, coitus interruptus, the use of a condom, and homosexuality, haunts people like witches and demons. Freud's follower Owen Berkeley-Hill wrote in the *International Journal of Psychoanalysis* of 1921 that "the anal erotism of the Hindu produces a congeries of character traits which are the very antithesis of those of Europeans, especially the English." Children and "primitives" share the anal stage. It is in accordance with Christian demonology, which depicts the Devil not only as lecherous, over-sexed, and sadistic, but above all as a bestial excrement loving creature. For Freud, the "anal personality" is characterized by being given to hoarding, sadism and pedantry, a secret lover of excrement. As a product of childhood, the child itself must be fundamentally evil, as, because of psychoanalysis's Haeckelian roots, the "childhood of humankind": history and "primitive peoples." It is not difficult to find examples represented by the chain Childhood ⇨ History ⇨ Primitives ⇨ Evil ⇨ Satan in the works published by Freud and his followers; the second part of Webster's *Why Freud Was Wrong* (1996) discusses example after example for over 150 pages. Webster shows that Freud identified his sinners and heretics based on this chain. He also formulated his own stake. Writing about a homosexual patient, Freud said that "in the most unfavourable cases, one ships such people [...] across the ocean with some money, let's say to South America, and there let them seek and find their destiny."[24]

One way to theorize the political mapping of all these ideas is by reading the work of linguist George Lakoff, in which we encounter a modeling that parallels one of the Orders, introduced above.[25] After studying rhetoric, literature, speeches, and the use of conceptual metaphors in ordinary language, the linguist juxtaposes a Strict Father Model versus a Nurturant Parent Model. Lakoff concludes that in the United States the nation is often conceived as a family. The State would be this family's home. It appeared that, in idealized form, the Strict Father Model mapped onto pure conservative politics and beliefs, and a Nurturant Parent Model mapped onto more progressive politics. The Strict Father Model is based on the presence of a strict father as the moral leader of the family, who is to be obeyed. The strict father protects his family against the evil in the world — or inside the head (in psychoanalytical terms the strict father can be the SuperEgo) — and educates the children who are naturally born without education and would be wild, selfish, and egoistic if left alone — narcissistic, say the psychoanalysts. The strict father punishes and demands discipline. He is authoritarian and patriarchal. To be self-reliant he coerces his children into self-discipline and a life of hard work. His wife is "other," subordinate and obeying. As we see, the Strict Father Model can be articulated to the Structuralist-Romantic Order, to Freud's psychoanalysis, to his political attitude and his running of the psychoanalytical movement. It also articulates to Western colonialism.

Androcentrism has nothing to do with the evolution of sex differences. Any "othering" of women must be a deliberate political act. It constitutes both gender and sexual identity. It has been in operation this way since the age of witch-hunters. Sexual identity speaks to the way people see themselves as male or female, while gender identity is the recognition of the perceived social gender attributed to them. Both identities combined result in the sexual orientation, which also refers to the sex of the erotic/love/affectionate partners people prefer.[26] Androcentrism established the hierarchy between the combined sexual and gender identities. Undeniably, as Bem concludes, it must be for political reasons that androcentrism is embedded in Western cultural discourses, social institutions, and individual psyches, not as just the historically crude perception that men — as sexual and gender identity — are superior to women, but as the *neutral standard* or norm of male identities and experiences. By consequence, female identities and experiences are sex-specific deviations of that norm, not simply inferior but basically as "other." In most cases, male power is concentrated among relatively rich, white, and heterosexual men, and reproduced through androcentrism. This means that boys and girls are, perhaps unwillingly, differently educated, which gives them an identity consistent with local cultural gender values. Here lies the foundation for the Strict Father Model.

The Nurturant Parent Model is based on the cooperative attitude of two parents, with equal responsibilities and as little gender constraints as is possible. Children arrive in the world without education but are in principle "good," and inherently know and learn what they need. They should be allowed to explore and need to be nurtured and mentored by being stimulated, by setting limits and explaining them. Discipline comes out of the child's developing sense of care and responsibility. The Nurturant Parent Model requires respect, mutually by parents for children, and vice versa. Restitution is preferred over punishment. The parents are protective and enable the empowerment of their children. The model can be used to describe family development in the period of the Cognitive-Evolutionary Order in the future of the West. In this sense, and apart from the fallible scientific status of psychoanalysis, readers who feel progressive politically and socially must feel themselves better at home in the cosmos of cognitive science than in the Freudian Edifice. This is the reason why it is difficult to understand writers like Žižek and Argentine and American intellectuals, who think that psychoanalysis would "liberate" them in some fashion.

Although it would be premature to label the Functionalist-Enlightened Order as politically progressive — leftist, Liberal — and the Structuralist-Romantic Order as its opposite, 19th-century Europe was a fertile breeding ground for the darker side of the Romantic attitude looking for universal political values that centered and privileged Western colonizing warrior cultures. Playwright Arthur Miller (1915–2005) expressed something similar, based on personal experience. In a 1963 interview, he said: "My argument with so much of psychoanalysis, is the preconception that suffering is a mistake, or a sign of weakness, or a sign even of illness. When in fact, possibly the greatest truths we know, have come out of people's suffering. The problem is not to undo suffering, or to wipe it off the face of the earth, but to make it inform our lives, instead of trying to 'cure' ourselves of it constantly, and avoid it, and avoid anything but that lobotomized sense of what they call 'happiness.' There's too much of an attempt, it seems to me, to think in terms of controlling man, rather than freeing him — of defining him, rather than letting him go! It's part of the whole ideology of this age, which is power-mad!"[27]

# 6

In the West, and perhaps even globally, feminism combats the Strict Father Model rather successfully. Nevertheless, some films still try to promote the old model. This is the case, for example, with *The Twilight Saga*, a series of feature films consisting of *Twilight* (2008), *New Moon* (2009), *Eclipse* (2010), and *Breaking Dawn* (Parts One [2011] and Two [2012]). The series is based on the novels by Stephenie Meyer, a Mormon author. The script is written by Melissa Rosenberg. There is no need to go through the stories in all their details and themes. It suffices to privilege a few characteristics to show that these films are androcentric. Despite the fact that she repeatedly says "I know what I want," the leading female character Bella Swan (Kristen Stewart) is obedient to the male characters. Furthermore, she desperately wants to have a family. In fact, she is empowered only when she finally has her family by marriage and giving birth to a daughter. Marriage and motherhood gives her equal powers as her husband. However, the modern attitude is also found in the female character, not because she actively strives for liberation and emancipation, but because she expresses not to believe in the soul. With this agnostic part of her, Bella embodies much of what is typical for the Cognitive-Evolutionary Order. However, lining up with traditional faith, the boys she loves do not. Bella is being protected and sought after by two male characters, Edward Cullen (Robert Pattinson) and Jacob Black (Taylor Lautner). Because the former is a vampire and the latter a werewolf, the boys belong to the European reservoir of witch-tales. Edward Cullen and his adopted family of six vampires were educated and raised in the early 20th century, which makes them culturally old-fashioned. Black and his natural family belong to the Quileute tribe in La Push, a small settlement within an American Indian reservation near the rainy town of Forks, Washington. The set is situated near this town and its surrounding forests. Both the Cullen vampires and the American Indian werewolves, being enemies, serve to protect Forks from evil vampires. In this sense, they resemble Ginzburg's "pre–Hammer" benandanti good-doers of Northern Italy. Although Hollywood traditions want to present werewolves especially as romantic figures, driven by impulses beyond their control — think of *The Wolf Man* (1941) or *Wolf* (1994) — Cullen and Black are in full rational control over their powers.[28]

In our time, very few viewers will take the supernatural aspects of characters like Cullen and Black seriously — not even young girls. However, in the early modern period, vampires were an Eastern European phenomenon emerging precisely at the time that the witch-hunts were forbidden by law. There were several trials involving vampires. Conversely, the belief in lycanthropy was widely accepted on the planet for centuries. At the time, lycanthropes were far from sympathetic figures. Werewolves were malign creatures who took a vicious pleasure in the harm they caused. They killed humans for flesh. Like witchcraft, lycanthropy was associated with magic and the presence of the Devil on earth — as witches who could transform themselves. No wonder that there was some discussion of it also in the *Malleus Maleficarum*. In fact, contemporaries could read that creatures like werewolves were illusions created by the Devil to deceive human senses. Demons could make an exterior object seem other than it is, like false bodies composed of air. Although intellectuals always had their doubts, it lasted until the 19th century before serious alternative causes of the belief were discussed. Interestingly, a pre–Freudian 1865 publication proposed that the lycanthropic symptoms arose from bestial desires, including what it called "sexual sadism," that were normally hidden in "civilized people."[29]

*The Twilight Saga* does not find its roots in medieval Eastern Europe but in Bram Stoker's *Dracula* (1897) and Anne Rice's *Interview with the Vampire* (1976). At the end of the 19th century, the vampire was an evil monster guided by the Devil. His behavior and interests were much like the witch-hunters believed to find in the demons they hunted. The evil world in Stoker's version was not connected directly to the female but to the East. At the time, the othering of the East was in full swing — and enjoyed by Freud, as we have seen, as an enthusiastic reader of H. Rider Haggard's novel *She* (1887) — creating an image of the effeminate or childish colonized by the colonizer, who was a "real man." The anxiety evoked by the novel was Dracula's plan to travel to England and conquer the Empire from within. This would cause the doom of the "civilized world," as they felt it. Even British soil would be contaminated because Dracula carried coffins filled with Transylvanian earth. As in the time of witch-hunters, Stoker's Victorian exogamic demon ultimately works by conquering English women. Dracula knew how to dress up like a perfect Englishman. His blood-rite to conquer the bodies of English women began with the draining of a woman's blood and ended with infusing her with his own. Because Dracula lacked a mirror reflection, his enemies had an instrument to recognize the vampire. Furthermore, he could be countered carrying

Christian symbols. He displayed inhuman physical strength and could transform into mist or a beast, but he would die in the sunlight.[30]

In Rice's novel, part of a series called *The Vampire Chronicles*, the reading public fell for humanized plantation owner Louis — played by Brad Pitt in the filmed version of *Interview with the Vampire* (1994), directed by Neil Jordan after Rice's script — who had become more humanized and much less part of an evil world. Significantly, Louis tells his own story, which makes "othering" difficult. Indeed, Rice breaks down the boundaries of the "vampiric evil" and the contemporary West. Louis has few supernatural powers and he is not exogamic. All this does not make Louis a "true" vampire, although he still needs to avoid sunlight and live in the dark, wandering restlessly and thirsty. Tortured by the death he causes, he refuses to kill humans. There is a bit of a Freudian psychomyth here, however: it seems Louis has repressed his homosexual side. Nevertheless, it is as if the empire of the Devil has lost ground today and vanished from our minds. Louis is pagan. Christian symbols are of no importance to him. On the other hand, as a plantation owner he is a colonizer, which impedes him from being truly modern. His slaves use black magic and love their master. Nevertheless, all these vampires are not living in the Devil's realm. They are still superhuman, but beyond the world of the inhuman beast. There is no need to exorcize anymore. Liberated from the division of Christian/pagan and Good/Evil, the vampires can now be breathtakingly beautiful. The Cullens are even more our Westernized contemporaries than Louis. Saving human lives, and showing strong ethical and altruistic values — yet culturally quite conservative — the vampires are socially competent. Like Louis, the Cullens deplore their state of being. Without a blood-rite, it is sufficient to suck blood out of someone to turn him or her into a vampire. Furthermore, the Cullens do not fear the sunlight, do not sleep in coffins — they do not sleep at all — and seem to be fully pagan. Despite Edward's belief in Bella's soul, expressing that his love for her soul is stronger than for her blood, she does not care.[31]

In general, *The Twilight Saga* is focalized through 17-year-old Bella. For example in *New Moon*, directed by Chris Weitz, she is in every scene, with the exception of a few scenes involving crucial actions by Edward or Jacob. It is appealing to consider the story as Bella's illusion, as a fantasy made up to compensate for her loneliness and isolation. We know from the first film, *Twilight*, directed by Catherine Hardwicke, that Bella had arrived in Forks alone, to live with her father. Her mother moved from Phoenix, Arizona, where Bella lived before as well, to Florida with a new partner. In Forks, Bella has problems fitting in. Imagine she falls in love with a beautiful boy, who, perhaps, is out of her league. At the same time, there is an admirer nearby her home, but he is too young for her. Perhaps, Kristen Stewart's natural beauty is misleading here, because Bella is childlike, clumsy, shy, self-deprecatory, and suffers from low self-esteem, but we can easily understand that day-dreaming about two handsome boys fighting to protect her is an effective way out; one lover sitting next to her at school, the other living in the forest. In her fantasies, she finds an explanation for Edward's frequent absence: he likes the scent of her sweet blood so much that he can barely control himself not to suck her dry. Sometimes he needs to skip school. Seduced by his voice, scent and "impossible beauty," Bella invents a relationship with the charming, polite, determined, and mysterious boy. The relationship is trouble — it should be, as is any good story — because the forest is dangerous. The woods had been a battle ground between cold vampires and hot werewolves. Because werewolves protect humans and vampires prey on them, the werewolves are the main hunters of vampires. In *Twilight*, Jacob Black merely served as a device through which Bella learned Edward's secret. Listening to his Quileute legends, she understood that the Cullens are vampires. After some interrogation, she hears from Edward that the they are not "true" vampires because they do not feed on human blood, but hunt animals.

In *New Moon*, we see Bella inventing that the forest still is a battle ground. In fact, she is herself the principal subject of constant danger. The story shows the efforts of Edward and his family to keep her safe from one "true" vampire: powerful Victoria. The creature searches to kill Bella as revenge for Edward killing her own mate in *Twilight*. As a traditional European, almost Victorian male — born in 1901, but turned into a vampire in 1918 and therefore forever 17, by his looks — Edward is protective by nature, even with a tendency to overreact. He overhears Bella's conversations and dictates her choice of friends — this is Strict Father Modeling. Although mind-reading is his specialty with other living creatures, he is not able to read Bella's. She has a very private mind. Edward realizes that he and his family cannot protect her sufficiently. Thankfully, he learns that Jacob is a werewolf. Jacob, as the son of a family friend of Bella's father, has been around from the start. He needs to recognize Edward as his major opponent. In *New Moon*, Jacob gains the ability to transform into a werewolf, although he is not the alpha male of his troupe. Because Edward knows that the werewolves, later including Jacob and his pack, are on constant patrol for Victoria, he decides to break with Bella in order to save her soul.

The decision leaves Bella deeply heartbroken and depressed for months. At night, she is plagued by heavy nightmares, and during the day she sits on a chair, absently looking through a window. After a few months, she starts visiting Jacob at home, and recognizes a jovial companion who eases her agony. She likes to live more dangerously, for example driving a fast motorbike, because at such moments a spirit of Edward appears to warn her. However, Jacob also disappears from her life: he has become a werewolf. After she makes contact again with Jacob, Bella learns that Edward is in Italy. She finds him and convinces him to return to Forks to help defeat Victoria. Bella's victory is almost complete when Edward finally agrees to turn her into a vampire himself if she will marry him first. This, however, does not take place until *Breaking Dawn I* (2011), because, to his delight, Jacob comes to the rescue for a second time. Long ago, the Cullens and the Quileute people had a agreed upon a truce: the werewolves will not attack the Cullens as long as the latter do not bite any humans. Jacob would see to it that neither Edward nor any other of the family would change Bella into a vampire, despite her willingness to join them.

Edward Cullen and Jacob Black share the same androcentric world as Father Michael Kovak and Father Lucas Trevant: Strict Father conservatives, confronting emancipating females. The idea to fully create 20th-century vampires that may convince a 21st-century audience works. Lining up with a centuries-old Western tradition of promoting the traditional Strict Father Model, *The Twilight Saga* at the same time grants the female character a strong will to follow her own goals. Teenage girls might feel empowered by Bella's disobedience and independence. No doubt, due to the demise of religion in the West, or at least the demise of the Devil, the series reflects the more modern assumptions of its viewers. Despite its romantic character — love is much more important than the supernatural — the soullessness of the males and the characterization of Bella as a deliberate agnostic affirm that the films' audience is sharing a worldview that stands much closer to the Cognitive-Evolutionary Order than the Structuralist-Romantic. Both Edward and Jacob are embodied characters who do not need a soul to love and care. As benandanti, the Cullens and the Blacks act in a social collaborative way as well, as part of the "social body" of the population of Forks. Seen from popular psychology, *The Twilight Saga* is a transitional series — from Freudian to modern — but with gender emancipation lagging behind seriously. By not being religious, Bella found a way to become what she wants: eternal life at the side of her beautiful lover. This is a 21st-century fairytale.

# 7

The reason to work with vampires, demons, and exorcists is not only to offer the viewer a series of exotic images full of special effects. It is also fun to view horror. *The Rite* and *The Twilight Saga* are suspenseful, at least temporarily, despite the clear facts that *The Rite* is full of ludicrous demon resistance and that *The Twilight Saga* cannot do without Bella, Edward, and Jacob, making all attacks on them harmless beforehand. "When you put your hand on a hot stove you experience pain," says Dirk Eitzen in an interesting blog. "Pain makes you recoil *after* you've been burnt, to prevent you from getting burnt worse. Fear, on the other hand, makes you pull back *before* you've touched the stove. It anticipates danger. It is a danger *avoidance* mechanism." Knowing that the stove is too hot, we realize that we should avoid even coming near. Psychologists have established that fear operates through separate circuits in the brain, independently of awareness. Most people believe that it works like this: "First, you see the oncoming car. Second, you recognize the danger. Third, your body springs into action and you leap out of the way." It does not. Experiment after experiments shows that it is more likely like this, says Eitzen: "First, your body springs into action. Second, you see the oncoming car. Third, you recognize the danger." Registering danger this way, the oldest and most "primitive" circuit of the brain triggers fear immediately, without conscious thought — also preceding conscious thought. This spurs general attention, orienting the body and the mind toward to the source of danger. The next step, of course, is for the mind to come into operation. For example, the brain releases adrenaline into the bloodstream, and tenses the muscles. With the body prepared for action, the danger enters the conscious part of our thinking into the forefront of awareness. "This is why it is extremely difficult, if not impossible, to turn fear off by simply willing it away," says Eitzen. "Horror movies and thriller novels show that, even though it is very difficult to turn off the fear response, it is not very difficult to turn it on."[32]

In short, the filmmaker (1) triggers attention to danger, (2) brings the body of the viewer in a state of arousal, and (3) keeps the viewer conscious of it. Håfström tried to push these "three buttons of fear" in *The Rite*, and also *The Twilight Saga* cherishes its horror scenes because of the audience's commitment. The vampire does not trigger fear anymore, as the ancient stories about vampires did. Looking at the movies, the vampires and demons cannot possibly touch the viewers, but most of the spectators feel anxiety. "Galvanized attention, tense muscles, mind focused on the possibility of harm ... these are exactly the responses that scary movies produce," Eitzen concludes. "It is the idea of danger that triggers the fear. [...] Still, the fear machinery churns away, beneath the level of this conscious stuff. We cannot turn this machinery off." There is something awkward happening here, Eitzen warns us. "Humans are the only creatures that actively seek out fearful experiences. We take roller coaster rides. We skydive. We go to scary movies. We even pay money to do these things. That seems irrational. Paradoxical." Informed by recent studies, he also supplies the answer. Adrenaline streaming through our brains gives us energy, makes us feel good. The safe chair in the cinema or in front of the television allows us to enjoy that feeling without actually being in danger. Experiencing "the rush produced by fear where there is minimal actual danger, particularly when accompanied by a sense of control, can be an exhilarating experience." Next there is the cognitive mastery: "A movie monster is not just a dangerous creature, it also typically invokes ideas that we do not like to think about because they are repellent (putrescent flesh, spiders, deviant sexual behavior, cannibalism, etc.) or ideas that are difficult to think about because they violate our normal conceptual categories (dead yet alive, artificial yet sentient, destructive mothers, vengeful birds, and so on). By imagining something disgusting or threatening, we take a step toward comprehending it and then to manage or control it. It addresses a biological need, by helping us feel and be safe."[33]

Stories address basic biological needs. This is why humans dive into narratives. This is why ideas, values, and behavioral and conversational solutions presented in films root in our brains as potential simulations to influence behavior. Films, especially the violent and frightening ones, help us manage danger by thinking about it. Improving the "fear schemas" means developing better survival skills. Fiction transports us into simulations of situations we may normally not experience, including unnatural dangers, in order to allows us this way to think them through and how to respond to them. Humans are hardwired to be transported into storyworlds; to imagine or simulate social responses. The threat appearing in scary movies affects groups and communities, but also connects us with other people, as this quintessential social act pleases us. Entertaining fearful ideas, says Eitzen, "is not just about cognitive mastery." It is also "about making connections to other people, real and imaginary, as a way of practicing social skills that are useful in coping with actual dangers." Because both *The Rite* and *The Twilight Saga* have left the traditional implications connected with demons, vampires, and werewolves behind, working with contemporary mental schemas, the Freudian link to hidden and haunting forces is lost as well. Although both films appeal to the metanarrative of the "deep," they somehow also witness the beginning of its demise. Judging from the reviews, *The Rite* does champion exorcism but seems to overdo it in our paganized eyes. Apart from strict Roman Catholics, few viewers would share Father Lucas's worldview. More than *The Rite*, *The Twilight Saga* is a challenge to Freudian essentialism because there is nothing to exorcize from Edward Cullen or Jacob Black.[34]

# 3

## *Carol's Predicament*

### The Body in *[SAFE]* (1995) and *Jennifer's Body* (2009)
Todd Haynes (writer and director); and
Karyn Kusama (director), Diablo Cody (writer)

1

Carol White (Julianne Moore) and Chris (James LeGros), a fellow patient, have prepared a meal for the other patients at Wrenwood Center — a series of wooden cabins and a communal center in the desert of New Mexico. Carol seeks treatment in the center for an odd disease. Late in the afternoon, the patients dance, but perform unusually: they distance themselves from one another, even while dancing together. Chris, Carol's cooking partner, announces that the following day is Carol's birthday. A cake is presented, candles are blown, a song is sung ("For She's a Jolly Good Fellow"). Some in the group shout at Carol to give a speech. This is difficult, for Carol is timid, shy, and retiring. She answers: "I can't. I've never made a speech. I want to thank Chris for doing this ... and everybody here so much. It just pulled me through a really hard period. Anyway, I couldn't have done it without you." She seems confused: "I don't know what I'm saying. I really hated myself before I came here ... so I'm trying to see myself ... hopefully, more as I am. More ... More positive, like seeing the pluses. I think it's slowly opening up now. People's minds, like ... educating and, and ... AIDS and ... and other types of diseases ... because, because ... it is a disease, because it's out there ... and we just have to be more aware of it. We have to make people aware of it ... and, umm, even ourselves ... like, uh, going ... reading labels and going into buildings." That night, she seals herself in a sterile, white, porcelain igloo on the Wrenwood compound. There, Carol looks in the mirror, past herself and into the audience, and says, "I love you. I really love you. I love you." It seems, this is the moment she is soon to be "born again," as a child locked in a protective womb. After the happy experience of cooking a meal with someone and enjoying it in the group, the film suggests Carol has finally found her way out of her negative state of mind.

# 2

This is a scene from *[SAFE]*, written and directed by Todd Haynes. (Today, *[SAFE]* should not be confused with Boaz Yakin's action film *Safe*, which premiered in 2011). Until the moment described above, character Carol White believed she was not herself. She had entered the Wrenwood clinic trying to see herself "hopefully, more as I am." This individual quest for the inner self is emblematic for the attitude of the Structuralist-Romantic Order. Although he does not characterize himself as a gay filmmaker, Haynes is the face of the New Queer Cinema movement. The goal of this movement has been to both explore and redefine the contours of queer culture in America and beyond. The question then is: who does Carol, who is an enigma to herself, represent? The answer is to be found in the illness. The film suggests that Carol is infected. But with what? She must have contracted something, somewhere. Outside? She hardly leaves the car. Inside? Is her house dangerous? The analysis in Susan Potter's article in *Camera Obscura*, "Dangerous Spaces" (2004), confirms Haynes's words uttered to his interviewer, Collier Schorr, a female queer photographer from New York. Interviewer Schorr found the film's opening sequence "shamelessly gorgeous and seductive." Haynes needed to transport the viewer into Carol's narrative world this way: "I wanted the opening to be a glossy, slow entry into this world. The way it is described in the script is that the viewer is driving up a hill and watching houses go from small to large to larger, all more and more simulated in their architecture [...]— fake Tudor, fake country manor, at night bathed in the iridescent blue-green glow of street lamps and landscape lighting, with that buzz of electricity in the air. Everything the film is about can be seen in those houses from outside at night." Potter points to the extension of the private space from the home to the car. Only in her car, Carol moves safely to visit her nearby friend Linda (Susan Norman), to the local health club's aerobics classes and to the dry cleaners. Carol's world is stunning and frightening at the same time. Haynes believes that Carol's Los Angeles is "like an airport: you never breathe real air; you are never in any real place; you are in a transitional, carpeted hum zone." Carol is like the buildings she moves through and she learns about herself by becoming ill. "I think the illness is the only thing that is telling her the truth in the movie," Haynes said. Being ill, she had been herself all the time.[1]

It is 1987. Carol seems to have it all in life: a family and a beautiful house in an affluent neighborhood of the San Fernando Valley, California. However, she is not only a seemingly unremarkable homemaker, she has a poor relationship with her stepson from her husband's previous marriage, Rory (Chauncey Leopardi). Furthermore, she lacks a strong personality and seems timid and empty during all of her interactions with the world around her. Her days go by gardening and attending aerobics classes. Every now and then she takes her clothes to the dry cleaners. Devoid of emotional intimacy, the relationship with her wealthy husband Greg (Xander Berkeley) seems stable. Earlier in Haynes' film, we have seen Carol in bed with him. The mechanical sex produces nothing in her, but she goes through the motions of kissing and petting him. The next morning we find her in the garden pruning her yellow roses. That day she has to stay at home to wait for her new couches to arrive. Carol walks through the spaces of her house like a fish in an aquarium — in fact, the house itself looks sort of like a dungeon set in an aquarium. Then, unexpectedly, horror strikes. Inhaling the smoky exhaust fumes from the truck driving in front of her, Carol suffers a coughing fit. In order to escape, she frantically seeks refuge in an underground car park, tires squealing as she drives around trying to find a free parking space. Potter notes a crucial scene: "The final shot of the scene is an extreme long shot as Carol opens the car door and doubles over coughing, while overhead the heavy, concrete beams of the car park weigh in on her. The toxic emissions of cars and trucks may be a cause of the illness that Carol eventually develops, but *[SAFE]* also implies that the private technology of the car and its associated infrastructure of enclosed parking spaces and wide multilane roads and highways compose an invisible social barrier that may be more dangerous than the protection it appears to offer."[2] Thus, Carol must have been infected from the *inside*.

*[SAFE]* is not about Carol, but about the "illness." What is it? Slowly, Carol becomes vilely inebriated by the blandness and inanity of her empty and isolated upper-middle-class life. The camera work underscores how her blues starts to break her, whereas the menacing electronic soundtrack gives the images a horror feel of a chilling dream. "You don't always notice it," writes critic Ebert, "but during a lot of the scenes in *[SAFE]* there's a low-level hum on the soundtrack." This is a conscious effect: "It suggests that malevolent machinery of some sort is always at work somewhere nearby." Think of air conditioning, electrical motors, and idling engines. This machinery is constantly sending gases and toxic fumes into the environment. "The effect is to make the movie's environment quietly menacing." The film, for

one, never clearly identifies any industrial or chemical origin for Carol's malady. By a series of deep-focus shots, Haynes wants to picture Carol coolly. He sets her in a materially comfortable but emotionally empty life as an almost invisible woman. The director never allows the viewer to get too close to Carol, making her predicament even more confusing and alienating. Haynes found the alternative difficult to film: "People who have chemical illnesses get really intense psychical reactions from chemicals. Some of the stuff I saw doing research was so extreme — cysts draining black discharge, for example — I couldn't put it in the movie because the audience would think it was just outrageous." Outside the home, human contacts are polite but distant. It is as if Carol White does not know who she is. The Freudian question urges itself upon us: Is there something subconsciously haunting her mind?

Haynes deploys seemingly contradictory modes of filmmaking, like this distanced style of cinematography combined with editing techniques that are ordinarily used to suture viewers into the narrative. "The effect of this combination," argues Potter, "is to withhold the identification with character that such classical techniques secure, while at the same time foregrounding their usual ideological effects." For Potter, one such moment occurs when Carol arrives home in the evening after having attended a meeting about "environmental illness," a disease characterized as a hypersensitivity to industrial chemicals and emissions. "Carol walks into the lounge and then pauses, her back to the camera. As she stands in the middle of the room, the camera performs a barely noticeable maneuver, tracking backward while zooming in. In this quiet moment, domestic space — and the female protagonist's place within it — is subtly altered." Haynes wanted to map Carol as a victim of her spatial surroundings: "I created a difficult situation for myself by providing the audience with all these ways not to care about Carol. But the ammunition the audience has just reiterates all the mean messages Carol is told: You are making yourself sick; it is all in your head; go see a shrink; you don't love yourself enough; you lead this empty life; you're not really stressed out. I wanted to touch that little bit in everyone where you just aren't convinced that who you think you are is really who you are — that moment when you feel like you're a forgery." Haynes refused to sketch a perfect home with a loving mother and satisfying sex. "A problem already existed," Haynes said, "and the illness was a circumstance that alerted her to it."[3]

Although this world Carol lives in would be considered safer than just about any other, there is a "monster lurking within her." As she goes about her routine working out at the gym, drinking mineral water, supervising her household staff and attending "benefit luncheons," she slowly begins to develop unpredictable and strange bodily reactions that apparently are allergic reactions. Starting with headaches and leading to a grand-mal seizure, Carol becomes more and more sick, claiming that she has become sensitive to the common toxins in today's world: exhaust fumes, aerosol spray, and so forth. At a baby shower with some friends or neighbors, she suddenly experiences an anxiety attack. When getting a perm at a hair salon, another restrictive environment overloaded by chemical fumes, her nose starts to bleed. At home, Greg's conciliatory embrace of Carol one morning after another small crisis ends with her physically shuddering in his arms and pushing against him to create space to vomit on the carpet. Does the constriction of Greg's embrace, a relation of sexual cause and effect or a negative androcentric gendering, contribute to her illness? Carol pulls back from Greg's sexual advances and spends her nights alone by the television or wandering around the outside of her well-protected home. At the dry cleaners, she has convulsions after noticing men spraying chemicals against insects. There does not seem to be a medical reason for her lapse. One specialist is able to identify only one true allergy: milk, which she drinks frequently in the movie without incident. Slowly, Carol starts to feel trapped by her own surroundings. The viewer, however, wavers between a sickness of the mind and of the body. Does suburban drudgery give way to a self-inflicted, existential crisis?

One feature Potter notes is the use of whiteness, tinged with pastels, as a metaphor of Carol's safe world — and blackness as the color of the danger coming in. The white is inside; black is outside. Although, at first, Carol believes that the contagion is black, soon she starts realizing that it must be white; in fact, a contaminated white. Her husband is Greg White, and when she comprehends that through marriage she has become a White herself, she starts to distance herself from her husband. Carol loves milk, perhaps she is a "milkoholic," until the finding of the allergy for milk. A white or light pastel sofa she has ordered appears to be black. The capacious rooms of her house are open to contamination without any barrier whatsoever. The maid is a Latina woman moving freely through the house. Taking pleasure in detailed descriptions of violent crimes and the weapons used to commit them, her stepson Rory reads about an essay he wrote for school suggesting that black gangsters are moving into white areas. Carol can never be alone in a private space of her own making. There is no defense against intrusion. As she begins to suffer various symptoms of illness, Potter notes, she breaks her domestic and social routines to find some solitude. "Walking in the garden one night, Carol is forced back inside the house by a mobile police unit that shines a searchlight on her and asks if she is all right. The soliciting question from the police connotes possible mental disturbance, adding to her unease rather than alleviating it. The moment ends with Carol drawing back inside the house as Greg appears on the second-story balcony above her to ask what she is doing." Sent back in by a male police force and being confronted by her husband above her, the scene exemplifies the way in which Carol is isolated while also continually under interrogation from the dominant forces around her:

"Being alone is inescapable yet unsustainable in surroundings that both enforce and deny privacy." Being a White submits her to her white surroundings — both the suburban lifestyle and the heterosexual androcentric submission to her husband.[4]

Attending psychotherapy sessions does serve Carol very well. This was undertaken to combat the haunting subconscious. But then, she watches a commercial on television, which strikes a nerve: "Do you smell fumes? Are you allergic to the 20th century?" She begins exploring environmental illness, thinking she is being poisoned by stray chemicals that are insinuatingly evident. The "illness" has no roots "inside," but "outside." Carol believes she has developed multiple chemical sensitivity (MCS), also described as the "Twentieth-Century Disease." Medically of course, MCS is controversial. The diagnosis is articulated from mild to severe non-specific symptoms, which are thought to be triggered by chemicals found in everyday household and industrial products. Carol eventually resorts to moving to the Wrenwood spa retreat in the semi-desert of Albuquerque, New Mexico. The settlement is communal and non-profit, founded by Claire Fitzpatrick (Kate McGregor-Stewart) and Peter Dunning (Peter Friedman). They designed it to help people suffering from MCS or similar diseases to recover. Probably Carol thinks that only by changing her surroundings, her "outside," making them less insular, more diverse and heterogeneous and more private at the same time, she can cure herself of her malady and gain a story of her own. Peter is the man that needs to lead her through this creation of a "toxic-free zone." Peter is HIV positive.

Does Haynes now show the film's true colors? Peter's character, Haynes explained, has a lot to do with a book that was very popular in the late 1980s: *The AIDS Book: Creating a Positive Approach* (1988) by Louise Hay. Her book was very popular among HIV positive gay men at the time. It puzzled Haynes: "What is it that makes people with AIDS read a book that says, If you loved yourself more you would not have gotten sick, and now that you are sick if you learn how to love yourself you will be cured? This puts the subjects in an impossible situation where they will never overcome their illness because they will never love themselves enough. I think I made Peter someone with AIDS not only because it is another immune-system illness, like environmental illness — they are often linked — but also because there was this history of New Age thinking and AIDS that I wanted to bring into the film." In *[SAFE]*, Peter preaches that the patients should act like him: accepting the toxicity of "outside," and taking responsibility for cleaning up the "inside." Haynes told Schorr that what Wrenwood ultimately provided Carol is as destructive and confining as her Los Angeles home and life she fled. In fact, Carol finds the highway is nearby; her attempts at meditation are disturbed by a rumble of jets, which also interrupt her group therapy sessions. At one moment, when she lapses into tears inside the ostensible privacy of her cabin, the center's director enters the cabin, offering therapeutic advice, thereby demonstrating that, like Carol's home in Los Angeles, this space is also potentially subject to interruption at any moment. "We leave Carol White almost where we found her in the beginning of the film — suffering in a repressive system that is supposed to have been the answer to everything."[5]

Although the spa is a self-help resort, Carol seems to be back at the "inside," back at the assumption that she somehow causes her symptoms herself. She seems to have traded one form of oppression for another; from the constricting identity as a homemaker to that as a reclusive invalid. This happens despite Wrenwood's spiritual approach, despite her allegiance to her cohort and the relationship with the other patients. Critic Roger Ebert writes: "To some degree, [SAFE] suggests that [...] maybe the blissful group leaders at the spa are doing to her mind what pollution did to her lungs. Or maybe it's a tripleheader: Maybe the environment is poisoned, and the group is phony, and Carol is gnawing away at her own psychic health. Now there's a fine mess." In 1995, talking to Schorr, Haynes said, "Wrenwood's answer for Carol is horribly cruel, for she is blamed for her illness and basically locked up in a sealed-up vault." Furthermore, Carol is never represented as a figure who embodies natural feeling and who is systematically evacuated of any interiority. Carol has no history. In fact, in several scenes Carol struggles to remember her past. "A psychological excavation of Carol's past is inappropriate," writes Potter, "since she is never presented as having an emotional or social history." Next to providing her with the identity as an upper-middle-class white woman, Carol's whiteness is also highly suggestive of her empty blank quality, her fundamentally unknown inner horizon. For Haynes, the film had to resist telling the viewers what to think and leave them without the kinds of rewards modern filmmaking usually assures. There is no romantic spark between Carol and Chris, for example. Carol is not fully accessible to the viewers, Haynes explains, and the viewers do not fully understand why the illness is happening to her.[6]

# 3

Focusing upon the "inside," Haynes emphatically opened the door to the Freudian Edifice. He confirmed this after interviewer Schorr asked him about Natalie Wood's character in *Splendor in the Grass* (1961, directed by Elia Kazan). "Both are models of restraint — with the exception of Natalie's breakdown in the bathtub and Carol's seizure at the dry cleaners. In [SAFE], does chemical illness replace hysteria, which seems ever stuck on the feminine?" Haynes answered: "Yes, of course. One thing about *Splendor in the Grass* is that Wood's character's sexual hunger is continually being tamed — by society and its rules of what a woman is supposed to be. Unfortunately Carol White doesn't have that hunger. The history of illness associated with women has been a continual interest in my films, from *Superstar* [subtitled *The Karen Carpenter Story*, 1988] to *[SAFE]*. I loved what seemed particularly inexplicable about environmental illness when I first read about it — how it was affecting housewives. [...] The ability to dismiss illness as feminine and the way illness completely undermines identity are what *[SAFE]* explores." In her *Other Voices* 2005 article "The Trouble with Carol," Julie Grossman argues that Haynes challenges traditional Hollywood narrative. We do not see a heroine taking charge of her life. As a victim of the repressive male-dominated society, Carol is a damsel in distress. The debilitating self-help culture, encouraging patients to take sole responsibility, only confirms her problems. In fact, Carol goes from bad to worse.[7]

Of course Carol is a hysteric? Is this her "inside" problem? Technically not. She cannot be a Freudian hysteric, because she demonstrates none of the typical features Freud wants her to have. True, suffering from or faking specific symptoms, Freudian hysterics imagine things wrong with their bodies, which were, said Freud, "to be found in the intimacies of the patients' psycho-sexual life, and that hysterical symptoms are the expression of their most secret and repressed wishes." Here is our problem. The viewers of *[SAFE]* have neither knowledge of Carol's past, nor of her supposedly repressed thoughts or wishes. It is therefore not easy to classify her as a classic hysteric, unless we accommodate Freud's basic proposition. Every working theory is modernized around proven basic propositions, as, for example, happens in *Theorising Desire* (2008) by Kristyn Gorton, a lecturer in the Department of Theatre, Film and Television, University of York, England. For her, Carol must be the typical hysteric from contemporary psychoanalysis in which, for example, chemical illness could replace repression. Gorton correctly says that if "the narrative of Oedipus is the central story within psychoanalysis, then the hysteric is its central feature." However, she does not mention the specifically classified symptoms of Freudian hysteria. On the contrary, she reviews writers' thoughts about contemporary hysteria and she hesitates to draw a firm conclusion. Her psychoanalytical colleagues point at hysteria's "obscene interpretability," from, among others, a physical disease, a mental disorder, a sociological communication to no illness at all; or they see a hidden hysteria manifested in our world and are not recognizing it; and that it is more contagious than in the past. So devoid of Freud, it seems that with every new publication the definition of hysteria becomes vaguer, until it almost vanishes.[8]

Any reader should be aware of this transformation. Is this loss consistent with modernization and progress? Freud wanted his followers to follow him strictly, to the letter. Therefore, we should not lose track of the basic psychoanalytical premises, like the idea that hysteria with its odd and assorted "neuroses" should be diagnosed as a symbolic representation of sexual "reminiscences." These are repressed because of their irreconcilability with the conscious ego. Repression in psychoanalysis is to defend unconsciously and energetically against remembering. It is a defense mechanism that puts memory out of consciousness. It is immanently part of the "sexual" in this theory. In her overview, Gorton refers to Freud's case of Dora to underscore that hysteria must be articulated to its intimate, repressed, and secret nature. In good Romantic fashion she adds that the "secret desires" of the hysteric "always and forever remain just out of reach." In addition, the jacket of her book reassures that she works from "psychoanalytical, feminist and film studies." Indeed, her sources of "feminist and film studies" include mainly psychoanalytically informed authors, who all seem to adhere to the ideas of a "subconscious," an "Oedipus Complex," and "repression," to name only a few of the chambers in Freud's Edifice. Feminist psychoanalysts, of course, working with the Oedipus Complex, see the hysteric as either a victim of patriarchal control or a heroine. However, Gorton begins her chapter on "hysterical desire" with the establishment that the "rise of an individualistic society also means an increase in the expectations placed on individuals to know what they want, to know their desires and to seek answers in everything from horoscopes, to TV talk shows to new age therapies." The hysteric answers questions about identity through "the 'psycho-boom' which, instead of relieving a sense of anxiety, works to create new problems, questions and hysterical symptoms." With this, she seems to disregard the sexual.[9]

For psychoanalysts, would Gorton's position count as progress? French psychoanalyst Elisabeth Roudinesco, Lacan's biographer, points at hysteria as "a protest against the bourgeois order that manifested itself through women's bodies." She believes that the modern world is plagued by depression as the 19th century was by hysteria. It is as if hysteria as a "contemporary neurotic conflict" no longer seems to derive from the unconscious and yet "the unconscious reappears through the body, opposing a strong resistance to the disciplines and practices seeking to get rid of it." Thus, it is the haunting unconscious disguised as depression. If the definition of hysteria is so general nowadays, so multi-interpretable, may we regard hysteria still as a credible diagnosis? Can it be used to discriminate against other diagnoses? Can we understand when some behavior is *not* hysterical? Any physician works with a typical scientific method in answering these scholarly questions, with theories that work, and with a therapy or medication that is tested and screened. Not all medical knowledge is sufficient; not all therapies work, but they are screened continuously and will be replaced if other therapies or medication proves better. This seems absent in psychoanalysis. There have only been less possibilities of theoretical discrimination.[10]

More than a decade ago, Borch-Jacobsen effectively questioned the idea of progress in psychoanalysis. His text was a review of a book by Juliet Mitchell on hysteria. It is common among psychoanalysts to react to criticism by saying that the opponents quote from outmoded texts — the one Freud tried to build. Today, they continue, psychoanalysts work with up-to-date concepts. By quoting Mitchell literally, Borch-Jacobsen shows this is not true. Mitchell suggests progress by stating that her work into the gendering of hysteria brought her to doubt Freud's vision on the "illness." "Thinking about hysteria has led me to a different reading of the Oedipus Complex and to the need to insert the experience of siblings and their lateral heirs in peer and affinal relationships into our understanding of the construction of mental life." The problem here is that Mitchell found no reason to leave the Oedipus Complex aside. By offering nothing but a "different reading" of it and adding a personal interpretation, she confirmed Freud's exorcist roots. Inevitably, "progress" in psychoanalysis means to move away from Freud. For example, it means a different understanding of curing patients. Following the classical methods some cures are reported, but the totals never rose above the average of the effects of placebo and spontaneous psychic recovery. "If there is no one reason for any particular recurring psychological phenomenon," writes Steven Hoenisch, a student in linguistic theory, "then psychoanalysis cannot impart a cure based on a scientifically inspired insight. At best, it can only put forth a possible reason, an invented cause, and persuade the patient to believe it." His conclusion: "The psychoanalyst's art, then, lies in finding, based on available information obtained from the patient and through transference, the most persuasive argument for the patient to see his problems in a different light — to be persuaded to see the world and his relation to it differently. In this change of perspective, brought about by argument, not insight, lies the cure. Or, to put it another way, the cure lies not in the insight but in being persuaded that the insight is right."[11]

Any session with a family member, a priest, or a friend has demonstrably the same result as psychoanalytic therapy. This means that, if successful anyway, psychoanalysis works for patients because of the talking, not because of the concepts, less because of some universal truths in its underlying theory. When individuals are asked to write or talk about their problems and traumas, significant improvements in psychic and physical conditions can definitely be found. Evidence of such a process was detected by professional psychologists in specific links between word production in the brain — detected through scans — and immediate autonomic nervous system activity, even in enhanced immune functions. However, although the well-known Boston psychoanalyst therapist Phyllis Meadow (1925–2005) concluded in her book *The New Psychoanalysis* (2003) that her trait "ceased to be a medical treatment and became a verbal one interested in understanding human emotion," she maintained that a talking cure is rooted in Freudian concepts. This is what she says about cancer: "Many possible causes have been documented in the literature, for example, an emotional loss is frequent prior to the onset of cancer. So, too, is a physical trauma. Preceding leukemia, researchers found a high incidence of flu and pneumonia. We know trauma can reduce the effectiveness of the body's immune system, thus establishing a readiness for cancer. In the analysis of cancer victims, the difficulty is in reversing the patient's tendency to discharge tension in life-destructive ways. The problem is that despite the patient's and the analyst's best intentions, the patient cannot say everything." The analyst must "de-block" this resistance. She continues: "Working with cancer patients has the further difficulty that the cancer is fast growing, so the treatment must be conceptualized as short term. Can we ask transference to unfold at a pace that will save the patient?" No, we cannot. This is the old way of pointing the finger to the patient: "Cancer is your own fault!" It might be true for lung cancer resulting from smoking — although this is not what Meadow means — but not for other cancers. In the medical profession, physicians are aware of the fact that mothers who catch influenza, pneumonia or a sexually transmitted disease during pregnancy run the risk of giving birth to a child that may develop leukemia.[12] Note, it is *not* the mother, as is indicated by Meadow, but her child. Is this child to blame? Definitely not. No medical specialists would agree with Meadow's remarks and might find them rather tasteless.

Like Freud, Fliess, and many of her precursors, Meadow was a medical nitwit. She studied English literature not medicine. She felt nevertheless confident enough not only to dismiss the hereditary causes of many cancers, without further research into the disease, but also to argue that the talking therapy would indeed cure cancer patients: "I had one patient who came in with a metastasized brain cancer and the belief that she should try everything on the off-chance that something might work. She was receiving chemotherapy concurrently with the analysis. In addition, she was encouraged to change her eating habits, which she did. This patient's personality fit perfectly the cancer personality profile: She was extremely polite but when she spoke revealed a great deal of repressed rage. When she learned that the cancer had been reversed, she left treatment. She did not want a treatment that would involve introspection, particularly regarding her inability to be close with others. She left without knowing what had caused the remission."[13] Medication, beyond a shred of doubt. For Meadow it would have been the analytic sessions or the change in diet. This echoes Freud truly — although, to my knowledge, he never mentioned the existence of the "cancer personality." The obituary in the *Villager*, a Boston newspaper, on January 26, 2005, stated that Meadow had "created a distinctive body of knowledge that earned respect for psychoanalysis despite much skepticism from critics in the medical field."[14] Her "distinctive body of knowledge" could not prevent her from dying of cancer herself. Would she have recognized her own "cancer personality," or her "repressed rage"?

Gorton also talks about insight, but she places it in a much wider context. She argues that hysteria is now more contagious and more prevalent than before, and that our world today, for example, manifests a "hidden hysteria" without recognizing it. One key element is what the theorists recognize as a wider anxiety within society over a loss of control and desire for safety. Illustrating this situation, *[SAFE]* reflects the "alienation and desire for security" that authors use to define contemporary hysteria. Gorton sees an articulation to the Gulf War Syndrome and Chronic Fatigue Syndrome. She notes that Haynes spends the first half of the film emphasizing the monotony and isolation of Carol's life, "so much so that we, as viewers, feel very little warmth toward her character or feel sympathy when she begins to experience hysterical symptoms." Gorton believes that the anxiety attack at her friend's baby shower must be diagnosed as hysterical, as is the collapse into a convulsive fit at the dry cleaners. In Wrenwood, Gorton sees Carol finally belonging, and becoming resistant to her husband's affections and desires to come home. At the end, Carol has transformed, but into what? Self-discovery, in Gorton's eyes, hardly encouraged empowerment. Nevertheless, awakened into some new consciousness, Carol is still alone and isolated.[15]

Carol does not show any of Freud's repressed desires, hence answering the questions of *[SAFE]* proves to be very difficult for Gorton. She thinks, for example, that Haynes presents a biological aspect of hysteria. Carol is convinced that her symptoms can be explained by a chemical overdose in her system — despite the fact that her doctors can find no rational explanation for this. She is in Wrenwood to strengthen her defenses, her immune system, by auto-suggestion and positive thinking. Gorton understands that at the end, Carol does not need to worry about questions like "Who am I?" or "What do I want?" for she has found a master answering them. Curiously, Gorton finds a way for viewing *[SAFE]* as somewhat variegated: by taking her own steps Carol goes against her husband's and her doctor's wishes and chooses her own path, which enables her to tell herself that she loves herself. Is she dismantling the patriarchal order this way? Conversely, Gorton also keeps open the possibility that Carol's desire is born from alienation and self-doubt, a "product of a society that continually emphasises fear — that reminds us that everything around us — from the food we eat, to the water we drink, to the people we live next to — are potential threats against our lives." The ability to answer the questions of "Who am I?" and "What do I want?" can only come from oneself. Gorton sees the closing scene of *[SAFE]* as evidence of this interpretation.

Far removed from Freud's original sexual theory, Gorton falls back on definitions of hysteria set down in dictionaries. Is there scholarly progress in consulting a dictionary? As we all know, dictionaries describe the actual use of words mostly in the public domain, accumulated from spoken language, radio, television, films, and the Internet, as well as from newspapers, magazines, plays, and novels. Most dictionaries also offer, outside of the definition itself, information alerting readers to attitudes that may influence their choices on words often considered vulgar, offensive, erroneous, or easily confused. The definitions in dictionaries are rarely taken directly from scientific literature. This can be easily verified. If someone, for example, tries to build a theory of economics based entirely on definitions given by dictionaries, the result will be inconsistent, incomplete, or simply awkward. Although careful research into the use of words and sentences — citations — gives dictionaries indeed their well-deserved reputation, the lemmas are eventually also a highly stylized dense abstract, perhaps overly compressed. In spite of many citations, a lemma always runs the risk of collapsing into a limited amount of statements about the behavior of the word in question. These features define dictionaries as typically artificial repositories of popular language, based on the changing meaning of words in spoken and written language. Not infrequently, dictionaries end up being outmoded, representing a consensus of words that belong to a time long past. Nevertheless, this is precisely what Freud frequently did with words used in popular language to describe a state of mind. Time and again the dictionary is invoked as an incontrovertible authority. It is as if psychoanalysis needs to articulate to popular psychology in order to underscore its validity — despite the dictionary's basic inconsistency, incompleteness, or simply the awkwardness of psychomythology.[16]

The dictionary as one major psychoanalytical instrument has a curious consequence: psychoanalysts begin playing word games to explain serious psychological problems. It does not improve their reputation. Take this game, recorded in an 1897 letter from Freud to Fliess in Berlin: "Mr E., whom you know, had an anxiety attack at the age of ten when he tried to catch a black beetle, which would not put up with it. The meaning of this attack had thus far remained obscure. Now, dwelling on the theme of 'being unable to make up one's mind,' he repeated a conversation between his grandmother and his aunt about the marriage of his mother, who at that time was already dead, from which it emerged that she had not been able to make up her mind for quite some time; then he suddenly came up with the black beetle, which he had not mentioned for months, and from that to ladybug [*Marienkäfer*] (his mother's name was Marie); then he laughed out loud and inadequately explained his laughter by saying that zoologists call this beetle *septem punctata* or the equivalent, according to the number of dots, although it is always the same animal. Then we broke off and the next time he told me that before the session the meaning of the beetle [*Käfer*] had occurred to him, namely, *que faire?* = being unable to make up one's mind. *Meschugge!*"[17] Furthermore, Freud's "analysis" also referred to the word "beetle" as a referent for women in Vienna and that the patient had loved a French woman who had been his nurse. Would a psychiatrist in our time pass his exam if he interprets the patient's frightening experience with an insect, using a dictionary on his desk, linking through a vocabulary game including two words from different foreign languages (here, French and Latin) a nurse, and first love with an anxiety attack? *Meschugge,* indeed.

## 4

If Carol's anxiety attacks are related to her identity in Los Angeles, her problem must be her autobiography. What has she told herself? Her autobiography is another reference to a narrative world, a "blueprint for world-creation." These "blueprints for world-creation" include stages, like the spacious rooms of Carol's Los Angeles home. As Carol experienced, this mapping procedure of the mind is strongly embodied. Today, cognitive scientists think differently about the problem of mind and body than in the days of *The Interpretation of Dreams*. In his *Descartes' Error* (1994), Damasio concludes: "The mind is embodied, in the full sense of the term, not just embrained." Reading Damasio, we learn that Western writing created the distinction between diseases of "brain" and "mind," reflecting "neurological" illnesses versus "psychiatric" ones. This distinction grew into another unfortunate psychomyth, which shows a basic fallacy of the functioning of brain, mind and body. This ignorance goes back to the erroneous *cogito ergo sum* (*I think, therefore I am*), formulated by the French philosopher René Descartes (1596–1650). Erroneous, for if you only look at the fear system in the brain of humans, shared with all animals, you will notice, says Damasio to his readers, that it is closely connected with the body — indeed, the rest of the body, for the brain is part of it, and not separate. The *cogito ergo sum* had separated the body and the mind, referring to the body as a machine made of "extended substance" and to the mind as made of "thinking substance." This so-called Cartesian Cut of the brain-matter, mind-body divide, which most authors lining up with the Structuralist-Romantic Order share, merged in Western thinking with androcentrism and the crucial and unparalleled significance of the human soul. It established the idea of a free mind or soul versus a coerced body, and may be related to the persuasion-coercion divide in Western social science. Damasio warns that his stance should not be taken for reductionism. "Realizing that there are biological mechanisms behind the most sublime human behavior does not imply a simplistic reduction to the nuts and bolts of neurobiology. In any case, the partial explanation of complexity by something less complex does not simplify debasement." The mind forms part of the body and, as a product of electric currents, is inevitably material.[18]

Today, the brain and hence the mind are seen as one bodily organ among many. Paul John Eakin reminds us of the recent find that individuals have a kind of built-in body map, keeping track of the position of their limbs in space and time. Because human individuals are social individuals, there is also a kind of built-in social body map, keeping track of the position of the individual in the social environment. More than a decade ago, Eakin followed the lead of developmental psychologists and traced the origins of autobiographical discourse to the young child's initiation into "memory talk," the homely little stories that parents and caregivers coach us to tell about ourselves. Eakin concluded that we learn as children what it means to say "I" in the cultures we inhabit. This training proves to be crucial to the success of our lives as adults. Our recognition by others as a normal individual depends on our ability to perform the work of self-narration. Thus, autobiographical discourse plays a decisive part in the regime of social accountability that governs our lives, and in this sense human identities could be said to be socially constructed and regulated. In recent years, Eakin added to this the insights of Antonio Damasio published in *Descartes' Error* (1994) or *The Feeling of What Happens* (1999). Damasio is one of the world's leading researchers in neurobiology and at the time head of the Department of Neurology at the University of Iowa College of Medicine. His work lines up with authors working within the Cognitive-Evolutionary Order. According to the neurologist, bodies have stories. Because we move in time, in fact, anything in the body itself moves in time, there is always a past, present, and future — the "imagetic representation of sequences of brain events," says Damasio, or pre-linguistic "wordless stories about what happens to an organism immersed in an environment."[19]

From Damasio's neurobiological perspective, the body emerges as a "homeostasis machine," and the body's homeostatic regulatory activities range from metabolism, basic reflexes, and the immune system at the lowest level, to pain and pleasure behaviors, drives and motivations, and finally to emotions and conscious feelings, feelings precisely that all these activities are taking place. The adaptive goal of all this manifold activity of homeostatic regulation, a great deal of it unconscious, is the well-being of the organism as it moves forward into the future. For Damasio the continuous attempt at achieving a state of positively regulated life is a defining part of our existence, one of our "drives." Eakin would extend this view of the human organism's homeostatic regulatory activity to include our endless fashioning of identity narratives, our performance of the autobiographical act. In addition, we would extend this to our social life, encouraged by Damasio: "Our life must be regulated not only by our own desires and feelings but also by our *concern* for the desires and feelings of others expressed as social conventions and rules of ethical behavior. Those conventions and rules and the institutions that enforce them — religion, justice, and sociopolitical organizations — become mechanisms for exerting homeostasis at the level of the social group."[20] Activities such as science, technology, and the arts assist the mechanisms of what Damasio calls "social homeostasis." Eakin thinks that we could say that autobiography's tracking of identity states across time serves a homeostatic goal. In this sense, the adaptive purpose of self-narrative, whether neurobiological or literary, would be the maintenance of stability in the human individual through the creation of a sense of identity. This is precisely the function of some "collective storytelling," social homeostasis, which is involved in feature filmmaking.[21]

Fear is one of the clearest examples of the mind-body integration. Hence, Carol's body experienced anxiety attacks. In our time, researchers link generalized anxiety to disrupted functional connectivity of the amygdalae, the almond-shaped groups of nuclei located within the medial temporal lobes of the brain in complex vertebrates, and their processing of fear and anxiety. In *The Emotional Brain* (1996), Joseph LeDoux says fear is pervasive — in both brain and body. Strictly speaking, he continues, the fear system is not one that results in the conscious experience of fear. It detects dangers and produces responses that maximize the probability of surviving a dangerous situation in the most beneficial way. In other words, it is behavior. Feelings of fear are a by-product of human evolution and that includes consciousness. People use fear to control. LeDoux displays how children learn to be moral to some extent by their fear of what will happen if they are not. "Laws reflect our fear of social disorder and, by the same token, social order is maintained, however imperfectly, by fear of the consequences of breaking the rules." Freudians will read this as the establishment of the SuperEgo and submission to the Father — the social order in the Freudian Edifice is androcentric. Too much or inappropriate fear, LeDoux concludes, accounts for many common psychiatric problems. Anxiety is a consciously realized brooding fear of what might happen. Phobic objects like snakes, spiders, open places, social situations, or, indeed, fumes, may be legitimately threatening, but usually not to the extent believed by the phobic person. Obsessive-compulsive behavior often involves extreme fear of something, with the patients engaging in compulsive ritualistic behavior to avoid the fear object or fear itself; a panic attack involves the rapid onset of a host of physical symptoms that will drive the patient to run away as quickly as possible, or collapse with the idea that death is near. Fear is a core emotion in psychopathology.[22]

We now have sufficient elements to defend a different vision of Carol's situation than that of hysteria. The first observation sounds much like Gorton's: Carol suffered from generalized fear, which probably originated in a strong feeling of being unable to cope. Thus, stress resulted. However, here ways depart, because especially in cases of phobias and anxiety and panic attacks, when stress has indeed developed into generalized fear, psychologists recognize the hyperventilation syndrome. This involves breathing too frequently, too deeply, or too rapidly, thereby accumulating too much air in the lungs. A good treatment is to teach patients how to deliberately slow down their breathing. With this kind of cognitive behavior therapy, if successful, most fears will disappear like snow in summer. In other cases, the origins of stress are genetic. People's tolerated stress levels are different and personal. In addition, the use of drugs and alcohol may be seen as causing a mental disorder like this. There is nothing of the Freudian "deep" here. Seen this way, the academic insights that come with the Cognitive-Evolutionary Order may be used as weapons against the persistent presence of the Cartesian Cut and the identity of women as the Second Sex in Western discourse.

# 5

But the task is huge. "Hell is a teenage girl," says Anita Lesnicky, aka Needy (Amanda Seyfried), to us, the viewer, in the first sequence of *Jennifer's Body* (2009), a feature film written by Diablo Cody and directed by Karyn Kusama. The sign cannot be missed: this is her film. She is our narrator. Every scene will be representing her thoughts. She informs us that "hell" is what society forces upon teenage girls. The theme is similar to *[SAFE]*, but elaborated differently. However, asked if the film was paired up underneath a certain promo, Cody chose *The Virgin Suicides*—a film discussed later in this book and also the concoction of the film's narrator. Cody remembers thinking: "What would actually scare me, what would frighten me?" She could only think of girls. "Teenage boys are pretty harmless." But teenage girls "can be really frightening, really ruthless, and irrational and evil." And: "So I thought about the most terrifying, aggressive female bullies that I had known in my life; the ones that just made my blood run cold when I was younger. I started to imagine them as literal monsters, and that's when I started writing." Her experience tells her that girls' "emotions are heightened when you're a teenager, so romantic relationships have a tendency to get really crazy and dramatic." This creates an "atmosphere of terror and intimidation." Apart from blaming it on hormonal fluctuations, Cody underscores the "fact that society pits women against each other," which "forces us to be in competition." And: "Women feel like there's a limited amount of space for them in every arena of life and so they have a tendency to try and tear each other down." This may cause severe stress. Carol in *[SAFE]* cannot breathe because of this kind of limited space; in *Jennifer's Body* the girl turns aggressive. Cody wrote a script full of memories that had given her reasons to be anxious as a teenager, and "just the hunger that society imposes on young girls, sometimes literally." She thinks of those things as horrific.[23]

The camera represents Needy's mind and shows her world. At the beginning of the film we learn that Needy suffers from hallucinations and has turned very violent. The hell brought up by Needy is hers. The film shows how Needy interprets her friendship with Jennifer Check (Megan Fox). The girls were playground "lovers" and remained friends at high school. "Sandbox love never dies," Needy says. They are connected through matching lockets engraved with the initials BFF, Best Friends Forever. The town the two grew up in together is bleak and small Devil's Kettle (Minnesota). The Devil's Kettle is also a local waterfall that goes in a sort of vortex that seems not to have a bottom. Scientists have been throwing things in for some time but no one knows if the things come out again. Interestingly, at the end of the film Needy accidentally passes a forest stream where we recognize some of these things. There must be an exit somewhere in the forest — or Needy thinks there is. Needy sees Jennifer as a sort of alpha girl, a pampered and sought-after cheerleader. For Needy, Jennifer acts as if she is shallow, dominant, and demanding. Needy follows her in her decisions and actions. In her story, Jennifer knows how to verbally shoot down boys and men. One moment, talking about a boy who has a crush on Needy, she virtually grabs the male phallus: "He is into maggot rock. He wears nail polish. My dick is bigger than his." Needy wears glasses. She is sensitive and smart; intimidated by her friend all her life, she is cautious not to upstage her. In short, Needy is the typical sidekick that gets bullied every once in a while. The important thing is that Needy has something that Jennifer does not: a devoted boyfriend. She even has a secret admirer. Both boys seem to go for the relationship and true love, not for sex — hence, for Needy's personality, not Jennifer's. Needy believes, however, that Jennifer has sex and nothing but. Needy fears that because Jennifer's boys are after her body and not her personality, the friendship has turned toxic. Jennifer must be jealous.

One night, Jennifer persuades Needy to leave her boyfriend Chip Dove (Johnny Simmons) at home. Jennifer wants to check out an indie band, Low Shoulder, at a local dive club. Needy believes that Jennifer is perhaps too insecure to go to places on her own and needs her for that purpose. Happily, once arrived at the club, Jennifer remains faithful and does not leave her friend alone. The girls stand together, but, as reviewer Mary Pols writes in *Time,* "the warring elements of Needy's relationship with Jennifer play across her face. She's pleased for her friend — finally ablaze with passion, rather than her usual cynicism — but simultaneously afraid for her, because Jennifer's craving for [the band's leader Nikolai (Adam Brody)] is so intense, and because she herself knows better than to fall for a poser like him." The band is trouble, Needy knows. The boys want quick sex, rape, or, as she becomes to believe: to offer a girl to Satan. Somehow, during the performance of a song entitled "Through the Trees," the stage is set on fire. The club burns down. Despite the panic, and the deaths of several people, the band members seem unimpressed by the tragedy. Because they believe Jennifer is a virgin groupie, the band disappears with Jennifer, despite Needy's protests, to rape her in the forest. No doubt speaking in hindsight from the asylum, Needy provides us detailed information about Jennifer's rape. In the forest, Low Shoulder's front man performed a satanic ritual on her which he had found on the Internet. In exchange for the offering, the band would be rich in the future — the classical Faust theme.

Needy also explains that the ritual backfires. The Devil refuses Jennifer, because she is not even "a back-door virgin." As a result, Jennifer becomes a demon. She moves on as a kind of undead with supernatural powers, which can move through the air and over the ground with unlimited speed. Needy tells us her friend has extreme strength and lives off human blood and flesh — a type of vampire. She chooses boys to eat. Needy's metaphorical thinking here is obvious. Cody explains: "I think if you have ever been in love or infatuated with somebody, you feel like you actually want to eat them." After every meal she tells the viewers that she is "full" again. On such moments, she is a beautiful, energetic, and quick-thinking girl, going to high school. But when she has not fed in a while — had sex — thus being hungry, she is bad looking and pale; her hair is dull and lifeless. Needy tries to explain to boyfriend Chip that Jennifer is Evil. Chip says he knows; she spoiled more than often his dates with Needy. "No, I mean, she is actually Evil," Needy continued, "not high-school evil." She tells her sweet, adorable, and caring boyfriend about Jennifer's curious behavior, about the horrors she has seen. She adds that she found out about Jennifer's new persona by going through the occult section of the library. She reads that only a knife in the heart can kill the demons. But, as could be expected, Chip does not believe her. Shortly before the school ball, she breaks up with the boyfriend for his own safety. Apparently, Needy has the feeling that Jennifer's victims do come from her own surroundings. She knows and tells Chip that he will be in danger walking around with her. It seems Needy has fallen into a psychotic state, suffering from a series of hallucinations or delusions.

Needy imagines Jennifer as a jealous demon not only out of psychotic anxiety that she will lose her boyfriend(s) to Jennifer but perhaps also out of guilt. Jennifer might truly have been raped but this was, she explains to herself (and us) because Jennifer neglected Needy's advice. Thus the rape was not Needy's fault. Although every time after Jennifer has fed herself, she is a loving friend, a person with feelings, who decides to inform Needy about what has happened to her, the food itself came from boys Needy likes and loves. Jennifer was never a good friend, as Needy tells her at the end of the film. She had been a jealous demon long before the kidnapping. Yanking off her BFF matching locket gives Needy all the power to kill Jennifer's body — her soul long lost in the forest during the satanic ritual. We realize that from the beginning, in Needy's mind Jennifer had basically been her body. "Hell is a teenage girl," because Jennifer has always thought that becoming a true woman means to be pretty, sexy and shallow, including "laxatives to stay skinny." Proving her social worth by spouting inside slang is usually a mark of insecurity. Despite her supposed sexual bravado, Needy creates a Jennifer who convinces as a sensational-looking girl, and how to use this asset as her main tool to influence people. Jennifer's demon role had been the fulfillment of her character. *Slate*'s Dana Stevens concludes that actress Megan Fox understood "the key gambit of Cody's script: Her character is less a teenage girl turned monster than an exploration of the monster that lurks inside every teenage girl." Needy, not Jennifer, is the victim of androcentric culture.[24]

Because *Jennifer's Body* is a horror allegory of a toxic female friendship, taken to its total extreme, Needy's view on the relationship between her and Jennifer is the key to this film. There is no need for Needy to fit in and cling to the lifeline of popularity of Jennifer's body and language. Through her delusions, Needy undergoes a transition from side-kick into a self-sufficient kicker. Out of their friendship, Jennifer does not kill her — Needy believes — but she does kill the boys surrounding her. Needy imagines that she telepathically knows what is happening because she is connected to Jennifer through the BFF chain. The friendship is only broken during the fight in Jennifer's home at the end of the film. Curiously, there is even a little bit of a lesbian angle halfway through the movie, when Jennifer seduces Needy and the two start kissing. This seduction, like the others, falls on fertile ground, so it seems. Earlier on in the film, when the two girls first appear in one scene together, they share a meaningful glance and a flirtatious wave. This prompts a student sitting nearby to suggest that they are lesbians. And perhaps Needy is. A little later, when Jennifer and Needy watch Low Shoulder in the club shortly before the fire, Jennifer, in full groupie admiration of the front man, takes Needy's hand. Needy looks at her friend with that same meaningful glance, revealing strong feelings indeed. Furthermore, the lesbian kiss scene ends with Jennifer explaining about her situation and the sentence: "Come on, Needy, let me stay the night. We can play boyfriend-girlfriend like we used to." We will encounter a similar scene in *Black Swan* later on in this book. Although she cannot fulfill the female ideal the way Jennifer can, the hallucinations are quite out of order. Could it be that Cody uses another Freudian Excuse here: Needy has repressed her lesbian side?

This would explain why *Jennifer's Body* is not truly a revenge movie. Jennifer is not getting back at the boys of the band who did this to her. Because the men were not the enemy here, the script shows elements of female empowerment. Jennifer's victims are not necessarily sexist. The people she eats are innocent, perhaps easy prey for her. Halfway through the film, Needy starts to catch on. As in many young adult high school movies, it must all come together at the school dance — the "Through the Trees Ball," named after the Low Shoulder song that meanwhile has become a national hit song. In fact, Low Shoulder is to perform at the dance, but we do not get to see them, because Needy, through her telepathic contact with Jennifer, feels what the demon is doing: she kisses Chip. She runs away, and knows where to go, to save her boyfriend. We have seen that Jennifer, in a beautiful spring dance dress, has indeed already seduced Chip. She had told him that Needy had let him down because she had been cheating on him with other guys — on a semi-regular basis — including one of the boys Jennifer had fed on a few weeks before. Jennifer has taken Chip to an abandoned building of the school, what used to be the pool but with the water still in it. It is a half-ruined building, in fact, with green water, and vegetation everywhere. Needy, also in a nice pink dance dress, climbs through a window and sees Jennifer sucking Chip's blood from his neck. When she looks up at Needy, we notice her bloodied snake mouth and teeth. What follows is the confrontation between the two girls. Unfortunately, the boyfriend does not make it, but Needy herself also appears to be bitten by Jennifer. The wound, however, has a reverse effect: it makes Needy a human with demon powers, as we will know within moments. As a hallucinatory image, the scene confirms Needy's fears of Chip having sex with Jennifer. For her, from that moment on, Chip is dead.

Needy decides to avenge her "dead" (?) boyfriend. Walking back into the town, she comes across the knife that the Low Shoulder front man had used to ritually kill Jennifer in the woods. We may conclude that the knife is there by accident but that in Needy's imagination it was the one used by the band. Needy takes it with her. She finds Jennifer at home, on her canopy bed, satisfied by the sex/blood, and attacks her with the knife without much beating about. We see how, during the fight, Jennifer lifts both of them up in the air. Then Needy rips off the BFF pendant, indicating their childhood friendship, and hurls it to the ground. Immediately, Jennifer seems to lose her power. She falls back on the bed, as does Needy. After some struggling, Needy drives the knife through Jennifer's heart. At first, Jennifer does not believe that she is actually being killed. She experiences the stabbing as just another scratch, "My tit!" No, Needy says, "It is in the heart." Shortly after this moment, Jennifer's mother enters the room and is horrified by what she sees. Of course, no one will believe Needy's explanation, and she ends up in jail. The film ends with Needy escaping from prison and going after Low Shoulder. She finds them after a show in their dressing room, feasting with booze and cocaine. She kills every member. This would also be Needy's fantasy.

# 6

In *Jennifer's Body*, there are good reasons to believe that we have been inside Needy's head all the time. The storyworld is her fantasized explanation for killing Jennifer. Where in *[SAFE]* we saw Carol's behavior but hardly had a clue about her thinking, in *Jennifer's Body* we are transported into Needy's fantasy and can only guess at what really has happened. If we are indeed dealing with delusions and hallucinations, the most obvious conclusion would be schizophrenia. This disease of the brain relates its origins with problems at conception and difficulties in the womb. For almost all patients, predisposition to the disease is genetic. Just as problems in the womb like poisoning by chemicals (e.g., mothers smoking cigarettes or taking drugs or medication) or food shortages predispose people for schizophrenia, so do mothers who are stressed because of the pregnancy itself. This is another factor we will meet in *Black Swan*. Studies of the brains of schizophrenics have demonstrated that in the area that develops early in life, the brain cells are arranged chaotically or in the wrong places. But genetics do nothing if not triggered. An unexpected huge increase in stimulation from outside, like learning new skills, combined with stress can be such a trigger. The first symptoms of the disease reveal themselves at the end of adolescence, precisely at Needy's age, triggered by rapidly changing hormone levels. The disease has nothing to do with upbringing, nurturing or education. In a letter sent to Princess Marie Bonaparte in 1930, Freud stated something very true: the future would bring chemical medication to treat psychoses. Until then, we should prepare such a treatment with psychoanalysis. There, he proved to be wrong.[25] *Jennifer's Body* shows us Needy's psychosis.

Carol is not psychotic. Her "illness" stands for something different. In *[SAFE]* there is not a trace of Freud's method visible; *Jennifer's Body* has nothing Freudian either, perhaps with the exception of Needy's repressed lesbian feelings. Seen from psychoanalysis as Freud conceived it, a talking cure must have made Carol conscious of her repressed haunting wishes or traumas — if she had any. Haynes carefully keeps Carol's history out of sight, however, and his film does not present us such a cure at all. The therapist, Peter, is no psychoanalyst. He simply repeats endlessly the same text: confront yourself, you must cure yourself. Without help, apparently — we see no therapy sessions, the "clean" surroundings themselves are supposed to be instrumental. Within psychoanalysis, Freud was the only one who was allowed to do this, which he did by analyzing his dreams — in order to recognize supposedly repressed thoughts. Carol's dreams are left unspoken in *[SAFE]*. Without repression and the haunting subconscious there can hardly be a psychoanalytical diagnosis. It cannot be repeated enough. Freud saw his "subconscious," the dustbin for repressed thoughts, as the key to all psychological problems ("neuroses"). Devoid of this principle, there can be no psychoanalytical diagnosis. Hysteria devoid of repression into the subconscious is not a psychoanalytical diagnosis. Taking the essentials out of psychoanalysis is a severe critique to Freud's modeling. If today psychoanalysts feel they can do without Freud's key concepts, they have effectively and profoundly set Freud's theory aside. This is not "progress," as some would have it. It is building a different theory on new fundamentals, which, once again, for Freud had done the same, is psychomythology as recorded by dictionaries.

Although Haynes agreed that Carol was a hysteric, he also acknowledged that *[SAFE]* is foremost a movie about AIDS — or, to be more precise, an abstracted simulation with disguised variables, for "fumes" are not AIDS, of course. The film is set in 1987, a period when the AIDS epidemic in the United States was rapidly worsening. Like AIDS, Carol's illness comes suddenly. There is no "deep" to dig up, no archeology of the mind. For that reason, Carol has no history. The psychoanalyst has no material to work with. Haynes wanted to make a film about AIDS but without gay men, because he did "find that the specificity of AIDS right now in our day-to-day lives gives everybody the ability to set it aside from their lives out of a survival instinct. There are always ways of separating ourselves from a completely overwhelming experience when we don't have the means to deal with it. When I set out to do *[SAFE]*, [...] I did have this instinct to take the metaphor of AIDS as far as possible away from the war zone [...] and instead to try to discover illness in the most unlikely place on the planet: in the safest, most protected, most comfortable, most sealed-off kind of life."[26]

Does it work? There is no problem if the viewers are constantly reminded of the historical setting — as in a costume or period drama — because they will fix the context to the interpretation of the film. In that case, *[SAFE]* could be screened as a metaphor for AIDS and HIV in the late 1980s, when the virus attacked people almost out of the blue as if it came with the wind and its fumes. However, the 1980s are still too close for us; they are difficult to distinguish in *[SAFE]*. Furthermore, *[SAFE]* is from 1995, a time when three major routes of transmission of HIV — unsafe sex, contaminated needles, and transmission from an infected mother to her baby — were already discussed in the media all over the world. The idea of being "contaminated by fumes" was over. It is here that *[SAFE]* fails. It cannot properly function as an AIDS simulator. For a post–1995 viewer, the AIDS/HIV metaphor is almost impossible to recognize. Besides, Wrenwood will not be of any help for patients suffering from HIV/AIDS — only exhaustive medication can. Furthermore, we know nowadays so much about cognitive psychology that Carol's anxiety attacks are recognized as they are: the expression of generalized fear, articulated to stress. For a case like Carol's, cognitive behavior therapy would help her to understand how thoughts and feelings influenced her behavior shortly before her attacks. To find rest and escape attacks, she may start in Wrenwood, of course, but cognitive behavior therapy means, eventually, that she must be treated in the spaces where she had experienced the attacks. It would help her to return home, and leave Wrenwood. A good psychiatrist would also treat her with the appropriate medication — like anti-depressives. For some, it helps indeed, looking in the mirror saying: "I love you. I really love you." For Carol it might be only the first step of her way out. Also Needy needs a psychiatrist to treat her hallucinations and psychotic behavior with the proper pharmacological medication. The Freudian Excuse of her repressed lesbian side, perhaps her bisexuality, needs a different discussion — screening the Argentine film *XXY,* for a start.

# 4

## *Alex's Decision*

### Gender Choice in *XXY* (2007) and *Chloe* (2009)

Lucía Puenzo (writer and director); and Atom
Egoyan (director), Erin C. Wilson (writer)

### 1

The setting is a fishing village at the shores of Uruguay, near the ferry to Buenos Aires. Young and skinny tomboy Alex (Inés Efrón), probably short for Alejandra, is lying on her bed. The bed stands in front of a window. At a short distance, we see the sea and the light of the sunrise. The previous day, Alex had been attacked by boys who wanted to see her genitals. She was not raped because a friend rescued her in time. Her father, called Néstor Kraken (Ricardo Darín), sits next to her bed. Alex just wakes up and sees him sitting. "What are you doing?" she asks him. "I am guarding you," he answers. Alex waits a few moments before answering: "You cannot always guard me." Kraken nods his head. He knows. "Only until you have chosen." Alex knows what he means, as does the viewer. "What?" "Whatever you want." Another silence. Alex turns around and stares at the ceiling. Her answer comes slowly, soft but outspoken and indicates that she already has chosen: "What if there is nothing to choose?" Kraken suddenly realizes that his daughter has indeed made up her mind. After another short silence, she returns his book about hermaphroditic animals and plants to him; "I have finished it." Her father nods again. He thinks a bit and says: "Did they rape you?" "No," Alex answers quickly.

And after a few moments: "Did you report it to the police?" "No," says Kraken. "That is up to you. If you want to, we will do it. But it must be your decision." The two stay silent again for a short while. Kraken continues: "But everyone will be informed, if you do." Alex does not need to think much now: "Let's inform them." Father nods affirmatively. He realizes what his daughter wants. She has found a way out of a struggle that must have cost her and her parents years of uncertainty.

## 2

This scene from *XXY* (2007; with the Y as an X with a mutilated leg), written and directed by Lucía Puenzo, takes place almost at the end of the film. Until then, viewers were witness to the sexual awakening of a young girl. However, the viewers also saw a film about a girl who has to learn to accept her body and not to allow others to make her feel awkward. This has nothing to do with the fact that Alex wears rubber boots, shorts, baggy tank tops and hooded sweatshirts, has a pet lizard, or lives a homeopathic existence as a vegetarian and plays almost the maximum expression of being different. These features Alex developed, Puenzo said in an interview, because she spent a very lonely childhood in this place where she made her own world, her own toys from the things she found at the beach. However, her exile from the crowded urban world has a different cause. The film's title *XXY* refers to her intersexuality. To be more precise, it refers to Klinefelter's Syndrome, a condition in which males have an extra X sex chromosome. Usually, men have an XY makeup, and women XX. With 1:1000 males affected, XXY is the most common sex chromosome disorder. The men tend to have small testicles and reduced fertility, some increased breast tissue and a little, rounded body type. Although most show hardly any other signs of affectedness, a few have the genitals of both sexes. The title suggests that Alex is a boy, not a girl. Perhaps the title is wrong. As an intersex person, 15-year-old Alex may not be affected by Klinefelter's Syndrome at all.[1]

Early in the film, Alex has fallen in love with Álvaro (Martín Piroyanski). He arrived by ferry with his parents from Buenos Aires. The boy's parents are friends with Suli (Valeria Bertuccelli), Alex's mother; they arrived on her invitation to investigate the prospects of an operation. It seems Suli is pushing for a decision: should Alex live as a girl or a boy? Soon after their arrival, Alex joins Álvaro, talks with him about having sex and gives him presents. The two youths live in an ordinary young adolescent world of experienced sensual romance. While falling in love they discover their identity. Their parents, on the other hand, inhabit a world of rational choice with preset boundaries and fixed roles. Kraken and Suli had left Buenos Aires many years ago, to live along the Uruguayan seashore to avoid society's negative stigma of their child, and to wait for the inevitable moment that a choice must be made between being male or female. Continuing as an intersexual seems no option. The surgeon, Ramiro (Germán Palacios), is a specialist who deals with "deformities." Álvaro explains to Alex: "He does not butcher people; he fixes them. He does tits and noses for money but he prefers the other stuff." "Such as?" Alex asks. "Don't know," says Álvaro. "Guys born with eleven fingers. My dad takes off the extra one." "And eats it," Alex responds quickly. However, after they understood why Suli has invited him, both Alex and Kraken succeed in avoiding a serious conversation with the surgeon during the rest of the film.

This strategy gives Puenzo space to handle the potentially explosive material of intersexuality with extraordinary grace and tact. Her camera does not get trapped by sensational images to tell the rich, emotional core of her story. The characters use minimal amounts of dialogue, staged as they are through long periods of silence conveying emotion and story through facial expressions and body language with subtlety and great sensitivity. More often than not, Puenzo chooses hints and intimations over frank explanations, adding a sense of mystery to the atmosphere, which somehow makes the film feel more believable. Of the central theme, Alex's parents waiting for a decision to finally establish her sex as male or female, Alex informed Álvaro with spare words he could not appreciate at that moment: "I feel sorry for mine. They are always waiting." No judgment is being made. Alex is painted not as a case but as a person. We are shown all kinds of symbols and artifacts that must convince us that Alex's intersexuality is only natural—as, indeed, they may serve to convince Alex and her parents. Kraken is a marine biologist studying the sexuality of sea animals. Part of his job is the treatment of wounded turtles found by fishermen. His name, Kraken, is also the name of a mythical giant squid. Alex keeps an aquarium full of clownfish—protandrous hermaphrodites that are initially male but may change their sex. She has also a collection of dolls with penises attached. On the one hand, the Kraken family looks like "freaks," with hardly a place in the modern world, but they care about each other and are not afraid to belong. The surgeon, his wife, and his son from Buenos Aires, on the other hand, although adapted at the "normal" side of the modern world, appear to be emotionally dysfunctional.

Emotions run high in *XXY*. Alex is an oddly seductive blend of confidence and confusion who wants to have sex, like any adolescent. The first thing she bluntly says to 17-year-old Álvaro, outside the wooden cabin on the beach: "You just had a wank." Álvaro reacts with shock. Alex continues: "There in your room." "How do you know?" he asks. "I can tell," she says. And somewhat later in the conversation, she says: "I have never fucked anybody. Would you like to?" Álvaro hesitates, gives no direct answer. We will learn that Álvaro has a sexual issue of his own; the film suggests he might be gay. Later on,

## 4. Alex's Decision

about half an hour after these scenes, he will reject her, but finally give in when she starts kissing him passionately. When they remove their pants, she suddenly turns him over with all her power and takes him from behind. Like a man. Álvaro is surprised but seems to like it. By coincidence, Kraken witnesses this encounter with his daughter acting the male part. This makes him seriously question what his role should be in the coming years. To clear his mind, he visits a gas station owner in the neighborhood who had to make a choice in his teens. The gas station attendant suggests not making a decision at all. Puenzo stages Kraken as undergoing this private crisis with a minimum of talk. Instead, she uses the rugged, striking beaches and low, blue-gray skies as a potent corollary to his lonely struggle. Suli also has an unexpected confrontation. Thinking about Alex's attitude and the opinion of her husband, she acknowledges that they had left Buenos Aires for good reason: "to get away from the opinions of idiots." These idiots she had met even before Alex was born, because, as Kraken finally tells the surgeon: "She was diagnosed two months before being born. They wanted to film the birth. For 'medical interest,' and to present the case to the ethics council. We said no, to all of it. Then, they wanted to operate. They said the only after-effect would be the scar." Meanwhile, Suli had clashed with the surgeon's wife, Erika (Carolina Pelleritti), who had told her that she could "not hide her for the rest of her life." "Hide her?" Suli asked her. "You think she is a freak?" For Suli, this was the opinion of an idiot. At the end of the film, saying goodbye to the invitees, the two couples separate without much friendship left, whereas Alex offers her arm to Kraken.

From the very first scenes of *XXY*, it is clear that while her parents are still waiting for a decision, Alex has indeed already taken one. She has stopped taking her hormones that were to suppress the development of masculine features—like a beard. The film suggests that it happened recently, but Alex is already capable of using her penis to have intercourse with Álvaro. She also urinates standing up. Kraken loves his daughter unconditionally and thinks she has always been "perfect" exactly the way she is. He treats her as a girl; but, in a row with a fisherman, he once calls her "son," *hijo*. With Alex into puberty, her sexual desires have led to a conversation, at least, with her friend Vando (Luciano Nóbile), one of the young men from the village. For some reason, she had punched him in the nose. Probably he had revealed Alex's secret to his friends, because that afternoon three boys from the village harass her on the beach. They forcibly pull down her pants to see her genitals. Vando comes to rescue her before the boys are able to rape her and finally consoles her. It becomes clear that Vando deeply regrets that he has betrayed Alex's confidence. In one telling scene, later in the film, Vando, Álvaro, and Alex share a drink; the first boy seduced by her female side, the second one by her male side. Meanwhile, Kraken wants to report the potential rape to the police, but realizes that reporting would cause everyone in their entire world to know about the anomaly. As we have seen, Alex decides that she actually prefers that it is known in order to be able to continue her life the way she is. Kraken seems to accept this, and Alex is comforted and supported by her parents, by Vando, and by Álvaro.

What is particularly interesting is that Alex had not shied away from exposing her body to friends. Most intersex persons are afraid to be viewed as freaks. They fear their bodies could not be the object of "normal" sexual arousal. Interestingly, Vando and Álvaro are probably not the only peers to know about Alex's secret. Next to her interest in these boys, she has a close relationship with the girl next door, Roberta (Allín Salas). When Alex cannot emotionally tolerate a situation at home, she runs to Roberta's house and frequently stays over for the night. The film shows girl talk — including a typical scene of sexual initiation tales. Roberta has "done it five times" with a nephew. However, her father expresses some discomfort and interrupts the scene by commanding his daughter to sleep on the floor and Alex in the bed. The next morning, girl talk may evolve into some juvenile lesbian making out when Roberta joins Alex in the shower — a standard trope for a sex scene with a steamy shower and the two naked bodies of girls. But Alex did not like this at all. Alex had woken up sullen after finding that Roberta had painted her nails while she was asleep. It is clear that she loves boys. When Roberta starts shampooing her hair, she abruptly pushes her away, and returns home irritated.[2]

Puenzo visited, sometimes accompanied by actress Inés Efrón, doctors, geneticists, teachers, parents of intersex children and young adults who had or had not been operated on when they were born. She used information from a German intersexual documentary filmmaker who realized that after years of operations and taking hormones to become a man, he would never be a man or a woman. Critics recognized that Efrón had seduced them with her adolescent search for both sexual desire and social acceptance. Aside from Alex's special body and Álvaro's troubling sexual orientation, the relationship between her and Álvaro is like any other at that age: confused, sweet, traumatic. "The sexuality in the film is the most important," said Puenzo in an interview, "and I thought that that was actually the only thing that moved the film all the time. I think that when people connect with their sexuality and what makes them feel desire, they are saved."[3] It is only natural that human beings deserve to be loved for who they are, regardless of their physical morphology, sexual being or gender. For intersex persons the problem rests with the binary position of rigid gender polarization, not necessarily with their bodies. A new Argentine society, rising up from the dark decades of the 1980s dictatorship, torture, and violence, needs to face dealing freely with bodies in the first place.

**3**

Literally possessing two sexes, Alex was born bisexual. Is this confirmation of Freud's theory? As early as 1905, two of Freud's contemporaries, Nettie Stevens (1861–1912) and Edmund Beecher Wilson (1856–1939), wrote independently about the XY sex determination. At conception, most mammals, including humans, and also some insects and plants inherit such a sex-determination program. It must be stressed that the gender differences result directly from the blending of the parents' chromosomes. The fetus has a gender from the very first moment. The XY sex determination means that from the very conception onward, girls have two of the same kind of sex chromosome (XX, the homogametic sex). Boys have two distinct sex chromosomes (XY, the heterogametic sex), because a single gene (*SRY*) on the Y chromosome acts as a signal to set the developmental pathway toward maleness. Next, the male hormone testosterone is added to guide the fetus, body and mind, into a boy. Only for the first six weeks after conception, there is no structural difference between genetically male and genetically female embryos. In week seven, informed by the information stored at the chromosomes, testes are beginning to be formed. After a week, the embryos have the same urogenital membrane and primitive phallus, which will grow into a future penis or clitoris. Certain male hormones, principally driven by testosterone, determine maleness of the entire body, including the brain. If testosterone is absent, the membranes start developing female external genitalia, female organs in the body, and a female brain. During the second part of pregnancy, another shot of testosterone guides the definite formation of the male brain.[4] In whatever way we like to discuss it, a person like Alex is and will be an exception. All this is evidence against Freud's theory of innate bisexuality.

The theoretical implications are profound. Remember that Freud, following Fliess, argued that every child starts out bisexual and that he would mature *phylogenetically* by "auto-erotic" movements including sucking (oral), excretion (anal), and masturbation (phallic). These stages were necessarily repressed, said Freud, and the sexual energy or libido would be organized under the primacy of the genitals to the purpose of sexual reproduction. As stated previously, this theory of the oral, anal, and phallic phases is not based on stories Freud heard from patients. He transferred the doctrines of Lamarck and Haeckel to his psychoanalysis. Following this procedure the psyche was to *subconsciously choose a gender* during the development of the Oedipus Complex. In her *Vice Versa: Bisexuality and the Eroticism of Everyday Life* (1995), Marjorie Garber — a Shakespearean scholar — made a case for bisexuality. Following the Freud-Fliess fallacy, she believes that most people are bisexual if not for "repression, religion, repugnance, denial, laziness, shyness, lack of opportunity, premature specialization, [etc]." Copying Freud, she writes that the human "libido is distributed, either in a manifest or a latent fashion, over objects of both sexes." Garber's is no voice crying in the wilderness.[5] Many will follow psychoanalysis in making people responsible for their own gender. We know now for sure that this reasoning is fallacious. It cannot be repeated often enough: the differences between the sexes are genetic, including the brain. Whereas Freud still theorized that females were simply males with hormones, we now know that the opposite is closer to reality. The brain is set female by default. However, after some eight weeks the brains of most boys turn male due to surges of testosterone. Contrary to psychoanalytical reasoning, people are not born bisexual; there is very little to choose after birth, either consciously or unconsciously.

Garber's suggestion resonates with a now almost forgotten time in which dolls were given in vain to little boys and fire engines to little girls in the expectation that this would neutralize sex differences and finish off the differences between the sexes. But it appears that these are not solely the result of upbringing. The sad story of David Reimer (1965–2004) is evidence of how serious the old mistake was. In 1967, the boy had suffered a botched circumcision. Sexologist surgeon John Money (1921–2006) amputated his genitalia. Next, he advised the parents to raise him as a girl. And so he was. But although Reimer was not informed of his early history, as a young child he behaved in a distinctively masculine way. All attempts to socialize him as a girl failed and Reimer began living as a male at age 14. He could not cope with the problems he encountered. First, there was his demanding relationship with his parents. Next, he separated from his wife. In 2002, his twin brother Brian had died. Two years later David committed suicide. Especially over the past decades, research has evidenced that children are already different and that they favor their sex roles from the very beginning. Today, social and psychological research can be complemented with scanning techniques to look at the workings of the brain. Using these techniques, scholars established the fact that male and female brains do indeed operate differently from the outset. And this at an age too early for any Oedipus Complex to develop — in the womb. Parents can see for themselves that baby girls look longer at faces and at mechanical mobiles, whereas baby boys do the reverse. Soon, boys prefer toys that can be deployed to satisfy their need for testosterone-fed play. Girls will look for toys to satisfy their nurturing needs.[6]

Whereas gender is by and large determined by the effects of hormones on the embryonic brain, this is not necessarily the case with specific gender roles. The brain is in general quite plastic and will change dramatically during life, mostly in response to bodily and social developments. We know that men's brains are about 9 percent larger than women's, but men are also bigger in general. Men's brains have more white matter than women and less gray matter. White matter is the manifestation of the long, thin filaments that connect nerve cells together; gray matter is the manifestation of the central bodies of nerve cells. Female brains pack their nerve cells more densely than male ones — they do not contain more cells, but they are simply orchestrated differently. Most IQ measurements of men and women with similar class and educational backgrounds show no differences between the sexes, but brain scans do suggest that men carry out the tests differently than women. For example, in cases where women use both hemispheres, men use only one. In fact, in men mathematical reasoning correlates with temporal-lobe activity. Not in women, however, who seem to rely much less on their gray matter for their IQ. Research by Janet Hyde from the University of Wisconsin–Madison, using available meta-analyses, has also shown that no significant difference could be identified between the sexes in vocabulary, in mathematical problem solving before puberty — although it can during puberty, when boys perform better than girls — and in reading comprehension. Out of 124 effect-sizes Hyde calculates, only 22 percent of reported behavioral differences between the sexes scored as significant. Men performed better in mental rotation and in physical aggression, while women did better in smiling, spelling, and indirect aggression. The latter point is interesting: when the women — performing a video game organized by the researcher — thought nobody was watching and judging them, and expected no physical consequences, they were even more aggressive than men. Other research showed that conflicts between men would end with physical violence; between women with gossip, knowing that a smear would not be less damaging than a blow. Although men perform better in imaginative use of three-dimensional objects, they do not excel in all spatial tasks. Contrary to popular myth and despite the fact women rely on remembering landmarks and men on their geometrical skills, men and women are equally good at navigating.[7]

This literature seems to have gone past the study rooms of feminist philosopher Judith Butler and her followers. Butler used the word "performance" to discuss Reimer's sexuality in order to question the rigid border between male and female, as if there is no singular, stable sexuality behind what are merely representations of gender roles. She was not only echoing the Oedipus Complex and its sex choice, but also the notion of performative utterances introduced by J.L. Austin (1911–60), first used in a 1946 paper "Other Minds," but better known from the 1955 William James lecture series *How to Do Things with Words* (1962), and elaborated further by sociologist Erving Goffman (1922–82), *The Presentation of Self in Everyday Life* (1959). Her piece is called "Doing Justice to Someone," and was first published in 2001 in *GLQ: A Journal of Lesbian and Gay Studies,* but later reprinted in her book *Undoing Gender* (2004). Of course, the "open" gender identities had been her argument from the start. As the title of her article indicates, she wanted to do "justice" to Reimer, in a *theoretical* way. Butler defends the question of identity as a question of power, "a power that determines, more or less, what we are, what we can be." Her question is: "What, given the contemporary order of being, can I be?" A major consequence is of course: "What can I *not* be?" "This relationship, between the intelligibility and the human, is an urgent one; it carries theoretical urgency, precisely at those points where the human is encountered at the limits of intelligibility itself." Butler "would like to suggest that this interrogation has something important to do with justice. Since justice not only or exclusively is a matter of how persons are treated, how societies are constituted, but also emerges in quite consequential decisions about what a person is, what social norms must be honored and expressed for personhood to become allocated, how we do or do not recognize animate others as persons depending on whether or not we recognize a certain norm manifested in and by the body of that other."[8] This is true. Beyond any doubt, the location of identity performance is crucial for someone's actions in time and space. But there are also crucial limits to this performance, like biology. For Butler, Money's choice to operate on Reimer, with all its tragic consequences, had been the end result of the gender border hegemony, the crucial machination of the Western power system that only leaves room for two genders. Point taken. Reimer might have felt better, Butler further indicates, if he could have had the choice to live his life as an intersexed person — in this case as a man in an artificially made female body. This would have done "justice" to him. It may also have been true. But poor David Reimer did not regard himself an intersexed person. Genetically, he had been a boy all his life and felt as such. He was not located in some in-between gender, as Butler wants us to believe; he was no transsexual. He was simply not born that way. He had a male brain. He was not an "Alex."

No wonder that several theorists of inter- and transsexuality, transsexuals and intersexed ventured negative reactions to Butler's all too performative modeling. In *Second Skins* (1998), Jay Prosser, for example, reminds feminist and queer theorists that even though linguistic and cultural representations may have immense power in our lives, people do live in real bodies — including the brains — made of substantial flesh, which characteristically carry more weight in their perceptions of themselves, and others, than words, texts, or abstract discourses do. This actual embodied gender experience may be delegitimized, he fears, if Butler's work leads to the collapse of sex into gender. In *Self-Made Men* (2003), the transgendered sociologist Henry Rubin also stresses the fact that many of his informants experience gender as permanently embedded in their bodies. Their struggle, affirms psychiatrist Vernon Rosario, "is not an arbitrary, ludic performance of gender masquerade but a hard-fought pursuit of an essential identity experienced as grounded in matter and construed through biology." Even the intersexed, with their discordant or ambiguous sex hormones, usually make individual and strongly motivated choices to have a definite gender identity as male or female. Psychiatrist Milton Diamond heard a transsexual informant say to him: "If there is anything I want to shout from the rooftops, it is that some of us want to change our bodies for reasons that have little or nothing to do with facilitating our acceptance as social women." They wanted to change their bodies because they wanted to *change* them, and this even though they know that they would *not* be accepted as women or have any social advantage whatsoever. Rosario adds that transsexual gynecologist Sheila Kirk has argued that research pointed to the role of intrauterine hormones in shaping the developing brain and determining gender identity.[9]

# 4

The case is clear. So, why in the 21st century are we still discussing this question? It is because of the influence of *Undoing Gender*. Beyond hesitation, we may acknowledge the Goffman-inspired background of Butler's argument. Although, differences in behavior between the sexes should be understood as reflections of systematically developed — evolved — differences between the brains of males and females, the gender *roles* are learned. The sexual identity of a person is an inner conviction of identification with his or her outward physical appearance and the sex-linked gender roles of his or her environment. People are not born sexually neutral, but it is also only relatively true that gender and sex exist in discursive locations. Males are usually perceived as boys or men, females as girls or women, but intersexed individuals are born with physical characteristics that are both male and female or ambiguous in character. Furthermore, note Butler's Freudian heritage. In the next chapter, discussing the Wolf Man Case, we shall see that Freud thought that homosexuality could be cured — he noted a "breakthrough to the woman"— because homosexuality was a deviancy of development. In his view, from "innate sexuality," the "correct choice" was heterosexual. The deviancy therefore was a kind of "own fault"— narcissistic, he called it. Psychoanalysis could correct this deviancy. Lacan, however, probably recognizing the sheer madness of such ideas, came with a simple solution: psychoanalysis cannot cure at all. But he did not correct Freud's idea of deviancy and must have seen homosexuals, like Freud, as "sexually not fully matured, *yet.*"[10]

To understand fully the depth of this problem, it will help if we know the critique on the Oedipus Complex. As with hysteria, we have to tackle its metarepresentational roots. Butler's is the Oedipus Complex and innate bisexuality — bodily differences between the sexes hide from view that the mind is born bisexual. Freud thought that the mechanism of the Oedipus Complex served to overcome this inborn sexuality through the active choices made by the children to confirm their psychic reality to their bodily realities. The

Oedipus Complex starts early in life, he thought, as soon as the child notes the bodily differences between the sexes. Furthermore, Freud speculated that the children assumed that the bodily differences were manmade, due to the girl's penis having been cut off. So for the girl something is missing; there is a *lack*. From the moment of sexual identification, the boy and the girl develop different theories. For boys, this developed into an anxiety, formed in early childhood, of their father intervening in their relationship with their mothers by cutting off their penises. To triumph, the boy must desire like his father. During the Oedipus Complex the boy works out the solution; because of his fear of castration the boy renounces his desire for the mother and enters the latency period. This marks the point of *exit* from the Oedipus Complex, its terminal crisis that will bring him closer to the father. The girl thinks, according to Freud, that her penis was cut off by her mother and that she can replace this loss by having a child because her attraction for her father must to a certain extent be conditioned by her desire to possess this missing body part. To triumph, she must be desired. The "penis envy" must emerge when they perceive themselves as lacking the penis. Freud thought that for the girl, blaming her mother for depriving her of the penis, penis envy marks the point of *entry* into the Oedipus Complex and redirects her so-called libidinal desires away from the mother and onto the father. For her there is no definitive terminal crisis, Freud argued. He imagined that during early childhood castration anxiety increased to unbearable levels. As a result, sexual thoughts and feelings supposed to be behind this were acutely repressed. Castration anxiety had been the exaggerated fear, in later life, of injury to any part of the body or of a loss of potency. It may be precipitated by everyday events that have symbolic significance and appear to be threatening, such as loss of a job, loss of a tooth, or an experience of ridicule or humiliation.[11] In all, castration causes lack, lack is caused by castration.

Human existence in all its facets was destined to replicate the Oedipus Complex or parts of it until death, including its inevitable repressions. Any human being was guided by the "Eros energy," or libido. The metaphor Freud needed to describe Eros was taken from the most advanced technology of his time: he chose to use either the steam engine or the electricity aggregator, concluding that psychological processes should be theorized in quantities and flows of energy. The libido is "loaded" into the brain like any battery in a car. It does not stop to load, apparently, because he argued that it needs to be released or discharged. If this does not happen, it builds up enormous pressures inside the brain, which could cause the mind to burst unless they were channeled into appropriate pathways. During sleep, Freud thought, the unconscious haunted the mind with these pressures by drafting narratives, combined with some experiences of previous days and some stimulus sensed during the night itself. A lot of this energy was used by instincts that want to reach their aims. Freud labeled this the Pleasure Principle. In his theory, unsatisfied instinctual desires forced humans into action because they created feelings of displeasure while their satisfactions create feelings of pleasure. Then, the energy level should be manageable again. The releasing of "steam," or the unloading of "electric pressures," from the libido was seen as sexual in nature but could be transformed into love for objects and persons (like mother, father, brother, or sister), passive or active (that is, female or male), or repressed. Over the past decades, psychologists have clearly shown that the mind does not work by fluids under pressure or by flows of energy, but by electronic processing of information. Neuroscientists have measured the energy level of the brain at approximately 40 Hz. This electronic processing is not like a battery — loading and unloading — but by continuous currents. A brain cell is a "firing" part of electronic circuits and does so from its creation to its death, apparently without stopping. No energy can in fact be built up in the mind, and consequently nothing needs to be released or discharged. The brain *consumes* energy on a constant level — consumption of food and fluids — without any sort of aggregation. The consequences of these by now truly established facts can be of considerable significance. For example, according to psychoanalysis a neurosis is the result of the lack of "unloading." If the aggregation idea is not correct, then the notion of the neurosis must be wrong as well. In academic psychology there is no room for psychoanalytic neurotic conditions.[12]

In a 1994 *Critical Inquiry* article, Borch-Jacobsen stresses once more that Freud was aware of the fallacy in his Oedipus theory and that he used most of his writings published after the First World War trying to solve it. The key word to understand the problem, says Borch-Jacobsen, is *identification.* Notice the original steps once again: first, a newly born boy immediately develops a so-called object-cathexis for his mother. The breast is therefore the "prototype of an object-choice on the anaclitic model." Also, the boy deals with his father by identifying with him. Then, when the boy develops strong sexual wishes in regard to his mother, the father is perceived as an obstacle that can better be removed. The boy thus changes his identification with his father into a hostile image, accompanied by the wish to take his father's place at his mother's side. Freud imagined "libidinal object-cathexis" and "identification" as two separate, parallel currents that only converged in the Oedipal Triangle of mother/father/boy later on. And this Triangle came out of the object (e.g., sexual wishes in regard to his mother) as the consequence of the reinforcement of sexual wishes. Thus, identification was in itself not sexual but the consequence of a sexual desire for the mother. This primacy of sexuality was also understood as object-desire or libido.[13] In the end, Freud had theorized the libido/object-desire as "normal" development: the boy wanted his mother instead of his father — he desired. Because he could not fulfill this desire, the boy was mourning his lack the rest of his life. For Freud, heterosexuality was the norm, hence, "normal"; homosexuality was not, and female sexuality was different or "another format." This would make the characters in *XXY* quite complicated, for Alex has a clear male sexuality but seems to love boys, whereas Álvaro has developed a gay sexuality, falling in love with her. In Freudian sense both characters had become homosexual, and it is true that in the film both Alex and Álvaro had a special relationship with their fathers, but Alex more as a daughter while Álvaro wished to be like his father.

Freudian theory is notoriously difficult to work with. On the basis of his official position, Freud left an important space to fill in. For example, he had noticed that the breast was an object of desire for both boys and girls — another "desire" not meant by Puenzo in *XXY,* for she refers to the "natural" adolescent drive to have sex. Curiously, the Oedipus Complex had a pre-history in which desire was not sexual. Following the bisexuality thesis, only through the oedipal processes of identification would gender differences become "normal." The first problem arising from this was that the lack of the penis then could not be sexual. As an alternative Freud imagined that the sexual organ of both sexes, the key concept of this "original bisexuality," was the *phallus.* The phallus described an emotional tie, not a gender tie. Borch-Jacobsen concludes that the phallus confounded love and identification. In Freudian eyes, the "real scandal" of the Oedipus Complex is not infantile sexuality, neither that the child harbors incestuous and patricidal desires, which are very difficult to recognize in toddlers anyway, but "that access to genital heterosexuality is not a foregone conclusion." Contrary to his Lamarckian-Haeckelian conviction, Freud concluded, with obvious discontent, says Borch-Jacobsen, that according to the interpretation of his own Oedipus Complex human sexuality would *not* spontaneously conform to the anatomical difference between the sexes. The real penis appeared to be less important than the original phallus. It deadlocked Freud's modeling. The Oedipus Complex teaches the child to desire in conformity with its biological gender and the instinctual mechanisms released at puberty *in order to avoid homosexuality.* A second problem Freud noticed during this phase was that his original idea of a difference between love and hate had to be wrong as well. Jealousy and hatred must be inherent in identification and, by the same token, says Borch-Jacobsen, in the pre-oedipal object relations. The later Triangle of the Oedipus Complex was merely a repetition of the ambivalent identification with the mother from the earlier stages. Freud had made his own Oedipus Complex, this "nucleus of neurosis," dependent of theories on earlier sexuality, which he had not written yet.[14]

Freud himself had seriously undercut his theory of "normal" development. The origins of neurosis might not have been its origins after all, for how can anyone gain access to "normality," Borch-Jacobsen asks, if it all starts with a fundamentally identificatory ambivalence in early childhood that will *not* be resolved during the crucial Oedipus Complex? The first "object of desire" for both sexes was the mother's breast but because of its non-sexual content it could not be a true "object" whatsoever. The Oedipus Complex had become both the repressed *and* the repressor. Freud's boy ought to be like his father but may not be like him at all. He has to escape the repressor inherent in the Oedipus Complex by the means given to him by that very same Oedipus Complex. How? By way of identification, says Freud. The reinforcement of the sexual that had to take place during that phase, he postulated, gave rise to what he called Ego Ideal or, later, the SuperEgo. As the internalized agency of social control, the SuperEgo was provoked because the boy identified with the father, "in order to respect that prohibition," stresses Borch-Jacobsen. If the boy succeeded, the Oedipus Complex was repressed. This was inevitable according to Freud's Haeckelian conviction. The same held true for the girl since she identified sexually with the mother, but not as a rival. However, says Borch-Jacobsen, the situation must be more complicated for her, because her "phallus" had been with the mother in the first place. Thus: "Because her first object is also the mother, her identification is originally virile, and, in order to arrive at femininity, it will thus be necessary for her to pass through the castration complex and penis envy, which will lead her to identify secondarily with the mother in order to obtain the phallus from the father in the form of a child." This is an eccentric detour, Borch-Jacobsen concludes, that again brings us to ask: How? In both cases, boy and girl, identification was precisely what needed to be escaped. There is no answer here why a "reinforcement" of the identification with the same-sex parent should *necessarily* lead to a heterosexual gender choice and not a homosexual one, nor why hate identification with the rival should *necessarily* be transformed into a respectful identification with the bearer of authority. Identification, to be surmounted only by "reinforcing" the same identification, therefore, precisely *is* the reason for such rivalry and gender choice. The Oedipus Complex cannot be "normalizing" at all.[15]

How could Freud be so wrong? In itself, there is no reason to doubt the scholarly qualities of a Romantic. Even the inspiration of a Rider Haggard could have led to valid scientific theories. Someone who puts his eggs in the wrong basket could nevertheless be a good scholar. Freud was not. Harris writes in *No Two Alike* (2006) that although Freud contextualized all his theories in the unconscious, his writing is almost entirely about open relationships. "The idea that the child learns how to behave by identifying with the same-sex parent is one of the few aspects of Freudian theory that generates testable predictions, and research has not supported the predictions." Boys growing up without a father are no less masculine than those in two-parent homes, for example. Children in two-parent homes do not resemble their same-sex parent in degree of masculinity or femininity. In fact, the evidence suggests firmly that boys resemble other children's fathers in behavior as much as they do their own. Children will imitate whoever is around. In her previous book, *The Nurture Assumption* (1998), Harris discussed a case of a child who was reared with a young chimpanzee and who had begun imitating that animal's behavior. If there are no children around — or chimpanzees — the child will imitate the adults. Even then, a child soon learns that behaving like adults does not work very well, even at home. A great amount of research indicates that children are largely socialized by their peers. This influence of the peers transfers the Oedipus Complex into a historical oddness, interesting for the historians of psychology but not for the psychologist, less for the therapist and psychiatrist.[16]

In short, Butler had not realized that Freud's Edifice was built on misdiagnosis, sheer ignorance, and the cocaine-fed delusion of grandeur, nor that the published claims of cures were in fact nothing but lies — a fact that can be found in all major libraries around the world. She did not realize either that from the exorcist paradigm specialists are needed if only because an exorcist needs something to exorcize. She did not realize, finally, that the history of European androcentrism had been rooted in a culture of fear, in a society of distress, misery, and pain. She will no doubt be pleased to learn that it had been gender indeed that stood at the roots of this anxiety and fear. But she should forget penis envy and castration fears. There is also no evidence for Freud's belief that boys rivaled their fathers intensely. Remember that this rivalry was to force the boy's sexuality into latency. It also created the SuperEgo, Freud added later on, the boy's moral agency. Freud historians and other critics made mincemeat of these ideas. In all, the Oedipus Complex cannot serve as a proper diagnosis for Alex's struggle with her sexuality. What about the results of clinical practice? Most psychoanalysts will write things like: "My material for these reflections comes largely from a clinical psychoanalytical practice." They learned to do so from Freud himself. Borch-Jacobsen surely is correct to lament that this trump card of psychoanalysts escapes scholarly evaluation thanks to a protection by medical confidentiality. In reality, he continues, the psychoanalysts appeal to their clinical results only in vain because their "observations" and "facts" are simple products of their method. They provide the "input" with the "output" firmly established. What cannot be tested by independent researchers are not confidential data but fabricated facts. The psychoanalysts see in the patient what they want to on premeditated ideas. Patients, in turn, are only too happy to confirm because they pay for their cures and believe in the authority of psychoanalysis. Thus, we are dealing with a co-fabrication of "data," which cannot be avoided.[17]

# 5

Although many psychoanalysts refuse to discuss the scientific standard of their trade — indirectly acknowledging that *The Interpretation of Dreams*, for example, is indeed closer to a novel than to a scholarly work — Butler's influence makes sure that we are not able to get around the question in this book. Freud wanted his ideas to be taken at face value and not be understood as metaphors or symbolic writing. Psychoanalysis was meant to be full-fledged medicine. It was not meant to be philosophy, not hermeneutics, not cultural studies. Freud and Breuer saw themselves as physicians, medical doctors who set out to *cure* their patients. This means that according to his standards, psychoanalysis can only be a mature theory and taken seriously if it serves to cure people. The theory should *work*. For that reason, from the outset, Freud expressed that beyond any doubt his patients *were* cured. Freud argued that with his theory he could cure hysterics, neurotics, and homosexuals. Because, outside the printing office, he was not so sure, Freud began revising earlier material that might have been distrusted by his readers. As early as 1896, he published new interpretations of his "material" in a series of papers in the Viennese review *Wiener klinische Rundschau* (numbers 22–26). This was purely on philosophical grounds because his patients had never told him anything of the kind and denied persistently when Freud confronted them with his interpretations. Freud did not worry about this because corresponding to Charcot's model of unconscious symptom-formation, a sexual trauma could only have a pathogenic effect if there was no conscious memory. There was no need to listen to the patients' accounts at all, for the theory supposed that Freud needed to "reconstruct" scenes of which they had no recollection and then to force these upon them as explanations of their physical sufferings. The patients did not need to go "into the deep"; it was Freud who did. He needed to play an active role in constructing such scenes.

One of the major studies going through Freud's work, and thus taking it very seriously in this respect indeed, is *A Final Accounting* (1996) by philosopher Edward Erwin. Interested in Freud's own standards, Erwin confirms a set of widely accepted epistemological standards and developed a comprehensive evaluation of Freud's theory and therapy, thereby referring only to Freud's work in discussing his experimental and non-experimental evidence. He came across no fewer than 1500 experimental studies of Freudian hypotheses in the pre–1980 literature alone, thus previous to Freud's Fall. The studies he privileged for his evaluation were the ones that have been regarded by Freud's defenders as most supportive. From the evidence Erwin concludes that psychoanalytical ingredients of therapies could make no significant causal contribution in producing some type of benefit for a certain type of patient.

"If 3 years of analysis are followed by the elimination of a patient's phobia, it would hardly undercut the analyst's claim of a cure to point out that a change in the weather or a change in government or excessive sunlight *might* have caused the result. Suppose, however, that the rival explanation holds that spontaneous remission occurred, and suppose that we have solid evidence that this type of phobia usually disappears without formal treatment within 3 years. Would not the failure to rule out this quite plausible explanation undercut the analyst's evidence for a cure?" Erwin concluded that psychoanalysis made no difference to ordinary talks and other talking cures and that "virtually none" of Freud's theoretical hypotheses could be considered true or approximately true according to Freud's own standards.[18]

It must be said, all this resembles astrology. Astrology is a cultural practice that was regarded as science for many centuries indeed. Considering the limitations of the scope and the flow of information in the late Renaissance, some astrologers could gain "world fame" as scientists. Italian Girolamo Cardano (1501–76), for example, had been such a celebrity of science. He recorded technical data on a form and divided them into categories, which enabled him to select, organize, and record specific "facts." The almanac was his essential desk reference: a work largely consisting of tables, which would provide him with all the data he was likely to need to construct and to interpret genitures and interrogations. But despite all the equipment and the almanac, the astrologer's success was built on only one assumption: that celestial events shape life on earth. Cardano investigated world history, wrote on the "nature" of man, worked as a prognosticator and as a political counselor, but in the end, was arrested by the Inquisition and condemned for heretical views.[19] Little remains of this tradition, for who would like to work with the assumptions of astrology to describe, for example, Andean narratives as a consequence of particular celestial constellations? Or to work with the assumptions that founded the theory of a flat earth, and celebrated the Universals of God's creation and the Earth in its center? Freud's surgery looked like a replica of the astrologer's: he was surrounded by instruments, many books indeed, and other paraphernalia of high status.

Some authors who trusted astrology are still popular. Anthony Parel's analysis of the work of Niccolò Machiavelli (1469–1527), the author of *Il Principe, The Prince* (written in 1513 and published in 1532), comes to mind. Parel's *The Machiavellian Cosmos* (1992) shows that this Renaissance political author and scholar firmly believed in the occult forces of heaven and bodily humors. Machiavelli focuses primarily on the "new prince"; the *principe nuovo*. This prince is a non-hereditary ruler who is confronted with the task to stabilize his recently established powerbase. In *Il Principe* the arts by which he could do so are extensively described. The main message seems to be that the end justifies the means. This is not all there is to say about it, because for

Machiavelli power for its own sake was not sufficient. This did not justify malevolent actions. The only acceptable end was the health of the state, and stable and enduring power. Even now in our poststructuralist days, political scientists would claim Machiavelli as a modern political thinker with a cynical view of political and personal power, for the purposes of presenting his concept of power based on a combination of the traditional, or classical, and Christian thought that was prevalent in philosophical circles of his day. However, Parel showed persuasively that Machiavelli's writing owed more to the astrological cosmology prevalent in the European Renaissance than to any Aristotelian, Platonic, or Christian world picture. Like many of his contemporaries, Machiavelli firmly believed that humans best follow the recommendations of astrologists, especially when their "natural" pursuit of appetites for riches and glory could be satisfied. A prince was "good" if he followed the opportunities provided by the stars and his bodily humors, although he should do so without any scruples whatsoever.[20]

# 6

The character caught between two genders is an attractive Freudian Excuse for filmmakers. It is, of course, not the Freudian part that arouses the viewers' interest. It is the conflict that may tear the character apart. Reading the literature, stories may evolutionarily be rooted in sexual selection as ways of getting sex by making gaudy, peacock-like displays of skills, intelligence and creativity. Other scholars stress the idea of stories as cognitive play, something similar to rough-and-tumble play for our motor skills. Stories may also delight in order to instruct, to learn about other minds without the "potentially staggering costs of having to gain this experience firsthand." Or they function as social glue for couples, families, communities, peoples or nations, bringing them together, for example, around common values. What all these possibilities have in common, however, is that stories concentrate upon arousing emotional moments or situations, in general of a conflictive nature. Stories are not to bore people by everyday routine; they need to attract attention by humor, sex, aggression, gossip, and the like. Stories are about trouble, Jonathan Gottschall reminds us.[21]

The character Chloe Sweeny (Amanda Seyfried) in Atom Egoyan's film *Chloe* (2009) — screenplay by Erin Cressida Wilson after the French film *Nathalie* (2004) by Anne Fontaine — both experiences trouble and causes it. The former becomes clear during the film: as a lesbian she falls in love with a non-lesbian married woman, gynecologist Catherine Stewart (Julianne Moore). The film's first focalization is through her desire and disillusionment. Interestingly, Chloe says that being a young high-end sex-worker she usually does not "do women." It seems that she has had her eye on Catherine from the first scenes onwards because the film is hardly started before she offers Catherine a hairpin: "I want you to have it." Catherine refuses. Later on, we learn that the hairpin had been Chloe's mother's. In the following hour and a half we see her efforts to seduce Catherine by telling stories, mostly about having sex with Catherine's husband David (Liam Neeson). In a way, she succeeds because she eventually has sex with Catherine. However, after this, Catherine sends Chloe home with no illusions whatsoever.[22]

The problem for Chloe is that Catherine never had any true interest in her at all. This is told through the film's second focalization: Catherine's agony of doubt. Seen from Catherine's point of view, the film is about a woman growing older and fearing that she cannot arouse her husband much longer. At the end of the movie, she says that she still believes herself to be only nineteen years old, although the mirror tells her something different. This is the Snow White Syndrome, of course, and of all ages. In fact, the couple seems to have lost interest in sex and has moved into the more general midlife situation of being intimate, supportive and very close friends for some time now. Catherine experiences this as a loss; David does not. Catherine constantly looks at her husband through windows, walking alone in open rooms and separate levels, and from a distance. In the music hall, looking at their 17-year-old son Michael (Max Thieriot) performing a piano concert, they sit in chairs separated from each other; in fact, they do not even arrive together. Furthermore, Catherine's relationship with her son is difficult, whereas David seems to be well-informed about his situation — that Michael has a girlfriend, for example. The situation escalates for Catherine after a failed surprise party at their house in snowy Toronto. David, teaching in New York, prefers to have a drink with some students instead of going home and be confronted as well with his advancing age. The next day, Catherine finds a photo of one of the students — an attractive young girl — on David's cellphone and immediately concludes that he is having an affair. From her office, Catherine has seen Chloe accompanying several men in and out of the hotel opposite the street. Catherine, possibly attracted by Chloe's appearance, invites her to investigate David by seducing him. The viewer sees only one meeting between Chloe and David, somewhere in a café, with Chloe cadging some sugar. All the other images of David and Chloe are from Chloe's narrative about her adventures with him — true or imagined, this is left open for most of the film.

In the meantime, Catherine has met Chloe several times, listening to her supposed adventures with David. Assessing the effect of her stories on Catherine, Chloe gives more or less details, working with cliffhangers and other narrative tricks. In the opening sequence, Chloe has told the viewer — in voiceover — that she is quite capable with words and that she knows how to plant a story in her client's head. Probably because her interest is not professional but personal, she misjudges the situation. She believes that she has found good breeding ground because Catherine is visibly aroused by Chloe's stories every time they meet. From Catherine's point of view, however, the arousal does not involve Chloe at all, but triggers memories of her own petting sessions with David. When she eventually joins Chloe in a hotel bed, she simulates sex with David, not with Chloe, although this escapade confirms to Chloe that she has finally conquered Catherine's heart. The rejection afterward, in their ride home, comes as a cold shower to the young woman. From then on, in an attempt to be as close to Catherine as she can, Chloe goes for Michael. Things get worse after Chloe is exposed as an imposter. Trapped in the bar, David did not recognize Chloe at all. Next, Catherine informs David about her mistakes. Shocked and disappointed, he nevertheless understands the situation and embraces her. Chloe sends Catherine an email with a photograph of their sexual adventure together, both naked on the bed and Chloe smiling happily. She visits Michael several times and has sex with him in his parents' bed — where she is aroused by all of Catherine's objects and pictures around them. Naturally, Catherine finds them there, sends the protesting and shocked Michael away and starts to convince Chloe to disappear from her life.

    This is the moment of the Freudian Excuse. During the discussion the filmmakers suggest that Catherine might be bisexual. Of course, Freudians would think, aren't we all? A few scenes earlier, Catherine had admitted to Chloe that she had been seduced and that she liked having made love to each other. Interestingly, Catherine and Chloe's lovemaking scene occurs after Catherine wears Chloe's perfume to trick David. David did not recognize the smell at all. Because this happens before the exposure in the cafe, the viewer has the idea that Catherine has realized that Chloe's stories had been fiction all the time. Nevertheless, she invites her to have sex in the hotel room. Now, at home, wanting to end it all, Catherine repeats: "I think you are very beautiful. You must know that." Reading her mind, Chloe asks for one last kiss and to Michael's horror, Catherine complies, as in a trance. Back to her senses, Catherine sees Michael's reaction and pushes Chloe away. The girl falls violently against the bedroom window, which is not very strong and breaks. Chloe grabs hold of the frame but rapidly concludes that she has lost perhaps the love of her life, and lets herself fall to her death. Curiously, she now stays with Catherine forever — in her mind. An alternative ending on the DVD reveals this motive for her death, again in a voiceover. At Michael's graduation party, with the family back on track again, Catherine walks around wearing Chloe's hairpin as a reminder of this lost love. On the DVD there is even another alternative ending, with Catherine's voiceover telling us that through the hairpin she continues to hear Chloe's whispering voice constantly.

## 7

By following Freud, analysts like Butler are on the same road of error as their master. It is a road built after the exchange of ideas Freud had with Fliess, while reflecting upon Western literature from their Romantic epistemic view. Because so much depended upon their ideas on bisexuality and the crucial moment of the Oedipus Complex in deciding the male or female gender, it is tempting to repeat that Freud knew that his Oedipus Complex was wrong, precisely because he could not find the proper answer to the question of gender choice. Why would a boy identify with his father and male sexuality and not become homosexual? Why would women not identify sexually with women? And Alex? Well, she had never struggled with identification with her father or mother. Neither did she go through an Oedipus Complex. Her choices were biological from the outset, as *XXY* so aptly demonstrates. She is limited by the social: the gossip and the scandal. Helmer Lucía Puenzo did a good job filming this story with no reference whatsoever to psychoanalytical popular psychology, and informed herself, and her leading lady, by intersex persons. As simulators, the film will do a very good job, no doubt. But Chloe and Catherine were either straight or lesbian, or one of them was bisexual, or accidentally both were. They must have been born that way, although in Catherine's case the incident might have been just an incident. Their behavior could not have been articulated to gender choice. Freud's idea that every "new arrival on this planet is faced with the task of mastering the Oedipus Complex; anyone who fails to do so falls a victim to neurosis," has always been simply wrong. Mental simulations based on this idea will not work. Every theory, every concept derived from the erroneous starting point of innate bisexuality should be considered erroneous as well. Theories based on the Oedipus Complex are in serious need of revision, or for the dust bin. For filmmakers, there is no ground to include the Freudian Excuse of inborn bisexuality in their simulators.

# 5

## *Wendy's Advice*

### Nightmares in *Mysterious Skin* (2004) and *Dioses* (2008)
Gregg Araki (writer and director); and
Josué Méndez (writer and director)

## 1

Night has fallen. Brian (Brady Corbet) arrives at Avalyn's place. She had called him that night and urged him to come over to her place: "I need to show you something. Can you come out here?" Avalyn Friesen (Mary Lynn Rajskub) is not an attractive girl. On top of that, she is lame in one leg. Brian shows her a framed picture of his Little League baseball team, which he had stolen from the local library. He tells her he has recognized the boy of his nightmares. Avalyn is not really interested, but by breaking the glass of the frame, she finds out the boy's name. "N. McCormick," Brian reads. Avalyn leads Brian into a meadow to the corpse of a cow, body ripped open. Brian looks at the lacerated part. "Sex organs," says Avalyn, "they're gone. The aliens experiment on cows because the poor things are so defenseless. Us, on the other hand, they can't kill us. They just leave behind hidden memories. Which in a way is almost worse." During these words, stimulated by Avalyn — "Can you feel that?" — Brian puts first his hand and then his arm into the corpse. He hardly hears her talk about the aliens. In fact, with his arm right up in the corpse, he begins to faint. An image from the past introduces itself to his consciousness. His nose starts bleeding. Avalyn calls his name: "Brian!!"

Almost fainting, he now remembers two important details. First, that this other boy not only had been present during this childhood event but also intervened somehow, saying to him, "Here we go. [...] Tell him you like it." Also the hand who caressed him during the event had not been an alien's hand, but human. Eventually, Brian passes out; Avalyn calling him constantly and trying to wake him up. "Oh, my God. Brian!!"

## 2

This is a scene halfway through *Mysterious Skin* (2004), a film by Gregg Araki, adapted from the evocative 1995 novel with the same name written by Scott Heim. Like Todd Haynes, Araki is known for his involvement in the United States New Queer Cinema. The film tells the story of a teenage hustler and a withdrawn young man obsessed with alien abductions. Both of them have to deal with the sexual abuse they suffered as eight-year-olds from their Little League coach when they were children. *Mysterious Skin* takes place in Hutchinson, Kansas, and in the city of New York. With this movie Araki found critical acclaim, also from the public. The story is basically told from the perspective of Brian Lackey (portrayed by George Webster as a boy and Brady Corbet as an adolescent) and Neil McCormick (Chase Ellison and Joseph Gordon-Levitt). Critic Wesley Morris of *Boston.com* speaks of a "brutal yet brilliant" film. For critic Ebert, *Mysterious Skin* is "at once the most harrowing and, strangely, the most touching film I have seen about child abuse." Set mostly in the late 1980s, the film guides the viewers through a world of pain, caused by Coach Heider (Bill Sage), who stole the boys' innocence. Coach is played by Sage "with surpassing tenderness," writes Morris, "who here sports a killer Mark Spitz mustache." Focalized through Neil's experiences in the film, Coach has been both a predator and the father perhaps Neil never had. As a friend, Coach seems to have been the love of his life. For Mick LaSalle of the *San Francisco Chronicle,* the virtues of the film go beyond the moment. "The movie lingers in the mind," he writes, "and there are things in it that only make complete sense upon reflection. There are also unresolved elements that are haunting. This is a serious piece of work that's even better the next day."[1]

The two characters reflect Araki's decision to picture the trauma of Coach's molestation in two different ways. Dark-eyed Neil is a nuisance. As a young boy, he was good at baseball, if only to become Coach's favorite. He must have known all his life that he fancied men, not girls. At an early age, he leafed through the *Playgirl* magazines of his unmarried mother (Elisabeth Shue). At eight, far too early in life, he interprets Coach's abuse as an initiation to love and sex. Even much later, Neil still remembers the moments with Coach as the most beautiful in his life; his sudden absence left a hole in his heart. Note what Neil tells his soul mate Wendy (Michelle Trachtenberg) later in the film, and indirectly to the viewers (and the writer of the film to his audience and the critics): "I know some people might think it's fucked up, or terrible. But what happened that summer is a huge part of me. No one ever made me feel that way, before or since. Like I ... I was special. [...] [H]e really loved me. I mean, there were other kids sometimes, but ... I was his prize. I was his one true love." The "relationship" had continued that whole summer. After Coach had unexpectedly disappeared, Neil developed a compulsion to please older men, no doubt to find this lost pleasure of his childhood — including the mental schema of sex for money, which in this case looks like the Freudian "compulsion to repeat." In short, the Freudian Excuse in this film is childhood abuse and castration anxiety.

Critics feel that the film demonstrates that the rapist is not some creepy monster on a bicycle or in a van that snatches a kid at a playground or walking home from school. "Almost every other movie dealing with pedophilia focuses on the abuser, on the adult in the situation," says Araki in an interview. "It 'humanizes' the monster, so to speak. This story focuses on the victims, the two kids and on the irreparable impact the abuse has on the rest of their lives."[2] Critic Dennis Lim of the *Village Voice* affirms that "instead of humanizing the perpetrator, Araki humanizes the victims — or more precisely, complicates them."[3] Ann Hornaday of the *Washington Post* confirms that the "scenes between the coach and Neil are sickening, as are the ways Neil later copes with his experience, becoming a kind of predator in his own right."[4] According to Stephanie Zacharek: "The scene in which the coach seduces Neil is shot in a way that's both horrifying and hypnotic — it has a dreamy quality that only intensifies its power. We recoil at what's happening to Neil, but we also understand completely why he responds to it."[5] Coach is someone the child knows very well and trusts, like his teacher, an uncle, a stepfather, a father, or a priest.

It does not take long for Neil to drift into petty crime and prostitution. Castration anxiety in Freudian thinking brings people to compulsively repeat behavior in the hope of a breakthrough. Neil has sex with older men hoping to find the type of love he felt with Coach. He does not realize that Coach's abuse has in fact "screwed up" his life. Prostitution does not bring happiness or joy. Interestingly, his male sexuality differs substantially from the queerness of his friend Eric (Jeffrey Licon), who creates a stereotype gay persona with flamboyant hairstyles and dark lipstick. But he does not seem to be sexually active. Neil's soul mate Wendy is his true companion. "I met Wendy when I was ten and she was eleven and a grade ahead," Neil tells us. "If I hadn't been queer, we would have had sloppy teenage sex and contributed more fucked-up, unwanted kids to society." She accepts his standoffish nature and warns Eric: "Where normal people have a heart, Neil McCormick has a bottomless black hole...." Passing Coach's former house, lit at night in blue light, Neil gets out of the car and starts talking to himself— to Coach, who he remembers living in that house: "You called me your fucking angel."

The story is different for Brian, and it is not. "The summer I was eight years old," says Brian at the beginning of the film, "five hours disappeared from my life." He can only manage to catch a few fragments of what might have happened: a lousy baseball adventure, an interested coach. His sister found him in the basement at home, with blood dripping from his nose over his face and shirt. In voiceover we hear Brian telling us: "Mom made me quit baseball the next day. This was when the nightmares began. And the nosebleeds. I wet the bed several times. And then there were the blackouts. I'd feel my eyes roll back in my head. I'd crumple to the floor like a dropped puppet." It sounds like hysteria. Brian reacts to the abuse by developing what one researcher called "psychogenic amnesia." After the initial abuse, there followed a second one, a few months later. Brian had lost his way during a Halloween night and Coach found him. In his teen years, Brian became nerdish and withdrawn, perceived by others as nearly asexual. Because of his strange, unsettling memories in recurring dreams, Brian suspects that he and another boy may have been abducted by extraterrestrials. He spends the rest of the movie trying to uncover the nature of the abduction.

One day, Brian sees a television show about Avalyn, who lives in a nearby Kansas town and who believes she was abducted by aliens. The television voice tells us that Avalyn is 32 years old, unmarried, works as a secretary, and lives with her father. Avalyn tells us more: "Under hypnotic regression, I learned I'd been abducted more than twenty times." This is a kind of Freudian language, of course. The two meet after Brian calls her. Telling his story about the nosebleeds, Avalyn links this to a scar on her leg. This is "mysterious skin," she explains, where a "tracking device" supposedly had been implanted. Brian's nosebleeds reflect an "old nose trick, so the scar can't be seen." He has this mysterious skin inside his nose? Brian reads a text to her from his dream book: "There is a blue light. I am in my Little League uniform and a tall alien is hovering over me. Someone else is with me. Another boy. Also in uniform. A Panther?" Brian explains to Avalyn: "That was the name of my baseball team. Let's see." He continues: "The alien has big black eyes. He's touching my face. I want to cry out for help, but ... I can't." The friendship lasts a few months at least. Unexpectedly, Avalyn tries to seduce him sexually. Brian, obsessed with his nightmares, cannot deal with this yet. Later on, in high school, he strikes up a friendship with soft, friendly Eric. Brian ends up living in a world of constructed, protective fantasies about encounters with alien beings.

While still trying to untangle his confused memories at 19 years of age, Brian sees the photograph of his childhood baseball team in the local library, recognizing a young Neil as the boy from his own dreams. When he starts looking for him, Neil has just followed Wendy to New York. There, in the early 1990s, Neil learns about AIDS. He quits prostitution, at least for a while, and tries several other jobs. One of his last activities as a sexworker is tending to a dying AIDS victim: "This is going to be the safest encounter you have ever had," the man says to Neil. "If you could just rub my back. I really need to be touched." Filled with empathy, perhaps for the first time in his life, Neil connects to another human being. One last encounter, this time with a brutal queer cowboy wearing a baseball cap, sends him fleeing home to Kansas on Christmas Eve. The return offers a crucial meeting with Brian. Does he remember the time they were both on the Little League team? He does. Neil takes Brian back to the place where it first occurred — the blue-lit house. There, during the final scene, Neil explains to Brian. First, there was the undressing and a kind of French kissing. This was followed by a more serious sexual harassment: Coach took the little penis and the scrotum of the boys in his mouth. The next step was Coach's satisfaction: "When Coach would ask me to do things, crazy sex things ... and if I could do them, he'd give me a dollar bill. And on that night, the dollar was mine if I could ram ... my little fist ..." Next, Brian had to do it, too. "And then we drove you back to Little River and left you in your driveway." So why was Brian's nose bleeding? "When it was over and we were getting you dressed, your face looked like you'd been erased. Like you were just empty inside. And you just fell. Face first on the floor. Bam. And when we pulled you up, your nose was bleeding."

If there is repression in these trauma stories, it would be in Brian's, although he does not seem to suffer like a 19th-century hysteric. He is also far from the anxiety of Carol in *[SAFE]*. Neil remembers very well, but he has this compulsion to repeat having sex with older men. The ending of *Mysterious Skin* looks like a Freudian talking cure, because, perhaps, Brian's nose bleedings will stop after Neil's account. Brian's reaction to this story is despair and sadness: he weeps and quivers severely, while looking for comfort and solace in Neil's lap. However, Neil appears as damaged by the experience in his youth as Brian, or perhaps even more. In an interview, filmmaker Araki said that it has always been his theory that Neil is more injured and delusional than Brian. "Neil's damage is very deeply internalized. He has shut down emotionally and is acting out his trauma on this hypersexual path of self-destruction. [...] Even though Neil was already gay and actually had a crush on the coach, their sex screwed him up forever, in ways that he's not able to understand fully." In voiceover, Neil regrets his part in this story. He describes from the inside what the viewer sees on screen: "And as we sat there [...], I wanted to tell Brian it was over now and everything would be okay. But that was a lie, plus, I couldn't speak anyway. I wish there was some way for us to go back and undo the past. But there wasn't. There was nothing we could do. So I just stayed silent and trying to telepathically communicate ... how sorry I was about what had happened. And I thought of all the grief and sadness ... and fucked up suffering in the world ... and it made me want to escape. I wished with all my heart that we could just ... leave this world behind. Rise like two angels in the night and magically ... disappear." What has been stolen from their youth — the innocence of children — has been confronted. Now, both boys can try to make a new start.

# 3

The Freudian Excuse of childhood trauma manifests itself in *Mysterious Skin* as a compulsion to repeat, both in conscious (Neil) and unconscious life (Brian). The details are so convincing that Araki may very well be a well-informed Freudian. This compulsion is founded in the idea of a quasi-natural transmutation of "bad," pre-oedipal identification into "normal" and loving post-oedipal identification. After the failures of the initial stage of his theorizing, Freud thought that it would help to present the Oedipus Complex as something very ancient. Therefore, after World War I he dedicated himself to publishing a series of articles and books with historical analyses of the Oedipus Complex. And to incorporate the horrors of the war, Freud borrowed ideas from his followers to identify the Death Drive ~~Thanatos~~ or Evil Within extensively in a 1920 book titled *Beyond the Pleasure Principle* (*Jenseits des Lustprinzips*). (We should indeed write Thanatos *sous rature*, under erasure, because one of Freud's pupils had coined the term and not Freud himself, which was reason enough for Freud not to use the term in his publications.) The Death Drive ~~Thanatos~~ needed to be tamed (i.e., culturally domesticated) by repression. The negative feelings and desires of death could only "return" to consciousness in dreams, fears, and aggression. They are "the return of the repressed." As its major behavioral feature, the compulsion to repeat would be the tendency or impulse to repeat traumatic events in an attempt to deal with them, like endlessly running up a wall in order to break through it. Or, perhaps, the blissful deflowering Neil experienced at an age too young to fully grasp its effects. In *Beyond the Pleasure Principle,* Freud writes that the patient "is obliged to *repeat* the repressed material as a contemporary experience instead of [...] *remembering* it as something belonging to the past. [...] The compulsion to repeat the events of his childhood in the transference evidently disregards the pleasure principle in *every* way." However, far from offering the desired solutions to the Oedipus Problem, the theory of the Death Drive ~~Thanatos~~ complicated things even further.[6]

In *Mysterious Skin*, we see Neil in growing despair thanks to his compulsion. Neil's behavior looks vintage Freud, as the so-called "destiny neurosis," which manifested in "the life-histories of men and women [as] an essential character trait which remains the same and is compelled to find expression in a repetition of the same experience." Opposite to the newly labeled Sex Drive Eros, the Death Drive ~~Thanatos~~ would turn the human psyche into a battlefield between the forces of life, integration, change, power, love, and lust — or "pleasure"— versus death, disintegration, stagnation, defeat, hate, and envy. Whereas Freud was understood to have originally placed the sex instinct or libido center stage in trying to convince his readers, after 1920 he went "beyond" this simple pleasure principle. The Death Drive ~~Thanatos~~ urged mankind to return to a time or phase prior to such conflicts, like a period before birth. The stronger the Death Drive ~~Thanatos~~, the more aggression necessary to subjugate it. In his 19th-century terminology, this is called *abreaction*, or letting off steam. It was the main solution in combating the pressures of society to repress thoughts, wishes, desires, and behaviors. Mankind has to abstain from these; *triebversicht*—a successful attempt is by sublimation of doing labor, for example. No society is without repression, Freud thought, because that is what culture does. It leads to despair, aggression, and general discontent. Because, Freud had argued, the "subconscious" could become "conscious" through language — *wortvorstellungen*, word representations — the compulsion to repeat was to be made conscious through the same procedure: talking about it.[7] For Neil this would mean that he had to deal with his childhood trauma first, recognizing it as a trauma by talking about it, and then get over it. Only then would he be able to follow Wendy's advice to stop with dangerous sex. The point is, of course, that there is no evidence of repression of Neil's trauma — in fact, if it is one in the first place — and that the notion of repression itself has been blown off by now.

If Neil's behavior looks like a caricature, so would Brian's. The "royal road" to understanding the unconscious activities of the mind, said Freud, is dream interpretation. In *Mysterious Skin*, the filmmaker portrays Brian's nightmares as precisely such a road. Brian suffers from a compulsion to repeat endlessly the same nightmare. Nightmares and dreams are a common theme in cinema.[8] Brian's is a unique nightmare, which we share with him on the screen: a *still*— a picture of the torso and head of the boy lying on the ground, upside down, with an alien hand caressing. Psychogenic amnesia in general is believed to be a memory disorder characterized by extreme memory loss caused by extensive psychological stress. In Brian's case it is combined with the Freudian Excuse of repressed memories haunting the mind in dreams because of childhood trauma. It is common in the psychomythological context to believe that contrary to ordinary memory, haunting manifestations of traumatic memory are invariable and do not change over time. These stills are believed to be disguised versions of *unknown* trauma.[9] From the Freudian Edifice we may look at Brian's quest to find Neil as the step of a patient toward his analyst: retrieving memory in order to be cured. In the final scene, Neil asks Brian: "Why now? Why did you search me out?" Brian's answer is in line with the Freudian Excuse of popular psychology: "I'm tired of it. I want to dream about something else for a change." For that reason, the ending of *Mysterious Skin* seems designed as a Freudian talking cure, although Brian can hardly be identified as a hysteric. The talking cure works only if there really is a haunting "subconscious" and if dreams — the basic "entrance" to the "subconscious"— and a free flow of thoughts spoken to the analyst on the couch, for example, actually are "outside of consciousness," as Freud assumed — and the exorcist is needed.

Little eight-year-old boys do not possess the cognitive-emotional equipment to deal with abuse like Coach's. *Mysterious Skin* demonstrates this confusion from scratch. Growing up leads to increased awareness. Neil especially eventually realizes how wrong his memories are. Critic Hornaday comments: "Of all the representations of pedophilia in movies recently, from *Mystic River* to Kevin Bacon's powerful performance as a recovering abuser in *The Woodsman* to Todd Solondz's treatment of the subject in the unsettling, if condescending, *Palindromes, Mysterious Skin* might be the most unflinching depiction of how sexual predation reverberates over time, like toxic ripples through a pond." It is not a message picture, critic Ebert agrees; it does not push its agenda; it is about discovery, not accusation. There is no graphic sex on the screen and the violence sometimes surrounding it is painful and unsentimental. Critic A.O. Scott of the *New York Times* writes: "To say that it is about child abuse is accurate, but incomplete. It is about the Midwest, about friendship, about the connections and disconnections between love and sex, and about a great deal more, all of it handled with clarity, simplicity and rare generosity of spirit." Critic Zacharek concludes that *Mysterious Skin* is not a film "*about*" suffering," but "a picture about getting on with things, about the freeing benefits of coming to terms with the past instead of being a slave to it." She sees the film as "a meditation on the necessity of making your way past, or through, any obstacle that prevents you from being a thinking, feeling person." For Hornaday, *Mysterious Skin* is "a startling portrayal of how the cycle of abuse plays itself out in the lives of its victims, who are in danger of either sliding into nothingness or becoming perpetrators themselves," adding that although Araki offers a "glint of redemptive hope" at the end, "its pervading mood of sadness nonetheless suggests that some wounds can never heal."[10]

This is the point. Despite of its curious Freudian undertones, *Mysterious Skin* does show that the same experience would have different outcomes. For one, there was some happiness and recognition; for the other, there was only anxiety. Neil's treasured memories had to give into what really happened and he might be conscious of his compulsion to repeat sex for money. For Brian, the memory of Coach freezes him in childhood. In fact, the ending suggests a *confirmation*, not a liberation. Neil might have left his destructive nihilistic road in New York already, after the queer cowboy had given him a serious beating followed by rape. After he has talked his past over with Brian, this must have ended his quest for love based on childhood memories of sex and money: there is no Coach in the violent queer cowboy or the AIDS victim. In fact, he is seen happy with his return tickets to Kansas. Scott thinks that a "lesser actor — and a less confident filmmaker — might have made him into a psychological case study, but the power of the character comes not from his status as a victim but from his resilient individuality." Ebert concludes that the film "hates child abuse, but it doesn't stop with hate; it follows the lives of its characters as they grow through the aftermath. The movie clearly believes Neil was born gay; his encounter with the coach didn't 'make' him gay but was a powerful influence that aimed his sexuality in a dangerous direction." Brian was also unable to process what happened to him. He had "internalized great doubts and terrors, and may grow up neither gay nor straight, but forever peering out of those great big glasses at a world he will never quite bring into focus." The moment Brian realizes what has happened, he seeks and finds comfort with Neil. Brian may be liberated from his decade-old dream, but anger and fury might be his fate now. This is not a Freudian triumphal exultation of rebirth — which, as we have seen, has probably never occurred at all.

# 4

To address the Freudian Excuse of childhood trauma in *Mysterious Skin*, Freudian-inspired researchers might like to turn to one of Freud's few case studies. Which one could be used? Contrary to present-day laws in many countries, in Freud's theory forcible oral sex was not considered rape. The boys in this film were seduced to do something rather strange — enter Coach's body through the anus with their arms — and had to endure Coach's kissing and touching. Is that sufficient reason for this kind of amnesia to develop in Brian and stimulate Neil's Death Drive ~~Thanatos~~? Critic Lim has his doubts: "Heim's scenario, a semi-knowing composite of mid-'90s daytime talk show topics, transfers a little unsteadily to a time when recovered-memory therapy is more closely associated with false-memory syndrome."[11] The Freudian case that comes closest to *Mysterious Skin* is the treatment of a patient he called the Wolf Man, the alias of Sergei Pankejeff (1887–1979). It is a case about an *unknown* trauma and is based, like Brian's, on a recurrent dream that involves a *still*. Freud published about this particular case during the period when he realized that more publications supporting the Oedipus Complex were needed. One of his most significant articles was "From the History of an Infantile Neurosis" (1918). He wanted to demonstrate that reconstructed scenes from dreams were "true unconscious memories of genuine occurrences." That is indeed what Brian tries to do in the film. What is also clear from this work is that Freud saw homosexuality as a deviancy from "normal development," and that psychoanalysis could cure this.

Freud tailored an old case that he recorded in the winter of 1914–15. Wolf Man Pankejeff was a wealthy Russian aristocrat, about 23 years old, who suffered from severe depression, which must have been, we know in hindsight, genetic in origin, because several members of his family had suffered from depression; a few had taken their own lives, including his older sister Anna. Freud began treating him not for depression but for an obsessional condition, resulting from debilitating compulsions and fears. He was, as it were, Neil and Brian in one. The suffering allegedly resulted, said Freud, from his sexual development having gone awry at an early age. Freud's text contains the following (verbatim) record of the Wolf Man's childhood dream that seemed to encapsulate Pankejeff's current fears, remembered at age four but told to Freud in 1914 — when he was 27 years old:

> I dreamt that it was night and that I was lying in my bed. (My bed stood with its foot toward the window; in front of the window there was a row of old walnut trees. I know it was winter when I had the dream, and night-time.) Suddenly the window opened of its own accord, and I was terrified to see that some white wolves were sitting on the big walnut tree in front of the window. There were six or seven of them. The wolves were quite white, and looked more like foxes or sheep-dogs, for they had big tails like foxes and they had their ears pricked like dogs when they pay attention to something. In great terror, evidently of being eaten up by the wolves, I screamed and woke up. My nanny hurried to my bed, to see what had happened to me. It took quite a long while before I was convinced that it had only been a dream; I had had such a clear and life-like picture of the window opening and the wolves sitting on the tree. At last I grew quieter, felt as though I had escaped from some danger, and went to sleep again.
>
> The only piece of action in the dream was the opening of the window; for the wolves sat quite still and without making any movement on the branches of the tree, to the right and left of the trunk, and looked at me. It seemed as though they had riveted their whole attention upon me — I think this was my first anxiety-dream. I was three, four, or at most five years old at the time. From then until my eleventh or twelfth year I was always afraid of seeing something terrible in my dreams.[12]

The Wolf Man had connected this dream with a tremendous fear of the picture of a wolf in a book of fairytales during his childhood. His sister Anna used to tease him by holding up a particular picture of a wolf in front of him on some excuse or other, so that he was terrified and began to scream. In the picture, the wolf was standing upright, striding out with one foot, with its claws stretched out and its ears pricked. He thought this picture must have been an illustration to the fairytale "Little Red Riding-Hood."[13]

Typical for his writing, arguing from one association to the next, Freud suggested that this dream represented an auto-censored version of a memory of an experience lived by the patient at a very young age, a year and a half old, in which he had been witness to his parents having sex, *coitus a tergo* (from behind). The early age was no problem to Freud. About the dream he wrote: "The dreamer, it will be recalled, said: 'I was three, four, or at most five years old at the time I had the dream.' And *we* can add: 'And I was reminded by the dream of something that must have belonged to an even earlier period.' The parts of the manifest content of the dream which were emphasized by the dreamer, the factors of attentive looking and of motionlessness, must lead to the content of this scene. We must naturally expect to find that this material reproduces the unknown material of the scene in some distorted form, perhaps even distorted into its opposite." In this speculative manner Freud continued: "*Suddenly the window opened of its own accord.* That is to be translated: 'Suddenly I woke up of my own accord,' a recollection of the primal scene. [...] *They were looking at him with strained attention.* This feature comes entirely from the primal scene, and has got into the dream at the price of being turned completely round. [...] *They sat there motionless.* This contradicts the most striking feature of the observed scene, namely, its agitated movement, which, in virtue of the postures which it led, constitutes the connection between the primal scene and the wolf story. [...] *They had tails like foxes.* This must be the contradiction of a conclusion which was derived from the action of the primal scene on the wolf story, and which must be recognized as the most important result of the dreamer's sexual researches: 'So there really is such a thing as castration.' The terror with which this conclusion was received finally broke out in the dream and brought it to an end." For Freud, "two factors in the dream had made the greatest impression on him: first, the perfect stillness and immobility of the wolves, and secondly, the strained attention with which they all looked at him. The lasting sense of reality, too, which the dream left behind it, seemed to him to deserve notice." Thus, Freud *assumed* the trauma of the "primal scene" or *urszene*—it originates in his theory, not in the patient's testimony. In fact, he saw the stillness of the wolves as a censored version of its opposite: a violent motion, as would occur in rapid coitus. The wolves were white as an allusion to the white of the parents' bedclothes and underclothes. The wolves were staring at the little boy because the boy was staring at his parents. The wolves had notably big tails as an indication of the recognition by the little boy of the reality of castration that would come from his viewing of this "primal scene" in the first place. Freud considered the primal scene to be traumatic because he believed the child would be over-stimulated to a point at which his defensive barrier would be breached: the scene proceeds from the sexual arousal of the child, through induced castration anxiety into oedipal development. Freud concluded that a hostile impulse directed at the father had been repressed, and that this repressed impulse was the basis for the Wolf Man's anxiety. As usual, he found the treatment successful. But the patient was not cured; many symptoms had not gone away at all.[14]

Interestingly, with the Wolf Man we have a patient who actively talked back. This is important because many readers of Freud's work are interested in what his patients thought of their treatments. We have seen people walking away due to a lack of results. We know that Anna O. in her mature life was always scathing about psychoanalysis. The Wolf Man gave a report of his treatment to a German reporter, Karin Obholzer, who spoke with him from September 1974 to January 1976. He remembered that he disagreed with Freud's speculations constantly. We must realize that, as the conversations with Obholzer reveal, the Wolf Man was no enemy of Freud. Take the following selection of his memory: "Freud was a genius, there's no denying! All those ideas that he combined in a system [...]. Even though much isn't true, it was a splendid achievement." Nevertheless: "If you look at everything critically, there isn't much in psychoanalysis that will stand up. [...] He was a witty, a very intelligent man, there's no disputing that. And that he made mistakes ... to err is human. And it's clear that he overestimated his work." Asked by Obholzer but sometimes given freely, the Wolf Man contradicted Freud on several critical points. For example, he had not been "entirely incapacitated [...] in a state of complete helplessness," but rather considerably improved by the time he came to Freud, and able to engage in a large number of social activities. He had not been in love with a peasant-one-night-stand, and merely gave her a present in return for her favors, as was usual. The Wolf Man remembered that the animals "were not wolves at all but white Spitz dogs with pointed ears and bushy tails."[15] He learned from Freud that a trauma was caused by some childhood experience and that if you remember this event, you get your health back. This was the prospect of Freud's treatment: "We have the means to cure what you are suffering from." For this reason alone, the Wolf Man would have tried to be as accurate as he possibly could be, of course, in telling his dreams — even though, as he told Obholzer, he "never thought much of dream interpretation." He did have that particular dream, but the "whole thing is improbable because in Russia, children sleep in the nanny's bedroom, not in their parents'." Not an exception, then? "It's possible, of course, [...] how do I know? But I have never been able to remember anything of that sort [...]. He maintains that I saw it, but who will guarantee that it is so? That it is not a fantasy of his? [...] I have always thought that the memory would come. But it never did." Perhaps not because of his resistance? "Well, that would also be a supposition, wouldn't it? But it is no proof." Freud tended to believe in determinism, Obholzer answered him. "Then he should have said that once all those childhood matters have been cleared up," the Wolf Man answered, "if they are the causes of inhibitions and symptoms, then it must disappear." They did not.[16]

Following psychoanalytical theory, Brian's psychogenic amnesia must have been caused by an attack of castration anxiety during Coach's touching of his tiny penis and scrotum. In fact, Coach took it in his mouth. For Freud, the "primal scene," real or imagined, of observing parental intercourse, of being seduced in childhood, and of being threatened with castration were "unquestionably an inherited endowment, a phylogenetic inheritance, but they may just as easily be acquired by personal experience." As Brian did. Freud further assumed that the intercourse between the Wolf Man's parents was *coitus a tergo,* and that the boy must have seen his mother without a penis, and, perhaps, interpreted the vagina as a wound. To underscore this assumption, Freud implies that the Wolf Man at that early age was able to recall real and extraordinary details of violent coitus, including rapid successive disappearances and reappearances of the penis. Three times repeated, Freud wrote. The result, according to Freud, was that the Wolf Man had developed a negative Oedipus Complex, for the "primal scene" meant that the boy thought he would have to be deprived of his penis if he were to gratify his feminine libidinal wish by satisfying his father sexually. The possibility of castration "was terror, horror of the fulfillment of the wish, the repression of the impulse which had manifested itself by means of the wish, and consequently a flight from his father to his less dangerous nurse." Although the phobic anxiety itself was transformed, repressed libido, the fairy story merely provided the occasion for the repression to begin; the real problem had been the fear of castration. Repression had caused anxiety.[17]

The Wolf Man remembered a situation in early childhood in which, according to Freud, his sister seduced him into sexual practices by taking hold of his penis and playing with it. "I can remember that we had sat down between the doors and she played with my penis." This was sufficient information for Freud to launch his traditional argument. The Wolf Man, Freud assumed, must have seen himself not as a passive player here, but in his fantasies, he must have been aggressive and he would have tried to see his sister undressed. Next, also in his fantasies as imagined by Freud, the Wolf Man was rejected and punished. He must have tried to win his nanny instead of his sister. Therefore, he must have begun to play with his penis in his nanny's presence. Of course, she would have disillusioned him and supposedly threatened him with castration. The Wolf Man is supposed to have said to Freud that he gave up masturbating very soon after this. Freud's Haeckelian and Lamarckian view of evolution is echoed in the only sentence in his piece that was italicized in the original: "*His sexual life, therefore, which was beginning to come under the sway of the genital zone, gave way before an external obstacle, and was thrown back by its influence into an earlier phase of pregenital organization.*" At the suppression of his masturbation, Freud stated, the boy's sexual life took on a sadistic anal character — homosexuality — and his libidinal expectation detached itself from the nanny and began to contemplate his father as a sexual object. Symptoms of anxiety, Freud concluded, only came after the occurrence of the particular event of the wolf dream. The Wolf Man, however, found his sister aggressive. But then, it was just children's play. And the nanny? She was hardly an object of his fantasy: "The nanny was an old woman." Obholzer asked the Wolf Man why he went to see Freud in the first place. What did he tell Freud he was suffering from? "Well, depressions." That was why he visited him? "Yes, actually it was because of Therese." This girlfriend was lower class and therefore not approved by his family. He had begun psychoanalytic treatment because he had fallen in love? Yes. And Freud approved it. He called it "the breakthrough to the woman"— because "ontogeny recapitulates phylogeny," and in a "correct Freudian way" this would mean the "cure" of the homosexual — and saw it as the step into the next phase. He stimulated the Wolf Man to stay with the girl. To the woman: not to his father anymore. "And if Freud had not said [...] that I could see Therese, I would not have stayed on."[18]

# 5

The Wolf Man did not dream the Freudian way. Confirming the Wolf Man's interpretation in his discussion of the case, Australian psychologist Malcolm Macmillan found little evidence for Freud's interpretations. The Wolf Man recalled events from some 20 years earlier, and the question, therefore, is why other direct "castration threats," which must have occurred, did not have the same impact. At age four he might have had knowledge of vaginas. Were it to be argued, Macmillan asks, "that these other threats of castration could have no effect because they occurred before the Wolf Man's childish feminine genital impulses were directed toward his father [...]?" If so, the problem arises, for example, as to why those threats did not prevent those impulses from being directed toward his father in the first place. The sequence of events, however, is difficult to verify. The Wolf Man first experienced anxiety during that dream about the wolves, said Freud. Trying to follow Freud's reasoning, it was, Macmillan answers, "at best, *simultaneous* with the repression." Macmillan sees both considerations mentioned here as tautological explanations. We know Freud stated that repression caused anxiety. Here, repression was actuated by fear of castration. Fear and anxiety are synonymous. So, what has been gained by explaining anxiety as a result of anxiety?[19]

Dream researcher David Foulkes discussed the Wolf Man's dream offering an alternative interpretation. Children's dreams, Freud thought, were reflections of the interaction between the child and its parents. Consequently, human unconscious is formed by the nurture provided by any individual child's family. Contemporary research tells a different story. A glimpse of recent dream research has established that children dream so differently from adults that it would be difficult to imply Freud's repression theory. The Wolf Man's dream dates from age four. Freud wrote about the stillness of the dream. And he added: "One day the patient began to continue with the interpretation of the dream. He thought that the part of the dream which said that 'suddenly the window opened of its own accord' was not completely explained by its connection with the window at which the tailor was sitting and through which the wolf came into the room." Children ages three to five do not have the capacity yet to dream as adults, Foulkes writes, to hide their experiences in symbolic language, or try to deny them. In general, children of that age group rarely dream at all in relation to older children or adults. Until they have achieved a certain level of competence in visual-spatial mental manipulation, they do not dream, or do not dream very well. Their dreams highlight only isolated events with distinctive static imagery and no active self-participation. In their dreams, social interaction, movement, and active self-participation are lacking. Animals hold a center stage but in the form of static "pictures" (a bird singing, a calf in its barn), but also the child's own body, and above all where the body was during sleep ("I am asleep in a bathtub"). In fact, children of this age group start "truly" dreaming frequently from age seven onwards — too late for Freud's Oedipus Complex to develop. Only then, they become capable of imagining small sequences of events and activities in their dreams, in the form of complex, kinematic narratives bit by bit, including their self-participation in social-interaction activities and settings. This is confirmed by reports coming from different cultures around the globe. The Wolf Man expressed this immobile image because at that young age he literally could not yet have imagined activity, and the animal characters were also typical for the contents of the static imagery characteristic for his age. According to Foulkes, the Wolf Man's dream was an ordinary one. He saw no hidden Freudian messages involved.[20]

In one of his earlier publications, Italian historian Carlo Ginzburg recommends an altogether different look at the Wolf Man's case. Ginzburg referred to it in his study of the Witches' Sabbath and the so-called benandanti, or good-doers, who told late 16th-century inquisitors that four times a year they fought the forces of the Devil during nocturnal battles over fertility. These benandanti, furthermore, argued that God had selected them because they were born with the caul. Ginzburg linked the stories of the benandanti with similar stories of other people who were born with the caul, born with their teeth, or born during the 12 days between Christmas and Epiphany, and who were therefore also "selected" for supernatural activities as participants or viewing a procession of the dead, working as shamans or being werewolves. Several of these cases were from Slavic and Baltic areas. Freud's Wolf Man fell into this category — as did, by the way, Freud himself, because he was also born with the caul and we know he felt the social-cultural pressure to perform as a "chosen one" as well. The Russian Wolf Man, born on Christmas Day, had told Freud about being born with the caul, perceiving the world from behind a veil, and considering himself as a special child of fortune whom no ill could befall. What is more, a nanny, or *njanja*, described as a peasant, pious and superstitious, and thus gifted in telling folkloric stories to the child, educated this wealthy Russian. She had comforted him after his anguished dream about the wolves. She might have told him about the extraordinary powers that were conferred by the fact that he had been born with the caul. Fables including wolves were part of Russian folklore, and one of them, for example, was included in a celebrated collection of Russian fairytales by Alexander N. Afanasyev (1826–71), who recorded and published more than 600 Russian folktales and fairytales, which is by far the largest folktale collection by any one man in the world. Beyond any doubt, this background would have fueled the Wolf Man's dream. Ginzburg believes that Freud, ignorant of Russian folklore, did not perceive that he could have found the answers he asked himself about the Wolf Man's dream in the works of Afanasyev. In fact, he did not recognize the element of folklore at all, ignored the cultural context in which the dream was rooted, and fell back on his own theoretical fabrications.[21]

In short, the dream must have been a reflection of cognitive input. As introduced above, from the late 1980s onward, psychologists began confirming the results of linguists about conceptual metaphor and schematic thinking. Nowadays, dreams are increasingly regarded as part of the information encoding system of the mind, one of the mind's major instruments to put experience into order, and evaluate its emotional impact. For Rosalind Cartwright dreams work to *avoid* neurosis, precisely the opposite to the traditional Freudian convention. (Although the word "neurosis" had better be avoided; since 1980, the word is absent from the DSM.) Cartwright researched people going through divorce who became depressed during that stage of their life. Depressed persons appear to cope better with their depression if they manage to incorporate their feelings and stressors in their dreams. The same way, these people were significantly better adjusted to their new life, thus demonstrably less depressed, if they had dreamt about their ex-spouses at the time of the separation. It was also made clear, as Ernest Hartmann later commented upon this article, that dreaming is considerably less benefit to people who prefer to wall it off or refuse to talk about their stress. In fact, according to Hartmann — and contrary to Freud's teachings here — traumatic or stressful events awaken strong emotions that take over the dreaming activity.[22]

Professional dream research went quickly in the opposite direction of Freud's theories. It is known that, during the so-called Rapid Eye Movement epochs, or REM sleep, numerous brain processes are going on at once, writes Susan Blackmore in her *Consciousness* (2003), "none of which is either in or out of consciousness." She continues: "On waking up a story is concocted by selecting one out of a vast number of possible threads through the multiple and confusing scraps of memory that remain." No version is "the right one." The waking up version is "concocted," using schematic reconstruction.[23] Furthermore, no hidden symbolism of "repressed" wishes could be affirmed. Emotions and moods guide dreams to beat "negative" intruders in the dreamer's emotional state because such negative emotions hinder the person's smooth functioning in society. In general, very traumatic experiences arouse alarming dreams of the kind in which the dreamer is believed to see his world near its end and survival is barely no longer possible. Then, during subsequent episodes, it is as if the initial dream of several nights in a row is used by the mind to look for other distressful events to try to find a similar mood, but one that suggests that the experience can be survived and that fear, loneliness, and guilt are not to be continued. This process can take years and sometimes does not end at all, but in most cases it works pretty well and releases the dreamer of "negative" emotions.

This was confirmed by psychologist J. Allan Hobson, who concluded from years of detailed empirical research that during REM sleep, the brain works on an activation synthesis, which relates the form of dreams to self-activated brain processes, spontaneous neural activity triggered by some external stimuli but above all by memories, whereby sensory and motor information is automatically generated and synthesized by the brain. The memories include random activation of two memory systems, dominated by events that have occurred in the recent and distant past. The Finnish neuroscientist Antti Revonsuo advanced a hypothesis from an evolutionary point of view, in which dreams incorporate current concerns, fears, and threats that may be preying on the mind of the dreamer in order to develop threat and fear avoidance skills. During most of human evolution physical and interpersonal threats were serious, giving a reproductive advantage to those who survived them. This means that dreaming evolved to simulate these threats and allowed repeated practice dealing with them. To support his claim, Revonsuo shows that modern dreams do indeed include far more threatening events than people meet in waking life, and that the dreamer usually engages appropriately with them. Nonetheless, if dreams encode experiences they do not always steer them toward a clear solution. It seems there are adaptive dreams that simply encode; there are dreams that solve problems within their own narratives, without linking relevance to the "working world"; and there are dreams that translate known solutions into the dream world. And, to quote one last study, a group of Belgian neuroscientists found sufficient data to confirm that all this is to "clean" the brain. Here the analogy might be made with normal computer routines — although the brain is not a computer — to liken dreams to updating memory files, discarding redundant data, rehearsing and checking routines. To sum up, then, daily experiences are stripped of harmful, negative emotions and are therefore "neutralized during dream-sleep."[24]

Dreams are bizarre or mundane thoughts. A thought is always about someone or something, expressed in language and images. These features result from the sensory inputs; sounds, sight, touch, taste, and smell. By "touch" we must understand the entire sense of the body in space, the complete mapping of bodily signals from within and without. Also, in its circuitry, no "messages" are exchanged. Neurons are simply part of the tracks of bio-electronic connections. Most of the 5,000 or so input lines to the average brain cell are parts of feedback loops returning via neighboring neurons, or from those higher up the hierarchy. In an introductory paper, John McCrone suggested that barely a tenth of all connections come directly from the sensory organs or from mapping levels lower in the brain. Dreams may be characterized by cognitive discontinuities in thoughts, incongruities, and uncertainties. Two perspectives can be explored. Milton Kramer believes that a nightmare should occur when the so-called integrative capacity of the dreamer is exceeded. In that case, the associated hyper-responsiveness of the dreamer has entered an altered emotional state. Kramer found that across the sleep period mood is being systematically and differentially transformed. He thinks that who and what the dreamer dreams about determines how happy he awakes in the morning. The mode of dream problem solving may be related to this if dreams are able to change the dreamer's mood during the sleep period. And when greater problems are to be solved — think of sexual abuse — the dreamers experience a higher frequency of nightmares and nightly terror. These dreamers have greater difficulty returning to sleep after awakening. This situation notwithstanding, research showed "little support for the hypothesis that 'worse' nightmares would possess the most bizarreness." No differences were found in bizarreness or realism when the length of dreams and nightmares was held constant in sleep-mentation reports. According to Jane Merritt, Robert Stickgold, and their colleagues, bizarreness can significantly be correlated with major shifts in emotion. They recorded no significant difference in the profiles of emotion of men and women. An analysis of about 200 dream reports shows that anxiety and fear were most common, followed, in order, by joy and elation, anger, sadness, shame and guilt, and, least frequently, affection and eroticism. The study by Merritt and colleagues has shown that as with any conscious thought emotion is a nearly ubiquitous feature of dreams, and as expected, is usually appropriate to the plot of the dream narrative. This is consistent with the findings that sleep "cleans" the brain.[25]

Thus, the bizarre character of dreams has no particular psychodynamic significance. No particular unconscious symbolism is involved, nor does their character necessarily result from a process of disguising inadmissible information. Rather it is the product of the brain's efforts to construct a story out of internally generated signals without the benefit of feedback from the external world and with only its own memories to guide it. On April 9, 2008, dream scholar G. William Domhoff gave a lecture at the University of California at Santa Cruz on "The Awesome Lawfulness of Your Nightly Dreams." He began his lecture with the "bold assertion" that it is not necessary any longer to study Freud and Jung in any detail. Domhoff recalled how, in 2002, he had told science magazine *Discover* that he had gone through Freud's work, "pulling out every assertion and comparing it with the systematic empirical studies conducted over the past 75 years, including my own. I don't find support for a single one of Freud's specific claims. Freud said all dreams are wishful, for instance, but there is a lot of evidence against that. I've given up on Jung as well. It's sad that these theories continue to attract so much attention when they are clearly not adequate. We ought to move on." Domhoff accumulated a database of more than 11,000 dream reports — Freud probably had not more than a few dozen of them in his entire career, and most of them were told to him much later, worked over by consciousness, suggestion, and Freud's expectations. It has struck psychologist Richard McNally in his book *Remembering Trauma* (2003) that even some psychoanalysts have questioned the wisdom of inferring repressed trauma from dreams. Indeed, if it were possible to dig up hidden trauma from dreams — as archeologists of the mind — then therapists should be able to sort victims from non-victims solely based on their dream reports. It would be cheaper for insurance companies to investigate their clients' dream reports than to finance their medication. There is no evidence that this can be done.[26]

Furthermore, suggestion does its work. If the patient and the therapist continuously talk about childhood trauma, the patient would sooner or later dream about it — as would the therapist. It is curious that Brian thinks and talks so much about alien abduction without having any other dream than the one he has involving little Neil and an unknown hand. Thinking about his dreams and explaining them consciously in terms of alien abduction would have changed his dream. Victims of severe violence and trauma also have the same dream recurrently. They know very well, and can explain in detail, the events behind the dream. Moreover, dream imagery does not follow the rules of language. This makes it difficult to decode and to distill some clarifying narrative, as we saw with the Wolf Man's dream. If Brian had truly forgotten Coach's assault on his innocence, he would not have dreamt about it, either. However, he did constantly, which means that the memory is there for consciousness to access as well. That is why we can make dream reports.

# 6

Considering the case against Freud by academic psychologists, there are few reasons to believe that Brian and Neil reacted psychologically to Coach's rape the way they did in *Mysterious Skin*. Brian had one recurrent nightmare and an unrealistic kind of psychogenic amnesia from the beginning and only slowly began recovering parts of his memory during the exchange with Avalyn. *Mysterious Skin* repeatedly indicates that Brian's experiences with Coach were "dumped into the unconscious," as the celebrated psychoanalytic trauma specialist Vamik Volkan called repression. Peculiar though it sounds, even in a few of his drawings, Freud represented the unconscious as a relatively small piece of the brain, indeed a dump bin for "repressed thoughts." Psychogenic amnesia is Volkan's domain. It is sometimes called dissociative amnesia, which in turn is a different word for repression. This type of amnesia is retrograde, which indicates an inability to retrieve stored memories up to the onset of amnesia. According to widely held clinical assumptions, "victims of a psychotraumatic event may protect themselves against the overwhelming exposure of threatening stimuli by inhibiting information processing." True psychogenic amnesia is extremely rare despite its frequent portrayal in films and novels, says McNally. It is extremely difficult for an academic to prove that someone has an *inability* to remember — as in hysteria, people may fake memory loss for personal reasons or because they are reluctant to think about the experience. The few cases that are described suggest that most patients spontaneously recover their memory within a matter of hours, days, or weeks; in rare cases, amnesia may persist for months — young children may forget the facts completely, and also not be haunted by nightmares. Others cannot retrieve their memories because the hurtful events were not encoded. This could have been the case for Brian. Recovery from psychogenic retrograde amnesia usually occurs suddenly.[27]

As recent as 1991, psychoanalysts Bessel van der Kolk and Onno van der Hart published a Freudian theory claiming that traumatic experiences cannot be organized on a linguistic level. They believe that this is a failure to arrange the memory in words and symbols, which leaves it to be organized on a somatosensory or iconic level. This theory was brought forward 45 years after the publication of an investigation of their colleague, psychoanalyst Theodore Lidz (1910–2001). Treating psychiatric casualties from Guadalcanal during World War II, Lidz had noted that when Marines exhibited amnesia it was usually for events occurring immediately after a traumatic event. The event itself was easily remembered. Preoccupation with the event had impaired encoding of events following it. Furthermore, following Freudian theory, Lidz had expected that he would need to uncover repressed memories of these events in order to cure them — for according to Freud knowledge of the trauma by liberating the repressed memory would do so. To his surprise, Lidz heard interminable narrations of event after event. The patients poured forth accounts of the episodes that had overwhelmed them with marked display of emotion. They had not repressed a single detail.[28] So, where is Freud's dump bin? Following Lidz and other researchers over the past 60 years, and in spite of van der Kolk's beliefs, academic psychologists have not found it.

Memories of trauma can recur in nightmares, McNally acknowledges, plaguing survivors while they sleep. Sometimes intrusive recollections are so vivid that it seems as if the trauma is actually happening again. This is what haunts Brian, of course. McNally refers to these nightmares as flashbacks. However, careful research indicates that only a small portion of the patients believe that the flashbacks are exact replicas of the event — although memory researchers doubt if people are able to make such spotless replicas at all. Traumatic nightmares are not a form of autobiographical memory. Despite patients' complaints about frequent nightmares, trauma survivors have seldom experienced them in sleep laboratory studies — perhaps they were less frequent than thought or the attention at the laboratory somehow suppressed their occurrence. Curiously, trauma patients seem to dream less than other people. In fact, replicative nightmares might be most common immediately after the trauma, but would wane in frequency soon thereafter. "Interpreting nightmares as symbolic evidence of repressed memories of abuse is a seriously flawed enterprise," McNally concludes. It is based on the notion that the trauma can only be re-experienced during sleep, while the person is entirely incapable of remembering it during the day. Not even Brian could be so limited, for in the meadow with the dead cow, he remembered very well some specific details. The Freudian idea, says McNally, "flies in the face of everything known about how people remember trauma — or anything else, for that matter." In fact, daytime intrusive recollection is the most common re-experiencing symptom. Anyone having traumatic nightmares will surely remember the trauma all too easily while awake.[29]

Emotions are always strongly involved in unconscious processing as part of thinking and decision-making, and not partly, as Freud reasoned. The unconscious is also not some kind of special place in the brain, as Freud had imagined. Academic research, critically tested over and over again, has shown that traumatic experiences cause the brain to stay in a constant state of arousal and store and retrieve information from the world differently than non-traumatized brains. In a way, *Mysterious Skin* effectively shows Brian's constant state of arousal from the beginning. In general, this kind of arousal causes the opposite reaction from amnesia. Victims of German, Japanese, Yugoslav, or Russian concentration camps, victims of gang violence in cities in the United States, victims of natural disasters, violence, abuse, and other mistreatment *cannot succeed in forgetting* and are haunted consciously and persistently by their memories, day and night. Interestingly, the people who *did* forget show malfunctions in the hippocampus. This is an organ of the brain consisting of two parts, located under the temporal lobe in each hemisphere. It plays a part in memory and spatial navigation. If someone is under stress and the influence of stress hormones too long, the hippocampus may begin to falter in its ability to control the release of stress hormones and thus in its ability to perform routine functions. Such damage to the hippocampus usually results in profound difficulties in forming new memories, and on average also affects access to memories prior to the damage. But this is not an ordinary situation. Research demonstrates that the more wounding an event is experienced and the more stress hormones begin circulating through the body, the *better* memory works. This series of investigations underscores why people cannot forget traumas: their encoding mechanism had been much better under stress.[30]

In short, academic investigations demonstrate that Freudian repression is highly improbable in cases like Brian's because stress factors damage the possibilities of the brain to process the memories in the first place. But if memories are processed, in general the human mind is unable to empty itself, even artificially into some basket for "dumped repressed thoughts." "Although humans may be quite able to distract themselves from unwanted thoughts under normal conditions," psychologist Daniel Wegner and his collaborator Ralph Erber write, "they can suffer from hyperaccessibility and the intrusive return of those thoughts when something happens to distract them from their distractions." Referring to Wegner's research Ziva Kunda adds: "In other words, when we try to control our thoughts, we often experience an ironic reversal; the more we try to suppress a thought, the more it plagues us [...] and], we continue to search for the thoughts we wish to avoid, but we are unable to defend ourselves against these thoughts when we find them." Suppression, a mechanism similar to the one imagined by Freud, leads in fact to obsession. Curiously, something similar happened in an investigation McNally discusses. Researchers found that having a clinician interpret a research subject's dreams as indicative of a frightening childhood experience — it was suggested that the dream indicated that the subject was lost at age three — increased the subject's preoccupation that this event had actually happened.[31]

# 7

One film that captures cognitive dream science very well is Peruvian filmmaker Josué Méndez's *Dioses* (*Gods,* 2008).[32] The dream sequence begins by picturing a girl from the well-to-do section of Lima, Peru, Elisa (Maricielo Effio), lying on the bed, with her head on the spread-out arm of her lover, the much older wealthy industrialist Don Agustín (Edgar Saba). Don Agustín is divorced and lives with his two very spoiled adolescent children Diego (Sergio Gjurinovic) and Andrea (Anahí de Cárdenas) in a coastal resort south of Lima. Recently, he had introduced Elisa as his latest paramour and probably soon-to-be wife to his household and his peers during a weekend fiesta. Elisa is a beautiful woman from a low-middle-class or poor family. Because of this background — a child of Andean migrants in Lima — Elisa is a *chola* and thus considered to be of lower rank than white Andrea and Diego. A chola in Peru is an "urban Indian" of Andean descent. Elisa eagerly sheds her lower class background. She opts for the opulence of Don Agustín's elite lifestyle. At breakfast, a few days earlier, after Don Agustín had introduced her — "Do you remember Elisa?" — Andrea responded: "The new maid?" To her dismay, Elisa realizes that she cannot slip into the glossy lifestyle easily. She has to come to terms with her future stepchildren. She works very hard at her new job of pleasing Don Agustín, walking around the house without a top on exposing her pert young breasts, and trying to keep up with all the other rich spouses by studying botany, the Bible, and Greek mythology to join in discussions about these subjects.

Elisa's greatest fear is displayed in a dream. Underscored by lovely soft chiming glockenspiel, we see her sitting in the house when she notices her mother and grandmother climbing the stairs. "You are going to love it," says mother to grandmother. Grandmother wears a traditional Andean costume and a pair of tresses. Mother is dressed as a poor chola from one of the popular parts of the city. Angry, Elisa walks toward the two women: "What are you doing here?" Her mother is happy: "Hello, my darling, I brought some *tamales*." This is Andean food of Amerindian roots. Mother continues to show the house to grandmother, neglecting her daughter. Arriving in the kitchen, the place where their "class" is supposed to be at home, they unpack some baskets. "Get out, Mother," Elisa says. "You are going to screw it all up. I told you not to meddle with my life. Look how Grandma is dressed! I could have bought her something." The two women feel embarrassed and angry. As Don Agustín enters the kitchen, mother wants to be introduced to him, but instead Elisa treats her as the new maid. When he leaves, grandmother steps forward and without uttering a word, slaps Elisa in the face. At that moment, she awakes. That day, anxious for a collision of worlds, Elisa cancels a lunch with her mother at the house. Only much later will she visit her in her mother's simple house at the fringes of the city, boasting about her new life with the wealthy Don Agustín and her upcoming marriage.

The marriage, however, is under the condition that she will present Andrea's child as her own. Shortly before this dream sequence, Andrea appeared to be pregnant and had been sent to Miami to deliver and never to return to Lima again. In exchange, Elisa demanded a stay of six months in Paris with Don Agustín — to hide her so-called pregnancy. In turn, Diego and Andrea joined a group of bums in the elitist outskirts to the South of Lima. Recently, Andrea had begun to earn riches of her own as a successful fashion model. However, she was also more concerned with nightlife and hanging out with the "right people" than her career. She was becoming famous enough to scandalize her father with her pregnancy. Diego loves his sister — as a *lover* — and hates his demanding father. He follows Andrea day and night from party to party, where she is seen spending a lot of money, drinking strong beverages, and consuming drugs. She must also have had several sexual partners, because she is pregnant and has no idea who the father could be. Due to his incestuous crush, Diego cannot fit in properly. *Dioses* seems to express that Diego had no alternative than to desire incest, for this should be typical for this milieu. The scene where Diego masturbates over his sister's passed out body is a dead giveaway of his impotence. However, incest might be the only taboo in this upper-class society, where everyone behaves as a god, beyond rules, morality or belief. The latter, says filmmaker Méndez, is a self-chosen isolation of the privileged. They are isolated geographically and intellectually from the economic and social problems affecting their country. Living isolated like gods, they choose to be at the fringes, raising their kids in a separate world. Méndez believes that "there is an urgency to deal with this issue, an importance to show how moral misery, and not only economic misery, is present in my society, and how it is not a quality exclusively owned by the lower classes, but a dilemma that defines us and prevents our society from evolving into a more inclusive, hospitable and sincere one." Andrea's and Diego's behavior can be seen as a revolt against their upbringing. Elisa wishes to embraces the possibilities that are now granted to her, but has also difficulties fitting in. Furthermore, she is terrified that her Andean family will spoil her fate.[33]

Ironically, after Andrea's departure, Diego does escape from this world. It appears that the only "real" people he knows are the maid and the housekeeper. One night, mourning about his lost love, he is sent by the maid to her home in one of the poorer parts of the city, riding there on an over-crowded bus. Diego sees the tightly packed slum houses where the Andean immigrants live. He stops and watches as the neighborhood kids play football on a sandy field. Then, we see him standing on a high ridge, looking out at the homes of the poor with a newfound respect, and we feel he has learned a valuable lesson. At the end of the film, we see Diego interact with guests at a fiesta going through all the social niceties and banal conversation he needs to participate in so as to remain amongst the privileged in Peru. But he has changed. He has lived some real life. He will study psychology and he is longing for a career in the social sector of the city. At the fiesta he meets a girl who, the camera suggests, might be his future bride. The fiesta is organized for the christening of the baby, now officially the son of Don Agustín and Elisa — although even the gossiping women know he is Andrea's. We do not see Elisa's family present. Perhaps due to her nightmare Elisa has been stimulated to keep the divide between her worlds as clear as it possibly can be. Méndez has integrated the dream in his film as a true feature, without Freudian undertones whatsoever.

# 8

Even if dream interpretation is not the "royal road" to learn about the unconscious — the analysis of behavior will do — it certainly does give us clues about our thinking and the use of our memory. Realizing this, the number of 21st-century films representing dreams or talk about dreams is surprisingly low. In the short 1995–97 period, James Pagel and two collaborators asked 62 filmmakers attending the Sundance Film Institute Screenwriter and Director Labs in Utah to complete a questionnaire regarding the use of dreams in their work. In this creative group of screenwriters, directors, and actors, dream recall was nearly twice what he had found among the general population in earlier studies. The frequency with which they said dreams had an effect on their creative activity in waking life was more than double the norm. This does not mean, of course, that they had the feeling of traveling the "royal road" into the unconscious.[34]

In *Mysterious Skin*, the characters of Neil and Brian are far from authentic. Contrary to the filmmaker's intentions, directed toward the experience of the boys, the Freudian Excuse in the film gives a distorted image of childhood sexual abuse, especially in Brian's case. Classic psychogenic amnesia is recorded to begin immediately after the hurtful event. This happened to Brian. Classical psychogenic amnesia is also recorded as involving loss of personal identity with the amnesia, a massive retrograde memory loss, not merely of the hurtful event, but rarely lasting more than a few weeks; it usually ends suddenly rather than gradually, even without psychotherapy. Brian's case shows nothing of these accompanying essential features of the amnesia. Freudian repression assumes that the traumatic events have been encoded by the brain — and then dumped — but due to high levels of stress this is not necessarily the case. There is a difference between encoding failure and retrieval failure. Cognitive psychologists have established time and again that people's memory of childhood is not as good as the people investigated thought it was — with the exception of people who truly experienced severe trauma. Brian's is a moving story; it serves a compassionate viewing experience, but it is misleading outside the diegesis.[35]

Today, the researcher, the critic, and the screenwriter can consult a vast amount of clinical case studies and academic literature on the Freudian fallacies, like the effects of therapeutic suggestion, stress and trauma on memory. There is only one conclusion possible: traumatic experiences are *unforgettable*.

Some victims succeed in avoiding thinking about their experiences for long periods of time, or even forgetting them. This is not the same as repression — the inability to remember — because, as McNally demonstrates, the evidence for repressed memories of trauma is weak indeed: "What has clinical research taught us about memory for trauma? Events that trigger overwhelming terror are memorable, unless they occur in the first year or two of life or the victim suffers brain damage. The notion that the mind protects itself by repressing or dissociating memories of trauma, rendering them inaccessible to awareness, is a piece of psychiatric folklore devoid of convincing empirical support."[36] Because a traumatic event has the power to affect emotions, these victims will try to avoid having the memory in the first place, more than just avoiding the traumatic event from recurring. They refuse to talk about it, develop strategies to think of other things, move far away to different places if they have the possibility to do so, or escape into drugs or alcohol. In general, they yearn to repress their memories, but fail to do so simply because thought suppression is a notoriously ineffective method for thought control. Their horrible experiences are very easily recalled despite distractions, because these psychologically wounded are constantly triggered to thoughts about past experiences by cues in everyday life: a face, a uniform, food, a sound, a light, a color, a smell, and such. In sum, these experiences are not repressed but are constantly available to the sufferer. Indeed, the victims might wish that Freud's theories were right and that their traumas could be hidden from conscious thought, even for a short while.

# 6

## *Clementine's Whisper*

### Consciousness in *Eternal Sunshine of the Spotless Mind* (2004) and *Drama* (2010)
Michel Gondry (director), Charlie Kaufman (writer); and Matías Lira (writer and director)

## 1

We are halfway through the movie as Joel Barish (Jim Carrey) starts running with Clementine Kruczynski (Kate Winslet). "We gotta go. We gotta go." "What? Where?" Clementine asks. Joel: "I have an idea of how to stop this." The sequence is confusing. The running is shortly interrupted by various short scenes: Joel and Clementine having fun in bed, sitting in the cinema, waiting at a train station. "Concentrate, Clem," Joel says to his imaginary partner. "We gotta get back to the office." Clementine is bewildered, but Joel knows where to go: "There was a tape recorder." Interrupted by a short scene, Joel painting a picture: "No, not the picture." This is not the memory he needs right now. At last, Joel meets the doctor. "Look, our files are confidential, Mr. Barish," the doctor says, "so I can't show you evidence. Suffice it to say that Miss, uh ... Miss Kruczynski ... was not happy and she wanted to move on." The doctor is busy with another version of Joel, talking to a tape recorder. The office is dark; several people are doing strange things. Joel interrupts: "Mierzwiak! Wake me up!" We are at the New York City firm Lacuna, Incorporated, owned by Doctor Howard Mierzwiak (Tom Wilkinson).

Mierzwiak notices him and responds: "Oh, I, I'm sorry, Mr. Barish. I thought you understood what was going on here." "I don't know. You're erasing her from me. You're erasing me from her ... I don't know. You've got this thing. I'm in my bed. I know it. I'm in my brain." Joel realizes that he is dreaming. It is a kind of lucid dream, but, as we know, one that is triggered by the medication the doctor had given him and the electric devices he put on his head. A lucid dream is a dream in which the dreamer knows during the dream itself that he is dreaming. The doctor leaves no doubt: "I'm part of your imagination, too, Joel. How can I help you from there? Uh, I'm inside your head, too. I'm you. Sorry." Then, Joel sees Patrick, the doctor's assistant, with eyes upside down on his face. That is Patrick, he learns. Joel says to the doctor: "He's stealing my identity. He stole my stuff. He's, uh, seducing my girlfriend with my words and my things. He stole her underwear. Oh, Jesus Christ! He stole her underwear."

## 2

At first sight, *Eternal Sunshine of the Spotless Mind* (2004), written by Charlie Kaufman and directed by Michel Gondry,[1] juxtaposes the Freudian Excuse of childhood trauma and the talking cure with novel insights from cognitive psychology and neuroscience, like the mapping of memory in the brain and lucid dreaming. Along with French performance artist Pierre Bismuth, who seems to have delivered the idea to Gondry suggesting, "You get a card in the mail that says: someone you know has just erased you from her memory..." Kaufman and Gondry did a wonderful job in setting his argument *vis-à-vis* this type of popular psychology and translating it into an ingenious narrative. The film could be about the idea of being able to return to the state of childlike innocence before adulthood starts hurting and reshaping us. Return to childhood, improve yourself and start again. This is truly necessary for Joel, because childhood experience has distorted his ability to bond and explore long-term loving relationships. The film gives a clear picture of Joel's almost chilly relationship with his mother. For example, late in the film we see Joel's childhood self saying about his mother: "She's not looking at me." And: "No one ever looks at me." "I want her to pick me up." The Freudian Excuse here teaches us that thanks to a distorted relationship with his mother, he has no confidence in Clementine to be a good mother either. The problem, however, these scenes tell us, is not Clementine's but Joel's. He has to "unlearn" his childhood experience in order to develop a new attitude toward women and toward Clementine in particular. Unwittingly, Mierzwiak's technology helps him do it. The talking cure he experiences is the dream we witness.

French director Gondry, legendary for some music videos, and his cinematographer, Ellen Kuras, visualized the script mostly without computer animations and other physical tricks. The film is told in a non-linear structure. In fact, it is partly circular, because almost at the end of the narrative we are back where it began — back to Paradise? To create the film's themes and moods, especially the nostalgia that dominates much of the narrative, Gondry built the *mise-en-scène,* the things happening within the camera frame or diegesis, including objects, furniture, dress, locations, and light. Evoked by the use of sunlight and a light haze in his home-centered memories, the nostalgia colors Joel's memories. The camera is steady or moves around depending on the situation. To reflect the awkwardness of the conversation of Joel and Clementine in the train, shortly after they met (again), the camera wavers around the train and shows the two lovers from different angles, yet it lingers on them just as they feel attracted to each other. Panic and fear, however, is shot from high and wide angles. Lighting, editing, and sound reinforce these images. Music and sound emphasize the preciousness of memory. For example, while Joel and Clementine talk we hear music, but when they are silent, so is the music. This is, as the DVD commentary points out, to call attention to the stilted rhythm of the conversation.

The story begins when emotionally withdrawn Joel Barish, a 30ish lovelorn nerd, awakes in the morning. Although this is an ordinary scene, the camera is shaking. Joel lives on Long Island, New York, and commutes to his job in Manhattan by train. It is near Valentine's Day. In the background, we hear a door being closed in a hurry, as if someone had been in Joel's apartment. The environment is clean, white, blank. Joel must be some office clerk, but he also loves to write and draw in a journal. Among his prior girlfriends, one had really been important to him. From the "deleted scenes" section on the DVD, we learn that after his break-up with Clementine he visits her again. Actor Jim Carrey played against type here; no grouchy quotes, contemptible humor, or weird antics. Anyway, it is Valentine's Day: "Today is a holiday invented by greeting card companies to make people feel like crap." Waiting for his New York–bound train, Joel impulsively runs from one platform to another to take the train to the Montauk beach, at the eastern end of Long Island. "I don't know why," Joel says in voiceover, "I'm not an impulsive person." In fact, this is a trip not lightly undertaken. Montauk is not just around the corner. The rail journey lasts some three hours, perhaps a little less from the platform where Joel boarded.

On the lonely, wintry beach of Montauk in February, Joel spots Clementine Kruczynski, although he has no conscious recollection of her. She passes him by, interested but not addressing him. Nevertheless, they soon meet on the station platform back to New York and share a compartment on the almost empty train. Like Carrey, Kate Winslet also plays against type. On the DVD she says that she had to play her as a "Jim Carrey part." Clementine is excited and wild. The chameleonic and lush young woman changes hair colors—blue, red, orange—according to emotional periods she thinks she is going through. The colors also reflect the historical periods of the film. The question now is: do opposites attract? These two lovers do. "Don't make any jokes about my name," Clementine warns Joel. She craves attention but needs intimacy. She has a job at Barnes and Noble. It takes some time before the viewers realize that the two had indeed been former lovers. They spent two years together, in fact. The separation came when Clementine, unhappy in the relationship and after a month of arguing, went to Mierzwiak's Lacuna, Incorporated. She hired the firm to erase all her memories of the relationship. Upon discovering this, through some unexpected mail sent to his friends, Joel was devastated. How do you cope with the notion of having been *erased* from your lover's memory? In a fit of rage and spite, Joel decided to undergo the procedure himself to forget both Clementine and the very hurtful idea that she had erased him. The process takes place while he sleeps. The morning in the first scene of the film is the one after this procedure, the door being closed hastily by Lacuna's staff.

For the procedure, the Lacuna staff needs stories and artifacts. The erasure, of course, will cause some brain damage, "on a par with a night of heavy drinking," Mierzwiak, the firm's manager, says. "Nothing you'll miss." In order to annul them one by one, we see how Joel had to gather all the objects that remind him of his lover and to revisit every corner of his brain to indicate where all his experiences of Clementine are located. A lacuna, of course, is a gap and *lacunar amnesia* is a selective gap in memory. The Lacuna, Incorporated staff will visit the client at night and place him or her into a dream-state, where they will then perform a brain-scan procedure and delete those parts of the memory where the undesirable information is located. The client wakes up the next morning, after the scientists have left, with no recollection of the procedure having ever taken place and with no memory of the deleted data. In the film, this is screened as routine. The staff had been there all night, indeed, but this time they did a lousy job. One staff member had to leave because he was called away by his new girlfriend in a panic—this girlfriend, by the way, is Clementine. Another had sex with Mierzwiak's secretary, who entered the apartment later that night and brought weed to smoke. Mierzwiak had to come over to save the job. The clinic itself is shown as a shabby second-floor office, tiny, with cramped corridors and disheveled piles of paper all around. The company's waiting room is populated by grieving clients who have apparently lost loved ones, even children, or pets. The doctor tapes Joel's stories on a cassette that is filed with the papers Joel signed. From this description it follows that Lacuna's memory cleansing was not exorcist, because the grief was conscious. Therefore, one way to review *Eternal Sunshine of the Spotless Mind* is as a film about bereavement.

For most of the time, the narrative of the film concerns itself with an internal view of the erasure of Joel's memory, which is cross-cut with an external view of the same. As his memories are erased, Joel finds himself revisiting the memories in reverse. Throughout the film, the artifacts reappear in their original contexts, showing how they first came to form his impression, and memory, of Clementine's vibrant personality. The erasure starts with the most recent memories. They are more or less nasty, so the sleeping Joel does not protest too much. Several techniques are used. We note that during specific sequences the quality of the image and sound deteriorates. Showing the disintegration of his memory, the objects and spaces associated with Clementine blur or are placed in disorienting contexts. Gondry uses very limited stage lighting. Subtle details fade from view, like her name from postcards, or the titles of the books in the Barnes and Noble. As most of the more recent memories vanish, so too does his memory of his brutal coldness toward his girlfriend and his unforgivable insults. "The effective target of the brain-wipe, apparently, is not the pain that she caused him," reviewer Stuart Klawans recognizes, "but his knowledge of the suffering he inflicted on her." It is important to realize that we are looking at Joel's memories of Clementine, at his view of her. What the Montauk meeting indicates is that the two lovers remember their relationship unconsciously. Philosopher C.D.C. Reeve says that a relationship "weaves lives into one another. Just how much unweaving you would have to do in order to erase all traces of one is unclear. And in that un-clarity, which the film subtly exploits, lie grounds for skepticism about the very possibility of what Lacuna purports to be able to do. Erasing a single traumatic memory is one thing. Destroying all recollection of a one-night stand — that's something heavy drinking or a concussion can accomplish. But erasing a long, intimate relationship and all its associations, no matter how far back or how deep they go ... what would remain?" For Reeve: "Two blue ruins — two sad wrecks," remembering still all that has not been erased because Mierzwiak did not have all the stories or all the artifacts.[2]

Going back in time, Joel strikes upon happier, older, memories of his life. Upon experiencing them, he regrets his decision and changes his mind. He wishes to preserve at least some of them. From that moment on, Joel is walking fast or running, looking for Clementine or trying to escape from erasure with her. The journey goes through rooms and public spaces and along several artifacts. One moment we see Joel and Clementine lying together under a blanket. She tells him how lonely she felt as a child: "Like you don't matter." She had thought she was ugly growing up, trying to make her ugly doll, named Clementine, be pretty so that she could "magically change, too." As Joel kisses her, telling her she is pretty, she hugs him, saying, "Joely, don't ever leave me," in a way that touches us as well as Joel. With these two scenes, the viewer experiences Clementine's vulnerability and fear of loneliness. One by one, Joel recalls other loving moments with Clementine, starting with a night in Boston in which she leads him out onto the iced-over Charles River. He is frightened walking onto the ice, but lying next to her, he tells her he is as happy as he can be. The film has played upon the viewer's own need for intimacy and the viewer's own fear of loss. From this point on, the lovers must be reunited. It is clear that bit by bit Joel must realize that he does not want to lose his memories at all. And he does. First, Joel tries to awake. For a short moment, he succeeds. Next, in his sleeping brain, he tries to save his memories by escaping with Clementine to memory "chambers" where she could not have been, introducing her, for example, to his childhood. This is where the technicians at his bedside lose him and they call in Dr. Mierzwiak to save the procedure. Eventually, Mierzwiak finds him again and succeeds in erasing Clementine, except for one last memory, in which she says: "Meet me in Montauk."

After the erasure, both Clementine and Joel awake with feelings of loss. Joel finds himself in an aimless, directionless state and is unable to attribute meaning to that particular morning. During a few days, Clementine felt an irrational distress, helpless fear, and meaninglessness. "I'm lost," she says. "I'm scared. I feel like I'm disappearing. I'm getting old and nothing makes any sense to me." One day Clementine does something impulsive again: she goes to Montauk, alone. She has no conscious recollection of this spot as the place where she met Joel before. However, unconsciously her memory has made her act. And Joel is there; he had also been guided by impulse. At her apartment, she offers him a drink to "ease the seduction." She laughs to avoid the intimidating effect of her words. Meanwhile, she touches his body. After some silence, not uncommon in situations when two people having crushes on each other have their first conversation, Clementine says she will marry Joel. He takes it in stride. The crux of the separation, as we will see, is immediately present again. Unconsciously, Joel recognizes his lover, but his conscious "interpreter" has no access to that information. It looks like Freudian repression, but it has nothing to do with it; I will opt for a different explanation below. Joel leaves. At home, after, in this deleted scene, having phoned his old girlfriend Naomi, he calls Clementine. She wants to know if he misses her already. Indeed, he answers. She responds laughing: This means that they are already married. Having "met" at the beach once more, after they both passed the erasing procedure, Joel and Clementine are again attracted to each other and renew their courtship. This brings their life in shape again. Finding each other means reconnecting with parts of memory that are not erased. The viewers must realize that their sense of self is too bound up in their memories and past events. In short, if you come to forget the bad times, the good times go, too.

Running parallel to the central story is a subplot involving the employees of Lacuna, Incorporated. Technicians Patrick (Elijah Wood) and Stan (Mark

Ruffalo) are commissioned to execute Joel's memory erasure, as they did with Clementine's only days before. Following their work, we learn that they are revealed as more than peripheral characters. For example, Patrick dates Clementine now, profiting from Joel's remembrances to trigger her most affectionate memories of happy days. However, his plagiarized lines disturb Clementine as one déjà vu after another, driving her to visit the places she has been with Joel. She does so first with Patrick, which turns out to be a failure. When she visits Montauk beach on her own, she meets Joel for the second time around. Unexpectedly, matters gain momentum when the viewers learn that Mary (Kirsten Dunst), the Lacuna receptionist, is Dr. Mierzwiak's former mistress. Stan has a crush on her. The girl has a penchant for pithy quotes from *Bartlett's Familiar Quotations* (1855).[3] Because Dr. Mierzwiak's spouse found out, Mary agreed to erase every recollection of the affair. Again, not all memories could be wiped out because during the troubled night at Joel's, she re-develops her crush on her boss and affirms her love for him. When Mierzwiak's wife discovers them once again flirting in front of the window, she tells Mary about the memory erasure. Angry and confused, Mary first investigates the firm's archives. Next, she takes the records home to send them to all the clients. Shortly after their (re)encounter at Montauk, Joel and Clementine find their files at home. They are shocked. Discussing the find, listening to the tapes, they try to reconstruct their memories. Joel tries to convince Clementine that they can start over, but Clementine states that it could inevitably end the same. Realizing that Clementine has a point, the couple decides to give their relationship a shot anyway.

For philosopher Michael Meyer, there is another interesting aspect. If you come to forget the bad times, he says, times wherein you have been wronged or hurt, you cannot remember enough to be able to forgive. For him, this point about memory and forgiveness is a key feature of the film. At the end of the film Joel and Clementine utter a series of apologies and share intense moments of sometimes unspoken and even uncertain forgiveness. This offers a merciful ending of the film, made possible because, after their unknowing "reunion" at Montauk, Joel and Clementine listen to the tapes that came with Mary's copies of their own memory files from Lacuna, Incorporated. In fact, the tapes are veritable litanies of complaints about the other and the sad state of their former friendship and they decide to listen to them near each other. It has the initial consequence of rendering them angry with each other and confused. Next, regret and reconciliation sets in. They realize that they love each other after all. A series of images of contrition and forgiveness passes over the screen, a situation that allows the two lovers to move forward, recover their friendship and their relationship, including boredom and irritations. By embracing their history, they have transcended it. *Eternal Sunshine of the Spotless Mind* subtly suggests that it is our memories that create us, making us who we are. The film also suggests that without memory there can be no reconciliation. In fact, we learn from the film that the formations and formulations of identity are so embedded in our personal, social, and cultural experience that they can never be fully erased or eliminated. "Shared experience can be dulled," reviewer Gary Simmons concludes, "but never forgotten, because it has been lived. There is no on/off switch in human beings."[4]

The film criticizes the idea that ignorance is bliss, says reviewer Vivien Silvey. This is another psychomythology: before trauma, childhood was Paradise. The film's title is drawn from the poem "Eloisa to Abelard" (1717) by the English poet Alexander Pope (1688–1744). Lines 207–210 could have been Freud's motto: "How happy is the blameless vestal's lot!/The world forgetting, by the world forgot./Eternal sunshine of the spotless mind!/Each pray'r accepted, and each wish resign'd..." Ignorance is, in this case, forced repression executed by the Lacuna, Incorporated. It is shown to lead to deception and pain. Reviewer Kim Edwards points at the roots of Pope's poem. Pope describes the ill-fated medieval story of two lovers, secretly married, which ended with Abelard being castrated by his family and Eloise leaving for a nunnery. There, Eloise imagines herself as an ancient Roman Vestal Virgin living in pure, simple, and sinless solitude. She believes that there must be happiness in being able to erase the "spots" from her mind and memory, for example, her traumas, her pains, her sins, and her regrets. She experiences a lack of this "spotless mind," and lingers for a return to this kind of virginal happiness. That is psychoanalysis in a nutshell, but told as the loss of the mother's breast. This background combines the Biblical state of innocence in Paradise and the Western philosophical theory about the *tabula rasa*, the blank slate. For centuries, psychomythology wanted to believe that people came into the world with a mind completely empty. Modern genetic research has made clear that this is far from the case. This has entered modern popular psychology, but interestingly without erasing the *tabula rasa* theory from top to bottom. In *Eternal Sunshine of the Spotless Mind,* Lacuna, Incorporated offers what Pope wrote, and what Freud thought the mind did with unwelcome feelings, wishes, and dreams.[5]

# 3

Seen through Freudian lenses, *Eternal Sunshine of the Spotless Mind* must be about repression. One psychoanalytical review of the film is by Herbert H. Stein, originally published in *PANY Bulletin* of 2005 (the bulletin of the Psychoanalytical Association of New York).[6] The choice of this author and review of course is arbitrary, but there is no more authoritative text; psychoanalysis is no theory but an accumulation of theories and notions, constantly being debated and disputed. Stein considers the cinema "close to the same thing" as a psychoanalytical consulting room. For him, Joel's texts can be understood as spoken to the psychoanalyst: "I ditched work today, took a train out to Montauk. I don't know why. I'm not an impulsive person." Joel also says to have discovered that there are two years of entries torn out of his diary, entries he does not remember making. He describes himself as shy ("If only I could meet someone now. I think my chances of that happening are somewhat diminished seeing that I can't make eye contact with a woman that I don't know.") and needy ("Why do I fall in love with every woman I see who shows me the least bit of attention?"). For Stein, Kaufman allows us to examine the relationship between memory and meaning as it unfolds in the psychoanalytic process, and perhaps even gives us a cinematic equivalent of transference, the unconscious redirection of feelings from one person to another — for example, from the psychoanalyst to the psychoanalyzed for better understanding of the latter's feelings.

For Stein, Joel is the victim of massive repression. The first memories Lacuna, Incorporated erases are Joel's memories of visiting Lacuna in the first place and contracting for the repression. This demonstrates, says Stein, what Freud wrote about for repression to work: the process must itself be repressed. As Joel's memories unfold, the viewer begins to piece together the dynamic history of his symptoms. These symptoms did not start with repression, because the viewer has seen that on the night before the procedure, Joel looks severely depressed, in anguish, crying and banging his arms on the steering wheel of his car. Joel's own visit to Lacuna, Incorporated is partly inspired by a desire for revenge — and to kill her intra-psychically by destroying his internal representation of her — and partly as a defense against his painful grief. "As viewers and analysts," Stein comments upon this stage of viewing the film, "we are already making excellent progress, having made sense of his use of repression." In a Freudian way, memory is revealed to understand how the patient came to grief, and working backwards, from effect to cause, it may be possible to piece together the underlying dynamics. One of the earlier memories to be erased, one of the most recent ones, gives a superficial idea: "In his memory, Joel is sitting alone at home waiting for Clementine. When she gets home, dressed for a night out, it is late. She has damaged his car, driving drunk. As the argument heats up, Clementine says, 'Face it, Joely, you're freaked out because I was out late without you, and in your little wormy brain, you're trying to figure out: Did she fuck someone tonight?' Frustrated and stung, he hurts her back, saying, 'Now, see, Clem, I assume you fucked someone tonight. Isn't that how you get people to like you?' This is the last straw for Clementine. Joel chases after her as she runs out, first apologizing, asking her to come back, sensing that he is losing her both in the memory and with his realization that she is being erased from his life. The scenery crashes and disappears. He screams, 'I'm erasing you and I'm happy. You did it to me first.'" In Freudian tradition, Stein recognizes this as a false surface, "a compromise formation" that serves as a defense against a "deeper" source of anxiety and shame. That source needs to be found, and it is to be found earlier that day, when, at the flea market, a happy Clementine says to Joel that she wants to have a baby and Joel responds with the question: "Clem, do you really think you could take care of a kid?" Clementine is severely hurt. This is why they broke up.

Of course, this is not a discovery made by the reviewer, because Kaufman and Gondry designed their script around this problem. The "deeper" source to look for, Stein suggests, is not the argument; neither is it Clementine's irresponsibility. In fact, the pair has broken up over a vicious argument about Joel's fear of starting a family in the first place. Joel is an anxious person, says Stein. Here the characterological symptoms can be found in Joel's confessions, uttered in the train and on the beach: "If only I could meet someone now. I think my chances of that happening are somewhat diminished seeing that I can't make eye contact with a woman that I don't know." "Why do I fall in love with every woman I see who shows me the least bit of attention?" Joel is inhibited, fearful, and needy, and his reaction to Clementine's wish to have a baby, for psychoanalyst Stein, is a further clue that will prove to be closely tied to the source of Joel's insecurity. Joel is afraid to reveal himself. In one of the first memories we see, Clementine tells Joel, "You don't tell me things, Joel. I am an open book. I tell you everything, every damn embarrassing thing." Joel reacts with defensive sarcasm, telling her that "constantly talking isn't necessarily communicating." She takes offense, at the same time pushing him, saying "I want to share things, Joel. That's what intimacy is." He in effect acknowledges the defense, saying, "My life just isn't that interesting."

The "deep" of Joel's conflict is not yet revealed. The process of repression becomes conflicted as Joel becomes aware of the overly loud and intrusive technicians through his sleep. Joel hears the technician who has fallen in love with Clementine talking about it and is startled to hear the technician using his pet name for Clementine, "Tangerine." Apparently stimulated by jealousy and rivalry, Joel moves to memories of intimacy with her. This is also the moment he begins to fight the repression. He enlists the aid of his internal representation of Clementine, the girl constructed from his memories, in his battle with Lacuna, Incorporated together in an attempt to keep ahead of the grim memory editor. Here Stein says to remember another feature of the analytic process. When the psychoanalyst finds himself pulled into a particular emotional issue, it is likely to be an important issue for the psychoanalysis. In this case, the central issue is attachment and loss, and it will prove to be central to our "patient's" character. As Freud stipulated, to get to the sources of this conflict, the psychoanalyst must find a way to childhood memories. In Joel's memories, Clementine suggests that he take his memory of her to places unknown to the memory erasers. Next, we see Joel in various childhood situations while Clementine accompanies him, sometimes as an addition to the memory, at one point playing the role of his babysitter. Baby Joel complains that his mother pays no attention to him. The film presents this subtly, but it gives us a likely source for Joel's insecurity and neediness. The Freudians call the blending of childhood and current memories — here Joel's memories of Clementine into his childhood memories — transference. It is in fact the normal way memories are reconstructed.

For Stein, this transference image in *Eternal Sunshine of the Spotless Mind* has a particular valence. Unlike his mother, he writes, Clementine is caring and attentive. Joel's internal image of her is blending with his childhood memories, with Clementine playing a positive, supportive role. She is becoming a gratifying transference image, a "good" mother. This reminds Stein of Joel's anxious accusation earlier, "Clem, do you really think you could take care of a kid?" And we are at the root of his fear to have a family: his question reflects his fear and anger about his mother's ability to take care of him. "In the process of having Clementine removed from his memory, Joel is also developing a transferent image of her by which she can take care of a kid, better than his own mother, and can undo his childhood fears." Earlier on, we have seen evidence of it in their adult relationship as well, with Clementine leading a frightened Joel out onto the ice where he finds he is very happy. Next, Clementine is with him as he is bullied by a group of small children. Clementine rescues him from this encounter, telling him, "They're not worth it" and reassuring him, "It's O.K., you were a little kid." This is like the process of psychoanalysis, Stein says, uncovering memories with their affect so that they can be reappraised in the light of adult understanding. In his memories, Clementine is now serving as a positive transference figure, helping to guide him through the traumatic memories. When he finally has found her again, and the two lovers force themselves to listen to their angry descriptions of the other, both Joel and Clementine experience a massive reconstruction of repressed material — making them aware of the relationship they have had without being conscious of the actual memories — finding a resolution to the original trauma: Joel now trusts Clementine to have a life with him — with children, no doubt — by accepting her as she is.

Joel and Clementine are not merely reunited, Stein concludes. They have found a way to overcome the angers, fears, and frustrations that caused them to lose one another. It is a happy ending for the viewer who has experienced their loss and their intimacy first hand. And, Joel, the "patient," has benefited from his "analysis." He understands his symptoms, says Stein, and, more importantly, has made gains in dealing with his character. For Stein, Joel is now more mature, able to trust the idea of having a family without being troubled by his frustrations with his own mother. "He has the confidence to enter into a commitment of intimacy without being certain of the outcome. As so often happens, he does all this without being aware of the influence of transference." Reeve has a similar conclusion: it is Joel who changed, who is now ready for a relationship with Clementine. Clementine "already has the sort of heart that Joel, through suffering, must acquire. Capable of intimate disclosure, eager to have children, able to understand that lovers must learn to take the bad with the good, she is already an adult, already aware of what she's like." She tells Joel constantly about this, inside and outside his dream. After the erasure procedure, Joel is indeed able to start afresh. He should be better able to perform, he has "grown," had a "break-through" to an open adult life with Clementine. It is his imaginative dream character Clementine who finally establishes this. In the beach house scene, at the very last moment of the erasure, Clementine comes up with her final suggestion for how to outwit Lacuna: "Meet me in Montauk," she whispers. It is, as we shall see, a whisper from the unconscious — not Freud's dump bin, but one of cognitive psychology.[7]

Were the filmmakers consciously working along Freudian lines? Is Stein's a reliable interpretation? Similar observations were made by authors like Reeve, who do not work from a Freudian perspective. Nevertheless, there is a hint in the film that Kaufman and Gondry know their Freud. Character Mary is surnamed Svevo, no doubt after Italian writer Italo Svevo (Ettore Schmitz, 1861–1928). Svevo is believed to have corresponded with Freud. In line with the idea of the Freudian cure is that Mary unlocks the repressed memories in order to "heal" Lacuna's patients from their suffering.[8] Humans require these memories to lead a normal life, no matter how painful or shameful they may be. In her review in *Screen Education* (2008), Kim Edwards hints at this, arguing that a spotless mind and the idea of eternal sunshine are both images of the "blank" slate, adding the synonyms clear, clean, unblemished, stagnant, and pristine, and the infantilized possibility of as-yet-unrealized potential. She informs us that the film abounds with visual blank slates like Joel's head on the white pillow from the opening scenes, the blank pages of his diary, the white sands and pale washing waves, the snowy landscapes and the ice lake, and, of course, the cold, stark spotlight that follows him and Clementine on their journeys through his mind. For Edwards, the white spaces become symbolic of the Lacuna, Incorporated brainwashing procedure. Next, she leads us through several meanings of lacuna, as they seem to have been used in the film. An anatomical lacuna is a gap or cavity between the tissues of an organism, including those created in the brain as a result of neurological damage. This is what Lacuna, Incorporated does, of course. In the literary sciences, the lacuna may point at a missing portion in a text or narrative. In *Eternal Sunshine of the Spotless Mind,* the lacuna cracks literally appear in Joel's brain, becoming both narrative gaps and a visual tabula rasa. "The word 'lacuna' thus reminds us that such blank spaces are meaningless voids: it is only the act of remembering and writing and experiencing that turns them into something significant." The act of erasing—repression—is violent and disorienting.[9] This is what Lacuna, Incorporated does. For Freud, repression was both necessary and sometimes pathological.

On closer examination, this violent act of erasing with the help of a spotlight hints at something different than the repression of thoughts as the crucial feature of the film. The spotlight in the dream itself empowers Clementine's whisper. This can only be done during a lucid dream. Joel knows he is dreaming; the dream must be lucid. In lucid dreams, critical thinking, dream control, and the sense of being a kind of conscious — the feeling of controlling the "I"— occur together. Lucid dreaming is a normal activity. Surveys show that about half of the people interviewed in the world about it acknowledge to have had at least one lucid dream in their lives. About 20 percent had one a month or more. Small groups consciously trigger such dreams after simple training.[10] Interestingly, Lacuna's staff can trace where "Joel" is by looking at a red dot on a map of his brain. In his lucid dream, Joel experiences this red dot as a spotlight. But most of the time he cannot control it. It is very difficult to establish if dreaming can be defined as a state of consciousness, but researchers have little doubt that lucid dreaming can. Indeed, in *Eternal Sunshine of the Spotless Mind* we see the dream-state pictured as part of consciousness. Reviewer Bert Cardullo writes that "many films have attempted to portray dreams as well as dreamlike memories, but usually they falter because they are either just conventional narratives of the flashback-kind or the very opposite: sets of symbols depicted in soft focus and embedded in surreal, or quasisurreal, imagery." Not this film, he adds, for "*Eternal Sunshine of the Spotless Mind* has the only dream or 'induced-memory' sequence I know that convinces — it is something like traversing a kaleidoscopic nightmare — and that is because of Michel Gondry's virtuosity." In fact, Cardullo concludes, Gondry shows "not only that film is primarily a visual medium, but, more important, that no other artistic medium can capture as well, in motion, serially and cumulatively, the unfettered imagistic workings of the human mind — workings that are beyond, or perhaps above, verbal expression."[11] Especially instructing is Gondry's work to visualize the recent state of the art developments in consciousness studies concerning lucid dreaming, a field populated by psychologists, neuroscientists, biologists, philosophers, and literary theorists.

We know that psychomythology is wrong about dreaming. Dream symbolism, expressed in signs and symbols, operates within an "everyday metaphor system" that structures thought. This system seems to be in line with the conventional modes of thought of a culture or a group. If dreams are culturally informed thoughts, why are thoughts cultural and not individually private? Next to the findings that sleep "cleans" the brain, interpreting the memory of daily experiences, the brain is also confronted with current sensory input, triggering thoughts. During sleep, the brain tries to make sense of this, including, among other things, the firing of motor commands. Sleep blocks them at the spinal level, however. If the brain has no corrective sensory data from the real world, it forms the best, most logical, interpretation about what is going on. It does so with the cultural resources at hand. For this reason, dreams can shed light on a culture's central metaphors. However, after comparing dream reports, another expert concluded that dream-language should be read as a rebus-like derivative of the experiences of the "waking world" and not as a set of metaphors at all. But this, of course, is not the full picture. Sensory inputs like sounds, taste, light, smell, and touch are nothing but sounds, taste, light, smell, and touch. They are first of all transformed into connections in the brain resulting in these 40-Hz. electronic circuits. The connections or circuits involve several specialized parts of the brain that are biologically designed to process and encode sensory inputs. These circuits are built up from the very first sensory experiences of the newborn child and probably as early as the fetal stage. Once a connection is made, it seems to remain permanently in the brain. The thought consists of that connection or circuit and should be seen as a series of brain cells that fire neurons to each other within that particular frequency. The power of this encoding system is enormous.[12]

The unconscious works with all its instruments to serve the conscious mind, precisely the opposite of a haunting unconscious. Dreams are bizarre and difficult to control with logic. They are built up with images, not with language or "like" language, as Lacan thought. These images come from daily experience and their articulations with memory — to clean the brain on double entries or unnecessary memory encoding. Forgetting, as we shall see, not encoding is the rule; and forgetting is not the same as repression. In addition, due to all these features, dreams are highly personal. They do not contain some general human dream symbols. These characteristics of dreams make filming them extremely difficult. Transposing these images into logical narratives, as filmmakers usually try to do, can never be more than tentative. Even filmmaker David Lynch, who is thought to film dreamscapes, for instance, in his features *Mulholland Dr.* (2001) and *Inland Empire* (2006), has stylized the stream of images in his films too much. Although it is difficult, these films can be re-told. In fact, there seems no other way. Kaufman and Gondry, like all filmmakers, need an audience for their film; *Eternal Sunshine of the Spotless Mind* is a story, not a true stream of images of Joel's dream. They have to build logic into it. For this purpose, they have chosen for the Freudian Excuse Joel's childhood problems with his mother. Contrary to what Stein thinks, Kaufman and Gondry used the Freudian Excuse to anchor an argument about the impossibility of repression. What they demonstrate with Joel's dream, however, is the complete openness to consciousness.

## 4

Before diving into this openness, a discussion of the second film of this chapter, *Drama* (2010) by Chilean helmer Matías Lira, may be helpful. Lira's film is an actors' film. Motivated by the techniques of the Theater of Cruelty, invented by Antonin Artaud (1896–1948) on Freudian foundations, Lira shows the experiments of three students of a theater school of a university in Santiago de Chile. Their experiments are part of an assignment to act from-the-inside-out, to use their traumas and desires from the "subconscious" for their stage performances. The students' teacher (played by Jaime McManus) says: "We're finding the truth, or at least we're close. This is Artaud, the artaudian technique. A real reaction, that's what we're looking for. To find the true 'I' that is what Artaud proposes. Rediscover the side that is connected to pain and suffering." The first assignment was: "The crime scene must be invoked. From this day on, you should experiment with yourself, so go out on the street, outside, to look for your truth, and tomorrow you'll go on stage with the experience you live today." The second assignment was: "For the next class, I want you to look into your heritage, your traumas. Replay the crime scene. Don't resist wanting to find the truth. Absorb the body and soul of a character that provokes you. Let him show you who you really are or want to be." The third: "The next exercise consists in copying the soul. Try to find a state of extreme commotion. Get lost in the reality, let your senses talk ... and let the gesture grab on to the subconscious ... and let the skin allow for every movement." This "technique" has a lot in common with Freud's — spontaneously digging "deep" into the "subconscious" — and a psychoanalyst might recognize the resemblances with *Eternal Sunshine of the Spotless Mind* as a filmed psychoanalytical session. The theme of the film came from Lira's own heart — he was educated this way. As could be expected, the only "truth" is believed to be found in the "subconscious." Curiously, what he said the assignments needed to teach the students was that they could wish or desire to be the best actors in the world and that they could go "deep" for it, but that in the end they needed to focus on their own psychological and physical health. They needed to know their limits and "act." Actors do not need to live to the edge in order to be successful. In this sense, Lira eventually dissociates himself from Artaud's principles.[13]

The heart of the film is focused on the nightlife of Santiago de Chile; its clubs and vacant sites where prostitution, artistic expression, censorship, and intolerance dwell. The three inexperienced students who seem to get to know this world for the first time are Mateo (Eusebio Arenas), María (Isidora Urrejola), and Ángel (Diego Ruiz). Mateo is the informal leader of the pack. He manipulates the others constantly, trying to find intimacy in their friendship but at the same time creating a distance when the two others come too close. María is his girlfriend, but he also has sex with another actress — the one playing his mother in an open-air stage performance. María seems rather successful with the first assignment but she denies this by acknowledging that she merely "exaggerated." Her performance had not been "real." Ángel is a friend who plays a queer role, who is obviously in love with Mateo but says he is not. Mateo decides to play the role of a drug dealer — he follows one actively — but ends up "discovering" a hidden history from the military dictatorship of General Augusto Pinochet (1915–2006; junta leader, 1973; president, 1974–90). He represents the void caused by the disappearance of his mother, who was arrested back stage after playing *Romeo and Juliet*. He blames his father for staying passive and actively puts him in a negative spotlight during the performance. One may have the idea that the assignments of his teacher "uncovered" a repressed trauma, but the images of his childhood are present in the film from the very beginning, even before the first assignment. In fact, we see an "open" memory, not one dumped in the "subconscious."

After seeing Mateo having sex with the other actress, María feels rejected and perseveres stronger than before in staging a prostitute. Her fascination with prostitution or paid sex brings her into a relationship with a rather dangerous underworld character — and indeed gets paid for her services. Ángel tries to flatter Mateo by playing a male prostitute, and is also invited by a client. However, watched by Mateo, he escapes with his friend before the actual deed. There is no indication that the two bring up something "unknown" from their "subconscious." From the beginning, Lira shows the viewer that María has had some peculiar sexual experiences involving strangulations and that Ángel knows he is gay. What they all found on the street, while searching for "real emotions," was something they had been preoccupied with for a much longer time in their lives. They were only prepared to carry it to the limits — and beyond. Their obsession with becoming better actors had led them to their darkest sides, surpassing boundaries that neither they nor their teacher could have ever imagined. Eventually, playing consciously and openly with their memory, the three found themselves through performance. In short, the performance in *Drama* has little to do with Artaud's Freudian inspiration, perhaps only with his techniques. This is not difficult to understand. The brain is open to all memory because of its open circuitry of connections.

# 5

To answer Freudian critics like Stein, we need to understand the unconscious as a dynamic activity: it is what we call "thinking." Where Stein sees repression — dumping thoughts in a closed part of the brain — academic psychologists see thoughts actively moving through the brain freely, without such hindrance. The three characters of *Drama* and the protagonist of *Eternal Sunshine of the Spotless Mind* demonstrate by their actions that they have access to all their fresh and recorded thoughts. Through a coherent collection of neural patterns thinking articulates "consciousness" and the "unconscious." One basic collection maps, moment by moment, the state of the physical structure of the organism across multiple dimensions. This is usually referred to as the *Proto-Self*. As experience increases, more and more circuits are installed in the brain. Because most experiences in childhood and adolescence are new, and the brain is still maturing—the brain at birth is less than half its mature size—the production of brain cells and new circuits goes hand in hand. The cells grow automatically, of course, but if no connections are made within some circuit of experience, they soon die off. This feature, almost absent in the non-human animal world, has led biologists, psychologists, and philosophers to conclude that the growing brain stores all new experiences physically, and vice versa. The brain is a physical unit of experience for more than half of its cells. And history is involved. The wiring of the brain, a sophisticated and exquisitely engineered device, is the result of evolution, including learned responses to specific stimuli, inherited over the generations. This means that culture (e.g., learned responses) is eventually rooted in genetics or the biology of the womb (the development after conception). The psychologist Steven Pinker traces the design through the millennial history of survival, as if the brain is shaped by the problems our ancestors faced in dealing with the world, his hypothesis goes. All this is true both before birth and in subsequent development with the fabrication of new connections. Therefore, each cell of the human body came to specialize in a particular function according to instructions encoded in its DNA, its developmental history from pre-history onwards, and chemical influences from other tissues.[14]

The emotions are attached to this articulation of translated and interpreted sensory inputs. In fact, no thought is without an emotional link in the circuit. LeDoux argues that the amygdala in the brain seems to arrange emotional memory of fear by adding feelings derived from experiences at every cognitive occurrence. No circuit seems to develop or thought to be made without the involvement of emotions. Large parts of the brain, as is true for other physical organs of the body, were pre-designed to encode specific sensory inputs, to control the eyes, the tongue, the ears, nose, and other sensors, to control hands and feet, reasoning, language, and so forth. Most species in the animal kingdom have neurons and neurotransmitters, but each one works with its own variety to develop its cognitive and emotional capacities. During the evolution of thousands of years, hundreds of millions of neurons in the human brain found specific ways for the production of specific connections. As Nico Frijda sums up from years of international research, the emotions and strong passions were included in this evolutionary process of problem-solving and survival. LeDoux makes clear that there is no single emotion system but many, each of which evolved for a different functional purpose and each of which gives rise to a different kind of emotion. Each part of the memory system contains emotions as well as interpretations and consciously developed experiences. Most of these emotions, or rather their bodily expressions and consequences, are consciously felt because the brain interprets them in connection with received inputs from the sensory system. It develops a "discourse of emotions" directly linked to specific feelings.[15]

Emotions typically occur when a person perceives positive or negative changes in his or her personal situation or that of related others. According to Damasio such perceived changes occur constantly, without interruption, forming the rule rather than the exception. All these emotions can be engaged automatically, without conscious deliberation, and they use the entire body as their instrument. People all over the world share a fundamental stereotypic, automatic, and regulatory purpose of the emotions, despite individual and cultural variation in shaping some inducers. In addition, a group of psychologists around Paul Thagard clearly demonstrated that emotions were involved in the decision-making process. Without emotions people would endlessly examine all the logical possibilities without reaching a decision. Only with the help of emotions are people able to cut the knot. Thagard and his collaborators propose a "coherence theory of decision-making" in which the decision-making process strives for coherence by weighing up the emotional impact. With the help of the emotions linked to experiences, the assessing and ordering of various competing actions and goals is made easier. Emotions influence the cognitive mechanisms that define goal states and choice of goals in a planning process. This can be very basic. Vindictiveness, a specialized subcategory of anger, may define "injuring the offending party" as its goal state. The motivational priority chosen by the emotion programs make this goal state satisfying in some situations but extremely unpleasant in others. The choices that eventually are made are those that are most consistent with currently held goals. Therefore, a decision can be described as an inference to the best plan where the desirability of previously formulated goals is determined by deliberative coherence. Motivation and affect color all decision making. They come from several different inputs, such as attitudes, beliefs, self-perceptions, accuracy, and, of course, coherence as a goal in itself. It is good to repeat what Kunda recently wrote: directional goals — the motivation to draw a particular conclusion — are reasons in themselves for coming to a decision. Humans are particularly likely to access those beliefs and rules that support their desired conclusions. And moods influence decisions because they bring to mind mood-congruent material relevant to judgment.[16]

At a 40-Hz performance, almost every brain cell is involved in several circuits, constantly ticking at a steady speed of three or four spikes a second. These spikes bouncing around the brain's connections must maintain it at a certain level of tone, giving each new input something to disturb. But it should be made clear that there is no single point of orchestration into which all the information is channeled and redistributed. Referring to this as "computing" may be confusing because the system is dynamic.[17] Where the architecture of the brain accepts parallel inputs from different parts of the sensory domain of the organism and sets up patterns of excitation in higher levels of the system, a huge interpretative process attaches meaning to it. The mind cannot transform sensory inputs into meaning directed toward behavior, without a conceptualization of that behavior and therefore, of the world at large. This is the reason why lucid dreams develop into lively memories of some actions. Sensory processing areas of the cortex part of the brain receive inputs about external events and create a type of perceptual representation of the stimuli. These representations are also referred to as "images," although they are nothing but electronic circuits combining information from sensory, bodily inputs and from memory; they are not "pictures." In humans, this can be transformed into language — but should not automatically be — which means the creation of a narrative, but its basic step refers to images or representations, as they are sometimes called. These images/representations are then channeled through the cortical regions and the hippocampus. The hippocampus communicates back to the surrounding regions and then with the neocortex. The information is stored in the hippocampus for a few years, but if little use is made of it, it gradually relinquishes control over this part of memory to the neocortex, where it remains possibly for a lifetime although usually out of daily use. Not repressed, not fully forgotten, simply stored far away from daily synapses.[18]

The images/representations and narratives are used to build theories about the world, including the Self. These theories are formulated and constantly reformulated from early childhood onwards in a fluid, accumulative process not guided by dialectics. All humans try to fit their thoughts based on experience to such theories. As this process seems to follow the pace of the expansion of the physical brain, it suggests that theories of the surrounding world in which we live are included as physical units of the brain. Bit by bit the sense of self is increased into a sense of *knowing* about self. This is the knowledge of our body and our experiences, our being in space and time. The explicit memory system is processed unconsciously — out-of-consciousness — through the hippocampus and consciously through an awareness of stored knowledge or personal experiences. The outcome is the expression of emotional responses, in general defensive for survival. However, humans, also in the non–West, usually experience both. They are conscious of an emotional arousal and consciously combine this with explicit learned memories of past situations of similar arousal. In this way, new explicit memories that are formed about past memories can also acquire emotional coloration, be it positive or negative. This is why talking about emotions can reduce the negative effects of feelings. During therapy a different, less frightening discourse is constructed to account for them. It does not mean that conscious retrieval of emotional memory is "authentic." Psychologists made crystal clear that people's memories of their past emotions are not very stable. In accounting for biases in emotional recall, changing appraisals can be attributed to a partial reconstruction or inference of the emotions on the basis of current appraisals of events. The organism tends to neutralize the negative evaluation in such a way that it is rarely recorded as it actually was. Autobiographical events associated with intense emotion and personal significance are generally, though not always, remembered more accurately or vividly than less personally significant events. The present moment biases memory retrieval. Shortly after a negative evaluation has subsided, counteracting processes start to reverse, minimize, or undo the initial response. Only if the present situation somehow requires the continuity of the intensive emotions, will the emotion be retrieved later in the same way although still colored by the present emotional state. The mind responds to negative events with *short-term mobilization,* says Shelley Taylor, but soon afterwards with *long-term minimization.* In short, "experience" governs retrieval and subsequent storage.[19]

# 6

Nevertheless, in *Eternal Sunshine of the Spotless Mind,* consciousness is cut off from specific parts of the unconscious. By showing this on screen, the film acknowledges that, first, the brain is open to its farthest corners, and, second, that the erased memories are dumped into some sort of wastebasket, but, indeed, erased forever. This is not repression. With the help of the ancient expressive metaphor of the mind as theater, neurobiologist Bernard Baars has developed a model of human thinking.[20] In reality, it is a model of consciousness, called Global Workspace Theory or GWT — scholars are more interested in consciousness these days than in the unconscious. According to GWT, consciousness is a spotlight on the stage of the theater of the mind. In fact, conscious contents of the brain are limited to a brightly lit spot of attention on stage only. The rest of the stage remains in the dark. The stage is working memory, which is constantly active during specific actions. The diegesis of a film shows the stage of the theater. The character on the screen is the one who has attracted the spotlight of consciousness of the viewers of the film. In GWT, next to the stage with its working memory players and the player in the spotlight, the theater is filled up with a very interactive audience. This image in particular contrasts Freudian thinking. The audience is constantly in connection and dialogue with the actors on stage and is not working unseen by the players, haunting their actions. The GWT posits an active audience, openly intervening or reiterating comments and suggestions to the players on stages. The audience is what popularly would be called the unconscious. It ventures goals and knowledge out loud; perhaps so close to the stage that we may speak of a subconscious automatic level.

The theater of the mind provides accommodation for many unconscious contributors. For example, there is a kind of director. There is the perceptual input from the senses to guide the players on stage. Most of the audience members are unconscious mechanisms like automatic routines and rarely, if ever, enter the stage. They are specialists though, guiding eye movements, dealing with speech, or hand and finger movements. Another group there operates autobiographical memory. There is a group managing the semantic networks that represent knowledge of the world. Next we find declarative memory for beliefs and facts. The audience members involved in implicit memory maintain social interaction, skills, and attitude schemas. From the context-data, players, audience and director try to answer the question of the Proto-Self: "What's happening to me?" Activities behind the scenes of the theater concentrate on executive processes. The director would be found there, leading a large number of context operators. They shape conscious experience but keep themselves out of the spotlight. They remain in the "dark," because contrary to the access to information structures in the brain, the information-carrying capacity of the conscious stream is limited. Within split-seconds, the brain has access to any of its required stored past experiences — real, imagined, or fictional. Hence the idea that the brain functions like a loom, as Reeve says,[21] weaving experiences into one another, and that "unweaving" is very difficult indeed in order to erase all traces of an experience. This is also the problem with Freud's repression: you cannot isolate or privilege specific parts of an experience in order to repress it and keep the other parts intact.

Every action in the theater of the mind is directed toward attracting the spotlight. Some players on the stage are in contact with networks of members in the audience; other players with other parts of the audience. They fight each other to position "their" actor into the spotlight. The idea is to prompt the actor with adequate scripts and other schemas for action. The spotlight goes over the stage of the theater of the mind. Studies of macaque brains indicate that the stage of Baars' GWT can be limited to the inferotemporal cortex and the superior temporal sulcus of the brain, where strong convergence of conscious visual-object information was recorded. Almost all the visual neurons in these areas responded differentially to the conscious flow in a binocular rivalry task, but not to the unconscious flow. Lower visual levels show low response rates to both conscious and unconscious rivaling input. However, even this makes the stage not a truly fixed place yet, as we can see in *Eternal*

*Sunshine of the Spotless Mind.* Joel runs over the stage — e.g. through the diegesis of the film — inside the spotlight thereby creating the "stage" under his feet. In *Drama,* the spotlight is the camera itself, following the actors leaving the stage and going into the world of Santiago de Chile looking for signs that activate their memories. The city becomes the stage of the mind. The brain is not a Cartesian theater, with a center point where all sensory input converges, like the pineal gland in Descartes's view of the brain. The only limit is the brain itself. Most current proposals about the workings of the brain involve "binding" of neurons and circuits, "convergence zones" also called "working memories" as a kind of stage for the integration of conscious input.[22]

Consciousness, says Baars, although limited in capacity at any single moment, does appear to offer a gateway to extensive unconscious knowledge sources in the brain. There is much behavioral evidence for this claim. Biofeedback control of single neurons and populations of neurons almost anywhere in the brain is well established. For example, the ability to access unconscious knowledge via consciousness applies to the vast number of automatisms that can be triggered by conscious events, including the automatic inner speech that often accompanies reading; automatic inferences in social judgments; and the automatic transformations of visual patterns on this page into letters, words, and phrases. Triggered by conscious events, none of these automatisms are conscious in any detail. No one is conscious about the group of vocal-tract muscles that are used to speak or sing. Nevertheless, most people feel that they consciously control a wide variety of parameters. In fact, conscious feedback — from the actor in the spotlight into the crowded hall — seems to give access to skeletal muscles and autonomic musculature in a rather spectacular way. Consider autobiographical memory, Baars advises us, which is believed to involve the hippocampus. The size of long-term episodic memory is unknown. But after a week we are able to spontaneously recognize almost every picture out of a series of 10,000 pictures we saw over several days, without conscious attempts to memorize them. When we use recognition probes other remarkable results can be recorded, like asking people to choose between known and new pictures. These probes appear to work because they reinstate the original conscious experience of each picture. With seemingly little effort, the brain does a remarkable job retrieving this amount of pictures from memory.

Understanding words seems to require the gateway of consciousness. "Conscious exposure to any printed word on this page is sufficient to access its meaning, syntactic role, inner speech phonology, emotional connotations, semantic and sound associates and imagery components, and to trigger automatic inferences," says Baars. Think of the vocabulary of educated English speakers, which contains about 100,000 words. Although they do not use all these words in everyday speech, they can understand them. Each vocabulary item is already quite complex. The *Oxford English Dictionary*, for example, has about 75,000 words dedicated to the meanings of the single word "set," but all we need to access such complex unconscious domains of knowledge is to become conscious of the word. It seems that humans create memories from the stream of perceptual input merely by paying attention, but because we are always paying attention to something, this suggests that autobiographical memory could be very large indeed. Mere consciousness of some event appears to help store a recognizable memory of it, and when we experience it again, we can distinguish it accurately from millions of other conscious experiences; both episodic storage and retrieval seem to require consciousness. The triggering function is hampered when conscious input is degraded by distraction, fatigue, somnolence, sedation, or low signal fidelity.

# 7

*Eternal Sunshine of the Spotless Mind* shows us the destruction of the network the actor in the spotlight — Joel — maintains with the members in the audience who have knowledge of Clementine. But, only this network is destroyed; not the audience itself. There are empty seats, so to speak, but the neighbors of the former "Clementine members" still have knowledge of Clementine-related actions. This means that audience members roughly connected to Clementine-informed-schemas can inform other actors on stage to attract attention and stimulate the body to go to Montauk. When that suggestion reached the actor in the spotlight, a new memory is created: the whispering Clementine. This phenomenon is known among psychologists researching sleep and dreams as the resolutive quality of dreams. If difficult problems are taken to bed, chances are that during sleep, because of these resolutive qualities, the sleeper awakes with a solution. The "meet me at Montauk" solution brought both Clementine and Joel together again, precisely what they wanted. Joel probably has no fear of having a family with Clementine because he believes that she would be a bad mother. No, his fear is to bond to her. He does not want to compromise. Joel fights Lacuna not only because he encounters love in his memories but also because he hears the technician in his room talking about Clementine. Jealousy makes him want to wake up from his lucid dream and reestablish contact with Clementine. Joel's actions in his lucid dreams suggest that he could go anywhere he wished, including taking Clementine to areas where she has had no part in, like his youth.

Memory in the characters of *Eternal Sunshine of the Spotless Mind* and *Drama* is built according to modern psychological insights. In *Drama,* the actors are looking for signs for both the characters and the audience to run simulations about the workings of the mind and discover cause and consequence relations that are closer to reality than Freud's. Kaufman and Gondry can simulate the dreaming process thanks to new knowledge of the workings of the brain. Over the past few decades, cognitive psychologists have been busy designing a mind different from the Freudian in architecture, in its workings and emotional dominance, that also found its way into the simulations fed by popular psychology. We realize that memory retrieval is a reconstruction made of information at hand. This is shown to us in *Drama*. Every memory is a blending of old and new information — and then stored in the most recent form. This has nothing to do with "transference." The new popular psychology of *Eternal Sunshine of the Spotless Mind* and *Drama* teaches us that it is better to remember, mourn, and honor personal loss, than to "repress" and thus to remain in ignorance of pain and earlier experienced happiness. In all, both films discussed in this chapter seemingly introduce the Freudian Excuse of the power of repression — and even look like filmed versions of the psychoanalytical technique — but on closer examination represent modern cognitive insights. We all know, and do not need Freud to inform us, that without awareness of the past, history is doomed to repeat itself. It also teaches us that we have to deal with our inner demons of the past by confronting them. This is very old knowledge, known long before Freud was born.

# 7

## *Melinda's Silence*

### Conceptual Metaphor in *Speak* (2004) and *Cosas Insignificantes* (2008)

Jessica Sharzer (writer and director); and
Andrea Martínez (writer and director)

## 1

It is the end of school; the students are cleaning their stuff from the classrooms and their lockers. We are in an abandoned janitor's closet where freshman Melinda Sordino (Kristen Stewart), barely 15 years old, has found some refuge and exposed her drawings of trees on the walls. She shows the trees to her free-spirited art teacher Mr. Freeman (Steve Zahn). Seeing them, his eyes fill up with tears of wonder and admiration: "They are very good." Almost for the first time in the film, we see Melinda smile. Shortly after Mr. Freeman has left, Andy Evans (Eric Lively) rushes into the closet. A moment earlier, Andy had been dumped by his girlfriend Rachel Bruin (Hallee Hirsh), Melinda's former best friend. Melinda had told Rachel that he had raped her at the end of last year. Andy is angry and confronts Melinda. "So, I raped you? I could have any girl in this school, if I wanted. Without forcing. Why would I rape you? You are not even attractive." The threatening becomes a beating, and it seems he moves to rape her again. Apparently, Rachel had informed the girls, perhaps the entire school, of Andy's earlier assault for now he yells at Melinda: "Go tell all the people of this school that you lied!" In fear, the girl fights back, screaming. She manages to beat him, splashing aerosol chemicals into his eyes. This blinds him, perhaps forever. The girls' field hockey team, including another of Melinda's former friends, Nicole (Tyanna Rolley), happens to walk by the closet and notices the commotion that is going on inside. They open the door and immediately defend her. Seeing that Melinda has overpowered Andy, Nicole confronts him: "Everyone knows what you did." Melinda's ordeal is over. In the car back home, sitting next to her mother Joyce (Elizabeth Perkins), she explains her hospital visit — where she was treated for her injuries — and finally finds the words to speak about the rape.

# 2

This is the final scene of *Speak* (2004), an American independent movie directed and partly written by Jessica Sharzer. The film is based on the novel with the same name by Laurie Halse Anderson, published in 1999. The book was a bestseller and won the Printz Honour Award. Most reviewers celebrate Kristen Stewart's performance in this film. Her non-verbal acting, communicating in very few words and mainly relying upon her face and body language, is acknowledged as impressive. This is nicely offset by the voiceover narration. The girl's blank face and her soulless eyes reflect the pain she is going through with gut-wrenching accuracy. The filmmaker opts for close-ups of her eyes and face to convey Melinda's sense of defeat and fear to the viewers. The choice is not random, because victims of rape are often much too hurt and full of shame to talk about the horrible event. When the pain gets trapped too much inside, the victims may suffer from severe bouts of depression. Furthermore, the viewers see Melinda's ordeal in flashbacks spread out over the film. Melinda is still a child, of course, and the filmmaker shows us the worst time of her life. She needs someone to get her through this, but she does not know how to find that someone. However, when she realizes that she cannot hide any longer, that she cannot run away from speaking, her struggle changes into a story of finding herself and facing her fears.[1]

What happened? A few weeks before her freshman year of high school, Melinda Sordino and her friends from 8th grade, including Rachel, were invited to a high school party at Kyle Rodger's house; he is the brother of Randi Rodger (Caitlyn Folley). There, Melinda met Andy Evans. He took her to his car and raped her. Afterwards she wandered through the house and the partying kids with the intent to call 911. In despair, however, she immediately left the house. The police broke up the party for underage drinking, arresting some of the kids. Numb and alone, Melinda walked miles home to an empty house. The film itself begins a few months later, when Melinda starts her freshman year at Merryweather High School. Because Melinda is psychologically unable to speak about the rape, the other students blame her for calling the cops. At the beginning of the year, Melinda had been nice to a new student, named Heather Billings (Allison Siko). Heather claims to be her friend but after a few weeks, realizing that Melinda is a kind of black sheep, she goes her own way. Melinda is particularly shunned by her friends, Rachel, Nicole, and Ivy (Megan Pillar), and is forced to deal with social rejection on top of her depression. The rape caused so much trauma that she cannot find the words to inform her parents either. She chooses to keep silent. In the first part of the film, she wonders (in a voiceover): "I wonder how long it will take [them] to realize that I stopped talking." But the choice is not of her own free will, because every time she wants to speak about it, her tongue freezes up. When she wants to inform a former friend we hear say to herself: "Ivy has been nice. Say something. My throat is dry, it hurts." For most of the time Melinda walks speedily through the halls of the school buildings. She holds her books tight to her chest, hoping that the seniors would not knock them away. One moment, the filmmaker shows us Melinda thinking about her childhood while smelling an apple: this girl is "swept from paradise," as young as she is.

Curiously Melinda's teachers seem to look much like her. For example, her English teacher (Leslie Lyles), nicknamed "Hair Woman," cannot make eye contact with anyone in class. The biology teacher, Ms. Keen (Kimberly Kish), also has difficulty communicating with students. The history teacher Mr. Neck (Robert John Burke), however, bullies Melinda constantly. One student has no problem talking to Melinda, her lab partner Dave Petrakis (Michael Angarano). Of course, he is a loner. He also kept his distance from some clique. During the year, Melinda's grades are plummeting. Her parents notice the change in their daughter, but they are unable to determine the cause. As Melinda's depression worsens, she begins to skip school, withdraws from home, and aspires to do nothing more than take a nap. After being informed about the bad grades, her parents prompt her to improve, at least the history grades. Mr. Neck assigns her an extra history essay. Melinda has no problem writing something valuable, but she fails to read the essay aloud to her class and Mr. Neck sends her to the school principal (Tony Roseboro). An important scene shows us Christmas morning. Her mother has been overworked all the time and cannot find words of her own to open her daughter up. Her father Jack (D.B. Sweeney) is unemployed, struggling to get a job. To her pleasant surprise, Melinda's major present consists of art supplies. Without speaking, she conveys her emotions. Her parents were actually aware that she was drawing! But the situation peters out quickly when they start a conversation about a stereo system. This triggers a flashback of their absence when she returned home in despair from the party. Even Christmas reminds Melinda of the rape.

It must be half-way through the year at high school when Melinda creates her personal place of refuge. The makeshift hideaway in the abandoned janitor's closet is eventually one of revelation. There, she hides when she is feeling anxious or sleeps during the day. There, she constantly thinks about the night of the party, and deals with her inner demons. There is a direct connection to her other solace, Mr. Freeman's art class. She may spend her lunchtime in his classroom and he stimulates her to express her inner struggles. Melinda feels encouraged to turn her depression and despair into works of art, both during class and in her hideaway. In fact, Mr. Freeman finds a way to translate this into words she needs to hear. One piece is particularly important. She made it with turkey bones and a little plastic palm tree she found in the classroom. She is seated near her little gem as Mr. Freeman and her former friend Ivy come close to look at it. Ivy reacts with surprise: "It's scary!" Not like clowns, she adds, but scary nonetheless. Mr. Freeman falls silent in admiration. Then he says: "This is excellent." And he realizes he must give an interpretation. "I see a girl trapped in a vacation that went wrong," Mr. Freeman begins. "Her meat is torn every day. The palm tree, perhaps a dream shattered.... I do not know, but it has a meaning. Pain." The camera is static as they discuss the project this way. But when Mr. Freeman says the word "pain," the filmmaker cuts to a tight reaction shot of Melinda's face as she registers the word. Her eyes look up at him in surprise. The viewers of the film are shown not just that he is picking up on her pain from the symbolism in her art work, but more importantly that she now realizes there is someone who understands her non-verbal communication and is interested in her well-being. This is a turning point. Melinda realizes at that one moment Mr. Freeman has to see the drawings that decorate her hideaway.

From that moment on, Melinda definitely wants her voice back. She needs to talk about the rape with someone — anybody. The second catalyst presents itself when she understands that her former best friend Rachel is dating Andy, the rapist. This cannot be! She must warn Rachel — which is almost impossible, because since the party disaster they treat each other as enemies. Melinda forces her rejuvenation to take off during an impromptu hospital visit. That day she skips school and takes a bus through the city. There, we learn from her voiceover that she is now convinced that she needs a breakthrough: "I should count on someone, anyone." It could be the nurse she follows from the bus to the hospital, but she puts herself to rest on an empty bed instead: "It is hard to sleep at home. How long would it take for these nurses to realize that I am here? Does that make me rest for a few days?" In a voiceover we hear her reflecting upon the change: "It happened. There's no avoiding it. No forgetting." Repression is impossible. At home, strong again, finding her voice back, she dumps Heather, plays a killer set of tennis, and bicycles to the scene of last summer's party where she confronts what happened to her. It seems, the tree that inspired her painting also helps tie everything together. Now she decides to tell Rachel. Her friend is at the library and still waving her aside. But Melinda insists so much that Rachel eventually gives in. Still unable to speak the crucial words, Melinda finds the strength to write them on paper: "I was raped." Outside, the two talk. At first Rachel doesn't believe her, and calls Melinda jealous. Eventually, she confronts Andy. Melinda is right. Soon, word gets out, which brings us to the final scene, described above.

# 3

A similar hideaway closet for refuge and eventual revelation was made by the protagonist of Andrea Martínez's little jewel *Cosas insignificantes* (2008). Again, in this film the main characters also struggle with a psychological blockade and cannot express their feelings to others, thereby running the risk of losing contact with their loved ones. Finally, revelation comes from outside as well, not by rape but by some magical dispensation: Popocatepetl Volcano covers Mexico City with a snow-like layer of volcanic ashes. The "snow" returns the power of the protagonists to take life into their own hands again by re-bonding with their loved ones because they now can "see" how to do this. For principal character Esmeralda (Paulina Gaitán), seemingly insignificant artifacts are the keys to organize her own world within Mexico City. These insignificant things she finds or steals from others include objects like a note, a paper arrow, and an origami seahorse. Because she finds them cast aside and scattered in the streets of Mexico City, the objects symbolize the lost opportunities of their former owners. Esmeralda keeps them in a hidden, locked case, a little shrine to the mundane and a sanctuary from her pressured and crowded life. Life in Mexico City is difficult, and due to the activities of the Popocatepetl Volcano, the city could be damaged or even partially destroyed. This sense of impending doom is emphasized by radio reports heard during the film. It is crucial that Esmeralda suffers from severe migraine attacks and sometimes sits suffering and crying on the street. She finds refuge in her objects, without knowing the mystery behind them, trying to establish why Mexico City causes her migraines. Hence, from the beginning there is a kind of sad feel to the atmosphere on the screen. This film unfolds as the stories of three of the items behind Esmeralda's finds are revealed in a series of connected and touching vignettes. It is the wonder and mystery of the movie's storytelling vehicle by artifact: these insignificant things carry heavily important stories with them, which tell us about human bonding and its crucial problems — not unlike the theme of *Eternal Sunshine of the Spotless Mind*. The artifacts have the same function as in Gondry's film: triggering stories.[2]

Despite the inconceivable enormity of the city, the filmmaker has introduced us to a series of four small worlds in which the characters live. Each story covers loss, love, fear, and betrayal. These are common themes for a film, but within *Cosas insignificantes* they take on an all-encompassing feel. It is in the balance between these stories that the film achieves its most impressive feat. The viewer comes to know a group of characters that, although somewhat flawed, are all convincing and worth exploring and remembering further. A small piece of paper introduces us to the story of a psychotherapist (Fernando Luján), who longs to speak once more with his estranged daughter. The note reads "Inés" and a telephone number. It was given to him by his ex-wife, who visited him for the first time in 20 years. The daughter had left her parents' home early in her life. She now lives in Aguascalientes, a city a few hours west of the capital. The psychotherapist calls her, only to find out that she has no interest in reestablishing contact with her father. Second, we meet pediatrician Iván (Carmelo Gómez), who must balance personal problems with the sexual desires of his devoted lover. He cannot make love to her because he finds out he has a son with a former lover. The boy suffers from leukemia and Iván, who is both his father and his physician, worries about his health. His object Esmeralda has found is a little orgami seahorse, which for her is a reminder of her work in a Chinese restaurant but for him a reminder of his love for his girlfriend — she has an aquarium with seahorses. Third, tortured mother Paola (Bárbara Mori), a wealthy woman, takes over the screen. It is her son Diego, aka Vaquerito, who is diagnosed with leukemia. He loses his hair. Because of the illness, her world also collapses. She decides to find help from the psychotherapist we met in the first story.

Near the end of the film, on the lowest point of the protagonists' histories, the fairytale snowy ash rain detonates the characters' change of heart for the better. Esmerelda has to care for her little sister Lina and her mentally sick grandmother Fani. They are migrants from the Amerindian Otomí region to the west of Mexico City. There is no mention of Esmeralda's parents, or what may have happened to them. The grandmother wanders within her own mind most of the time. She is nearly blind but hopes to one day see the volcanoes surrounding the city. She seems obsessed with an old tale, representing Popocatepetl as a sad warrior, waiting for his lover to awake, the Ixtaccihuatl Volcano next to Popocatepetl. Ixtaccihuatl is a little princess that is in a "Sleeping Beauty" sleep. The film suggests that Esmeralda might be the princess's reincarnation. A picture of a sunset behind Ixtaccihuatl passes through the screen frequently, especially when one of the protagonists is in despair. It seems, interpreting the film this way, that it is Esmeralda who needs to be awakened to rescue the others — and herself. Looking for "snow" to cure her migraines — she heard of this solution earlier in the film — Esmeralda accepts an invitation by her two brothers to join them in Canada. She has some tough decisions to make and she handles them with maturity and compassion. However, the "snow" catches up with her just in time. Popocatepetl's ash rain awakens her and transfers this power to the objects in the case, thereby immediately improving the fate of the people involved in the stories behind the artifacts. They all came to see what actions are needed to solve their problems. This renders Esmeralda's case unnecessary and Esmeralda gives it to the psychotherapist with the assignment to call his daughter, which he does — and with good result because the daughter has also opened her heart after seeing the "snow" over Mexico City. Pediatrician Iván tells his lover about his son, and she forgives him. And thirdly, Paola reconnects symbolically with her suffering son by cutting her hair and bonding in baldness. And the box-keeper herself concludes that she could not leave her little sister and her blind grandmother behind. As in *Eternal Sunshine of the Spotless Mind*, the viewers come out of a screening of *Cosas insignificantes* with optimism and hope. They feel that the characters will be all right and life will work out for them. And, of course, there are the occasional extraordinary takes of a Mexico City that rarely has been portrayed as so beautiful and yet so dramatic.

# 4

Both *Speak* and *Cosas insignificantes* confront us with a play of metaphors: opening your heart as if the heart is a house, and empowerment through seeing as if the eyes provide control. Or, we can see it another way: in *Speak*, Melinda blinds Andy to make him impotent. Note the image here, because we are not dealing with the Freudian Excuse of the penis but with the scrotum. The eyes as balls are an image much older than the Viennese psychoanalyst's ideas about the phallus. For one recent author, Gary Taylor, psychoanalysis reflects the Rise of the Penis in Western culture, accompanied by the corresponding Fall of the Scrotum, which means that reproduction has steadily ceded the floor to pleasure.[3] We may wonder if Freud was aware of the difference. It could be another misconception. He knew nothing of conceptual metaphor as a phenomenon in its own right and he is not to blame for this because the Theory of Conceptual Metaphor is recent. The theory owes much to the work of George Lakoff and his collaborators, including linguists Mark Johnson and Mark Turner in the late 1980s, and, more recently, Rafael Núñez. "We may not always know it, but we think in metaphor," Lakoff wrote at the time. Metaphor is not a purely linguistic construction. Cognition is vitally dependent on metaphor. Reasoning is not abstract but physical and does not fit the world as it is, but it does so via conceptual metaphors and cognitive cultural schemas. Emotion is an implicit part of the same brain circuitry used for reasoning. Metaphor is primarily a conceptual construction, central to the development of thought. It includes all kinds of thinking: about emotion, society, human character, language, the nature of life and death. Lakoff defines metaphor as the mapping of so-called preconceptual structures from one domain onto another, thus making experience possible. Such preconceptual structures are directly meaningful concepts that provide certain anchors in the evaluation of situations.[4] Thinking of Baars' GWT: conceptual metaphor must occupy the first rows of the theater of the mind, maintaining direct connections to the actors in the spotlight.

Where we were trying to understand the actor on stage in the previous chapter, now we are more than ever in the darker areas of the theater of the mind. Conceptual metaphor seems to be a pretty active member in the audience. The literal provides the building blocks of thought, says Lakoff in his *Women, Fire, and Dangerous Things* (1987). "Cognitive models derive their fundamental meaningfulness directly from their ability to match up with preconceptual structure. Such direct matchings provide a basis for an account of truth and knowledge." But "where there is no clearly discernible preconceptual structure to our experience," Lakoff states, "we import such structure via metaphor. Metaphor provides us with a means of comprehending domains of experience that do not have a preconceptual structure of their own." A large proportion of our most commonplace thoughts make use of an extensive system of metaphorical concepts, mined unconsciously from our brain. These are concepts from a typically concrete realm of thought that are used to comprehend another, completely different domain; from one world to another. They are often reflected in everyday language, but, says Lakoff, their most dramatic effect comes in ordinary reasoning. For example, the underlying metaphor of scholarly debate is: Argument Is Struggle ("He won the debate." "Her claims cannot be defended." "His criticism was right on target." "I will shoot down your reasoning.") Melinda is silent because she cannot defend herself.[5]

It is crucial that most metaphors go back to the human body in space and time. Lakoff was one of the first to speak about an embodied mind. Up to the most abstract reasoning, human cognition makes use of concrete, low-level facilities as the sensorimotor system and the emotions and depends on them. Even the most abstract reasoning is rooted in the language of moving around with our bodies through space. As neural beings, human brains take their input from the rest of their bodies. "What our bodies are like and how they function in the world structures the very concepts we can use to think. We cannot think just anything — only what our embodied brains permit." Although Lakoff further shows that non-metaphorical thought is only possible when we talk about purely physical reality, he demonstrated that the basic concepts of causation used in the physical and social sciences are primarily constituted by a system of some two dozen distinct metaphors, each with its own causal logic. It is perhaps impossible to say many things literally, for there are simply no appropriate conceptual primitives.[6]

All meaningful perception and action is mediated by our brains, whether physical, social, emotional, or interpersonal. There is no abstract meaning floating in air, nor in empty symbols that are just manipulated. It is the brain, extending throughout the body via the nervous system, and connected to the body functioning in the physical and social world, that gives meaning and grounds reason. Among the major mediating systems in the brain, language consists of circuits linking meaningful, embodied thought to physical linguistic form, including speech, writing, gesture, and signs. Lakoff shows, for example, that you cannot *not* think of an elephant if asked to because you cannot consciously control your own neural system. Triggered, a word like "elephant" activates an image of an elephant and knowledge about elephants. Since, in North and South America, Europe, and Australia there is little experience of directly interacting physically with elephants, the word "elephant" does not activate a motor program in humans living there. This is different from the word "cat," which is connected to motor programs for petting and dealing with cats. This motor program is part of the meaning of "cat." It has been demonstrated that people with inferior temporal cortex lesions, near the motor area, may lose the ability to recognize cats, but not elephants.[7] Melinda cannot *not* think of the tree as dangerous. While being raped, she saw a tree. The tree is her ordeal. Drawing a tree, as Mr. Freeman asks of her, is feeling the pain, experiencing the assault on her body again. This is not just the memory. The tree was a stabbing weapon in male hands long before Freud: A Stick Is Dangerous.

Metaphor is a natural phenomenon. As a matter of course, by language learning and the conflation of conceptual domains in everyday life, children born at a certain place and among a certain people automatically acquire a mastery of everyday metaphor in use at that place by that people. The Knowing Is Seeing metaphor, for example, important to understand the effect of the "snow" in *Cosas insignificantes,* is learned by first using "seeing" literally — about vision only: "See the snow"—and next deflating seeing and knowing into "See the snow opening our hearts." The use of knowledge only is the third step, not connected any longer to literal seeing: "See what I mean." Some of these metaphors belong explicitly to one place and one people — culturally limited or enclosed — others can be found cross-culturally. Our bodies are central and thus not incidental to what we are as human beings. Because language arises from everyday experiences and a basic neural learning mechanism, grammar consists of neural circuitry pairing embodied concepts with sound, sight, smell, signs and so forth. Grammar itself is first learned by pairing sound combinations with familiar experiences.

Conceptual Metaphor Theory involves the mappings of one domain onto another. In the source domain important metaphorical reasoning takes place and it provides the source concepts used in that reasoning, whereas the target domain is constituted by the immediate subject matter. Take the expression "Melinda was raped close to the beginning of summer holiday." In this expression we note the metaphor close to, with time as the target domain and space as the source domain. In the sentence given, the relationship between the two events is given metaphorically in terms of space (close to). Here time is the subject matter of the sentence, while space is only the conceptual source. It could be demonstrated that conceptual metaphors are computed via neural maps. These neural maps consist of neural circuitry linking the sensory-motor system with higher cortical areas. This makes the conceptual metaphor a *physical* unit, part of our brains. The theory has become a *material* theory. The scholarly description of this makes use of another metaphor, however, taken from topography: "In the visual system of the brain, neurons *project,* that is, extend, from the retina to the primary visual cortex (v1), with neurons that are adjacent or nearby in the retina projecting to neurons that are adjacent or nearby in v1. The neurons active in v1 are said to form a map in v1 of the retinal image. [...] Similarly, the motor cortex is said to contain a map of the body. Neuronal clusters throughout the body 'project' (that is, are connected) to neuronal clusters in the motor cortex, with neuronal clusters adjacent or nearby on the body projecting to neuronal clusters adjacent to or nearby the corresponding clusters in the motor cortex. Maps of such types are common in the brain." The retina is "territory," and v1 is the "map." But the mappings are physical links; neural circuitry links neuronal clusters, which are called nodes. The domains are highly structured neural ensembles in different regions of the brain. Through so-called neural recruitment, the neural maps are formed by the long-term potentiating of neurons connected to the source and target neural ensembles that are coactive during conflation. For example, the metaphor Affection Is Warmth is a conflation of the simultaneously active neuronal ensembles devoted, on the one hand, to emotion (Affection), and on the other hand to temperature (Warmth). The metaphor is grounded in the childhood experience that affection literally corresponds to the physical experience of the warmth of being held closely. Because this is so close to our primary experience, it is called a primary metaphor. Largely universal, says Lakoff's colleague Jerome Feldman, primary metaphors provide the grounding for much of the metaphor system. In all, they form a stable, conventional physical system of metaphors in the brain, articulated to the conceptual system and independent of language as such.[8]

Interestingly, in the 20th century linguists concluded that the "language of the psyche" was closer to metaphor than to stories. Curiously, Freud's so-called hidden signs of the unconscious consisted of metaphors that he did not notice. In his "dream article," "How Metaphor Structures Dreams" (1993), Lakoff takes a shot at several dreams. Stressing the importance and extensive knowledge about the life of the dreamer, he includes dreams of dreamers he personally knew very well. The metaphor series Knowing Is Seeing, Testicles Are Eyes, and Impotence Is Blindness helped him to interpret a dream of a friend about blindness. One of the banes of his friend's existence was the feeling that he lacked power and influence, and was therefore unable to get things done for himself and others. His recurring dream occurred several times just before he took on his first important administrative position, about which he feared that he would spend a lot of effort and not accomplish anything significant. Lakoff recognized a few other metaphors as well, all combined in the dream: Knowing Is Seeing, Worldly Power Is Sexual Potency, and Genitals Are Eyes/Impotence Is Blindness. When Freud talked about the sexual, he did not mean the testicles. The theory of the phallus was essential to him. Before Freud, "castration" did not mean removal of the penis, but of the testicles. The metaphorical sequence discussed by Lakoff— Knowing Is Seeing, Testicles Are Eyes, Worldly Power Is Sexual Potency, Powerlessness Is Impotence — is constituted in the learning of language. Our everyday system of conventional metaphor is employed in ordinary thinking about the world. It can be thought of as a kind of collective or social language of the unconscious. For the most part, it is not idiosyncratic. It defines conventional modes of thought within a culture and is expressed in the lexicon and grammar of languages — thus a kind of "social thought." For *Speak*, the Testicles Are Eyes metaphor may be the idea behind the film's ending. In most ways, feature films are collective enterprises of the director, writer(s), actors, producers, and the like. In the novel behind the film, written as a purely individual work, Melinda does *not* blind Andy.[9]

# 5

The body shapes the mind thanks to culture. Cognition is not the representation of a pre-given world by a pre-given mind but is rather the enactment of a world and a mind on the basis of a history of the variety of actions that a being in the world performs. Worldviews live in the minds of people. "Everything we know is physically instantiated in the neural system of our brains," says Lakoff. To perceive is not merely to have sensations, but to have sensations the brain understands. Therefore, philosopher Alva Noë looks at perceiving as a way of acting. "Perception is not something that happens to us, or in us. It is something we do." It is not a process in the brain, he says, but a kind of skillful activity of the body as a whole. The perceptual experience acquires content thanks to our possession and exercise of practical bodily knowledge. People *enact* their perceptual experience. Viewing a film is in a way participating in it. This is a bodily active process. We feel the movie. This works literally and metaphorically at the same time. This reaction, says Lakoff, is grounded in the "mirror neurons" located in the prefrontal cortex of our brains. Such neurons fire either when we perform an action or when we see the same action performed by someone else. There are connections from that part of the brain to the emotional centers. Such neural circuits are believed to be the basis of empathy. Our systems of metaphorical thought — Genitals Are Eyes — interacting with our mirror neuron systems make us feel empathy with Melinda and the ending of *Speak*.[10]

By pointing at the mirror neurons — one of the major discoveries of neuroscience over the past decade — Lakoff truly made the embodiment of the mind physical. Mirror neurons play a crucial role in learning and understanding, but also in understanding and interpreting cinema. They are important in feeling empathy with others, including fictive others, like characters in novels, in films, and on television. In the cinema, the moment we see Melinda spraying the aerosol on Andy, we do it in our brains as well, and because we have learned to share Melinda's feelings, we may also feel relieved. Imagine, says Lakoff: "You're walking through a park when out of nowhere, the man in front of you gets smacked by an errant Frisbee. Automatically, you recoil in sympathy. Or you're watching a race, and you feel your own heart racing with excitement as the runners vie to cross the finish line first. Or you see a woman sniff some unfamiliar food and wrinkle her nose in disgust. Suddenly, your own stomach turns at the thought of the meal. For years, such experiences have puzzled psychologists, neuroscientists and philosophers, who've wondered why we react at such a gut level to other people's actions. How do we understand, so immediately and instinctively, their thoughts, feelings and intentions?" Mirror neurons are part of circuits in our brain that suggest that when we watch others performing actions we are in a way performing those actions ourselves. This is why people get involved with anguish, pain, and tension, both in real life and in films.[11]

The mirror neurons were discovered by accident, at a laboratory in Parma, Italy, in the early 1990s, where a group of neurologists led by Giacomo Rizzolatti was working with macaque monkeys. The group was testing a neuron that fired whenever the monkey would grab for a peanut. The researchers called it a motor neuron, for it had to do with the motion of the monkeys grabbing the food. Yet, one day, the monkey was not moving at all but his neurons were firing by just watching a researcher grabbing a peanut. The researchers concluded that seeing and doing made use of the same brain cells. Over the years, this was widely corroborated. Watching somebody do something is like doing it yourself. Because the brain was obviously mirroring the action it sees, they labeled the cells involved "mirror neurons." In his *The Ape and the Sushi Master* (2001), biologist Frans de Waal discusses the apprenticeship of the Japanese sushi master. The apprentice slaves in the shadow of masters of an art requiring rice of the right stickiness and delicately cut ingredients. His education seems a matter of passive observation; cleaning the dishes, mopping the kitchen floor, bowing to the clients, fetching ingredients. In the meantime, he follows from the corners of his eyes everything that the sushi masters are doing, "without ever asking a question," says de Waal. This lasts at least three years. He is not allowed to make actual sushi — an extreme case of exposure without practice. But then, invited to make his first sushi, he will do so with remarkable dexterity. Witness to the hundreds of times he had made sushi in his head, aided by his mirror neurons. In 2002, Lakoff had the opportunity to work with Vittorio Gallese, one of the original discoverers of mirror neurons. They found that the information needed for the frame structure characterizing the concept of grasping can be found in the mirror neurons governing the action and perception of grasping. In other words, a conceptual structure for physical actions exists in the neural system governing bodily movements and the visual perception of those movements. For Lakoff and Gallese, this was evidence that the most basic concepts characterized in frames could be physically embodied at the level of mirror neurons.[12]

For the moment, the human brain is still too complex to locate the exact place of the mirror neurons. The premotor cortex, an inferior frontal, and the inferior parietal cortex are identified as eligible candidates. When a person looks at someone else performing a specific action, these areas are increasingly activated. It is as if parts of the body — muscles above all — are made ready to perform. Furthermore, data show that the brain of participants — in a psychology laboratory experiment — who look at someone who feels disgusted activates a particular segment — the anterior insula — that is also triggered when the participants themselves feel disgusted. When experimenters touched one of the participants' legs with a feather-duster-like contraption the same part of the somato-sensory cortex was activated as when the participants saw pictures of a person being touched on the same spot. In 1995, Rizzolatti and another neuroscientist at the University of Ferrara, Luciano Fadiga, recorded motor-evoked potentials: muscles are ready to act. They were recording hand muscles from participants who were watching the researcher grasping things. The participants' potentials matched the potentials which were recorded when they were grabbing the things themselves. Researchers investigating eye-tracking in babies concluded that the system might be active at a very young age indeed. It helps the infants to understand other people's actions. In due course, research went beyond the motor action systems of the brain. Other research has confirmed that mirror neurons tie us not only to other people's actions but to other people's feelings as well — especially empathy. For example, neurologist Marco Iacoboni of the University of California at Los Angeles has demonstrated that the part of the brain that is working when we make a face is the same as the part busy when we see a face. Because faces tell us about someone's feelings and emotions, our emotional system is triggered.[13]

Mirror neurons can send messages to the emotional system in our brains, which helps us tune in to each other's feelings. Actors and actions in movies, on television, and in novels, for example, can do the same. Our brain may mirror the thinking and experiences of Melinda and Rachel in *Speak*, of Joel and Clementine in *Eternal Sunshine of the Spotless Mind,* of Neil and, perhaps, Brian in *Mysterious Skin,* or Alex in *XXY,* to mention only a few, but less readily, due to the distance, with Carol in *[SAFE].* It links them with our other experiences and insights — for example, with our knowledge of the assumptions of Freud — and uses them as simulators. This system is a unifying mechanism, and probably the most basic social brain system that allows people to actually connect at a very simple level, even if some of the people are fictive characters on a screen. However, cognition through mirror neurons is less embodied as it is grounded. The discovery of the mirror neurons, the embodiment of thinking, and the revival of simulation theory come together in the Theory of Grounded Cognition (TGC) as advanced by psychologist Lawrence Barsalou. The TGC proposes that cognition works through modal simulations, bodily states, and situational action. It is founded on evidence from research on perception, memory, knowledge, language, thought, social cognition, and development. This is not the place to go over this theory more intensively. It suffices to conclude that simulation plays increasingly important roles in contemporary theories of social cognition, which is significant for understanding feature films as simulators, and that mirror neuron circuits typically underlie social simulation theories.[14]

# 6

The endings of *Speak* and *Cosas insignificantes* can also be articulated to another psychological mechanism: our drive to bond. Or to re-bond, as in *Speak*. Precisely because Melinda blinded Andy, she confirmed the conceptual metaphor of her peers. She struggled with her friends' lack of empathy and with her helplessness to explain why she called the police. It seems her peers were not interested. This damaged her mental health, which, in fact, deteriorated during that year at high school. One reviewer concluded after seeing *Speak,* "anyone knows just how cruel and unfeeling pubescent teenagers can be, more specifically how oblivious they are to the truth behind their classmate's behavior. Melinda's choice to refrain from informing even her closest friend of her plight proves to be an exceptionally appropriate vehicle in illustrating these harsh realities, revealing to us as viewers that she'd rather not speak at all for fear of further social backlash."[15] It is not a problem typical for pubescent teenagers only. Evolutionary psychologist David M. Buss, in his *Evolutionary Psychology* (1999), notes that for hundreds of centuries people seem to have devoted tremendous effort to avoiding disrepute, dishonor, shame, humiliation, disgrace, and loss of face out of attention to status, prestige, esteem, honor, respect, and rank. "Empirical evidence suggests that status and dominance hierarchies form quickly." In fact, one study has found that in half of the cases of 59 three-person groups of individuals, previously unknown to each other, a clear hierarchy emerged within one minute. This happened for the other half within the first five minutes. Most members of groups could accurately evaluate their own future status within the group after they had merely encountered the other members and before anyone had uttered a single word.[16]

Coming out of the same pool, the rapist's aggression must be biological (a slightly damaged fetus in the womb), genetic, social, or all at the same time. Psychologists have found no evidence for a class of biological explanations that argue for the Freudian building up of "negative" energy until explosion — neither from frustrating the sexual instinct nor from some inborn drive. Scientists have not discovered any reservoirs of aggressive energy in the brain or elsewhere in the body. Aggression is found to be a typical action tendency in response to anger and goal-pursuing struggles as part of emotional arousal. Solid evolutionary arguments predict that aggression is likely to emerge more strongly among young men, both as aggressors and victims. Some of its origins can be attributed to observational learning mechanisms, mimicked from important others as well from television and cinema. Others are programmed from status, reputation, and power contexts, or from sexual jealousy and intrasexual rivalry: More Is Up, Worldly Power Is Sexual Potency. In short, aggression represents a collection of strategies that become manifest under specific contextual conditions and may be viewed as solutions, albeit sometimes repugnant ones, to several distinct adaptive problems. Reading important studies covering different cultures and a history going back to 4000 B.C.E., Buss concludes that if "there were ever a reasonable candidate for a universal human motive, status driving would be at or near the top of the list."[17]

Psychologist Denise Cummins shows that a so-called dominance hierarchy forms, allowing some people to gain greater access than others to key resources that contribute to survival or reproduction. This hierarchy principle has developed by evolution and is transitive, meaning that if A is dominant over B, and B is dominant over C then A will also be so over C. People high on the scale of social dominance orientation — the A's here — endorse an ideology involving the legitimacy of one group's domination over another, the deservingness of discrimination and subordination of one group by another, and, as Buss says, the allocation of more perks to one group than another. Empirical evidence discussed by Buss and Cummins supports the evolutionary rationale for predicting a sex difference in the strength of the motivation to achieve high status. The hormone testosterone and the neurotransmitter serotonin have both been linked with dominance, although the direction of causality is uncertain in both cases. Nevertheless, high status in men leads directly to increased sexual access to a larger number of women — witness Andy in *Speak*, and the behavior of the girls. Women would have been selected to choose high status men, since this would have led to a greater bounty of benefits for themselves and their children. Men tend to be more hierarchical and tend to express dominance for personal gain and ascension, like getting others to do menial tasks rather than doing them themselves. Women, however, tend to be more egalitarian and express dominance through pro-social actions like settling disputes among others in the group. Also, when given a choice of roles to take, dominant men take the leadership role for themselves, whereas dominant women tend to appoint men as leaders. Across studies, males form hierarchies as early as age three. We may find some conceptual metaphors in Lakoff's work that might articulate this — Control Is Up, Divine Is Up, Freedom Is Up, Good Is White, Bad Is Black, More Is Up, Mortal Is Down and many more — but the principle is clear: to be better off, you'd be better "up" and "white."[18] Hence Melinda's fight with the tree. The moment she has control over the tree, she is able to blind the rapist, and earn back her status among the girls. Today, the times of *Totem and Taboo* are long forgotten.

Sharzer's focus on the peers in *Speak* is supported by Harris' book *No Two Alike* (2006). Harris writes that her colleagues at several universities demonstrated convincingly that the context-specific socialization of the child takes place basically outside the parental home, in peer groups of childhood and adolescence. An increasing number of studies show that there is "very little impact of the physical environment that parents provide for children at home and very little impact of parental characteristics that must be essentially the same for all children in a family," like education. After reviewing all the data on the variation of personality with birth order and doing a huge research of their own, two Swiss psychologists found no birth order effects on personality. In the late 1980s, again two other scholars concluded that siblings are probably hardly more similar than children chosen at random once genetic relatedness has been taken into account. For these researchers, differences between siblings may be explained by what they called *nonshared environment;* that is: nonshared by siblings. Intra- and inter-group processes are responsible for the transmission of culture to the next generation, and not only dyadic relationships between parents and children. A large list of published parent–child socialization research, studies on sibling differences, birth order, adoption, language acquisition, and child-rearing practices across time and culture does indeed point to a *limited* — that is, not absent — influence of the parents on the development of their children's personalities and behavioral habits outside the parental home.[19]

It was not Harris' theme to underscore the work of behavioral genetics but to uncover the complicated and subtle mechanisms through which the environment in its broadest senses leaves its mark. She shows that her colleagues mainly determined which aspects of the environment should be excluded from their conclusions. Furthermore, she affirms that the "aspects of the environment that do not seem to matter are all those that are shared by all the children who grow up in a given family — which includes most of the things the word 'home' makes you think of. Whether the home is headed by one parent or two, whether the parents are happily married or constantly rowing, whether they believe in pushing their children to succeed or leaving them to find their own way in life, whether the home is filled with books or sports equipment, whether it is orderly or messy, a city flat or a farmhouse — the research shows, counterintuitively, that none of these things makes much difference" — counterintuitively due to the long roots of psychomythology.[20] The error made before is based on the psychomythological assumption that what a child learns in his home environment is automatically carried along with him to other settings. This assumption is built into most theories of personality development, including the Freudian, with the assumptions about a child's attachment to its mother in infancy setting the pattern for all later relationships. On average, a child growing up in a well-run orderly family is no more conscientious later than one growing up where chaos rules the family. A child who has inherited a predisposition to be aggressive or conscientious will display these traits both at home and at school. Researchers have found that when children display the same characteristics in a variety of settings, it is usually because of genetic influences. It is this carry-over of inherited predispositions from one environment to another — along with the fact that these predispositions tend to show up early in life — that gives the false impression of a lasting effect of the home environment.[21]

Status is universal but can only be played out on particular stages. First, time and space are important, the stages where the character acts. Harris gives us the example of a boy named James. His mother, she asks us to imagine, is a poor disciplinarian. Popular psychology makes us believe that James would be a problem child at school and at home. But at school, James may have established himself as a very different boy. His teacher, says Harris, may tell us that he behaves acceptably, "on a par with the rest of the class." James would have known this from when he was a baby. In their simple, underdeveloped way, babies are able to understand, perhaps from birth, that people are different from each other. They know that their mothers' caring behavior does not imply that other persons would treat them well — not even if their faces are familiar, like their sisters' or brothers'. The babies realize at this early age that they have to get to know each human being one by one, environment by environment, sooner or later. Harris tells us also that some babies, living the first weeks of their lives with mothers who suffer from postnatal depression, behave quietly, still and subdued in their company, but much more animated and noisy in the company of other people. They seem to know that their mother's depression is not the general human state and that this allows them to be cheerful and lively with others. What works in one setting will not necessarily work in another. Children learn quickly that crying brings one response from their mothers, but quite a different one from other children at the daycare center. The idea of environment and company seems inborn.

Children seem to know instinctively that patterns of behavior acquired at home must be cautiously tested, and perhaps modified or abandoned, when they start to have a life outside the home. The influence of peers does not begin in the teenage years. It can be seen as early as age three. For Harris, this ability to behave differently in different social settings and with different social partners is a built-in survival mechanism. Think of the child of immigrants who learns to speak one language at home and a different language outside the home, including an accent that outside the home will be the same as that of the other children in her neighborhood. There is only a limited necessity to continue to believe in the potency of the home. In fact, the home is only one stage on which to perform out of many.[22]

Culture as a conglomeration of schemas and conceptual metaphors is limited to specific stages. Of Harris' many examples, this one is particularly revealing, based on the work of developmental psychologist Carolyn Rovee-Collier. With her colleagues, Rovee-Collier performed several experiments with babies lying in cribs, a mobile assembled above them. The researchers were interested in the babies' learning abilities. They tied a ribbon to one of the babies' ankles. The babies could kick that foot to jiggle the mobile. Very quickly, six-month-olds were delighted to discover that they could control the mobile that way and two weeks later they still remembered how. However, when the researchers changed the details of the experimental setup, the babies appeared to have lost this knowledge. Different doodads hanging from the mobile, a new liner surrounding the crib with another pattern or color, or a different crib altogether placed in an altered room caused the babies to gaze up at the mobile clueless, as if they had no memory at all of the previous joyful activities. Harris believes that the babies have an inborn warning label attached to their learning mechanism: one context is not the same as the other. The label will never be detached from this either. Every parent knows that their child can be a different person outside the home, when they are with their peers, for example. They recognize their child's tailored language or speech and behavior. If immigrant children come outside the home, Harris asks us, and find out that they speak a different language, would they be surprised? Knowing about the babies and the mobile, the answer must be: probably not. Change the liner surrounding the crib and they think they are in a different world, a new world with different rules, yet to be learned: language learned at home may prove to be of no use whatsoever outside the home. Immigrant children know this all too well. "You would think a picky eater in one setting would be a picky eater in another, wouldn't you?" Harris asks her readers. "Yes, it has been studied, and no that's not what the researchers found." One third of the children in a Swedish sample were picky eaters *either* at home or in school, but only very few were picky eaters in *both* places. The latter figure, no doubt, was due to genetic effects like food allergies or a delicate digestive system.[23]

In each of the different social contexts, status is a separate arena with different contestants. It is learned and experienced early, perhaps a kind of innateness. Despite the recognition of the influence of genes, Harris warns, it is wrong to overestimate the power of inherited predispositions. Identical twins provide a good illustration because they have identical genes, and therefore they should have exactly the same inherited predispositions. Now, stressing the genetic factor, most of the stories about identical twins emphasize their peculiar similarities, but what also needs to be aired is that identical twins are not nearly as alike as the genetic sounds suppose, because even when identical twins are reared in the same home by the same parents, most of them differ noticeably in personality. The differences are as peculiar as their similarities, especially because as identical persons their environment usually treats them identically. Some differences might be the result of random biological processes in development—there are slight physical differences between the brains of identical twins, just as there are in their fingerprints, Harris notes—but beyond any doubt, genes cannot account for them. "Attachment theory, for example, derived from psychoanalysis, stubs its toe on the question of why one identical twin but not the other would form a secure attachment to their mother." Neither can it "explain why identical twins separated at birth and reared by two different mothers are as similar in personality as those reared by the same mother. As for birth order theory, it's a non-starter. Identical twins are well matched in size and strength and generally don't regard each other as rivals."[24]

A few years before Freud's first major publications, William James, the father of American psychology, had written in his *The Principles of Psychology* (1890) that "*a man has as many social selves as there are individuals who recognize him* and carry an image of him in their mind."[25] Harris concluded from more recent psychology: "But as the individuals who carry the images fall naturally into classes, we may practically say that he has as many different social selves as there are distinct *groups* of persons about whose opinion he cares. He generally shows a different side of himself to each of these different groups. Many a youth who is nice and polite to his parents and teachers, swears and swaggers like a pirate among his 'tough' young friends. We do not show ourselves to our children as to our club-companions, to our customers as to the laborers we employ, to our own masters and employers as to our intimate friends."[26] In other words, people behave differently in different social contexts — different stages — unless the experience is a terror on several stages, like Melinda's. She is not able to speak to her peers, nor to her parents.

The explanation Harris comes up with in her *No Two Alike* (2006) rests on an assumption made by neurobiologists and evolutionary psychologists: the human brain is a toolbox of various basic devices, each designed by evolution to perform a specific function. One might call them "modules." These "modules" were probably first developed by learning and then became inborn.

Nowadays, different parts of the brain work according to their own rules and each of them responds to a specific type of information provided by the environment, and uses that information in a particular way. Harris confirms that the mind has at least three different motivational modules to collect and process information from the social environment and to design "appropriate" behavior in response. These are the status system that makes one want to stand out; the socialization system that makes one want to fit in; and the relationship system that makes one want to conform. Time and again, researchers found these in their data. They are also easily recognizable in *Speak* and in *Cosas insignificantes*.[27]

First, there is the Relationship System, or RELS, which frames the collection and storing of data about the individuals people meet, like the way in which they store words and their meanings. The RELS allows them to distinguish and recognize others as certain individuals, not as classified people like a partygoer, woman, activist — it is a splitter, not a lumper. The RELS identifies the other actors on a certain stage as specific persons. Harris maintains that "we never lose our curiosity about people. Gossip is a popular sport even in the old people's home. It is the relationship system that fuels our hunger for biographies and novels, and makes us want to look at photos of movie actors and sports stars." Second, the Socialization System, or SOCS, frames behavior that is appropriate to living among groups of people. It means to learn the locally "correct" behaviors and customs, with the prevailing attitudes and beliefs, and of course, to acquire language, accent and (some) slang. Children need to figure out what sort of person they are — child or adult, male or female, serf's son or princeling — how other people in their social category behave and adjust their behavior accordingly. This is why children acquire the accent of their peers rather than that of their parents. The SOCS tends to make people of the same group — on the same stage — more alike. On the conceptual level this blending creates prototypes that define categories into a kind of stereotype in order to self-categorize in relation to others. Thus someone may self-categorize as girl, as member of a school, and so forth — depending upon which prototype is functional — and switch behaviors accordingly. Unconsciously, the SOCS works self-motivatedly and takes place as the adjustment of someone's behaviors to the expectations of the central tendencies of a category — following the appropriate script on a specific stage.[28] Through flashback we learn that before being raped, Melinda acted appropriately in the SOCS of her school.

Though the SOCS can explain some of the behavioral differences between cultures, it cannot account for the non-genetic differences in personality between reared-together twins or siblings. As they grow up, children become more like their peers in some ways, but less like them in other ways. The uniqueness of each child's personality is due to Harris' third system, the Status System, or STATS. This one frames the competition with fellow group members on a stage.

Without other rewards as self-esteem or external reinforcers, the outcomes of that competition constitute status. Harris relates studies that show that people react separately to social acceptance and social status. The most conceptually complicated part of determining someone's own status is being able to read what others consider her or his status to be. This is a matter of picking up on sometimes subtle clues involving eye contact, posture, speech, and the like. It is this system that shapes personality. Children by age three, but most clearly by age six or seven, have an idea, through pair-wise competitions, of their status in their groups — like for boys being the strongest, the fastest, the toughest, the funniest; or the bulliest, who may fail at acceptance but succeed at status to acquire adequate self-esteem.[29] Almost any scene at Melinda's high school involving the behavior of the girls can be articulated to the STATS.

The purpose of the STATS is to enable people to compete more or less suitably with their peers. Therefore, they need to acquire a sense of self-knowledge and to discover in what way they can be compared to these peers. There are several questions that linger on; for example: Am I tall or short, strong or weak, pretty or plain, smart or dull? Answering such questions is important to be able to compete, to dominate or to avoid being dominated, to take the lead or to follow others, to turn down mates or friends or to join in, etcetera. Harris argues that self-acceptance derives from this STATS — the portion that is not genetic — and that for adolescents it is status that is determining. Like other organs, the systems vary somewhat from one individual to another. For some children, the SoCS generally takes priority; for others, the STATS often gains the upper hand. "Every child has to find out what he is good at and place his bets on the things that are most likely to pay off. Even identical twins will find different niches to occupy." But these differences become visible only when the two goals of fitting in or standing out conflict. At other times the two goals can peacefully coexist, Harris concludes, for the child in school sits quietly in her seat like her classmates — she conforms — whereas at the same time she may try to stand out by excelling in reading or mathematics.[30] In short, one of the first mappings a child experiences is the status difference between children and parents, between their peers, as well as between male and female.

# 7

The audience in the theater of the mind has a strong embodied focus. Lakoff's conceptual metaphor and Harris' three systems can be found juxtaposed in *Speak* with Melinda thrown out of her clique as well as out of any larger community at school for the reason that she could not inform them why she had called the police. Her "horizontal" exclusion (from her communities) damaged her SoCS, and brought her to the bottom of the social ladder

STATS. The conceptual metaphors here are orientational with the embodiment clearly imagined: sleeping lying down, awaken standing up: Conscious Is Up and Unconscious Is Down. These metaphors go with Happy Is Up and Sad Is Down, More Is Up and Less Is Down, Having Control/Force Is Up and Being Subject to Control/Force Is Down, High Status Is Up and Low Status Is Down, in fact, Good Is Up and Bad Is Down. Freud assumed that "evil" in the form of repressed thoughts, wishes, or trauma was hidden "deep" in the unconscious. We know now why he thought this way: following Western conceptual metaphor, it *had to be* down, deep, and low. He was simply in line with metaphorical thinking. People do behave accordingly, of course, as we see in *Speak* with the rapist as having Up: High Status, More and Having Control, but by Force. Criminals — who are morally Low, of course — are therefore usually represented as people of the Dark of Death and, eventually, Less, despite the fact that most criminals, for example in the drug trade, are very rich, live in the wealthier neighborhoods of our cities and operate in broad daylight. In the movies they will lose, eventually, as does the rapist in *Speak*, and perhaps even be punished without trial, as happened to him. In fact, he is metaphorically punished with one of the most powerful images we have: castrated by blinding.[31]

However, the decision to *speak* was made separately. When she spoke out to her friend, Melinda had reached the bottom of the possibilities of her social relationships; she could not be more Down. Pressed by the circumstances — her former best friend had begun dating Andy — she found the strength to make Andy's crime public. A similar analysis — pressed by the circumstances on the lowest point in their relationships, the protagonists decided to open their eyes — can be made of *Cosas insignificantes*. Although *Cosas insignificantes* gives us a Mexican version, in which the heart opens thanks to the magical intervention of the Popocatepetl Volcano. It is a by-product of Mexican culture, one might speculate, to await such an intervention. But any viewer may also conclude that the protagonists involved all came to the conclusion that this downward spiral had gone on too long. And they took their steps. The filmmaker accentuated this watershed: she filmed them looking out of their windows in agony to Ixtaccihuatl, their point of reference. The moment (Down) and the loneliness fit very well with the desire to get Up again and re-establish social relations. For this reason, *Speak* and *Cosas insignificantes* can be viewed as excellent films to explain modern cognitive science, blending contemporary linguistic research into the conceptual metaphor as well as the psychology of relationship, socialization, and status. If anything would invoke and feed mental simulations it would be conceptual metaphors. At least two of Harris' three social psychological systems, the STATS and the SOCS, are likewise recognizable in such simulations. In this sense, *Speak* and *Cosas insignificantes* are exemplary simulators.

# 8

## *Nina's Double*

### The Illusion in *Black Swan* (2010) and *The Virgin Suicides* (1999)

Darren Aronofsky (director), Mark Heyman,
Andrés Heinz, and John McLaughlin (writers);
and Sofia Coppola (writer and director)

## 1

Dressed as the White Swan, ballet dancer Nina Sayers (Natalie Portman) returns to her dressing room. She is crying, because she has just made a terrible mistake on stage. It seems she cannot cope with the stress of dancing the major part. "Rough start, huh?" she suddenly hears. "Must have been pretty humiliating." In front of the mirror, she sees sensual and liberated Lily (Mila Kunis). Lily is her understudy, preparing to take over the role of the Black Swan. Nina tells her to leave. Lily answers that she is worried about the next act. "I'm just not sure you're feeling up to it." That is the point, of course. Nina is desperate. "Stop, please, stop!" Lily rises: "How about I dance the Black Swan for you?" Nina loses control and attacks Lily, thereby shoving her into a mirror, shattering it. Unexpectedly, Lily has changed into Nina's double — Black Nina. It is Black Nina who fights back. White and Black Nina start wrestling. Black Nina shouts several times: "It is my turn!" Nina's "Black" side needs to destroy her "White" side. In a final attempt to save her life, White Nina grabs a piece of the broken mirror and stabs Black Nina in the stomach. "It is *my* turn," she says angrily. Upon realizing what she has done,

White Nina recognizes Lily. Black Nina, her double, has switched back to her adversary. Crying and breathing heavily, almost hyperventilating, but determined, she hides the body in the bathroom. Her eyes turn bloody red and she returns to the stage as the Black Swan.[1]

# 2

This is a world of illusions. We have seen this before in *Jennifer's Body*. Nina's fate is not much different from Needy's. Therefore, the scene above must be the key to *Black Swan* (2010), a film directed by Darren Aronofsky and based on a story by Andrés Heinz, with script revisions by John McLaughlin and Mark Heyman. The scene is also a key to cognitive film criticism. We are now trying to settle permanently outside the Freudian Edifice. Humans are the storytelling animal, Jonathan Gottschall tells us. Stories make us human; like fish in the ocean, we live in a sea of stories. The better we can deal with stories the better we can "swim." Or, said differently, stories — based on real experience or fictional — can make us behave better. Through simulation, they prepare us for future behavior because they provide us with an assortment of actions. Recorded in memory, stories are articulated to emotions, which help us decide what to do. A fiction film is such a story. Films offer simulations by the "brain's left hemisphere interpreter," especially when they are focalized through a limited number of characters. A film focalized through one character gives us the vision of this "interpreter."[2] And as we shall see, even in "healthy" circumstances, the "interpreter" would saddle us with illusions.

Pushed by neuroscientist Michael Gazzaniga, the "brain's left hemisphere interpreter" broke cover. This is a module of the brain that is designed to seek logical explanations or causes for events a person experiences. It provides us with a comprehensible vision of the world and us in it. By generating "explanations about our perceptions, memories, and actions and the relationship among them," it gives us a coherent identity. Gazzaniga met it in split-brain patients — patients who suffered so horribly from epilepsy that the surgeon decided to cut the links between the two hemispheres of their brains. Investigating the effects, Gazzaniga and his collaborators found out that the left-hemisphere put experience into words and was designed to do so — the right-hemisphere could do it as well, but only with a lot of difficulty. Furthermore, the story that the "interpreter" uttered seemed in all cases to have been fabricated. "It made up a post hoc answer that fit the situation," Gazzaniga concluded. "It interpreted the response in a context consistent with what it knew, [...] using the inputs that it has from the current cognitive state [based on memory and mental schemas, AO] and cues from the surroundings." Gazzaniga passed a clear judgment: the "interpreter" "fudges." It never said

"I don't know," which would have been the correct answer in many of the experiments. This has consequences for our evaluation of film viewing, because the "interpreter" is probably the actor on the stage in the theater of the mind that most of the time attracts the spotlight of consciousness.[3]

A feature like *Black Swan* is consistently focalized through its main character Nina. The camera makes us experience the world through her eyes and mind. This interpreter bears on the audience as a partner. The camera shows us Nina's doubt and insecurity, and her hunt for a meaningful and positive story about what seems to happen to her. The information comes to Nina through her senses, but we basically are partners in sight and sound — in the cinema we (still?) do not smell and we cannot touch. We also get information from Nina's brain itself: her hallucinations. Almost from scratch, Nina sees herself as the Black Swan. We see how sometimes her fingers start to bleed unexpectedly. Nina notices the scars on her back and we learn from her caring but sometimes also overbearing mother, Erica (Barbara Hershey) — who is a failed dancer turned amateur artist — that Nina suffers from a kind of obsessive-compulsive scratching behavior. The viewers realize that the double cannot be there and that her fingers do not bleed. The scratches are real though, but Nina has no recollection of making them. She has to reassure her mother that she did not relapse into her compulsive behavior. The thing is, as viewers, we know better; but the "interpreter" who tells us this story, seems not to. Because we humans make so much use of our "left-hemisphere interpreter," most stories told by us would be from it. That is why when we are looking at Nina, for example, we do not see a documentary of an ambitious young dancer at a prestigious New York City ballet company. We see what her "interpreter" wants her to believe and what our "interpreter" makes of this story. In the flesh, her "interpreter" is the combined view of the filmmaker and the screenwriter.

It is this "interpreter" that provides us with the Freudian Excuse, which in this case is again childhood trauma — caused by the overbearing mother. The "interpreter" tells us that Erica believes that controlling Nina's life is indispensable, since ballet demands from its performers years of rigorous physical and mental perfectionism. Remember, stories are about trouble. Hence, the film takes off when the company's main choreographer, Thomas Leroy (Vincent Cassel), announces a new version of the classical ballet *Swan Lake*, but with a new leading ballerina — and he dismisses the company's star dancer Beth Macintyre (Winona Ryder). The lead must be able to present in person the conflicting characters of the delicate White Swan and the malicious Black Swan. The choreographer doubts Nina's capacity to be that person. Thanks to her rigid technique she is ideal for the White Swan, but she lacks the passion to dance the Black Swan. When she bites him after he forces a kiss on her, he sees her potential and gives her the role. In addition, choreographer Thomas tells Nina that he wants her to masturbate or involve herself in other sexual activities, to liberate herself. Interestingly, both good and evil are needed for the end product — the performance — to be better. This is not a traditional good versus evil feature film, which would make good triumphant and evil disappear. In a way, those times are beginning to be over. The title, of course, is ambiguous because the expression *black swan* suggests that Nina's assignment will be virtually impossible — an expression dating from the time black swans were supposed to be nonexistent, meaning a logical fallacy.

Nina's "interpreter" has to make sense of psychotic symptoms, including delusions and visual hallucinations — which we see on screen. Because Nina fears that her stand-in Lily wants to be more than a substitute, Nina's "interpreter" connects the hallucinations with Lily as the Black Swan. Lily is new in the troupe. She comes from the "liberal" West Coast, and fascinates Nina, not only as a rival, but more as a role model. We understand that due to very strong pressure, Nina develops the beginning of disintegration of thought processes and of emotional responsiveness so typical for schizophrenia. Lily acts as a catalytic agent, however, by inviting her to go out at night and have a drink with her and some friends. During the evening, Lily offers Nina drugs. This lowers Nina's inhibitions and awakens her sexual interest, not so much in the men as in Lily. Back home, Nina's "interpreter" gives us an almost violent version of her meeting with her worried mother. She runs into her room, closes the door firmly, and begins to masturbate. At least, fed by the hallucinatory images, that is what my own "interpreter" makes of the scene, because Nina's "interpreter" suggests having sex with Lily. The next morning, Lily is nowhere to be found. Nina is late for rehearsal. At the studio, she notices that the choreographer had already started, with Lily of course as her substitute. Envious, Nina defies Lily. Why did she not wake her up this morning? But Lily had gone home with a guy from the club. She teases Nina: did she have sexual fantasies about her?

In consequence of the tension at home, the stress at the studio, and the hallucinations caused by her brain, Nina's condition deteriorates within hours. The night before the ballet's opening several hallucinations make her pass out. Erica calls the ballet company to inform them that her daughter has been ill. Angry with her mother, Nina leaves for the theater. On arrival, she ignores that Thomas has asked Lily to dance in her place. She convinces him that there is nothing wrong. However, during the performance, hallucinations distract her again and even cause the dancer who is lifting her to drop her. Back in the dressing room she finds Lily as the Black Swan. Another hallucination is plaguing her: during the conversation Lily transforms into Black Nina. White Nina kills her — the scene described above — and then dances the Black Swan passionately. She feels black feathers growing on her back and her arms. This transformation is also an illusion, of course, but the performance must be virtuoso because the audience rewards her with a standing ovation. The perceived impossibility encapsulated in the *black swan* identity had been disproven. But at what cost? Her "interpreter" gives us a scene of a dying Nina, as if fatally wounded during the fight in the dressing room. But Nina is pleased: "I felt it. Perfect. I was perfect." The "interpreter" probably tells us that White Nina has died.

## 3

Since at least 1972, in *The Psychology of Anomalous Experience* by Graham Reed, we know that the doppelganger is an ancient phenomenon in human history probably caused by severe disruptions of the brain's left temporoparietal junction, which causes the sensation of self-attribution to be broken and be replaced by the sensation of a foreign presence or copy of oneself displaced nearby. This copy mirrors the real person's body posture, location, and position. A group of Swiss neurologists was able to trigger this experience by inserting electrodes into that part of the brain. For these researchers, this mechanism might help to explain schizophrenic feelings such as paranoia, alien control, and the notion that parts of one's body belong to somebody else. It is important to realize that the patient of the Swiss doctors had no history of psychiatric problems. This means that this type of illusion can be caused by a very simple switch in the brain.[4] The "switch" inside the brain is stress. But genetics, early environment, neurobiology, and psychological and social processes are also important contributory factors to this mental disease. Some recreational and prescription drugs appear to cause or worsen symptoms. However, Nina does obviously suffer from extreme stress during the time covered by the film. During that period, she came to realize that she could not remain the Victorian prudish White Swan and needed to be introduced to the world of sex, drugs, and rock 'n' roll by seductive Black Swan Lily.

Thus, beyond doubt, Nina's double was caused by attacks of schizophrenia, a prolonged psychosis. Nina behaves like an insecure girl, suffering under the rod of her demanding mother. Genetically, she seems to have inherited compulsions — most of her childhood she scratched her skin until it bled. The mother, however, would be more "guilty" of causing her daughter's sensitivity to schizophrenia by being stressed during pregnancy — she had to give up her own career — but that can hardly count. There is information about her smoking cigarettes or taking drugs during pregnancy. However, in the stressful situation, Nina must have collapsed under the pressure to perform. Hence, Nina herself triggers her Devil Within by taking drugs, having intense sex with herself, and fighting off the "external" Black Swan — the "image" of Lily, real or a virtual hallucination. It is a Devil that is far from in need of being exorcized, because by transforming into the Black Swan, Nina finally realizes that she is perfect. The audience of the film, however, knows that she has to visit a psychiatrist and take medication to control her schizophrenia. We also realize that schizophrenics cannot perform on this level, certainly not in a prestigious New York City ballet company. The image of a bleeding and dying Nina at the end of the film indicates that by becoming a schizophrenic, she has indeed figuratively killed herself as a dancer.

In his time, Freud, of course, had a different view on the doppelganger. He coined this experience of the double as another performance of the "return of the repressed," which he labeled as *unheimlich,* or uncanny. Since cultural scholars have discovered "the uncanny," there is something with doubles in films. Take for instance this remark by Andrea Sabbadini, from the introduction to a collection of essays on psychoanalysis and film: "Articles of textual psychoanalytic criticism are sometimes concerned with movies (e.g., those by François Truffaut) which display a special sensitivity to the psychological factors contributing to their characters' behaviour, or which deal with powerful feelings, for instance the fear often associated with a realistic or paranoid sense of being persecuted (e.g., those by Alfred Hitchcock); or more generally with films, such as those by Luis Buñuel, which use a cinematic language deliberately reminiscent of unconscious functioning and even conveying a disturbing sense of what Freud (1919) described as 'the uncanny,' especially in relation to the phenomenon of the *Doppelgänger.*"[5] Far from being forgotten, the "double" is indeed a popular concept nowadays in cultural and film studies, but also one that as full of problems as all the Freudian Excuses discussed in the preceding chapters. Hence, there is no need to dive into this too deeply. It suffices to recall that a return of the repressed is highly unlikely. We have seen that if filmmakers wish to give a special sensitivity to the psychological factors contributing to their characters' behavior, or wish to spotlight powerful feelings like fear, they do better to inform themselves about recent insights in academic psychology and neglect the work of Freud, Lacan, and others. If something is truly haunting the mind, it is during daytime as well as nighttime, and it has nothing to do with repressed thoughts, feelings, or wishes.

Freud had described the "uncanny" as a manifestation of the Death Drive T̶h̶a̶n̶a̶t̶o̶s̶. The idea for "the uncanny" stems from the time he worked at the formulation of the Death Drive T̶h̶a̶n̶a̶t̶o̶s̶ in *Beyond the Pleasure Principle* (1920). The essay "Das Unheimliche" contained a summary of this book. Apparently both pieces form some kind of a dyad. Why death? Repression, as we know, was rooted in the assumptions about energy and its discharge that underlined Freud's early theories and thus went back as far as the cocaine-fed speculations with Fliess in the mid–1890s. In *Beyond the Pleasure Principle* Freud returned to the stipulation that this system strived for balance and constancy, a provision ventured by several authors as early as the 1840s. It was hypothetically argued that if the energy level increased too much, abreaction or discharge was needed. To restore constant energy levels, Freud argued, the

Death Drive ~~Thanatos~~ would counterbalance the tendency of beings to do only what they find pleasurable. A good example is the orgasm as a pleasurable discharge. "The ejection of the sexual substances in the sexual act," Freud wrote in 1923 in his fake biological style, "corresponds in a sense to the separation of soma and germ-plasm [...]. This accounts for the likeness of the condition that follows complete sexual satisfaction to dying [...]." Thus, orgasm is the "little death" that follows intercourse. Contraception, the condom, coitus interruptus, masturbation, and the like hindered this kind of healthy and necessary discharge and formed a kind of unhealthy misdirected energy, causing frustration and eventually neuroses. The Death Drive ~~Thanatos~~ was the organism's instinct to return to the phase previous to this external disruption of "healthy" evolution in order to master the disruption coming from the external pressure. In short, the principal function of the Death Drive ~~Thanatos~~ could be to restore an earlier state of things. This "mastering" effort was done by compulsively repeating unpleasant experiences. It was also done socially. In Haeckelian terms, evolution was an illusion since life ontogenetically stored up "phylogenetic" past developments as stages that need to be repeated under a compulsion. Psychoanalysis "cured," only to prepare the patient for his or her own death in good health. Because one is always becoming-dead, one lives to die. However, Freud realized that *Beyond the Pleasure Principle* was his most speculative work: "In it I am saying things that are quite unclear," he wrote to his Hungarian disciple Sándor Ferenczi (1873–1933) in March 31, 1919, "out of which the reader has to make the right thing." In 1937, he wrote to another disciple, Princess Marie Bonaparte: "Please do not overestimate my remarks about the destructive instinct. They were only tossed off and should be carefully thought over if you propose to use them publicly." In *Beyond the Pleasure Principle* he further stated: "We make this assumption [about the existence of the Death Drive ~~Thanatos~~] thus carelessly because it does not seem to *be* an assumption. [It was] speculation, often far-fetched speculation."[6]

Curiously, as with most of Freud's key writings, the personal imagination laid down in *Beyond the Pleasure Principle* is rooted in the autobiographical. As always, the prevailing Structuralist-Romantic Order focused upon this "death and sex" in literature and the arts — Symbolism was very popular. Its brooding, introspective nature might have been characteristic of the Viennese elite witnessing the demise of the Austrian empire — perhaps fortified by the growing anti–Semitism in Vienna. In fact, there was so much "death and sex" in the air at the time, following public discussions after the disastrous World War I, Freud must have felt obliged to say something about it as well. Although the origins of this book must be found in the ongoing "duel" with Jung, Freud had some dark thoughts to dig for. First, his disciple Otto Rank (1884–1939) had written an essay "Der Doppelgänger" ("The Double") in 1914, which curiously still inspires therapists to diagnose split personalities in our own time. Three more disciples were preoccupied with death: Alfred Adler (1870–1937), Wilhelm Stekel (1868–1940), and Sabina Spielrein (1885–1942). Adler had developed an idea about aggression, Stekel had invented the term "Thanatos," and Spielrein had read an important paper about it to the Vienna Psychoanalytical Society in November 1911. World War I, with its trench warfare and several million deaths, came close to home when Freud's two sons had to go into the army, causing worries at home. In January 1920, his beloved daughter Sophie died. She had been his Sunday-child, so this must have been a true mortal blow. Freud had become an aged man with a persistent dark mood full of depressive pessimism. But then, most of his life Freud had suffered from *todesangst,* anxiety about death and dying. A grandson and one friend died from diseases and 15 (!) of his followers committed suicide. In this way, the Death Drive ~~Thanatos~~ had stuck to psychoanalysis firmly and would become an approach to cope with fear and guilt or even to deny responsibility for the deaths in the movement. All these failures made *Beyond the Pleasure Principle* nothing more than a kind of rhetorical strategy, whereby blame and responsibility could be assigned elsewhere — the patient is accountable, not the therapist. This way *Beyond the Pleasure Principle* can be read, Daniel Burston, a historian of psychology, concludes, as "a confession of impotence in the face of baffling complexities of mental illness." The formulation of the Death Drive ~~Thanatos~~ permitted its creator to live with the reality of death around and inside him.[7]

Nevertheless, the double fascinated people during the dawn of the Structuralist-Romantic Order. Think of Robert Louis Stevenson's *The Strange Case of Dr. Jekyll and Mr. Hyde* (1886), in which the character of Hyde was a personification of Dr. Jekyll's unconscious, if not a split-off of his death drive at war with his life drive. It is worthy to note that Stevenson's book was published a decade before Freud's crucial dream book. At that time it was already known for quite a while that the fearful double caused this anxiety not because of a problem in the brain's left temporoparietal junction, but because it was a sign of something "bad," or "destructive" of a "divided" or "double" consciousness. The idea had taken root that the Mr. Hyde character was typical for the Devil Within, a character that would better be hidden from sight. At the time Freud wrote about the uncanny/Unheimliche, he used dictionaries for its definitions. The dictionary stated that the word "heimlich" as "belonging to the house, homely, comfortable, familiar and agreeable" *and* "what is concealed, secretive, deceitful, and kept out of sight" exhibits a meaning that is identical with its opposite "unheimlich" (although "unheimlich" was not customarily used as the contrary of the latter meaning). Then second, in a telling quote by philosopher Friedrich Schelling (1775–1854), "unheimlich" was intoned as the name for "everything that ought to have remained secret and hidden but has come to light." Furthermore, one could find confirmation in *Grimm's Dictionary* of 1877, in which "heimlich" meant, among others, "as withdrawn from knowledge, unconscious [...] that which is obscure, inaccessible to knowledge [...]." These dictionaries all reflect the state of the Romantic mind of the time.[8]

All this has little to do with Nina's double in *Black Swan*. First of all, a Death drive goes right against all evolutionary thinking — a species "driven" to self-destruction would never have survived evolution[9] — and, second, the more down to earth explanation of psychosis and schizophrenia works better. Nina saw her double because of her collapsing state of mind. In fact, the filmmakers do their work well in representing this state of mind. Nina's mental illness caused a series of hallucinations because under severe stress her brain derailed from a more realistic tracking of imaging the world. Such a derailment is usually a minor step from the "normal" workings of the brain, especially if we consider the constructions of memory through time. The film shows us how an "interpreter" works in a frightening situation like this. Even the scholarly popular theory of the "Uncanny" cannot match this. Instead of confirming theories rooted in the Structuralist-Romantic Order, critics would do better to work with cognitive-evolutionary theories.

# 4

As artists, filmmakers play with the "interpreter" they set on stage. In the films discussed previously, the viewers experience one or two alternating "interpreters"— most of them not mentally ill. However, *Jennifer's Body* is a film comparable to *Black Swan*, with the "interpreter" giving us the experience of a seriously ill mind. In a more moderate way, *Chloe* and *[SAFE]* fit into the picture as well. We find an interesting game with the "interpreter" in *The Virgin Suicides,* a 1999 American drama written and directed by Sofia Coppola and produced by her father, Francis Ford Coppola. The viewers accompany Coppola's "interpreter" in the film when it tries to make sense of the past. Taking place "25 years ago" in "Michigan," *The Virgin Suicides* tells the story of a group of teenage boys and their memory of the Lisbon sisters, whose suicides ended the boys' childhood.[10] Because of this shared past, instead of individual stories the "interpreter" gives the history of a group of boys who shared their childhood in the same neighborhood. The film's "interpreter" is therefore a "group interpreter," trying to record this group's experience with the fate of the Lisbon family — their neighbors. The viewers get acquainted with the "interpreter" from the vantage point of the teenage boys growing up as disillusioned men in their thirties. Next to the images and the musical score, the "interpreter" also speaks to the audience as a retrospective voiceover. We learn that after 25 years, the "group interpreter" has trouble finding accurate memories that can pass by common consent. The voice of this "choral narrator" is uncertain, puzzled, and melancholic. Like in all memories, over time things are left out; details are distorted; other events are added. This is the "normal" workings of the brain. Where psychoanalysis had been pathologized thinking, the cognitive sciences look for regularities, systematics, and procedures.

Coppola's film is a dreamscape of cooperative recollection. The film shows us how the boys lusted after the girls. Trying to solve the mystery of the Lisbon sisters, they met several times over some 25 years. They contributed individually to the voice of the "group interpreter" with their stories and the paraphernalia they collected over the years. Their interest is to discuss the "proper" memory. *The Virgin Suicides* is based on a 1993 book with the same title, by Jeffrey Eugenides. The book impressed the filmmaker: "It was just so beautifully written, and it seemed so accurate with its basic theme about being a teenager, and all the epic feelings of first love and obsession. Also, the realistically melancholy atmosphere of the story has such a profound presence throughout, that I felt it would be a beautiful film if I could transcend that unique tone on to the screen." Further: "I thought he wrote beautifully about being that age, about being a teenager and about being at that age where you're first thinking about love and mortality." And: "That's what I liked about the book. That kind of etherealness. It's memory and not reality." From the book, Coppola took the story about young boys dealing with the world of girls. She copied how they tried to comprehend what it must have been like to be a girl or an older woman at the time. *The Virgin Suicides* shows us that this baffled collective never knew what had been going on. One thing the boys agree about is their frustration that the girls appeared to have understood them much better. It was as if the boys' world was ablaze with light for the girls, whereas the boys stumbled through a dark room. Coppola: "I wanted to emphasize that the whole film is a memory of the past as opposed to a reality of the present. A lot of it was shooting it from afar and the camera work was real simple and not aggressive at all. Also, the [...] music really helped a lot to add feeling. When I watched it for the first time with the music it added a whole extra dimension."[11] For reviewer Graham Fuller of *Sight and Sound,* she succeeded. He says that Coppola's fable "delights in the layers of mystique and accretions of physical detail with which it surrounds the loss of beautiful schoolgirls sucked before their time into the crevices of oblivion," which "has resulted in nothing less than a timelessly romantic suburban myth that could become a cult classic."[12]

A scene near the ending of Coppola's film shows the "group interpreter" at work — camera, score, voiceover. We hear soft piano music. On the screen is a calm, suburban house of an upper-middle-class Midwestern community, shot in various seasons; fast moving pictures from summer to autumn, night and day, back to spring. While the music continues its melancholic tune, and the camera moves inside the house, focusing in on a girl's hand playing with the water in a small aquarium, which is placed on a book entitled *Sacred Well of Sacrifice,* the voiceover returns. It is the voice of an adolescent boy: "For the next few weeks, we hardly saw the girls at all. Joe Hill Conley didn't call Therese as he had promised. And Lux never spoke to Trip again." We see four girls in one upstairs room. Two of them are softly discussing the potential of a make-up box, a third one is reading on the bed, and lovely Lux is looking out of the window full of desire. We hear Trip's voice: "You're a stone fox." One morning one of the girls resisted the cold to walk to the mailbox in her pajamas. "The girls' only contact with the outside world was through the catalogs they ordered that started to fill the mailbox with pictures of high-end fashions and brochures for exotic vacations. Unable to go anywhere, the girls traveled in their imaginations to gold-tipped Siamese temples or past an old man with a leaf broom tidying a moss-carpeted speck of Japan." Next, we see four boys on their knees in another upstairs bedroom, looking at catalogs as well. "We ordered the same catalogs and, flipping through the pages, we hiked through dusty passes with the girls, stopping every now and then to help them with their backpacks, placing our hands on their warm, moist shoulders, and gazing off at papaya sunsets." This is precisely what we see: a series of holiday snapshots of the boys and the girls as in happy days, including Cecilia, the fifth sister who had committed suicide. "We drank tea with them in a water pavilion. We did whatever we wanted. Cecilia hadn't died. She was a bride in Calcutta. The only way we could feel close to the girls was through these impossible excursions, which have scarred us forever, making us happier with dreams than wives." During the last sentence, the image turned foggy, rapidly white and black. Back in the boys' room: "Collecting everything we could of theirs, the Lisbon girls wouldn't leave our minds, but they were slipping away. The color of their eyes was fading along with the exact locations of moles and dimples. From five, they had become four, and they were all the living and the dead becoming shadows."

In Coppola's eyes, the neighborhood boys were especially interested in the Lisbon family's sexually precocious 14-year-old middle sister Lux (Kirsten Dunst). The film begins with the golden vision of Lux, polishing off a strawberry ice against the backdrop of a sunlit avenue before she drifts out of frame. The trait of "women understanding men devastatingly well" is perfectly personified in Dunst's portrayal of her. Within minutes, the viewer gets a quick shot of Lux, sucking on a popsicle at the side of the frame, briefly considering the audience before moving on, as if bored. There, removed to some heavenly world in the clouds, she gives us the sauciest of come-hither winks before the story of the neighborhood's decline is resumed. There is a world of complicity in that wink, Fuller thinks, for "it offers the audience a pact — a promise that, if we watch carefully, *The Virgin Suicides* has a secret to share, that it is only ostensibly a film about teenage wasteland." As a distant ambulance siren starts to slice through the French DJ-duo Air's insinuatingly ominous music theme, shots of a man watering his garden and women walking a dog are followed by the less reassuring — and blatantly symbolic — sight of workmen designating a diseased elm for removal. This last shot, Fuller concludes, tells us the rot has set in: "Cecilia was the first to go," we hear the voiceover saying, and the filmmaker cuts to the bluing face of Lux's 13-year-old sister Cecilia (Hanna R. Hall) lying face upwards in a bathtub — not unlike the *Ophelia* (1852) of British painter John Everett Millais (1829–96) — blood colored from slitting her wrists.[13]

What is going on? Through the thoughts of the neighborhood boys we learn that Cecilia had been a "daydreamer" and "completely out of touch with reality." But this does not explain her suicidal tendencies, of course. In recent studies, scholars have found that depression is a material condition that is typically the result of an imbalance in brain chemicals. Back in the 1970s, of course, there was no real explanation for this. Hence, we get no clarification. In fact, after the first attempt, the hospital doctor examining Cecilia had asked her why she would try to kill herself. Cecilia had given him dutifully the response expected by him, by her parents, and by the viewers: "Obviously, Doctor, you have never been a thirteen-year-old girl." But her face suggested that the true answer must have lain somewhere beyond her mockery. Soon, the viewers learn that the film is not about this deed at all. Neither does the attempt serve to prepare us for the suicides of all the girls; serious Therese (Leslie Hayman), sphinxlike Mary (A.J. Cook), pious Bonnie (Chelse Swain), libidinous Lux, and morose and religious Cecilia — all between 13 and 17. Swiftly, the story continues with an introduction to the Lisbon family, who were living in a house in Grosse Pointe, an affluent suburb of Detroit, Michigan. In the boys' memory, the parents (James Woods, Kathleen Turner) judged the world too evil and cruel for their five beautiful daughters. Father was an out-of-touch mathematics teacher at the school the girls attended. The "group interpreter" suggests that the parents wanted for their daughters, and especially Cecilia, the best they could offer but also that they were increasingly out-of-joint with the spirit of the age.

The generation gap getting out of hand as the cause for suicide? That sounds unrealistic. Cecilia continued to withdraw from family events. Psychiatrist Dr. Hornicker (Danny DeVito) found no way to deal with her disaffected boredom either and he informed the parents that Cecilia simply wanted attention. Given their conservative Roman Catholicism, he advised them to open up and allow the girls some space. Perhaps Cecilia wished for more intensive contact with boys her own age. It was in vain. Precisely the day the parents followed this advice and organized a party, inviting boys from the neighborhood, Cecilia jumped out of the bedroom window. The party had been nervous, of course, and only lightened up when a boy with Down syndrome, Joe (Paul Sybersma), entered, doing his "tricks." But soon, Cecilia had excused herself and made her way upstairs. After the noise of her jump, Mrs. Lisbon, the rest of her daughters and the boys had gone upstairs and out the front door, finding Mr. Lisbon holding Cecilia, draped over a fence, the spikes in her back. Following Cecilia's suicide, we learn from the "group interpreter" that the boys across the street tried to make sense of the repercussions of Cecilia's act, as well as of the way her sisters and parents tried to deal with it as well. But perhaps the suicide was not that important. What mattered was their social gathering.

The first major act of the neighboring boys was to begin a collection of Lisbon souvenirs, including diaries, clothes, and hairpins — not unlike the memory-aides from *Cosas insignificantes* and *Eternal Sunshine of the Spotless Mind*. Next, they began to speculate. Many minor details help the viewer feel what it must have been like living through the experience, like Cecilia "haunting" those around her and the diary — memory disguised as a ghost. Reading her diary, the neighboring boys found no clue as to why Cecilia had slit her wrists and then jumped from her window. The banal entries revealed nothing about her state of mind at the time she killed herself. For the boys, this perturbing situation permeated the daily lives of the family afterward as they tried to settle into some obscene form of normality but never could quite settle down, nor would others allow them. The "group interpreter" tells us that Mr. and Mrs. Lisbon changed the rules to be stricter and to hold their daughters to scrupulous moral standards. The "group interpreter" believes that there must have been a failure of communication at home. The father always deferred to "the missus" to make family decisions. As an old-school disciplinarian, the mother was so discomfited by her daughters' sexuality that she changed their homecoming dance dresses until they looked like "four identical sacks"— at least in the boys' memory. The family priest (Scott Glenn) visited the Lisbon residence only to find the master of the house passively drinking beer in front of a television screen and the mother upstairs in a near catatonic state. The parents could not converse well in these times, which, in fact, is in accordance with normal mourning. But the "group interpreter" preferred dull apathy above ordinary grieving. The neighborhood boys longed to be with the beauties but had neither the social skills nor the courage to charge the invisible moat surrounding them.

Virtual prisoners, the daughters had been made housebound. The viewer is confronted with the contrast the boys imagined between the formal external control dominating situations and dialogues, and the sense of devastating anxiety and despair that must have been hiding behind that exterior stillness. The gentle light pervading the oneiric moments, the soft tenderness of these refined and attractive girls make everything appear too calm, with a strange premonitory sense that something tragic would have to happen and make this surreal atmosphere explode. Of course, like any memory, this is recalled with the knowledge of the final suicide of the girls at the end of the movie. The boys merely imagined how suicide affects people and how their lives change due to someone's selfish act. They saw it as a nightmare, told in hindsight when their loves were lost within themselves, never to return. Filmmaker Coppola as writer and director captures the mystery that entwines itself with suicide. The film creates a haunting portrait of a time when sexual mores were loosened more than in perhaps any other period, due to increasingly widespread use of the pill (approved for use in the 1960s), the passage of the abortion law in 1973, and the upswing of divorce. Edward Lachman, the director of photography, shoots the bright colors of the 1970s as if through a layer of gauze. His dimmed, fuzzy tones suggest the darkening shades of the boys' memory.

Interestingly, even in the boys' memory, the parents were not those bad monsters that any kid would see as faceless villains. The "interpretation" in hindsight gives us the parents as a mild-mannered father and a strong-willed mother, quick to develop into a gutless slob and a shrew, projecting their fiasco upon their offspring. Was it the fault of the parents? Or, was it the sisters, their school, their friends, or ultimately the society in which the family interacted? No one had the answers, least of all the boys next door spying on them. In their eyes, so the "group interpreter" tells us, the girls must have begun hating their lives, hating their stern mother and powerless father. The girls wanted to have their lives, of course, but with these stiff parents that would be difficult. The boys remember that because of this life of isolation they thought that the girls should have been trapped in their own minds, in their own thoughts, unable to escape the blackness that had poisoned their lives after Cecilia's death. Most kids learn by adolescence how to rebel, and although we do not know about the early youth of these five girls, you can clearly see that all their lives they had no cause to rebel. Thus, the boys agreed, they didn't know how. The Lisbon parents communicated constant tension and mild anger, the boys think, driving the girls to their deed. But, as journalist Bree Hoskin says, this punishes them with undue severity because, in this nostalgic view of childhood and adolescence, parents are by rule doomed never to understand excessive teenage passions and the angst of their children. She continues: "Indeed, Coppola's film can be seen as a dark artistic expression of the experience of anyone who has looked back on the obsessive crushes or rebellious actions of their teenage years and thought to themselves, 'What was I thinking?'"[14]

Through voiceover, the "group interpreter" tells us that the neighborhood boys date not only the demise of their childhood but also the status of their neighborhood from the suicides of the girls. The area lost its innocent character of the childhood playground. It stands allegorically for the destruction of childhood for an entire generation of Americans born in the early 1960s. With adolescence come feelings of mystery, loss, despair, and the anxiety of the future. The 1970s saw the first conscious signs of environmental degradation — the trees in the front yard of the girls' house were dotted for removal on account of Dutch Elm disease. Later, the remaining four sisters protested the removal of one of these trees. Shortly before her suicide, Cecilia had mourned the fact that another animal had been added to the endangered species list. Indeed, in *The Virgin Suicides,* the longing for a lost childhood goes hand in hand with the demise of a part of the American dream. Through the condemned action of the voyeuristic nature of the press and the lack of attitude from the "respectable," bourgeois neighbors and school community, the meaninglessness, hypocrisy, and hollowness of suburban America are criticized. These agents see and comment on the abnormal behavior of the Lisbon family but take no attitude to help the girls. All this makes *The Virgin Suicides* a fairytale with a bad ending: childhood will be lost.

Following Disney-fed expectations, a fairytale on film needs a ball, and a ball needs a prince. The "group interpreter" gives us the school's Prince Charming in the figure of the handsome football player Trip Fontaine (Josh Hartnett). The "group interpreter" tells us that "all the girls at our school were in love with Trip." In the film, the boys are supported and perhaps even corrected by filmmaker Coppola. The prince needs a princess. Aloof and yet very aware of her beauty, Lux is considered the fairest sister. She causes Trip to turn to mush. She knows she has that effect even for a hunky guy who is "never one to pursue." With an apt sense of humor underscoring the moods of the time, the music in *The Virgin Suicides* is chosen to assist the "group interpreter" in its memory reconstruction work. Viewers would appreciate the joke of Heart's "Magic Man" (1976) accompanying Trip's entrance in the storyworld, with dozens of girls turning their heads in his direction. A modern magical prince, he wears a wig and smokes a joint in his car.[15] Invoking some magical imagery, the "group interpreter" confides the belief to the viewers that even Lux must have had his name written in magic marker on her underpants. The boys know from Cecilia's diary that Lux had done so with the name of an attractive garbage man. Trip managed to talk Mr. Lisbon into allowing the daughters, notably Lux, to go to the homecoming dance by promising to find dates for the other sisters and go as a group. Critic Zacharek comments: "The dance sequence sparkles from the moment the boys pick the girls up at the Lisbon house: the sisters filed down the stairs in their oddly shaped, matching homemade dresses, a procession of fairytale maidens decked out in Butterick finery."[16] During the dance, Lux decided to break the rules with Trip. In the company of one of her sisters and her date, she drank peach schnapps hiding behind a curtain. To the sounds of "Strange Magic" (1975) by the Electric Light Orchestra and "I'm Not in Love" (1975) by 10CC, the homecoming dance took on a kind of surrealist tenor. After they were crowned Homecoming King and Queen, Trip deflowered Lux on the football field. Until that moment it had been a happy tale.

The boys later speculate that Trip must have abandoned Lux during the night afterwards. Therefore, we see her left alone on the field. Three of the sisters had returned safely home. After one of the boys said goodnight to one of the girls, she entered the house. The girl left the boy sitting in the car. Partly intimidated and partly satisfied, he took a deep breath. But losing Lux this way, the girls had broken the curfew, and consequently they were punished by their furious mother. Lux's arrival at dawn set off the second stage of the family crisis. The boys remember that the girls were taken out of school. Mother forced Lux to burn all of her rock 'n' roll albums. Somehow, however, the boys agree later, Lux managed to make love regularly to new boys. In their reconstruction this would be inconsistent, because she was kept in. Therefore the "group interpreter" projects her on the roof of the house with one lover after another. To confirm this image, the neighborhood boys are shown looking through the telescope witnessing this. The image is of course also a reconstruction in hindsight, 25 years later, built on the previous reconstructions, on information added later on, and the inevitable nostalgia for a lost youth. These reconstructions made the boys outsiders forever, the girls insiders, trapped "in those rooms where they went to be alone for all time." The reconstruction of Lux having sex on the roof could very well be based on stories of or experiences with a promiscuous Lux at school.

After his repulsive post-coital abandonment of Lux, young Trip is never seen again in the film. Coppola stages his comeuppance as a 40ish guy in rehab (Michael Paré), where the boys interview him about Lux. The older Trip is decrepit-looking and wasted, withering in some bleak drug rehab center but still wearing the same ultra-fitted cowboy shirts. He remembers that he never loved anyone as much. Coppola talked with author Eugenides about this and he told her that "the character of Lux was based on some girl that he was in love with back in high school. I have heard stories of guys who fell in love in second grade and never found anyone that was quite the same." The boys recorded Trip saying about Lux: "I liked her a lot. But out there on the football field, it was different." The football field had meant the end of youth for him. The love and the sex had confirmed his loftiest ambition, which meant that there was nothing left of the dreams of adolescence. A new life of adult compromises, disenchantments and other drawbacks awaited him. Reviewer Ebert concludes: "Trip left Lux not because he was a pig, but because he was a boy and broken with grief at the loss of his — their — dream." In short, grown-up Trip suggests that the film addresses the absurdity of clinging to misremembered adolescence.[17]

The "group interpreter" settled with the idea that the girls were obliged to stay in their room all day. Informed that the girls received all these travel catalogs in the mail, the neighborhood boys speculated the girls were poring over them as a means of escape. The boys agreed that they imagined themselves doing likewise, sharing their imagined vacations in exotic locales, including the resurrected Cecilia. The girls were also believed to have sent letters to their dates for the homecoming dance, excluding Trip. The boys think they have answered these letters. Finally, after months of confinement, the boys transmitted a more concrete signal to the girls: through the phone. The messages were in the language of music. In hindsight, the girls must have made the decision to follow Cecilia on the anniversary of their sister's first attempt. This would make the game of songs an acid one. After Todd Rundgren's "Hello It's Me" (1972), the girls chose Gilbert O'Sullivan's "Alone Again (Naturally)" (1972). The boys countered with the Bee Gees' "Run to Me" (1972), answered by Carole King's "So Far Away" (1971). Finally, the Lisbon girls signaled by Morse code to the neighborhood boys to come over one night — presumably to help them escape from the house. The boys went over to the Lisbon household where they met Lux in the living room, smoking a cigarette. She opened the door and told them the other girls were upstairs and that she would go out to her parents' station wagon and wait for them. This sounded as if they planned on going for a ride to get out of the house.

But they did not. The boys went down to the basement and found Bonnie there, hanging. While they rushed back out of the house, terrified, they bumped into the lifeless bodies of the other Lisbon sisters. Later they were informed that Mary stuck her head in the gas oven. Therese took sleeping pills. Lux had gone to the garage to die there of carbon monoxide poisoning. Garage door shut, she had left the car engine running. The viewer notes that before they died, the girls had given out prayer cards to the boys that were similar to the one Cecilia had in her hand when she made her first attempt — in fact, in the novel, we read it is the anniversary of Cecilia's first suicide attempt. Devastated by the suicides of all their children, Mr. and Mrs. Lisbon quietly fled the neighborhood, never to return. The Lisbon house was sold soon after. The boys were left wondering what had happened and why; and what they could have done differently. But life in the upper-middle-class suburban town went on. The elms in front of the girls' house were cut down. Television reporters transmitted their clichés. And, of course, the neighbors went on with their lives. The boys grew older but no wiser. They found no answer, no justification, no meaning to the tragedy of these five girls. The viewer has gone with them through a nostalgic journey hoping "for a return to an authentic past" while hopelessly realizing that "this past is lost forever."[18]

## 5

*The Virgin Suicides* is a fully modern film. The movie offers no Freudian Excuse. Someone could have suffered from childhood trauma after Cecilia's suicide, but nobody did. In fact, their recurrent meetings of the boys imply a warm nostalgic bonding between them because of their shared past in this suburban area. Reviewer Todd Ramlow, for *PopMatters Magazine,* thinks that grasping at psychoanalytical answers must be seen as "a function of the interpretation and retelling of the story through a male perspective [...]." He adds: "The story turns into one about the lapses and anxious reassertions of male prerogative and access to knowledge/power. For these boys, this is a story of their own victimization, of their inability to put the suicides behind them, or to move on with their own lives." The "group interpreter" informs us through voiceover that "unlike boys, girls suffer various confinements that encourage their mental development, making their minds 'all dreamy and active.' While the Lisbon girls 'knew everything about us'," the "group interpreter" informs the viewer, "we couldn't fathom them at all." Yet, Ramlow concludes, "fathom them is precisely what the boys attempt, as the narrator claims their story as his own. And this is the final independence taken away from the Lisbon sisters, the ability to tell, or, more pointedly and importantly, not to tell, their own story."[19]

A psychoanalytical viewing has to fail, reviewer Fuller suggests. For example, Mr. Lisbon is not only a weak-minded father, but "he has, naturally, been emasculated by his domineering, maternalizing wife and the tide of oestrogen that sweeps through his house each day." Fuller invites us to see Mrs. Lisbon as "the Freudian evil mother, vengefully jealous of her girls' sexuality now her own beauty has waned." However, as he finds out, neither Eugenides in his novel nor Coppola in her film shows much interest in explicating the girls' suicides from Freud's theories. For example, "there is no return of the repressed because, in the world of the Lisbon girls, there apparently is none to return." Fuller again: "Trip's desertion of Lux on the school football field after he's devirginised her triggers her desperate bout of promiscuity on the family roof, but we do not get the sense she's going to kill herself over him." Although the other girls are almost, in Fuller's words, "slates as blank as Cecilia's diary," as viewers we can only guess at their supposedly repressed thoughts. Such thoughts would not include sexual wishes and desires, which are there constantly to be appreciated even by the most innocent of spectators. The pronouncements made by the psychologist in the novel are platitudinous. In the film he is played by Danny DeVito as a caricature. In all, Mrs. Lisbon's decision to withdraw the girls from school and keep them permanently at home is an unsatisfactory rationale for their determination to take their own lives. Interestingly, Fuller notes, Coppola sends the camera twice tracking over the girls' "puddles of girlish memorabilia — sunglasses, a lipstick, a prayer book, a Kiss LP, a brooch, a bloodstreaked laminated picture of the Madonna and Child — as if she were Tarkovsky tracking over the submerged detritus in *Stalker*." This suggests, Fuller believes, a downright celebratory passionate depiction of female adolescence. One boy, who gets to visit the girls and "pauses to sniff an illicit scarlet lipstick" in the bathroom, is confronted there by Lux, who throws him out so she can insert a tampon. For Fuller it is as if Coppola seized on the material with the intent of enfranchising teenage girlhood in all its hormonal glory, a subject glossed over in most Hollywood high school flicks.[20]

Eventually, for reviewer Fuller, the film's mythic quality is achieved through Coppola's playful *mise-en-scène*, which gives corporeal shape to the boys' memorialization of the Lisbon girls, gazing from an eerie spot across the street at the sisters' protracted demise — as we in turn watch them watching. In fact, as Fuller also concludes, the mythic level on which Coppola's movie operates suggests it is not about teen suicide but "about the monumental loss incurred by everyone with the passing of the teen years — [Coppola] has stated as much." He adds: "The suicides are a full-blown metaphor for the death of the teen experience — the non-stop emotional rollercoaster and the agonies and ecstasies of first love, the heinous parents, the unrepeatable aliveness, the sense of living inside a melodrama. We have, most of us, had a Lux or a Trip, that idealized projection of our own desires and inadequacies, that departed beauty who could never have maintained his or her inflated status in adulthood but whose unassailable perfections multiply with the passing years. The knowledge that this is what the film is about is the secret in Lux's wink." In short, *The Virgin Suicides* can be nostalgically viewed as far from an American dystopia as it can be. At the end, a "time-lapse sequence of the Lisbons' house reveals little change through the seasons, but as the girls recede from the foreground of the movie so Coppola endows them with an otherworldly aura." They are, says Fuller, "as lovely as living ghosts as they were as radiant schoolgirls." And this, despite all the signs of decay, dissonance, and universal malaise of the first years of the 1970s that are symbolized so well by talk about nasty smells and the cutting of the elms in front of the house. Jenny Cooney Carrillo of *Urban CineFile* asked her if the girls' suicides were realistic. Coppola answered: "It is not realistic to me because they are not real girls. I always saw them as symbolic and I did not want the parents to be the villains. They are not ideal parents that I would want to have but what I liked about the story and the book is that there isn't one good reason about why they do it. In life there are so many things that don't make sense and can't be explained. To me it was about these things in life that happen that there are no good reasons for — and how the survivors left behind deal with it."[21]

Reviewer Ramlow informs us that the year 1976, possibly the date of the diegesis, the bicentennial of 1776, marks "the frenzied end of one of the most turbulent eras in U.S. history, and the end of a 'traditional' American way of life and industry." He points at what the narrator remarks: "neighbors saw in the Lisbon girls' tragedy the 'wiped-out elms, the harsh sunlight, and the continuing decline of our auto industry.' The year was also [...] characterized by the energy crisis, and the increasing import of cheaper, more gas efficient foreign cars, that would shortly lead to the demise of Flint, Michigan, and Detroit auto workers, one of the historical backbones of the U.S. economy." For this reviewer, 1976 ended the turbulent sixties and seventies. It was final chord of the myth of national interest and a unified citizenry. In *The Virgin Suicides* the "group interpreter" presents us with Mrs. Lisbon as the archetypal reaction to the new times embodied in her daughters; or in her depiction of what they might be. Better to retreat in homeschooling and hiding away from radical social, political and sexual novelties. Ramlow: "The failure of the Lisbon family reflects the failure of the American Dream and the conservative values that underpinned it." On the other hand, Fuller informs us about a coincidence, which, at least partially, informed Coppola's filming. In May 1986, the elder of Sofia's two brothers, Gian-Carlo Coppola, was killed in a speedboat accident at the age of 22. Sofia told Fuller that "although she wasn't thinking of him when she chose to make *The Virgin Suicides*, she had been forcibly reminded during filming of how she too had gone over her memories time and time again to try to understand what had happened." In the end, she had stopped trying, but was left with "an essence" that persuaded her that his short life had had a purpose. Thus, Fuller winds up, "although fictional, Coppola's American beauties also have a purpose: to remind us all that our teenage triumphs and traumas, and the phantoms who provoked them, are as alive as they ever were." In short, despite the end of an era in U.S. culture, in general the American beauties are there to stay.[22]

In Eugenides's book, and in the script Coppola has reverently carved from it, Lux Lisbon and her sisters exist only insofar as they are the objects of masculine nostalgia. The narrator of *The Virgin Suicides* is "we," an infatuated segment of the adolescent male population of the affluent Michigan suburb. By making it her own, Coppola made Eugenides's book somewhat also an "inside" view with the girls on the "inside" of what we may call "girl culture," by stressing details like their dress and zooming in on Trip's behavior. At the same time she posits the boys on the "outside" of this world, although the narrator is "inside." Reviewer Zacharek wrote in *Salon Magazine,* April 2000: "What's interesting in particular about *The Virgin Suicides* isn't just that it was made by a woman, but that it's a case of a woman's adapting a novel about a group of young men's nostalgia for the unattainable girls of their youth. In the old days, you might have said those girls were imprisoned in the male gaze. But Coppola's picture is completely nonjudgmental about the narrators' love for the Lisbon girls (although it should go without saying that love shouldn't be subject to *anyone's* judgment). [...] The picture has a feminine sensibility in terms of its dreamy languor, the pearlescent glow that hovers around it like a nimbus."[23]

More than simply a "male gaze," the film shows us a dreamscape of cooperative recollection, which gives the filmmaker a series of liberties usually attributed to fairytales. Next to the image of Lux writing with a magic marker the name of an attractive garbage man in her underpants, the neighborhood boys conjure up images of the girls in a field with a unicorn. They could only feel close to the girls by the fantasized excursions around the world offered in catalogs, and we witness the traipsing off to these exotic locations with the girls; finding Cecilia back, living as a bride in Calcutta. Someone jumps off a roof and survives without a scratch. We see Cecilia's ghost at the foot end of a bed. Scenes like these suggest that major pieces of information are lacking. We automatically and unconsciously fill them in — like Mona Lisa's legs. Although beginning with the procurement of Cecilia's diary, the boys collected anything they could lay their hands on — yearbook photographs, invitations, eyelash curlers, lipstick, music records, hair brushes, nail polish, and more artifacts — recollection after 25 years makes it possible that eroded or lost scenes can be filled in at random. In fact, memory may take on an independent life colored by fantasy. Over time, on several occasions this memory must have been re-built and re-encoded with "new" information brought up during conversations. The voiceover tells us that whenever the boys ran into each other at business lunches or cocktail parties, they discussed the evidence over again. After all these years, they could not get the five girls out of their minds.[24] All this is much closer to a popular psychology of Cognitive Schema Theory than to Freud's Edifice.

# 6

What the neighborhood boys were actively conceiving was a mental schema of a crucial moment in their childhood. This is what memory and the unconscious are about. According to Cognitive Schema Theory memory consists of schemas as the major units of cultural memory. In 1932, psychologist Frederick C. Bartlett (1886–1969) was among the first experimental psychologists to address the question of culture and memory. He assumed that cultures are organized collectivities whose members form "strong sentiments" around shared customs, values, and institutionalized activities. These values and their expression through culture shape psychological tendencies to commit certain kinds of information to memory. Cultures assimilate knowledge through their operation and then constitute the schemas through which the universal process of reconstructive remembering operates. Psychologist Hiroko

Nishida defines schemas as "generalized collections of knowledge of past experiences which are organized into related knowledge groups and are used to guide our behaviors in familiar situations." A schema is a mental representation of a class of people, objects, events, situations, or behavioral codes, which are used to describe knowledge about how to act and behave. Experiences and other information stored in the brain bind together to form memory. Neural binding allows simple information and narratives to be combined into larger, more complex ones.[25]

Not repression but forgetting is the rule. New information that can be retrieved from already registered knowledge can be skipped. Think of a blue square, says Lakoff. It "appears as a single object, yet the color and shape are registered in different parts of the brain." For example, blue is known; square is known. All new information containing blue and square will make use of stored memory. However, every time a part of memory is triggered, it seems reinforced. This way the so-called "schematic narratives," serving like models for many others, become fixed in the brain. For the neighborhood boys of *The Virgin Suicides,* the film's story is such a schematic narrative. The synapses of the neural circuits characterizing schematic narratives have been so strengthened that they form permanent parts of our brains. Lakoff argues that "neural binding allows these permanent general narrative structures [including conceptual metaphor and cognitive schemas, AO] to be applied to ever-new special cases." Perceiving and thinking in terms of schemas enables people to process large amounts of information swiftly and economically. Instead of having to perceive and remember every detail of each new person, object, or situation encountered, their most distinctive features are placed within an already encoded schema. And it does not change very easily. Schema-refuting information is generally disregarded or reinterpreted. Only gross inaccuracy will lead to schema change. Those schemas that can be logically or practically refuted are the first to fall. This is not usually the result of general-purpose reasoning but is tied to other schemas in relation to a wider body of "knowledge." In general, though, schemas are fairly resilient. They tend to incorporate exceptions before being reformulated. Resilient schemas adapt to new information that "fits" and forget or neglect non-standard information. This way worldviews come into existence and become resilient. This is "one of the things cognitive science teaches us," says Lakoff. When "people define their very identity by a worldview, or a narrative, or a mode of thought, they are unlikely to change — for the simple reason that it is physically part of their brain, and so many other aspects of their brain structure would also have to change; that change is highly unlikely."[26]

This shows how active the "audience" in the "theater of our mind" is. That is the place where schemas work as devices to order and group thoughts, and the emotions and bodily feelings associated with them. They provide the categorical rules or drafts of scripts that are adapted, stored and maintained by the brain, and that are drawn on to interpret the situation a person is in at any specific moment and to predict what will happen next. They are simultaneously driven by structure and meaning and represented propositionally. Consequently, they are actively constructed networks, cognitive-emotional structures of neuronal connections that represent real or imagined knowledge about a concept or a type of stimulus, including its attributes, attitudes, and the social location of those attributes. Schemas function within a set of interrelated cognitions that allows individuals quickly to make sense of another person, a situation, an event, a place, a space, on the congruency of limited information. Such "knowledge groups" can also be regarded as neural networks; patterns of interaction among strongly interconnected neural assemblies. Instead of having to perceive and remember every detail of each new object or event, people simply note that it is similar to pre-existing schemas—and encode. They later remember only its most prominent features. Schematic encoding occurs rapidly, automatically, and unconsciously.[27] Although schemas depend on individual experiences and cognitive processes—and are thus unique to specific individuals—they are clearly "social" because they originate and are shared within a particular ecology of human development; that is, they originate from certain moments and within certain spaces among people who bring in their memories, emotions, and feelings. Hence, for the neighborhood boys the articulation of their childhood ending, the girls' suicides, and nostalgia of suburbia.

While every scene of *Black Swan* confronts us with the increasingly tense mind her "interpreter" needs to explain, *The Virgin Suicides* is brought to us as a collaborative, nostalgic narrative of a "group interpreter." Technically, there is no difference, however, because similar to the conceptual metaphor, individual schemas are cultural and collaborative. The influences shaping individual cognition and thought are social and interpersonal. A human being will locate behavior that is meaningful for him and near others and posit the thought where it acts; wording and actions give it a significant place. Personhood or personality cannot exist independently because the development of the individual takes place in an ecological setting, which necessarily ties it to specific cultural arrangements and historical change, which literally build up the brain cells of the individual. Humans, like most other animals, are wired to learn most from social sharing, including emotions. Adults tend to share more than adolescents, who are more cautious about sharing their emotions because their primary concern is how the group will view and evaluate certain experiences. Despite inner threats to mental functioning—disorders—all thoughts, including emotions, tend to fit the cultural conventions of the person's meaningful place and significant others in a way that are deemed appropriate. Therefore, thoughts in general, including private emotions and dreams, are social acts, the unique individuality of each person notwithstanding. Despite our ability to remember, the entire system is directed toward current and future behavior, including the accomplishment of goals, wishes, and desires. Memory works by seeing the ways in which current imaginative, symbolic, or real behavior displays continuity with the behavior and associated symbolizing of the past. This is a social question — for Nina in *Black Swan* as for the neighborhood boys in *The Virgin Suicides*. Memory does not work like a computer system of storing and retrieving. In short, the thought is directed toward communicable properties, involving ways of describing stabilized uses of signs and symbols, as well as inference-making abilities for those who have to grasp the communicative words, acts, and behavior that result.[28]

Rooted in the mirror neuron system, this "social thought" implies a systematic and essential association between someone's personal and unique use of concepts and the use made by others of that concept. The association must be systematic so that from the links between individual thoughts made at different times and places people can build up knowledge of the world, which is shared by the participants-in-communication. Psychologist Monisha Pasupathi reminds us once more of the fact that we live our lives "immersed in talk, providing others with stories of what happens to us and ideas [about] what we think our experiences mean." This talking includes dreams and talking to ourselves. Talking about past experiences, for example, is a process by which autobiographical memories are socially constructed because they are co-constructed with partners and they then gradually become represented internally. First, the storyteller reconstructs the experience or event during the conversation itself. In general, people tell listeners about events in ways which, they hope, will gain and hold attention. They concentrate upon norms, values, goals, and emotions that are accepted by their audience. Some details or perhaps the entire story might be recounted as being more exciting, sadder, or drearier than it actually was. In short, the account conforms to the community's cultural expectations. The listeners contribute to the storytelling by presenting their own insights, and reactions to it, be they positive, negative, or neutral. Their reactions influence which events are talked about and what sorts of interpretive statements, details, and emotions are connected with the event as it is discussed. The storyteller then encodes the effects of the conversation about the experience together with his or her memories of the original experience. The memory is reconstructed in the light of the conversation. This reconstruction of past experience is consistent with notions of development and cultural values. "People choose (or are asked) to talk about certain types of events and interpret those events in ways consistent with their own character in order to achieve particular aims with respect to particular listeners."[29] This is precisely how *Black Swan* and *The Virgin Suicides* are built up.

Growing evidence suggests that although memories are dynamic, fluid, and constructions bound to specific "stages," which are influenced by the context in which they are produced, reconstructed memories become relatively stable after the initial period of malleability. This means that they are also consistent with social and personal experience over time. Thus, because subsequent personal memories of events talked about in conversation are co-constructed, any personal memory is consistent with its socially constructed version. In the end, the content of autobiographical memory is a result of both experiences and social reconstructions of those experiences. The neighborhood boys of Coppola's film experience the same.

The physical characteristics of the social thought are, of course, chemical. It is pedestrian to say that human bodies, including their brains, are nothing but a chemical industry, but in Freud's Romantic thinking this would go too far. The chemicals that can be attributed to social thought are the "bonding hormones" oxytocin and vasopressin. Oxytocin is best known for roles in female reproduction. It is released from the posterior pituitary, which triggers milk letdown in the nursing mother. This is called the Milk Letdown Reflex, started off by the stimulation of the mother's nipple. Also the role of oxytocin in anxiety, social recognition, pair bonding, orgasm, and maternal behaviors has been confirmed. Interestingly, oxytocin levels in the brain increase during specific bonding activities like talking, listening, and even thinking of important others. It is the messenger of trust, affection, generosity, and peace of mind. Vasopressin levels are high in the brain while defending children against outsiders or standing for the rights of families and communities. High levels strengthen mating and other forms of social bonding. Here gender and sex merge, for oxytocin is more important for females than for males; vasopressin is more important for males than females.[30] This is not "performative."

The idea of social thoughts as being physically rooted in human minds should not distract us from someone's personal *conception* of reality. This so-called Theory of the World is retrieved from memory to deal with different realities, some 6,000 times a day. The thought that incorporates the reaction to one of these 6,000 instances comes into existence a few split seconds *after* the sensory input. This neuronal assembly of spikes within an electronic circuit in the brain, as the articulation of translated and interpreted sensory inputs, has no predetermined particular center, no fixed area in the brain, and is not always evenly distributed between individual brain cells. It acts in a spatially multiple way, but it is temporally unified around an epicenter, like a stone in a puddle, large enough to develop concentration on an input. The neural assemblies are highly transient throughout the brain and highly dynamic. As concentration grows, the assembly recruits more and more neurons. Neurotransmitting chemicals flow through the brain to keep it alert, and facilitate prompt reaction of the neuronal assemblies. Neurologist Oliver Sacks looks at memory as the imagination of the past. A retrieved past experience, emotionally evaluated, is subjective and individual and never a literal, photographic, or filmic copy of the inputs once received. It is, as suggested, also part of the present situation in which it is retrieved, and subsequently encoded and stored again under the influence of that present. In so far as we can indeed grasp memory retrieval as imagination, this restoring includes that imagination, and adds therefore another considerable bias.[31]

We have already seen that memory—as mainly developed in the form of schemas—can be activated at will and at random to guide future behavior. "All thinking is for doing," psychologist Susan Fiske wrote. Despite their voiced intentions, the neighborhood boys of *The Virgin Suicides* reconstruct their memories for present-day nostalgia. The film shows their 1999 mind; it is not a historical reconstruction of the late 1970s. For present-day use, schemas are set, stored, reset, and maintained by the encoding process. Retrieval cues of encoded events, experiences, moods, motives, emotions, and feelings are all combined in schemas. Experience leads to the formation of a kind of prototype schema S and all kinds of subsequent and derivative schemas $S^1$, $S^2$, $S^3$, ... $S^n$; although a final $S^n$ probably does not exist because the derivations never stop. In reconstructing memories, missing details are fitted into the retrieval apparatus by *schematic logic* with the help of already encoded schemas; for example, $S^2$ is reconstructed with the help of the chain $S + S^1 + S^3$. This quality helps the brain to reconstruct memories by providing a cognitive-motivated emotional notion of what memory *should* look like. Coppola's film shows what the neighborhood boys now think their past experience *should* look like. In effect, filling in—Mona Lisa's legs—is very important because most memories are imperfectly or poorly encoded. Perceptions are in themselves biased by expectations and preconceptions, which also form part of the schemas. Imagination like this could dominate memory astoundingly. When someone hears a sentence or a story, he often relies on his general knowledge about how the world works to fill in any missing details. For example, in the sentence "Trip broke a bottle in a barroom brawl," someone, using his knowledge of barrooms, is more likely to infer that it was a beer or whiskey bottle than a milk bottle that was broken. Constructive memory, as this property is called, is a by-product of the need to understand a world. It is a powerful addendum to the input statements that are *expected* to follow from them, expected in a subjective, culturally structured way.[32] We recognize the "interpreter."

As more instances are encountered, the schemas become more abstract and less concrete. They also become richer and more complex as more data have to be processed. At a certain point, however, a split is inevitable and several tightly organized schemas are organized, including more and more complex links between them. This is the chain $S^1$-$S^2$-$S^3$, ... , but also the chain $Ss^1$-$Ss^2$-$Ss^3$.... As said, once formed, people tend to keep their schemas intact and protect them from change by uncritically relying on their earlier judgments. The idea of all the girls committing suicide, and not just Cecilia, came to constitute the memory of the neighborhood boys in *The Virgin Suicides,* and there is no way for us to judge from the film if they actually occurred in their worlds or not. Memory does not serve history, it only serves contemporary and near future behavior. In this case, it serves the nostalgia and continued bonding of four neighborhood boys, which is perhaps the only world they share.

Why these four neighborhood boys cling so strongly to the girls' history is not explained in the film, although an important hint is given. After their youth, they spread out over the country. This means that they lost their bonding, the experiences of their Socialization System—SocS. People need to bond, and in modern Western societies with all this migration and movement of people, it is stressful and feeds general anxieties to cut off bonds that were once made. The historical narratives of youth recapture the origins of their SocS; it gives the people involved back their belonging.[33]

The individual thought as a memory device needs cueing. The social thought needs social cueing, perhaps by mirroring. In individuals, cueing occurs basically by the senses and the context of recollection. All else being equal, people are more likely to recall something when the context of remembering resembles the context of encoding. "Information may be available in memory but not accessible," writes McNally in his *Remembering Trauma* (2003), "because of the absence of potent reminders." He adds: "Yet seemingly long-forgotten events may immediately come to mind when cues present at encoding are present once again [...]."[34] Cueing schemas is culturally dependent, a feature of those groups who share language, religion, ideologies, and norms and values, in sum, of those who share a cultural memory.[35] We have seen that people also use instruments, or artifacts, to assist the process—as we indeed witnessed with the blue-lit house in *Mysterious Skin,* Melinda's tree in *Speak,* and many other signs in *Eternal Sunshine of the Spotless Mind, Drama, Cosas insignificantes, Black Swan,* and *The Virgin Suicides.*

By artifact, Michael Cole, one of the leading cultural psychologists, suggests we understand both the material object manufactured by humans, thus produced by material culture, and the conceptual or ideal products, thus, texts. An artifact is an aspect of the material world that has been modified over the history of its incorporation into goal-directed, human action. The "properties of artifacts apply with equal force whether one is considering language or the more usually noted forms of artifacts such as tables and knives that constitute material culture. What differentiates the word 'table' from an actual table is the relative prominence of its material and ideal aspects and the kind of coordination they afford. No word exists apart from its material instantiation (as a configuration of sound waves, hand movements, writing, or neuronal activity), whereas every table embodies an order imposed by thinking human beings."[36] This principle includes geographical features like mountains — landscapes. For Cole, Cognitive Schema Theory must be at work in the *narratives people tell themselves* — this is what the "interpreter" does — narratives that are passed on and learned by succeeding generations with the aid of artifacts, until "something better" is found. Cole sees this as the culture people inherit and can be described as "living" in a certain place in space and time. This is why cultures are bound to localities and social groups, more than to individuals.

# 7

With *Black Swan,* the viewer enters the mind's flight simulator of the protagonist and becomes acquainted with the consequences of increased pressure and stress. Also *The Virgin Suicides* could be seen as a simulation par excellence — of current group identity. For psychoanalysts, the question of identity had involved a *personality theory.* Recent research has demonstrated it is not. Identity is a theory of oneself, acting at a certain place (stage), in the company of a group, in a certain moment. This theory is based on schemas — these mental representations of people, objects, events, situations, or behavioral codes, used to describe knowledge about how to act and behave. As stated previously, information stored in the brain binds together to form memory and to form codes about how to perform at a certain location, influenced by tradition — thus, time — and numbers, like majority versus minority. Worlds are sometimes colliding because if people move from one place to another or change group belonging, their identity changes. They *plug in* to a new identity, so to speak. In addition, they run the risk of forgetting their roots. Schema Theory in a way predicts how to perform at a certain location, influenced by tradition — thus, time — and numbers, like majority versus minority. The theory can be used to explain why Nina falls into mental illness: in her world she first needs to acquire a status as high as possible, therefore she needs to perform and this brings her to go beyond her limits. Nina's predecessor Beth Macintyre needs to live outside this culture — this complex of interrelated schemas — but still cannot and thinks she is a failure. Outside the theater, outside the stage, the situation is different, and people are running different schemas. In a way, Nina's own stand-in, the West Coast girl, runs other schemas and does not seem to feel the pressure this way. This is genetic — Nina's predisposition may be different — but can be cultural as well. If people move in numbers, chances are that they replicate customs from their place of origin, fully or in part, at their new location. It is also possible, though much more complicated, to force a change of identity of certain places. This is what happens if, in a short time, an entire generation chooses to adopt new norms, values, codes, and such. The origins of this can be phenomena like globalizing influences, radio, television, the Internet, and, indeed, political projects.[37]

Freud thought that his psychoanalysis was a "great blow to human self-esteem." We should now look at it as a Structuralist-Romantic critique of the Functionalist-Enlightened portrayal of man — not something progressive but conservatively looking back, perhaps even a reactionary retrieving of something from older times. The Cognitive-Evolutionary psychology of Schema Theory and the conceptual metaphor of the linguistics provide us with a picture of human identity that may be much more shocking than Freud's ever was: people may *plug-in* and *plug-out* of identities, even without consciously realizing this, like robots, bounded to space and time. They can do so automatically and easily, or with considerable difficulties — as Beth Macintyre's case shows in *Black Swan,* and, in a way, Nina herself. Furthermore, conceptual metaphors that seem to work from the "deep" are simply learned and programmed by language. Finally, even the past is fabricated as a perpetual fantasy and memory does not serve like a historical archive — but that is known to human kind as long as we know. And it serves the present, as Coppola shows in her film.

# *Afterword*

## Out of the Deep

### 1

In Season 1, Episode 2, "Ah, But Underneath," first aired on Sunday October 10, 2004 (Prod. Code: 101), Bree Van de Kamp, a character of the well-known ABC television series *Desperate Housewives,* and married to character Rex Van de Kamp, convinces her spouse to attend marriage therapy instead of filing for divorce. Rex is frustrated by his wife's perfection-seeking nature. And indeed, she keeps the greenest lawn on Wisteria Lane, her cupcakes are always baked to perfection, and when she plans a dinner party she even upholsters the dining room chairs herself. It makes Rex state that he cannot stand "living in a deodorant commercial."[1] During the therapy sessions, however, the threadbare buttons of the coat of the therapist, Dr. Goldfine, continuously distract Bree's attention. When Dr. Goldfine recommends a series of private sessions, Bree refuses but then realizes she may seize the opportunity to fix the buttons and accepts. As she stitches the therapist's blazer, Dr. Goldfine hesitates: "I'm sure Freud would not approve of this." Bree is not impressed at all: "Oh, who cares what he thinks. I took psychology in college. We learned all about Freud. A miserable human being." If true, this could take the bread out of Dr. Goldfine's mouth. He tries to find ways to rebut her. "What makes you say that?" Bree, however, has thought it over carefully: "Well, think about it. He grew up in the late 1800s. There were no appliances back then. His mother had to do everything by hand, just backbreaking work from sun-up to sun-down, not to mention the countless other sacrifices she probably had to make to take care of her family. And what does he do? He grows up and becomes famous, peddling a theory that the problems of most adults can be traced back to something awful their mother has done. She must have felt so betrayed. He saw how hard she worked. He saw what she did for him. Did he even ever think to say thank you? I doubt it."

## 2

Bree's perception of Freud is not truly Freudian but it captures the Freudian Excuse pretty well. And I think we should not turn a deaf ear to her advice: "Oh, who cares what he thinks." If film critics and filmmakers want their viewers to offer insights into human nature, all evidence and interpretations indicate that they do better without psychoanalysis. That is this book's conclusion. Because viewers tend to be transported into the films' narratives, filmmakers can be quite successful in inviting them to use their work as simulators for future solutions for problematic or challenging situations in their lives. As we have seen, these simulations will not venture into something mysteriously deep. Filmmakers correctly dedicate a lot of attention to their actors, for viewers tend to identify with them and store their actions in memory. Thanks to their mirror neurons, viewers exercise a series of skills that are shared by these actors. What they need is a broad point of view (openness), a readiness to interpret the life of others, even from the past or the future, and the ability to observe, to conjecture, to experience, and to be carried away by emotions. In giving substance to the psychological lives of characters, the viewers must use their own experiences, encoded in mental schemas, to bridge gaps in narratives, including bringing facts and emotions to bear on them. On the basis of acquired mental schemas and personal temperament, different viewers use the space provided by these individual differences to various interpretations of performances. One of the main products of such performances is an inference to bridge gaps of various sizes in the narratives. Because we continually draw inferences and exhibit participatory responses in everyday life, we may look at our reality as constructed as much as any narrative world. Knowledge outside the narrative is often critical to the adequate construction of a narrative world — think of Mona Lisa's legs.[2] As previously mentioned, the human psyche does not go that deep; it is programmed by culture — including language — and it runs simulations to deal with emotions in a social reality.

Conscious forgetting (i.e., not willing to think about something or someone) is not the same as Freudian repression. It cannot be written off that Freud's haunting unconscious, the passive mind, repression, and many other connections between "facts" and assumptions did not succeed in passing serious scholarly testing over and over again — perhaps they were never meant to be. What is more, Onfray argues that Freud's reasoning was *magical*, underpinned by shamanistic rituals on and around his couch — what he called his "technique."³ No wonder that, academically speaking, the Freudian assumptions and its ensuing concepts could not make it to the status of hypotheses. This problem haunted the United States during the Memory Wars of the 1980s and 1990s concerning the possibility of recovering "lost" memories of sexual abuse. The result was that the popular media as well as juries and judges in the United States came to realize the fictional nature of the narratives of supposed victims of sexual abuse they had recorded. The authoritarian character of psychoanalysis was unmasked when people recognized that repressed memories were suggested to the "patients" by the all-knowing therapists during psychotherapy. Hundreds of psychologists — and this is not an exaggeration — testing human memory have shown that although people do forget, although never completely, instead of repress, but that with some concentration all memories can be brought back. Memory is open. It has no concealed rooms for "repressed" thoughts. Memories of traumatic experiences, in fact, could always be remembered better than any other experience; better indeed, and for a longer period of time. Curiously, our contemporaries have mostly neglected the work of William James (1842–1910), a distinguished psychologist at Harvard University, and author of *The Principles of Psychology* (1890), a book that despite some flaws due to its antiquarian character is still often quoted by common consent by scholarly psychologists today. James thought that the art of remembering is the art of thinking, using the brain and concentrating upon particular characteristics; in short, James made clear that memory is not repressed and never lost. Freud knew James' work but decided to neglect it. He preferred Sophocles.

Today, psychologists, linguists, philosophers, and other cognitive scholars agree that fictional narrations meet the human tendency to organize information in the form of stories. As a result, stories are supposed to yield better than abstract accounts such as rhetoric or expository texts. At the end of this book, perhaps Freud's standard mode of operation can be most fruitfully summarized by an anecdote. In 1910, in one of the first attempts to "prove" the Oedipus Complex by historical cases, Freud took on a reading of material provided by Leonardo da Vinci (1452–1519). The case was to answer the basic question of the Oedipus Problem: Why does the boy turn heterosexual and not homosexual? The Leonardo materials he gathered consisted of a few autobiographical notes Leonardo left about his childhood. Freud translated these notes himself. Going through them, the main dilemma Freud recognized in Leonardo was his supposed inability to finish projects. In the notes, Leonardo had written about the memory of a bird that landed on his cradle. The vulture, Freud read in Leonardo's words, opened his mouth with his tail and touched his lips with it a few times. It was not a true memory — it still is rather problematic for humans to remember cradle experiences — but a projection, perhaps fictive. Freud concentrated on the vulture. He stated that vultures in ancient Egypt were a symbol for motherhood and that vulture chicks matured without a father. For Freud this was a sign of homosexuality: boys could not properly choose their own gender. In short, Leonardo's note was evidence of his homosexuality. Leonardo drew a lot more young men in his notebooks than women. The male figure was more interesting to him than was the female, especially because some of the young men he drew were nude. Typically, Freud cheated, for he had prior knowledge. Authors in his time were well aware of a near-contemporary (15th-century) description by a biographer, who mentioned two beautiful young men as "beloved" of Leonardo at various points in his life. It was also known in Freud's days that Leonardo was twice charged with sodomy in 1476, together with two other men, and imprisoned for two months. The charges were dropped for lack of witnesses. In Leonardo's time, accusing someone anonymously of sodomy was sometimes a successful tactic to cause trouble to someone else.[4]

Because he dismissed other evidence, it seems that Freud found he knew enough. The historical logic of his argument, even of the errors in his own reading, were of no relevance anymore. Should we believe that Renaissance Leonardo shared a symbolic world with Ancient Egypt? Freud's major error was his translation. In the Italian original of Leonardo's note, there is no mention of a vulture but of a kite, an altogether different bird. Thus, exit vulture symbolism, right? But then the case turns really worrying. Dutch Freud historian Han Israëls found in Freud's consultation room in London — where Freud spent the last year of his life — a correct German translation, underlined by Freud himself. This means that Freud was familiar with the error in his translation. He must have stuck to the vulture translation only in order to pursue the homosexuality thesis. In fact, he never acknowledged the mistake and did not even bother to remove his underlining of the German translation or remove the German translation from his library in order that no one would later discover the painful mistake. Homosexuals, Freud supposed, have developed in childhood such a strong bond with their mother that they refuse to leave them — and be "adulterous" to them with other women — that they project their sexual desires on their own sex. This is quite unlikely for anyone studying homosexuality today. Freud concluded that the image of the vulture's tail meant that his mother must have kissed him many times on the lips. The fact that Leonardo, when he was older, did live with his father in a real family made no difference to him because this came too late. The damage was done: no experience past the age of three could change the formation of the child's personality. This, of course, sounds equally bizarre nowadays to any psychologist. But Freud was convinced that he had solved Leonardo's "neurosis" of the unfinished projects: it was in line with the role model of the absent father. He believed to have skillfully practiced the art of filling in details that are not at all in the data. In 1919, he declared that his book on Leonardo was the only *treasure* he ever wrote. In short, Freud not only bent the facts to his will but seemed not to have cared about the possibility of an unmasking of his deceit.[5] Of course, if Freud really saw himself as a "magician," which would have been in line with his Structuralist-Romantic thinking, there was no need to prove things at all. A magician works by doing things ritually, not by accurate logic.

# 3

However, sometimes, critics and scholars have no choice but to enter the Freudian Edifice. The author of a piece of art — be it a novel, a painting, a feature film, a documentary film — might himself be fully enrolled in psychoanalysis, hence the reason to identify the Freudian Excuses in films. It means that gaining insights into such a work of art — but not in the human condition in general — requires the discussion of Freudian theory. What is needed is knowledge of the source of information. Where does it come from? If we know this metarepresentation of the message, we know how to value the information. For this reason, in this book the origins of several Freudian Excuses were examined. One last example recapitulates how this works. It is borrowed from one of Italian historian Carlo Ginzburg's more recent essays, "The Sword and the Lightbulb" (2001). This is a translation from a small book published previously in Germany, *Das Schwert und die Glühbirne* (1999), about the identity of *Guernica,* a large painting by Pablo Picasso (1881–1973) in 1937. The world famous painting is a mural-size canvas in oil, 11 feet 6 inches by 25 feet 8 inches in black and white and nowadays kept at the Centro de Arte Reina Sofía in Madrid. The absence of colors was meant to set a dark mood. The small village of Guernica is located in Spain's Basque country. During the Spanish Civil War (1936–39), the village was considered to be a stronghold of the Republicans or the communist, socialist, and anarchist resistance. On the afternoon of Monday, April 27, 1937, for some two hours in the late afternoon, the village came under attack by German warplanes that supported the Nationalists, led by General Francisco Franco Bahamonde (1892–1975). The painting depicts suffering people, animals, and buildings wrenched by violence and chaos. Therefore, it is known as modern art's most powerful anti-war statement, a perpetual reminder of the tragedies of war, and an embodiment of peace.[6]

Curiously, though his sympathies clearly lay with the new Republic, Picasso generally avoided politics — and disdained overtly political art. But by May 1, 1937, news of the massacre at Guernica reached Paris, where more than a million protesters flooded the streets to voice their outrage in the largest May Day demonstration the city had seen. Eyewitness reports filled the front pages of Paris papers. Picasso rushed through the crowded streets to his studio.

Appalled, enraged, and stunned by the stark black-and-white photographs, he quickly sketched the first images for the mural. The overall scene is within a room where, at an open end on the left, a wide-eyed bull stands over a woman grieving over a dead child in her arms. A horse, falling in agony as it had just been run through by a spear or javelin, occupies the center. The shape of a human skull forms the horse's nose and upper teeth and under the horse we see a dead soldier, seemingly dismembered. His hand on a severed arm grabbing a broken sword from which a flower grows. A lightbulb blazes in the shape of an eye over the suffering horse's head. The lightbulb is thought to represent the sun, whereas the broken sword is thought to symbolize the defeat of the people at the hand of their tormentors. When pressed to explain the bull and the horse in the painting, Picasso said that "this bull is a bull and this horse is a horse." And he added: "If you give a meaning to certain things in my paintings it may be very true, but it is not my idea to give this meaning. What ideas and conclusions you have got I obtained too, but instinctively, unconsciously. I make the painting for the painting. I paint the objects for what they are." In July 1937, *Guernica* was exhibited at the Spanish Pavilion at the Paris International Exposition. The Pavilion was financed by the Spanish Republican government at the time of the civil war. After the Exposition, *Guernica* toured Europe and North America to raise consciousness about the threat of fascism. From the beginning of World War II until 1981, the painting was housed at the Museum of Modern Art in New York. Although it was taken to such places as Munich, Cologne, Stockholm, and São Paulo, Brazil, the one place it did not go was Spain, until the country had become truly democratic.[7]

By carefully discussing detail after detail, Ginzburg concludes that the painting was rooted in European imaginary and not necessarily had been antifascist or even anti-war. This does not contradict Picasso's political sympathies, of course, broadly shared, by the way, by Ginzburg himself. For his canvas, Picasso initially chose the scenery of his studio: the painter and his model. It is significant that Picasso is known to have been painting by "destruction": he painted a first version of a picture, which he then destroyed by painting another one on the same canvas and so on. In the end, nothing seems to have been lost, for one piece may have been taken away only to return somewhere else on the canvas. In spite of these changes, in the end, the original sketch — or "vision"— had remained almost intact. The original sketch of the painter and his model can indeed be recognized in the finished *Guernica*. But, of course, the topic had changed immensely after the newspapers had brought the news of the Guernica slaughter. A bull had entered the "studio," as did a horse, and there is the dismembered ancient soldier with his broken sword. In an attempt to reconquer elements from Greek and Roman mythology from the hands of the fascists, Picasso re-issued the winged horse Pegasus — used by him earlier on in his career, when he painted a curtain for the ballet

*Parade* made by Erik Satie (1866–1925), Jean Cocteau (1889–1963), and Sergei Diaghilev (1872–1929). The Classicist influence is particularly remarkable because at the time Classicism was considered conservative, anti-modern, and fascist. As well, the broken sword came from this mythological background. It could be that the interest to communicate with this "public painting" had forced Picasso to work with the widely shared public language of classical mythology. This must have brought him, Ginzburg suggests, to look at the work of Classicist and Rococo painters like Nicolas Poussin (1594–1665), Jean-Baptiste Greuze (1725–1805), and Jean-Baptiste Pierre Topino-Lebrun (1764–1801). The head of the fallen warrior, says Ginzburg, seems copied from an 11th-century Spanish manuscript on the Deluge, known as "The Apocalypse of Saint Sever."[8]

For such a large work like *Guernica,* Picasso found a traditional composition unavoidable. Perhaps, Ginzburg suggests, the painting's major influence had been Surrealist or, perhaps, a Romantic-Mystic text by Georges Bataille (1897–1962), "Soleil pourri" (1929; "Rotten Sun"). The latter was a piece about the so-called pineal eye, a gland at the top of the man's head, which seeks to drive him and his thoughts upward toward all that is noble. However, this compulsion to be forever driving upward simultaneously forces the man to stare directly into the sun, resulting in blindness and insanity. The friendly yellow circle loses its symbolic quality and becomes a ball of gas starved for an Icarus. As Bataille argues, art revealing the sun should be "a mental ejaculation, foam on the lips, and an epileptic crisis." This event was the collapse of the vertical axis into the horizontal. Art, Bataille wrote, provocatively exposes the grotesque elements of human nature. Artists have historically employed the aesthetic counter tradition of the grotesque to engage with the ambivalence and contradictions of the human experience. "In contemporary painting, the search for that which most ruptures the highest elevation, and for a blinding brilliance, has a share in the elaboration or decomposition of forms." Bataille ended by identifying the productive full sun with academic painting, as a form of balanced spiritual elevation, and the rotten sun with modern painting, especially the work of Picasso, since the latter aimed at excess and the rejection of elevation. Picasso had indeed painted first a full sun, then destroyed it and transformed it into a lightbulb — or better, an oval, eye shaped "sun" with the lightbulb as its iris. Through a sequence of destructions, he had by the very act of painting followed Bataille's method. The *Guernica* now exposed a rotten sun that figured in, as Bataille had put it, "the horror given off by an incandescent arc-lamp." A child of his time, Bataille rejected the opposition between fascism and anti-fascism and welcomed tragedy and death as instruments of life. Thus, *Guernica* is an anti-fascist painting without the fascist enemy and populated by humans and animals connected by tragedy and death.[9]

At this point, for some reason Ginzburg refuses to take the final step. The obsession with death and violence Bataille exposed in his work and that Picasso had re-worked in *Guernica* through his sequence of destructions is nothing else but the acting-out of the Death Drive ~~Thanatos~~. As we have seen, Freud had invented the Death Drive ~~Thanatos~~ shortly after World War I to deal with publications by his major opponents and to outbid his younger followers. Already during the war, Freud had written that if "you want to endure life, prepare yourself for death" because "the aim of all life is death." Although Freud wrote to his friends, telling them "not [to] take it too seriously," most of his followers actually did. Writers and artists, especially, would use the Death Drive ~~Thanatos~~ as a theme of their work. Bataille had been a member of the Freudian-inspired Surrealists but privileged the Death Drive ~~Thanatos~~ even more than his friends. He thought about desire as a kind of pre-birth situation without suffering. This was the period of Christian Paradise, of course. He learned from Freud that the crucial way to get rid of suffering is paradoxically to pursue it intensely and then to endure it thoroughly: catharsis. Exhaustion would be the ultimate sort of liberation, and, like orgasm, a kind of "little death" or the refractory period after fulfilled copulation. Bataille wrote as if acting out the Death Drive ~~Thanatos~~ and the Sex Drive Eros were liberating the mind of its negative energies, making man autonomous of limits, rules, and fears. This was also the way Picasso said he painted. Through this Freudian line, then, *Guernica* ends up more as an illustration of the Death Drive ~~Thanatos~~, based on "evidence" from the Civil War in Spain ("see what humans do thanks to their death drive"), than as a demonstration of anti-fascist struggle. It is as if Picasso did not paint the Guernica experience but his own discovery, through Bataille, of the Death Drive ~~Thanatos~~. In that case, the *active painting process* of *Guernica* would first and foremost simulate the thinking of the Parisian circle of Picasso and much less the events of the Spanish Civil War. Picasso saw the photographs taken of his painting activities as evidence of his acting out of what we now regard as psychomythology. This is the way critics need to view films: identifying and discussing Freudian practices, Freudian Excuses, to explain the artist's motives but with the afterthought that it is just a trope from psychomythology.

# 4

Due to the long traditions of Structuralist-Romantic thinking, most notions and theories based in Cognitive-Evolutionary thinking still feel rather counterintuitive. Several of these, however, did make it to be included in popular psychology. Think of the idea of the many identities a person can demonstrate. This is directly derived from Cognitive Schema Theory and the performances at various stages. There is no discussion that our behavior at work or at school or among friends is different from the world at home. A wonderful example of how this system operates is regularly on television. Episode 118 of the *Seinfeld* sitcom, titled "The Pool Guy," is from season 7; it first aired November 16, 1995, and was written by David Mandel.[10] Central is the character George Costanza, a neurotic and self-loathing, flagrant coward; he is paranoid, selfish, abrasive, and frugal, and an expert liar. He is arguably the show's most amoral character. George had been best friends with Jerry Seinfeld since middle school. Also involved in the episode are Elaine Benes, Jerry's former girlfriend who frequently hangs around in Jerry's apartment in downtown New York; and Cosmo Kramer, Jerry's neighbor. Elaine is looking for company to go to an exposition. Jerry and George refuse. After George leaves, Jerry suggests asking George's fiancée, Susan Ross. Elaine reacts with enthusiasm and rushes out the door. Shortly before George's exit, Kramer had entered and overheard the conversation: "That's gonna be trouble." Jerry does not understand. Kramer responds: "Jerry, don't you see? This world here, this is George's sanctuary. If Susan comes into contact with this world, his worlds collide. You know what happens then?" Kramer raises his hands into the air and slowly brings them together in an explosion. He is holding some food in one hand, so when his hands come into contact food flies all over. The next day, George confronts Jerry: Did he know that the night before Elaine had spoken with Susan on the phone?

> JERRY: Oh yeah, I know.
> GEORGE: How do you know?
> JERRY: Well, it was my idea.
> GEORGE: Your idea?
> JERRY: Yeah.
> GEORGE: Wha'd you do that for?
> JERRY: She was looking for someone to go to the show with.
> GEORGE: Well that was a really stupid thing! You know what's going to happen now?
> JERRY: Worlds collide.
> GEORGE: ... Well, ... yeah!
> JERRY: Because this world is your sanctuary and if that world comes into contact with ...
> GEORGE: YES! It blows up! If you knew that, what did you tell Elaine for?
> JERRY: I didn't know. Kramer told me about the worlds.
> GEORGE: You couldn't figure out the "Worlds Theory" for yourself? It's just common sense. Anybody knows, ya gotta keep your worlds apart.

George is gesturing with his hands going outward. Jerry says: "Yeah, I guess I slipped up." Kramer comes in while George is ready to leave in protest.

George says to Jerry, pointing at Kramer: "He knows the Worlds Theory." Kramer asks, "What. Is it blowing up?"

Later that day, in George's apartment, Susan talks about her day out with Elaine and appears to use a few words that are typical of Elaine's way of thinking. George is upset by this: "Well it's a little strange. You are going to start to talk like Elaine from now on?" Susan answers: "I don't know. Anyway, I thought we'd all go to a movie on Friday." To the movie together? This is the confirmation George needed: "This is not good. Worlds are colliding! George is getting upset!" He walks out distressed. The next day, George faces Jerry in his apartment: "Ah, you have no idea of the magnitude of this thing. If she is allowed to infiltrate this World, then George Costanza as you know him, ceases to exist! You see, right now, I have Relationship George, but there is also Independent George. That's the George you know, the George you grew up with — Movie George, Coffee Shop George, Liar George, Bawdy George." Jerry responds: "I love that George." That is obvious for George: "Me, too! And he's dying Jerry! If Relationship George walks through this door, he will kill Independent George! A George, divided against itself, cannot stand!" Elaine enters, and George warns her: "You are killing Independent George! You know that, don't you?" However, Elaine is not impressed. George confirms to Jerry: "You see. You see what I am talking about. It is all just slipping away. And you are letting it happen." He leaves, slamming the door. A few hours later, at Monk's Coffee Shop, Jerry notes Kramer, Elaine, and Susan at a table. Then he realizes indeed the magnitude of the Worlds Theory and the collisions that might take place. Jerry stands a few paces from the booth, looking around for George, and feeling uncomfortable about the upcoming events. Kramer invites him to join them. Jerry answers: "Ah, you know. I'm supposed to meet, eh, someone — I'll, I'll wait for him outside." But he has no choice but to sit down. When George enters, Susan says: "Oh, hey, hey, Georgie boy, over here." Extending his arm, counting to Elaine, Susan, Kramer, and Jerry, putting his hand under Jerry's chin, George makes a fist and presses it to Jerry's cheek. He cries, "Ha! Ho!" He turns and walks out the door. Susan and Jerry try to stop him: "Hey, George!" "We'll pull up another chair." In a desperate attempt to keep Independent George alive, George eats his lunch alone in Reggie's Diner. In preventing Worlds from colliding you may feel forced to do unusual things. Ultimately, the crisis is abated when Susan "breaks up" with Elaine because she finds the trivialness of the group's interactions unappealing.

Made up by clusters of schemas, typically bound by time and space, the Worlds are identical to the "stages" mentioned previously in this book.[11] Some eight years earlier, feminist philosopher María Lugones, of white Argentine descent but living in the United States and self-identified as a woman of color there, struggled with these Worlds as well. In a well-read piece published in *Hypatia: A Journal of Feminist Philosophy* (1987), she notes how she developed a "playful" identity among certain friends described as "far away people" who knew her well — one of her Worlds — whereas people "who were around her," like close friends and family members said to her: "No, you are not playful. You are a serious woman. You just take everything seriously." Lugones realized that there were different Worlds that triggered different personalities for her to act. She also realized that she could "travel" from one World to the other and thereby switch personalities.[12] This is what George Costanza did all the time, from Movie George to Coffee Shop George, to Liar George, to Bawdy George and back again, or somewhere in between. We may read it as the story of our life. For Freud, this would be pathological.

Several films discussed in this book witness such colliding worlds or the attempts to avoid collisions. For example, avoiding collisions with the world of their bonding is the main reason for the neighborhood boys to tell to *themselves* the story of *The Virgin Suicides*. Telling this story time and again recreates this particular narrative world, probably named "Youth World." It is a kind of Lost Paradise for them, which they try to preserve as part of their mature Worlds that began globalizing, and began becoming realistically polluted and abused. But it is not *desire* of the Lost Paradise because the reason to recreate this narrative world is their 1999 bonding — the present, not the past. Bertie's World is another resisting world. His consists of an honorable monarchy where strong manliness prevailed. He wanted to preserve it as well as he could, but being a stammerer was no part of it. Preserving traditional worldviews was also the vampire's task, conforming to the androcentric worldview that is still ours, as did Bella in *Twilight* and Michael in *The Rite*. Poor Carol's small world was not *[SAFE]* at all, colliding with an invisible world full of fumes and pollution. Needy feared her world would collapse with the one in *Jennifer's Body*. Not coping with the fears caused her hallucinations. The intrusion of Nina's Black Swan world into her White Swan World resembles Needy's situation quite closely. *XXY*'s Alex protected her world from colliding with the androcentric dominant world by preferring her transgender body above any mutilation; as *Chloe* fought for the prospects of a lesbian relationship. Clementine's whisper was to reconstruct from the remnants of memory a world that had almost been wiped out. With something similar in mind, Esmeralda collected *Insignificant Things* to map her neighborhood in one of the world's largest cities, in fact, to create a world. Melinda's world was a disaster and had to last as short as could be. She could terminate it by speaking again. The characters of these films wander around in relatively small worlds, keeping the worlds apart, if only because this is our human instinct. These are narrative worlds and we, as viewers, have been transported into them by the power of cinema to trigger our mirror neurons.

## 5

Scholarly works are important for critics and filmmakers, especially in a time when popular psychology is turned upside down. The Western world started the previous century in a Romantic magical mood, giving so much weight to the ingenuous idea that mind and body are separated. According to the culture of the Structuralist-Romantic Order, the belief about a dark hidden force haunting our minds was particularly strong. It had survived more than a century, when it started off as a reaction to the Enlightenment. At the beginning of the present century we experienced the demise of this Romantic storyworld. We have learned to see our mind as an organ of the body. We know that we are nestled ecologically in the immediate world that surrounds us, and that our thinking is influenced much more by this outside world than we realize. If we see a cookie, we want to eat it; if we see someone grabbing something, we want to grab it also; if we see a face in disgust, we like to run away; if someone we like utters a sentence, we tend to agree.... Furthermore, scholars discuss free will. Tested and verified data show that our decisions are made in the brain — by the "audience" in the "theater of the mind" — a split-second *before* the "actor" on the stage of that theater, our conscious self, knows about it. Our conscious mind *follows* our actions and it is still puzzled about them. However, the "interpreter" in the left-hemisphere does not want to be puzzled, and concocts an explanation. To prevent our behavior from always remaining an enigma to ourselves, the "interpreter" turns out explanations that are in line with previous knowledge; with locally acquired mental schemas; with locally or globally recorded information; with attitudes, knowledge and ideology; with our innate nature — and all this to provide us with a coherent image of ourselves, and our functioning as a social being. Although, as Daniel C. Dennett famously said in *Freedom Evolves*,[13] the idea that we actually may not be entirely in conscious control of ourselves ever, that we are acting, doing, performing upon preconceived schemas in our mind, programs delivered by the audience in the theater of our mind, based on chemical compounds and tiny electronic synapses, that we can be cured by correcting the chemical substance and rewiring the electronics in our brain, is more shocking to Freud's Romantic image of the Self than his Edifice ever provided.

In filmmaking and film criticism, this shift is also the topic of the day. And it must be. If you have seen a movie recently and want to talk about it with a friend, chances are that the friend is interested primarily in the film's subject matter. Only rarely, the friend would like to know about its *mise-en-scène*, its cinematographic style, the rhythm of the editing, the manipulation of lightning, and other technicalities. It is the story content that matters. And, as I have shown by frequently quoting well-known critics, this is also the case for professional moviegoers. However, to heighten the degree of likelihood that the films connect to the viewers, many filmmakers still think that they need to use elements of psychomythology and popular psychology, and, if possible, are fed by Freudian notions and concepts. By wandering through the same Edifice, critics support or extend this practice. They will not much longer. The Cognitive-Evolutionary Order is interfering actively with this ancient narrow-minded outlook, demonstrating that the Freudian Excuse throws nothing into the discussion of human nature. Psychologists, sociologists, neuroscientists, philosophers, linguists, and other cognitive scholars have firmly established that the mind works differently than Freud had ever imagined. Although he confirmed popular psychology, in the academic world Freud has achieved very little indeed. Rooted in misdiagnosis, fabrications, and lies, the answer to identity formation should not be found in Sex or Death Drives; neither in Eros nor ~~Thanatos~~, Greek framings that are being skipped from our Cognitive-Evolutionary logic. The current Cognitive-Evolutionary Order focuses on the present. The past does not serve the past anymore. There is nothing to exorcize from some "subconscious." There is no need to study the Oedipus Complex, to tackle the Oedipus Problem, or to read into it in order to review and interpret films or other works of culture. It seems inevitable to start over again and find a route along or away from the quagmire, into new framings led by contemporary psychologists, or linguists, as guides. At present, we notice around us that popular psychology is being fed already with these novel ideas, concepts, theories, stories, and narratives. The Freudian should be displaced and dismissed. This is a good task for storytellers like filmmakers.

Desperate Housewife Bree Van de Kamp is no fool. She gives us the standard of metarepresentational thinking. Looking at the roots of an utterance, a remark, a concept, a theory, and the like is important. Crucial for our judgment of accurate behavior and correct information, mind-reading, including any reading of fictional narratives in print or on screen, relies on, manipulates, and titillates our tendency to keep track of who thought, wanted, and felt what and *when*. Our judgment, however, is cultural and personal. Bree is a mother — this says it all. Her mental simulations are born in this identity. In this book I have discussed metarepresentation of Freudian psychomythology in order to avoid the inference of a mutilated version of Mona Lisa's legs, as has happened with several films discussed or with criticism of them. It is good to repeat that even when we interact with what seems to be a complete photograph or film, we show a systematic bias toward expanding their boundaries and imagining a continuation outside the diegesis, hard at work filling in around the edges. This filling in includes the psychology of the characters in the movie.

Indeed, forget Freud. But in order to do this, we also need to keep psychoanalysis in our archives as psychomythology, as we do with astrology and similar kinds of master narratives. There is so much psychoanalysis around that we need knowledge of its roots, its failures, and basic notions to be able to recognize it and unmask cheap Freudian Excuses. There is nothing lost here. We may think with Richard Webster and regard the large following of Freud's work as "an intellectual tragedy." Let us go with new currents in film studies and wholeheartedly welcome the Freudian Fadeout.[14] "We learned all about Freud."

# Chapter Notes

*For various reasons I tend to combine references for entire paragraphs. One is because arguments of authors are blended or discussed in combination, which makes it difficult to separate the references. Also I wanted to keep the number of notes manageable. Although the system attempts to be as precise as possible, and quotations are always indicated in these notes, they are only separately mentioned from other quotes by author, title, year, and page numbers in the paragraph endnote. The electronic sources below are indicated by URL and, if known, a copyright date. Access dates for electronic sources are listed in month/year format.*

*In preparing the synoptic sections that open every chapter in this book, I saw the film in question several times, segmenting them to the level of scenes and acts. Next, I made profitable use of interviews, reviews, articles, and book chapters written about the films and the filmmakers. I used remarks, insights and ideas that matched mine and helped to focus my argument. Some works and interviews stand out because I learned much from them or because they voiced a vision particularly close to my own.*

## Preface

1. Oatley, Mar, and Djikic, "Mind's" (2008).
2. Gerrig, *Experiencing* (1998), p. 29.
3. Mar and Oatley, "Function" (2008).
4. Gazzaniga, *Who's* (2011), pp. 77–78, 81–94, 98–99, 103.

## Introduction

1. In this paragraph, most information comes from *Television Tropes & Idioms*, at tvtropes.org_pmwiki_pmwiki.php_Main_FreudianExcuse (01/2011; [01/2011 means: website accessed January 2011]), and tvtropes.org/pmwiki/pmwiki.php/PlayingWith/FreudianExcuse (01/2011); also, Gottschall, *Storytelling* (2012).

2. Lilienfeld, Lynn, Ruscio, and Beyerstein, *50 Great Myths* (2010), passim.

3. Persson, *Understanding* (2003); Lilienfeld, Lynn, Ruscio, and Beyerstein, *50 Great Myths* (2010), pp. 1–20.

4. Lilienfeld, Lynn, Ruscio, and Beyerstein, *50 Great Myths* (2010), pp. 1–20.

5. Mar and Oatley, "Function" (2008), quotes from pp. 173 and 187;

6. D. Herman, "Editor's Column" (2009), p. viii. Herman recapitulates that mapping semiotic cues onto worlds is a fundamental requirement for narrative sense-making.

7. Oatley, Mar, and Djikic, "Psychology" (2012), including the references to these investigations. To have this kind of results, for philosopher Scott Stroud simulations involve three important steps. First, the viewers or readers are confronted with a specific fictional situation on screen or described in a text. Second, they place themselves in this specific fictional situation via simulation. Third, general values and mental schemas are adopted, which they can use in a variety of real situations. See Stroud, "Simulation" (2008), especially pp. 24–33.

8. Gilbert, *Stumbling* (2006); Oatley, Mar, and Djikic, "Mind's" (2008); Persson, *Understanding* (2003), p. 7; Johnson, *Body* (1987), pp. 102, 104.

9. The concept of anchoring is discussed in a book published some fifteen years ago by three Dutch psychologists, Willem Wagenaar, Peter van Koppen, and Hans Crombag. See Wagenaar, van Koppen, and Crombag, *Anchored Narratives* (1993), pp. 4–5, 10–11. See also B. Verheij, "Anchored Narratives and Dialectical Argumentation," at www.ai.rug.nl/~verheij/publications/evidence2001.htm (12/2007).

10. Wagenaar, van Koppen, and Crombag, *Anchored Narratives* (1993), pp. 39–40.

11. Zunshine, *Why* (2006), for example, pp. 6–10, 47–54.

12. Although I am not able to do justice to his carefully argued study, for the sake of my argument I will first mine it to juxtapose the Romantic Order with its immediate precursor, the Enlightened Order. Doorman, *Romantische orde* (2004), see p. 21. See also Munck, *Enlightenment* (2000); Darnton, *Mesmerisme* (1988/1968).

13. Doorman, *Romantische orde* (2004), quote on p. 15, referring to I. Berlin, *The Roots of Romanticism*, London, 1999 (quote from p. 1).

14. On these terms in anthropology, see Layton, *Introduction* (1997), pp. 27–29, 37–39, 63–97.

15. Muir, *Culture* (2007), pp. 6–7, referring to Martin, *Myths* (2004).

16. Doorman, *Romantische orde* (2004), pp. 101–2.

17. Abbott, "Narrating" (2010), pp. 3–5.

18. See, for example, Cioffi, *Freud* (1998).

19. One quote is contrary to Hofstadter and Dennett, *Mind's* (1981), p. 12. Other quotes from Cioffi, *Freud* (1998), pp. 161–66; Webster, *Why* (1996), pp. 108, 109; Spinoza, *Chief Works* (1955); Whyte, *Unconscious* (1960); Ellenberger, *Discovery* (1970); Crombag and Merckelbach, *Hervonden* (1996), pp. 13–17, 80–82. Against the traditional claim that repressed emotions could engender psychological distress, Freud believed to have "discovered," as Webster noted, "an aetiological theory which could explain the origins of a particular *disease* and cure this disease by uncovering repressed *memories*"—although even this was, as is adequately demonstrated in our time, a well-beaten path by then. The problem, in fact, was that it was not enough any longer for Freud to "just" confirm older theories of the origin of hysteria—and certainly not enough to have confirmed Hack Tuke's *Dictionary*. Webster's online texts: "The Cult of Lacan: Freud, Lacan and the Mirror Stage," www.richardwebster.net/thecultoflacan.html#_edn47 ( 1996; 07/2007; 10/2007); "Flirting with Freud," *Times Higher Educational Supplement* (November 1996), www.richardwebster.net/print/xflirtingwithfreud.htm (06/2003; 10/2007); "The Bewildered Visionary," *Times Literary Supplement* (May 1997), www.richardwebster.net/print/xthebewilderedvisionary.htm (06/2003; 10/2007); "Lacan Goes to the Opera," *New Statesman* (July 1997), www.richardwebster.net/print/xlacangoestotheopera.htm (06/2003; 10/2007)

20. J.D. Anderson, *Reality* (1996), pp. 23–24.

21. Personally, I believe that statements like this distract us from the real liberating work of combating capitalist elites and their structures of repression. Dufresne, *Tales* (2000), p. 92, quoting Herbert Marcuse.

22. Schorske, *Fin-de-siecle* (1981), p. 185; Freud, *Interpretation* (1996/1900), p. 309; Cioffi, *Freud* (1998), p. 167; Praz, *Romantic* (1970/1933), pp. 199–300; Mazlish, "Triptych" (1993), pp. 726–45, especially pp. 728–31, 734, 737, 740–41, quote p. 733. Freud, "Zeitgemässes" translated in 1915 as "Thoughts" (1915). Also: Onfray, *Crépuscule* (2010); because my French is not as good as my German, I also consulted the German translation, *Anti Freud* (2011).

23. Dufresne, *Tales* (2000), pp. 6–9, quote on p. 8 (italics added), quote by Jones p. 7. As the first English-language practitioner of psychoanalysis and as president of both the British Psycho-Analytical Society and the International Psychoanalytic Association in the 1920s and

1930s, Jones exercised unmatched influence in the establishment of its organizations, institutions, and publications in the English-speaking world. See also Cioffi, *Freud* (1998), pp. 163, (including quotes by F. Scott Fitzgerald and D.H. Lawrence), 169–177.

24. Carus *Psyche* (1851/46), p. 1.

25. Altschule, *Origins* (1977), p. 199.

26. The cradle stood in the literature of Joris-Karl Huysmans (1848–1907), Charles Baudelaire (1821–67), Stéphane Mallarmé (1842–98), Paul Verlaine (1844–96), or Edgar Allan Poe (1809–49). Important painters were Pierre Puvis de Chavannes (1824–98), Gustave Moreau (1826–98), Arnold Böcklin (1827–1901), Henri Fantin-Latour (1836–1904), Odilon Redon (1840–1916), Ferdinand Hodler (1853–1918), Félicien Rops (1855–1898), Fernand Khnopff (1858–1921), Franz Stuck (1863–1928), Jan Toorop (1858–1928), Gustav Klimt (1862–1918), and Jean Delville (1867–1953). It is here that Freud saw a role for himself and developed his other, more famous, writing about the unconscious and how to access "the deep."

27. Webster, *Why* (1996), pp. 71–102, quote p. 81; Carus, *Psyche* (1851/46), p. 1; Dufresne, *Killing* (2003), pp. 7–9, 16–18. On Symbolism, see the catalog *Het Symbolisme in Europa*, Museum Boymans-van Beuningen, Rotterdam, January–March 1976, also Grand Palais, Paris, May–July 1976. Good information is provided by: www.tendreams.org/symbolism-art.htm (05/2008); and the Wikipedia lemma at en.wikipedia.org/wiki/Symbolism_(arts) (05/2008). See also Ivey, "Sex" (2006), p. 871; Esterson, *Seductive* (1993), p. 220. During the twentieth century, seduced by Freud's borrowing of elements from popular psychology, a series of scholars joined the bandwagon inferring an entire narrative world of psychoanalysis. One of the best-known works is the *Civilizing Process* (1978/1939) of Swiss theorist Norbert Elias (1897–1990), in which steady tribute to psychoanalysis is made to constitute that process. More recent, in his *Outline of a Theory of Practice* (1977/1972), pp. 72, 89–95, Pierre Bourdieu used the work of Erik Erikson, a pupil of Freud's daughter Anna (1895–1982) and Melanie Klein, to constitute the "psychology" of the *habitus* concept. The tiny but much-celebrated book *How Societies Remember* (1989) by British sociologist Paul Connerton has explicit psychoanalytic overtones. In his *Freud and the Non-European* (2003), Edward Said mistakenly believed that Freud was a "*scientist* looking for objective results in his investigation [...]." See Said, *Freud* (2003), p. 28. According to Bourdieu, the structures of a particular environment, like the material conditions of existence characteristic of a class condition, produces *habitus*, which embodies systems of durable, transportable, so-called *dispositions*, defined as "structured structures predisposed to function as structuring structures." This means that they function as principles of the generation and structuring of practices and representations that can be objectively "regulated" and "regular" without in any way being the product of obedience to rules. They are objectively adapted to their goals without presupposing a conscious aiming at ends or an express mastery of the operations necessary to attain them. Being all this, they are collectively orchestrated without being the product of the orchestrating action of a conductor.

28. This and following paragraph: Webster, *Freud* (2003), pp. 15–19; Esterson, *Seductive* (1993), p. 15, reference to S. Freud, "The Interpretation of Dreams," in *The Standard Edition of the Complete Psychological Works of Sigmund Freud*, ed. James Strachey (London: Routledge and Kegan Paul, 1953; orig. 1900), 4:263; and "Introductory Lectures on Psycho-Analysis," in *The Standard Edition of the Complete Psychological Works of Sigmund Freud*, ed. James Strachey (London: Routledge and Kegan Paul, 1963; orig. 1916–1917), 6:335. On psychoanalysis as hermeneutics and so forth, see Robinson, *Freud* (1993); Billig, "Dialogic" (1997); Hollan, "Suffering" (1994); Tyson and Tyson, *Psychoanalytic* (1990), p. 7. See also Littlewood, "Science" (1989).

29. Israëls, *Geval* (1993), translated into German as *Der Fall Freud: Die Geburt der Psychoanalyse aus der Lüge* (Hamburg: Europäische Verlagsanstalt, 1999). For a review by Mikkel Borch-Jacobsen, see *London Review of Books* 22, no. 8 (April 5, 2000), or www.lrb.co.uk/ (06/2000). In this paragraph I quote from this review.

30. In this paragraph, quotes from: Webster, *Freud* (2003), p. 64; Goldschmidt, "Perspective" (2001), p. 794; Haslam, "Race" (1999); Perring, "Forlorn" (1998); Nelson, *Finger* (1999); Healy, *Creation* (2002). See also, for example, what Mayanist Carol Hendrickson wrote in the *Anthropological Quarterly* 74, no. 3 (2001): 149–50.

31. Sabbadini, "Introduction," in Sabbadini, ed., *Couch* (2003), pp 1–15, quote p. 2; Weismantel, *Cholas* (2001), p. 8 (italics added), and p. xvii;
32. Robinson, *Freud* (1993), pp. 7, 12, 14–19; Gay, *Freud* (1987/1985), pp. 19, 22–23, 33; Epstein, "Integration" (1994), p. 709; Hollander, *Love* (1997); Britton, *Sex* (2003); Roudinesco, *Why* (2001/1999); J.B. Jones, "Time" (2004); Gedo, "Enduring" (2001); see also the articles in *The Journal of the American Psychoanalytic Association* 44, no. 2 (1996): 573–99. Roustang, *Lacanian Delusion* (1990/1986), p. 12; Funder, "Personality" (2001), p. 199, and www.apsa-co.org/ctf/pubinfo/about.htm (04/2002). More examples in Israëls, "Pathologische" (1996), p. 21. See also Obeyesekere quote in Littlewood, "Science" (1989), pp. 10–11.
33. Robinson, *Freud* (1993); Billig, "Dialogic" (1997); Hollan, "Suffering" (1994); Tyson and Tyson, *Psychoanalytic* (1990), p. 7; Webster, "Flirting" (online, 1996); Littlewood, "Science" (1989), p. 6. Also, for a comment, see Zeddies, "More" (2002); or Ogden, *Subjects* (1994); Phillips, *On Flirtation* (1994).
34. One simple Internet search, for example, shows that not only Metz and Lacan are still widely popular, but also the authors who work with them. In 2000, Ravi S. Vasudevan compiled eleven essays on *Making Meaning in Indian Cinema*, which took Freud, Lacan, Žižek, and Metz very seriously indeed. See also Currie, *Image* (1995); Tan, *Emotion* (1996), p. 20; Grodal, *Moving* (1997), pp. 6, 20–21; Bordwell, *Making* (1989), pp. 76–78, 83–94, 197–201, 235–39, and "Contemporary" (1996), pp. 6–8; Anderson and Anderson, "Introduction," *Narration* (2007), p. 1; Freeland, "Cognitive" (1997); Manlove, "Visual" (2007). See also Sperry, "Impact" (1993), see, for example, pp. 878, 879, 881; Zimbardo and Leippe, *Psychology* (1991), pp. 92, 173, 187, 256–57.

## Chapter 1

1. Writing the summary, I profited from the readers' comments (358, March 3, 2011) published at the IMDb site, www.imdb.com/title/tt1504320/usercomments/ (03/2011); and, of course, the Wikipedia plot summary at en.wikipedia.org/wiki/The_King's_Speech/ (03/2011). Also lines from Colin Covert, www.startribune.com/entertainment/movies/112389004.html?elr=KArksD:aDyaEP:kD:aUnc5PDiUiD3aPc:_Yyc:aULPQL7PQLanchO7DiUr/(03/2011). Reviews by: James Berardinelli, www.reelviews.net/php_review_template.php?identifier=2238 (03/2011); Amy Biancolli, www.chron.com/disp/story.mpl/ent/movies/mobile/7349534.html (03/2011); Ty Burr, www.boston.com/ae/movies/articles/2010/12/17/firth_is_royalty_even_if_kings_speech_is_a_little_stiff/ (03/2011); Peter Debruge, www.variety.com/review/VE111794 3430?refcatid=31 (03/2011); Roger Ebert, rogerebert.suntimes.com/apps/pbcs.dll/article?AID=/20101215/REVIEWS/101219985 (03/2011); David Edelstein, nymag.com/movies/reviews/69690/ (03/2011); Rob Gonsalves, efilmcritic.com/review.php?movie=20527&reviewer=416 (03/2011); Bill Goodykoontz, www.azcentral.com/thingstodo/movies/articles/2010/12/16/20101216kings-speech-review-goodykoontz.html (03/2011); J. Hoberman, www.villagevoice.com/2010-11-24/film/the-king-s-speech-how-therapy-saved-monarchy/ (03/2011); Ann Hornaday, www.washingtonpost.com/gog/movies/the-kings-speech,1162190/critic-review.html (03/2011); Lisa Kennedy, www.denverpost.com/movies/ci_16929036 (03/2011); Anthony Lane, www.newyorker.com/arts/critics/cinema/2010/11/29/101129crci_cinema_lane (03/2011); Bob Mondello, www.npr.org/2010/11/22/131512433/for-a-king-s-speech-commoner-helps-find-a-voice (03/2011); Andrew O'Hehir, www.salon.com/entertainment/movies/our_picks/index.html?story=/ent/movies/andrew_ohehir/2010/11/23/kings_speech (03/2011); Michael Phillips, www.chicagotribune.com/entertainment/movies/sc-mov-1214-kings-speech-20101216,0,7434298.column (03/2011); Claudia Puig, www.usatoday.com/life/movies/reviews/2010-11-26-Kingsspeech26_ST_N.htm (03/2011); Nick Schager, www.slantmagazine.com/film/review/the-kings-speech/5164 (03/2011); Kenneth Turan, www.latimes.com/entertainment/news/la-et-kings-speech-20101126,0,4898019.story (03/2011); Chris Vognar, www.dallasnews.com/entertainment/movies/reviews/20101216-the-king_s-speech-b.ece (03/2011); and Colin Covert's review mentioned above. In addition, for *The King's Speech* I consulted the well-known Rotten Tomatoes website shortly after the U.S. 83rd Annual Academy Awards (Oscar) Presentation for

the best film of the year 2010 (February 27, 2011). Launched in the summer of 1999 as a website where people can get access to reviews from a variety of critics in the United States, it keeps track of all of the reviews counted. On Oscar night, the website tabulated *The King's Speech* as 95 percent "fresh," based on 201 reviews. Today Rotten Tomatoes offers the standard of the critics' evaluation of current feature films. The percentage of positive reviews is tabulated. If this makes up 60 percent or higher, the film in question is considered "fresh"; but if the positive reviews are less than this figure, then the film is considered "rotten."

2. See the note above, but especially: Ebert, rogerebert.suntimes.com/apps/pbcs.dll/article?AID=/20101215/REVIEWS/101219985 (03/2011); Edelstein, nymag.com/movies/reviews/69690/ (03/2011); Hornaday, www.washingtonpost.com/gog/movies/the-kings-speech,1162190/critic-review.html (03/2011).

3. References to specific reviews in previous notes. Interview with Hooper in *USA Today* can be found at www.usatoday.com/life/movies/news/2010-11-26-kingsspeech26_CV_N.htm (03/2011).

4. References to specific reviews in the previous notes.

5. See blogs.wsj.com/ideas-market/2011/01/24/re-thinking-stutterers/ (03/2011).

6. This paragraph and the next are my reconstruction of the case on the basis of literature. See, for example, Webster, *Why* (1996), pp. 103–7, 242–45. In recent times it has been suggested that Anna O. suffered from a subleuritic tubercular abscess, because one of her arms was paralyzed as a result of complex seizures.

7. On Anna O., see among others Ellenberger, *Discovery* (1970), and "Story" (1972); Hirschmüller, *Physiologie* (1978); Malcolm, *Psychoanalysis* (1988); Macmillan, *Freud* (1991), pp. 3–24; Esterson, *Seductive* (1993), pp. 2–5, 115, and 131; Israëls, *Geval* (1993; *The Freud Case*), pp. 122–215, and *De Weense kwakzalver* (1999; *The Viennese Quack*), pp. 28–37; Crews, *Memory* (1995); Webster, *Why* (1996), pp. 103–35, and his *Freud* (2003); Borch-Jacobsen, *Remembering* (1996), and "How" (1996); Erwin, *Final Accounting* (1996), pp. 30–38; Cioffi, *Freud* (1998); Bénesteau, *Mensonges freudiens* (2002); Dufresne, *Killing* (2003), pp. 4–25; and Borch-Jacobsen and Shamdasani, *Dossier Freud* (2006). Many curious "improvements" can be found in the literature.

8. Israëls, *Geval* (1993), pp. 36–43, and *Weense kwakzalver* (1999), pp. 39–40; Crombag and Merckelbach, *Hervonden* (1996), pp. 13–17, 80–82; Webster, *Why* (1996), pp. 242–45; Thornton, *Freud* (1983); see also Freud, *Ueber Coca* (1885), and "Ueber" (1885).

9. Freud, "Three" (1949/1905), and "On Narcissism" (1981/1914–16).

10. Masson, ed., *Complete* (1985), see, for example, pp. 57–58, 90–91, 131, 200, 243–44, 261, 284, 299, 341; Webster, *Freud* (2003), pp. 10–14.

11. Webster, *Why* (1996), p. 89. For more information, see the lemma "phrenology" and its links at Wikipedia, *the free encyclopedia*, en.wikipedia.org/wiki/Phrenology (05/2008). Gall's theory included also ideas like this: moral and intellectual faculties are innate, and their exercise or manifestation depends on organization; the brain is the organ of all the propensities, sentiments, and faculties and is composed of as many particular organs as there are propensities, sentiments, and faculties, which differ essentially from each other. See also LeDoux, *Emotional* (1996), p. 76.

12. Webster, *Why* (1996), pp. 108, 109, *Freud* (2003), p. 10, and Breuer quoted by Webster on pp. 111 and 196.

13. Breuer's notes in: Hirschmüller, *Physiologie* (1978); Edinger, *Bertha Pappenheim* (1963, and 1968).

14. Freud in Israëls, *Geval* (1993), p. 129, from: *Studien über Hysterie* (1895), pp. 111, 247, 264. See also Micale, *Approaching* (1995); Borch-Jacobsen, *Remembering* (1996); Crombag and Merckelbach, *Hervonden* (1996); Esterson, *Seductive* (1993), p. 131; Dufresne, *Killing* (2003), pp. 16–18; Kaplan, "O Anna" (2002), p. 66; Wegner, *Illusion* (2002).

15. See for this paragraph: Webster, *Why* (1996), pp. 214–40, and, *Freud* (2003), pp. 19–25; Dufresne, *Tales* (2000), p. 55; Davis, "Freud's" (1990), p. 185. Masson, ed., *Complete* (1985), passim, see letters by date (on the Breuer debt, see p. 59–60, p. 60 note 1; on Delorme, p. 76 note 2); Borch-Jacobsen and Shamdasani, *Dossier Freud* (2006).

16. Masson, ed., *Complete* (1985), p. 117, next remark on p. 118.

17. This is one of the main reasons Freud transformed the Seduction Theory.

18. Masson, ed., *Complete* (1985), pp. 117–25, 182–83; Israëls, *Weense kwakzalver* (1999), pp. 44–48, and *Geval* (1993), pp. 117–21, Freud quote from 1923, "Psychoanalyse." In Marcuse, ed., *Handwörterbuch* (1923), op p. 377; Israëls and Schatzman, "Seduction Theory" (1993). On Fliess and Eckstein, see also Esterson, *Seductive* (1993), pp. 5–8; Webster, *Why* (1996), pp. 224–25; Tyson and Tyson, *Psychoanalytic* (1990), pp. 255–56.

19. Webster, *Why* (1996), pp. 198–99; Malcolm, *Psychoanalysis* (1988), p. 73.

20. Webster, *Why* (1996), pp. 197–200, 272–77, p. 198 footnote; Eysenck, *Decline* (1986/1985), pp. 62–64; Erikson, *Identity* (1968), pp. 251–52; Lakoff and Coyne, *Father* (1993); Crews, *Memory* (1995), pp. 5–6, quote from p. 34. On Dora's case, see also Billig, "Freud" (1999); Decker, *Freud* (1991).

21. Onfray, *Anti Freud* (2011), pp. 348–350. In 1925, so Onfray found out, Freud charged $25, which in our contemporary times would be about $500.

22. The letters to Fliess can be found on their dates in Masson, ed., *Complete* (1985).

23. Masson, ed., *Complete* (1985), pp. 57–58, 90–91, 131, 200, 243–44, 261, 284, 299, 341; Israëls, *Weense kwalzalver* (1999), p. 50.

24. Darnton, *Mesmerisme* (1988/1968); Dufresne, *Killing* (2003), pp. 5, 9, 25; Macmillan, *Freud* (1991), pp. 25–37; Wegner, *Illusion* (2002), pp. 278–81.

25. This and the next paragraph: Richards, *Tragic* (2008). There is also a quote from Wikipedia: en.wikipedia.org/wiki/Ernst_Haeckel (05/2008). For introductory students, this is a good source with much more details about Haeckel's odd theories and many mistakes.

26. Bruer, *Myth* (1999); also, see Plomin, Manke, and Pike, "Siblings"(1996); Routledge et al., "Exploring" (2001); Markus and Nurius, "Possible" (1986); Maccoby, "Role" (1992), and "Parenting" (2000). Important is the collection edited by Borkowski, Ramey, and Bristol Power, eds., *Parenting* (2002). Hardy, *Mother Nature* (1999); next to the book, the reader might also consult an interview with the author in the E-zine *Author Interviews* at www.randomhouse.com/knopf/pantheon/qna/hrdy.html (04/2000) (quote); or the review by Helen Fisher in *Scientific American*, issue 1299 of 1999.

27. Pomata, *Contracting* (1998/1994); Entralgo, *Curación* (1958); Waddington, *Power* (1978), and *Medical* (1984).

28. Shorter, *History* (1996), p. vii; Borch-Jacobsen, "Little Brother" (2001), and his voice on p. x of Dufresne, *Tales* (2000); Macmillan, *Freud* (1997/1991), pp. 618–19 (quotes); Cioffi, *Freud* (1998), pp. 17n.39, 294; also Frederick Crews, "Unconscious Deeps and Empirical Shallows" (1998), paper published at: www.human-nature.com/freud/fcrews2.html (08/2007). Harris, "Where Is the Child's Environment?" (1995), then her *Nurture Assumption* (1998), and finally, her recent paper, "Why Home Doesn't Matter" (2007). See also John D. Mullen's review of Judith R. Harris' book *No Two Alike* (2006), in *Metapsychology Online Reviews* 10, no. 10 (March 8, 2006), mentalhelp.net/books/books.php?type=de&id=3039 (06/2007).

29. For Lehrer, see his *Wall Street Journal* blog at blogs.wsj.com/ideas-market/2011/01/24/rethinking-stutterers/ (03/2011); Yairi and Ambrose, *Early Childhood* (2005), and Yairi on www.stutteringhelp.org/Default.aspx?tabid=169 (03/2011).

30. Quotes from Lehrer, see previous note.

31. Roach, *Bonk* (2008).

# *Chapter 2*

1. For reviews: Roger Ebert's at rogerebert.suntimes.com/apps/pbcs.dll/article?AID=/2011 0126/REVIEWS/110129982/1023 (04/2011); Chris Pandolfi's, popzara.com/pages/1519/ (04/2011); Stephanie Zacharek's, www.movieline.com/2011/01/review-the-rite-is-a-super-serious-movie-about-a-hottie-in-a-cassock-and-its-not-anthony-hopkins.php (04/2011); Ami Biancolli's, www.sfgate.com/cgi-bin/article.cgi?f=/c/a/2011/01/27/MV9V1HE7A0.DTL (04/2011); James Berardinelli's, www.reelviews.net/php_review_template.php?identifier=2257 (04/2011); Andrew O'Hehir's for *Salon,* www.salon.com/entertainment/movies/andrew_ohehir/2011/01/27/the_rite (04/2011); Michael Phillips,' www.chicagotribune.com/entertainment/movies/sc-mov-0125-the-rite-20110126,0,3336539.column (04/2011).

2. The letters can be found on their dates in Masson, ed., *Complete* (1985), pp. 224-29.
3. Masson, ed., *Complete* (1985), pp. 224-29.
4. On the publication dates see Apps and Gow, *Male Witches* (2003), pp. 168-69. Most of the following paragraphs of this section follow Apps and Gow, *Male Witches* (2003), especially pp. 25-42, 45, 118-50; Clark, *Thinking* (1997), pp. 106-133; Stephens, *Demon Lovers* (2002); and Thurston, *Witch* (2001), and "World" (2006). A few data come from the introduction by Wicasta Lovelace to the online publication of the *Malleus Maleficarum*, www.malleusmaleficarum.org/ (06/2012).
5. Bem, *Lenses* (1993), pp. 2-3, and, "Gender" (1981).
6. Solomon, *Signs* (1988), p. 203. Solomon refers to de Beauvoir's famous book *Le deuxième sexe* (Paris, 1949), translated as *The Second Sex* (New York, 1973).
7. Thurston, *Witch* (2001), pp. 42-65, quote from p. 43; Clark, *Thinking* (1997), pp. 119-21, 131; Apps and Gow, *Male Witches* (2003), pp. 128-29, 136-37.
8. Thurston, *Witch* (2001), pp. 44-65.
9. Bartlett, *Making* (1993); Tilly, *Coercion* (1990), pp. 42, 54; Hale, *Civilization* (1993); Thurston, *Witch* (2001), pp. 19-24.
10. Bartlett, *Making* (1993); Tilly, *Coercion* (1990), p. 54; Hale, *Civilization* (1993).
11. Pateman, *Sexual* (1988); Mills, *Racial* (1997).
12. Thurston, *Witch* (2001), p. 16; R.I. Moore, *Formation* (1987). I read Moore's Spanish translation, *Formación* (1989/1987).
13. Thurston, *Witch* (2001), pp. 18, 23-24, 27-31, 37, 38.
14. This challenge was partly wrong. In my book on the Mexican Amerindian rebel Antón Pérez the Shepherd, *The Flight of the Shepherd* (2005), I argue that such testimonies might in fact have gone back on dream experiences that were interpreted by the people from a common framework. Ouweneel, *Flight* (2005), pp. 62, 69-72, 184.
15. Thurston, *Witch* (2001), pp. 5-7, 11, and "World" (2006); D. Elliott, *Fallen* (1999), another "Freudian" work, by the way; Apps and Gow, *Male Witches* (2003), pp. 118-50.
16. Thurston, "World" (2006), and *Witch* (2001), pp. 51-53; Apps and Gow, *Male Witches* (2003), pp. 100-101, 131-32; Ruggiero, *Binding* (1993), p. 71.
17. Stephens, *Demon* (2002), quote on p. 10, italics in the original. See also Muir, *Culture* (2007) about the skeptics in Venice. All this makes the witch hunt and the features of what was called witchcraft at the time a typical European phenomenon, and obviously difficult to compare with witchcraft and magic as it occurred in what we now call the Third World.
18. Armstrong, "*Oedipus*" (1999/1998); Ruggiero, *Machiavelli* (2007), p. 47. Freud, *Interpretation* (1996/1900), p. 70, quote, pp. 419 and 421, italics in the original.
16. Freud, *Interpretation* (1996/1900), pp. 185, 186, 187.
19. On the Oedipus Complex, see Freud, *Interpretation* (1996/1900), for example, pp. 185-91; Freud, "Three" (1949/1905), p. 226; Crombag and Merckelbach, *Hervonden* (1996), pp. 39-40; Macmillan, *Freud* (1991), p. 232, see pp. 231-329; Crews, *Memory* (1995), p. 207; Eysenck, *Decline* (1986/1985), pp. 24-25; Freud, "Three" (1949/1905), p. 226.
20. Ruggiero, *Binding* (1993), p. 71.
21. Armstrong, "*Oedipus*" (1999/1998); Harris, *Nurture* (1999/1998), pp. 2-7, 352-53; Freud, *Interpretation* (1996/1900), p. 187; Ferro-Luzzi, "Female" (1980), p. 45. Dufresne, *Tales* (2000), p. 7.
22. The underpinning for his ideas in *Totem and Taboo* he found in the work of the anthropologist James George Frazer (1854-1941) who had done research among the Australian Aborigines. Yet, bizarre as it all sounds, the tiny book is still popular among anthropologists and it even served for the article "Myth and Mythology" in the *New Encyclopædia Britannica* (1992), vol. 24, p. 720. Roazen, *Trauma* (2002), p. 119; Onfray, *Crépuscule* (2010), or *Anti Freud* (2011). See also the discussion in De Swaan, "Dyscivilization" (2001); and, Gómez, *Introduction* (1997). Quotes from: Freud, "Civilization" (1989/1930), *Interpretation* (1900), pp. 364, 371, 372, more in general: pp. 364-76, chapter 7, "The Psychology of the Dream-Processes," section b; Tyson and Tyson, *Psychoanalytic* (1990), p. 45. It must be supplemented here that in scholarly psychology textbooks, like in the fifteen-page subject index of *Hilgard's Introduction to Psychology* 12th ed. (1996), the notion of regression is not mentioned at all; neither in Frijda's *The Emotions*

(1986), Hogg and Vaughan's *Social Psychology* (1995), Cole's *Cultural Psychology* (1996), LeDoux's *Emotional Brain* (1996), Hatfield and Rapson's *Love and Sex* (1996), Smith and Bond's *Social Psychology across Cultures* 2d ed. (1998), Buss's *Evolutionary Psychology* (1999), Kunda's *Social Cognition* (1999), or Damasio's *Feeling of What Happens* (1999) and *Looking for Spinoza* (2003). Working on this part of my theory, I consulted the *PsychCrawler Website* on March 26, 2002 — "indexing the web for the best in psychology"—maintained by the American Psychological Association. It gave me negative results; the search on "regression" produced no hits at all, indicating that theories on regression do not belong to "the best in psychology." Serious psychologists do not work with the concept of regression. www.psychcrawler.com (03/2002).

23. Noll, *Jung Cult* (1994) and *Aryan Christ* (1997).

24. Webster, *Why* (1996), pp. 324 (quote on homosexual), 325–26.

25. This paragraph and the following: Lakoff, *Political* (2008), pp. 73–91, referring to a previous book: *Moral Politics: How Liberals and Conservatives Think* (Chicago, 2002, a revised version of a book published in 1996). The argument can also be found at Wikipedia, en.wikipedia.org/wiki/Moral_Politics (10/2008). Perhaps it must be stressed that these are idealized mental structures to favor interpretation and analysis. There is not always a direct link to actual conservatives or liberals; neither should it be concluded that all liberals and conservatives are the same.

26. Diamond, "Sex" (2002), pp. 326, 329.

27. The quote is from 1963, but I found it in a British television documentary film, *The Century of the Self, 2: Engineering of Consent* (2002). The documentary was written and produced by Adam Curtis; see also hareloco.spaces.live.com/blog/cns!E7089CD7CF32AA20!243.entry (01/2011). Lakoff, *Political* (2008), pp. 1.

28. For reasonable summaries of *The Twilight Saga* films, see Wikipedia at: en.wikipedia.org/wiki/ (03/2011), special sites: /The_Twilight_Saga_(film_series), Twilight_(2008_film), /The_Twilight_Saga:_New_Moon, /The_Twilight_Saga:_Eclipse, /The_Twilight_Saga:_Breaking_Dawn, Stephenie_Meyer, /Melissa_Rosenberg, /Bella_Swan, /Edward_Cullen, and /Jacob_Black. Again, Wikipedia can be established as a useful tool; see also the paper by Frank Schulenburg, LiAnna Davis, and Max Klein, "Lessons from the Classroom: Successful Techniques for Teaching Wikis using Wikipedia," (2011) at: www.wikisym.org/ws2011/_media/proceedings:p231-schulenburg.pdf (06/2012). However, see also: Sarah Baker, "A Place for Wikipedia or Putting Wikipedia in its Place," at: //education.jhu.edu/newhorizons/Journals/Winter2012/Baker (06/2012), including a short bibliography.

29. My thirteen-year-old daughter loves *The Twilight Saga,* but when I suggested she could write on werewolves and vampires for her history class, she answered me that it must be "real history." Oldridge, *Strange* (2005), pp. 96–111, 170–72. True-believers found confirmation in the Bible. In the Book of Daniel, it states that when King Nebuchadnezzar was sent into exile, God helped him to eat grass like an ox and to grow his hair all over his body "like eagles' feathers, and his nails like birds' claws." If God could do this, why not the Devil as well?

30. This paragraph owes a lot to Elizabeth Catalán-Morseby's excellent paper, "Vampires" (2010), including the references to other authors researching the theme. The novels mentioned are Bram Stoker, *Dracula* (London, 1897); Anne Rice, *Interview with the Vampire: The Vampire Chronicles Part One* (New York, 1976).

31. Also Catalán-Morseby's "Vampires" (2010).

32. See the blog by Dirk Eitzen, "The Fun of Fear: Horror, Suspense, and Halloween," SCSMI site, October 2, 2010, at scsmi-online.org/forum/the-fun-of-fear-horror-suspense-and-halloween (03/2011).

33. Quotes from: Eitzen, "Fun of Fear" (2010).

34. Quotes from: Eitzen, "Fun of Fear" (2010).

## Chapter 3

1. The brackets in the title of *[Safe]*, as seen in the film's promotional artwork, suggest enclosed protection. For reasons of continuity, and the distinction from *Safe* (2011), for example, I inserted the brackets within quoted passages if they did not appear in the source. Frequently

used in this chapter are Potter, "Dangerous" (2004), quote from p. 128; the interview with Todd Haynes by Collier Schorr, published as "Diary of a Sad HouseWife," *ArtForum,* Summer 1995, found at *bNet* of CBS IBN, findarticles.com/p/articles/mi_m0268/is_n10_v33/ai_17239572/ (01/2011); and Gorton, *Theorising* (2008), pp. 5, 40, 53–59, 62–63, 143, 148. Furthermore, writing this synoptic section, I have profited from articles by Jeremy Justus, "What You Are Seeing Outside Is a Reflection of What You Are Feeling Within: Space, Ideology, and Biopolitics in *Safe.* "*Magazine Americana* Online, www.americanpopular culture.com/archive/politics/safe.htm (01/2011); Reid, "UnSafe" (1998); Grossman, "Trouble" (2005); and, of course, the *IMDb* site, including a large series of viewers' reports, www.imdb.com/title/tt0114323/ (01/2011); somewhat poor is Wikipedia, en.wikipedia.org/wiki/Safe_(film) (01/2011); better is the article on Haynes, Wikipedia at en.wikipedia.org/wiki/Todd_Haynes (01/2011). See also the reviews by Roger Ebert (1995), at rogerebert.suntimes.com/apps/pbcs.dll/article?AID=/19950728/REVIEWS/507280304 (01/2011); Sal Cinquemani for *Slant Magazine,* www.slantmagazine.com/film/review/safe/288 (01/2011); Jeremy Heilman for *MovieMartyr.com,* www.moviemartyr.com/1995/safe.htm (01/2011); Christopher Null for *FilmCritic.com,* www.filmcritic.com/reviews/1995/safe/ (01/2011); Todd McCarthy for *Variety,* www.variety.com/review/VE1117903657?refcatid=31 (01/2011); Rob Gonsalves for *eFilm Critic.com,* efilmcritic.com/review.php?movie=2255&reviewer=416 (01/2011); Janet Maslin for the *New York Times,* movies.nytimes.com/movie/ (01/2011).

2. Potter, "Dangerous" (2004), p. 128.

3. Schorr, findarticles.com/p/articles/mi_m0268/is_n10_v33/ai_17239572/ (01/2011); Potter, "Dangerous" (2004), p. 126.

4. Potter, "Dangerous" (2004), pp. 128–32.

5. Schorr, findarticles.com/p/articles/mi_m0268/is_n10_v33/ai_17239572/ (01/2011); Potter, "Dangerous" (2004), pp. 140–42.

6. Ebert, at rogerebert.suntimes.com/apps/pbcs.dll/article?AID=/19950728/REVIEWS/507280304 (01/2011). Also, Schorr, at findarticles.com/p/articles/mi_m0268/is_n10_v33/ai_17239572/pg_3/ and /pg_4/ (01/2011); Potter, "Dangerous" (2004), pp. 137–38.

7. Schorr at findarticles.com/p/articles/mi_m0268/is_n10_v33/ai_17239572/pg_1/ (01/2011). Grossman, "Trouble" (2005); Wikipedia at en.wikipedia.org/wiki/Todd_Haynes (01/2011).

8. Gorton, *Theorising* (2008), pp. 39, 41, 47, 142.

9. Gorton, *Theorising* (2008), pp. 38–40.

10. Roudinesco, *Why* (2001 [1999]), pp. 6–7, 13–14, 15–16, 149n14. Roudinesco believes that in modern debates psychoanalysis is in competition with psychopharmacology, whereas the real problem for it lies in the results of scientific psychology. See also the discussion in Borch-Jacobsen, et al., *Libro negro* (2007 [2005]). Gorton, *Theorising* (2008), pp. 38–40.

11. Mitchell, *Mad* (2000), p. 7; Meadow, *New Psychoanalysis* (2003), p. 13; Borch-Jacobsen, in *The London Review of Books* 23, no. 10 (May 24, 2001), or http://www.lrb.co.uk/v23/n10/mikkel-borch-jacobsen/little-brother-little-sister (01/2011); Hoenisch, "Myth" (1996).

12. Meadow, *New Psychoanalysis* (2003), p. 35, also p. 1. Merckelbach, "Probleem" (1996); Pennebaker, "Putting" (1993); McNally, *Remembering* (2003).

13. Meadow, *New Psychoanalysis* (2003), pp. 35–36.

14. www.thevillager.com/villager_91/phyllismeadow.html (06/2007).

15. On *[SAFE],* see Gorton, *Theorising* (2008), pp. 41–45, 54–59, 62–63, 143, 148.

16. From Erin McKean's essay, published in *The New York Times,* December 17, 2009, "On Language: Redefining Definition," see www.nytimes.com/2009/12/20/magazine/20FOB-onlanguage-t.html (01/2011).

17. Masson, ed., *Complete* (1985), p. 290.

18. Damasio, *Descartes'* (1994), pp. 118, 125–26; Atmanspacher, "Complexity" (1994); Feldman, *From* (2008), pp. 78–82.

19. D. Herman, "Editor's Column" (2009), p. viii; Eakin, "Living" (2005), pp. 2–3; quote from Damasio, *Feeling* (1999), p. 189, and *Looking* (2003), pp. 30–31, 36. See also Eakin, *Living* (2008).

20. Damasio, *Looking* (2003), p. 166, italics in original.

21. Eakin, "Living" (2005), pp. 3–4, and *Living* (2008).

250  Notes — Chapter 4

22. LeDoux, *Emotional* (1996), from p. 128 onwards.
23. Quotes from interviews with Diablo Cody and Megan Fox for *MoviesOnline*, www.moviesonline.ca/movienews_17327.html (03/2011); Diablo Cody with *Examiner.com*, www.examiner.com/personalities-in-los-angeles/unleashing-the-devil-ms-cody-a-personalities-interview-with-diablo-cody-on-jennifer-s-body (03/2011); Diablo Cody for *Fandango*, www.fandango.com/commentator_interview:jennifersbodydiablocody_272?source=ca_title (03/2011); Diablo Cody with *Horror.com*, www.horror.com/php/article-2524-1.html (03/2011). Furthermore, see: *Slate Spoiler Special:* Jennifer's Body, hosted by reviewer Dana Stevens and her guest Lindsay Robertson, broadcasted September 18, 2009, at www.slate.com/id/2228708/ (03/2011); Noah Berlatsky, www.chicagoreader.com/chicago/a-supernatural-bitch/ (03/2011); Mary Pols, www.time.com/time/arts/article/0,8599,1924473,00.html (03/2011); Roger Ebert, rogerebert.suntimes.com/apps/pbcs.dll/article?AID=/20090916/REVIEWS/909169996 (03/2011); Dana Stevens for *Slate*, www.slate.com/id/2228708 (03/2011).
24. Dana Stevens at: www.slate.com/id/2228708 (03/2011).
25. Arzy et al., "Induction" (2006); Reed, *Psychology* (1988/1972); Swaab, *Wij zijn* (2010), pp. 236–47.
26. From the interview with Schorr, "Diary," *ArtForum*, at findarticles.com/p/articles/mi_m0268/is_n10_v33/ai_17239572/ (01/11).

## Chapter 4

1. To write this summary of *XXY*, I have profited from Bijan Tehrani's interview for *Cinema Without Borders*, www.cinemawithoutborders.com/print.php?a=1477 (10/2009); Pablo Goldbarg's interview for *Realfic(c/t)ion*, pablogoldbarg.blogspot.com/2008/04/interview-with-luca-puenzo-xxt.html (10/2009). The film is based on the short story "Cinismo," written by Puenzo's spouse, Sergio Bizzio, also published at lomioesamateur.wordpress.com/el-cuento-del-mes/cinismo-de-sergio-bizzio (01/2010). See also the reviews by: Nick Schrager, *Arts & Opinion*, www.artsandopinion.com/2008_v7_h3/schrager-xxxy.htm (10/2009); Andrew O'Hehir, *Salon*, www.salon.com/ent/movies/btm/feature/2008/05/02/xxy/ (10/2009); Tamsin Whitehead, *JGCinema*, www.jgcinema.com/single.php?sl=xxy-puenzo-gender-sex-sexuality (10/2009); Mike Vokins, www.xtra.ca/public/Toronto/XXY_Argentine_director_Lucia_Puenzo-4731.aspx (10/2009); *Filmlot*, thefilmlot.com/tflblogwp/?p=104 (10/2009); Michael Tully, *Hammer to Nail*, www.hammertonail.com/genre/drama/xxy-cruel-summer/ (10/2009); *The Spanish Dilettante*, spanishdilettante.wordpress.com/2009/11/21/xxy-a-film-by-lucia-puenzo/ (12/2009); Howard Schumann, user review on *IMDb*, www.imdb.com/title/tt0995829/(10/2009); Peter Smith, *ScreenGrab*, www.nerve.com/CS/blogs/screengrab/archive/2008/05/02/screengrab-q-amp-a-lucia-puenzo.aspx (10/2009); Wesley Morris, *Boston.Com*, www.boston.com/movies/display?display=movie&id=12029 (12/2009).
2. Article by Tamsin Whitehead, *JGCinema*, www.jgcinema.com/single.php?sl=xxy-puenzo-gender-sex-sexuality (10/2009).
3. Interview at www.nerve.com/CS/blogs/screengrab/archive/2008/05/02/screengrab-q-amp-a-lucia-puenzo.aspx (10/2009), by Peter Smith for *ScreenGrab*.
4. Cole and Cole, *Development* (2001/1989), p. 87.
5. Garber, *Vice Versa* (1995), pp.204 and 249.
6. This section is largely based on the popularized version of the contemporary research published in *The Economist* (August 3, 2006), pp. 70–72, "Differences Between the Sexes: The Mismeasure of Woman." This article is a review of a few other popularizing articles and books.
7. See again from *The Economist* (August 3, 2006), "Differences Between the Sexes," referring to Hyde et al., "Gender" (1990) and Hyde, "Gender Similarities" (2005), all three mentioned in previous note.
8. Butler, "Doing Justice" (2001), reprinted in *Undoing Gender* (2004), pp. 57–74. Weismantel works with Butler; see Weismantel, *Cholas* (2001), pp. 110–16.
9. Diamond, "Sex" (2002), pp. 325–26, quote p. 329; Prosser, *Second Skins* (1998), pp. 43–44; Rubin, *Self-Made* (2003); Rosario, "Biology" (2004), pp. 280–82.

10. Onfray, *Anti Freud* (2011), pp. 434–436, with references to Freud's work of course (*Drie Abhandlungen zur Sexualtheorie* [from Sigmund Freud, *Gesammelte Werke,* Fischer Taschenbuch Verlag, 1999 (Imago Publishing 1950), V, pp. 37, 44–45], *Abriss der Psychoanalyse* [XVII, p. 78], *Zur Einführung des Narzissmus* [X, p. 154]. Onfray speaks of Freud's "ontological homophobia."

11. Evans, *Introductory* (1996), pp. 20–21; Webster, "Bewildered" (online, 1997); Esterson, at www.deakin.edu.au/hbs/freudcriticism/ (06/2003). See, for example: Erikson, *Identity* (1968), pp. 22, 85–86, 117, 121, 145–46, 171–72. Keep in mind that Freud's self-analysis is based on an interpretation of his dreams. Other evidence is not given. Erikson found the oddity of the source of no importance, for he described Freud's dreams as "a superb record of his suppressed selves," that brought his "negative identity" to haunt him at night. It should be stressed once more that Freud's writing is full of neurological, medical, and evolutionary assumptions, which are never expounded. On the contrary, as expressed above, the texts Freud published furnish evidence that much of the "data" on which he ostensibly based his theories was, in reality, the product of those theories; not arrived at through patient observation, but through his own wishful interpretations and fanciful reconstructions. We should not stop repeating that Freud's clinical "findings" were nothing more than his own conjectures. See Erikson, *Identity* (1968), p. 22.

12. Freud and Bullitt, *Thomas Woodrow Wilson* (1967), pp. 45–56; Webster, *Why* (1996), pp. 142, 168–70, 173–75, 180.

13. Borch-Jacobsen, "Oedipus" (1994), quotes on p. 267 (italics added here), 268.

14. Borch-Jacobsen, "Oedipus" (1994), quotes on p. 271.

15. Borch-Jacobsen, "Oedipus" (1994), pp. 271–75, especially p. 273.

16. Harris, *No Two Alike* (2006), pp. 255–56, and *Nurture Assumption* (1998), pp. 98–100.

17. Borch-Jacobsen, *London Review of Books,* at www.lrb.co.uk/v23/n10/mikkel-borch-jacobsen/little-brother-little-sister (01/2011).

18. Erwin, *Final Accounting* (1996), quote from p. 51, other paraphrases from pp. 44, 45, 46, 49, 50, 53, quote p. 282; Erwin and Siegel, "Is Confirmation Differential?" (1989).

19. This fate looks analogous to the picture Freud painted for himself: the lone fighter against some Inquisition of psychologists who did not wish to recognize his views out of political reasons. Grafton, *Cardano's* (1999). See also Dooley, *Morandi's* (2002).

20. Parel, *Machiavellian* (1992). See, for example, the papers collected by a specialized website, Niccolo-Machiavelli.com, at www.niccolo-machiavelli.com/ (08/2004); Dooley, *Morandi's* (2002).

21. On stories: Gottschall, *Storytelling* (2012), pp. 27–28 (quote), 39-, 49–59.

22. On *Chloe,* see the film's website at www.sonyclassics.com/chloe/ (04/2011). Consulted reviews include Dave Campbell's blog at smellslikescreenspirit.com/2010/03/chloe-2009-review/ (04/2011); Ebert, rogerebert.suntimes.com/apps/pbcs.dll/article?AID=/20100324/REVIEWS/100329990/1023 (04/2011); Liam Lacey, www.theglobeandmail.com/news/arts/movies/chloe/article1511986/ (04/2011).

## Chapter 5

1. See reviews by Roger Ebert (with an excellent summary), rogerebert.suntimes.com/apps/pbcs.dll/article?AID=/20050602/REVIEWS/50531003 (01/2011); Wesley Morris, www.boston.com/movies/display?display=movie&id=7624 (01/2011); Owen Gleiberman, www.ew.com/ew/article/0,,1060113,00.html (01/2011); A.O. Scott, www.rottentomatoes.com/m/mysterious_skin/ (01/2011); Peter Sobczynski, efilmcritic.com/review.php?movie=10568&reviewer=389 (01/2011); Mick LaSalle, www.sfgate.com/cgi-bin/article.cgi?f=/c/a/2005/05/27/DDGSBCUNL71.DTL (01/2011); David Rooney, www.variety.com/review/VE1117924801?refCatId=31 (01/2011); *IMDb,* www.imdb.com/title/tt0370986/ (01/2011); and the article by Davies, "Imagining" (2007). There is an interview with Araki in *IonMagazine,* online at www.ionmagazine.ca/2005/03/gregg-araki/ (01/2011); and, in the *Rather Ronge* blog, at www.ratherronge.co.za/html/sub_content.aspx?reviewid=198 (01/2011).

2. In the interview with the *Rather Ronge* blog, we read that when Araki hired Chase Ellison

to play the young Neil and George Webster to play the young Brian he made it conditional that their parents must read the whole script; see text: www.ratherronge.co.za/html/sub_content.aspx?reviewid=198 (01/2011). They then were given a detailed breakdown of how the scenes would be shot. "Chase and George had separate scripts from the rest of the cast," says Araki. "In a sense they shot their own mini-movie within our movie. We filmed them from emotional beat to emotional beat without ever really telling them the full story or explaining what they were reacting to. The 'other half' of those scenes that involved the coach (Bill Sage) seducing the boys, was shot with Bill alone on the set. The boys were never with him in those seduction scenes. When I watch the film now it amazes me how natural and nuanced the young boys' performances are because I know they were alone on set. They did not even know what they were reacting to," says Araki. He adds that the young boys have never seen the completed film, only the scenes in which they appeared. Their parents will decide when they should see the whole story.

3. Dennis Lim, www.villagevoice.com/2005-04-26/film/the-lost-boys/ (01/2011).
4. Ann Hornaday, www.washingtonpost.com/wp-dyn/content/article/2005/06/23/AR2005062301873.html (01/2011).
5. Stephanie Zacharek, www.salon.com/entertainment/movies/review/2005/06/17/mysterious_skin (01/2011).
6. A summary of this book was added to another essay of that epoch, "Das Unheimliche" (1919). Apparently both pieces form some kind of a dyad; Freud, "Uncanny" (1955/1919), p. 218, translator's note. Borch-Jacobsen, "Oedipus" (1994), pp. 274–75.
7. Freud, "Civilization" (1930). Curiously, in her book about pishtacos and cholas in the Andes, anthropologist Mary Weismantel poignantly refers to Thanatos. This probably meant that the Andean population has repressed the discontent of Conquest and has been guided by the Death Drive ever since, but especially in contact with Whites. This discontent, Weismantel must think, explains the aggression against pishtacos. Weismantel, *Cholas* (2001), pp. 8–16, especially p. 8.
8. See Halpern, *Dreams* (2003).
9. McNally, *Remembering* (2003), pp. 111, 179.
10. Quotes from successively: Hornaday, www.washingtonpost.com/wp-dyn/content/article/2005/06/23/AR2005062301873.html (01/2011); Ebert, rogerebert.suntimes.com/apps/pbcs.dll/article?AID=/20050602/REVIEWS/50531003 (01/2011); Scott, www.rottentomatoes.com/m/mysterious_skin/ (01/2011); Zacharek, www.salon.com/entertainment/movies/review/2005/06/17/mysterious_skin (01/2011).
11. Lim, www.villagevoice.com/2005-04-26/film/the-lost-boys/ (01/2011).
12. Freud, "History" (1972/1918), p. 173, italics in the original. Remembering a childhood dream all these years is quite exceptional, but let us give it the benefit of the doubt.
13. Freud, "History" (1972/1918).
14. Freud, "History" (1972/1918), pp. 177–78, 187–88,n.18; Esterson, *Seductive* (1993), pp. 67–76, 76–93; Macmillan, *Freud* (1997/1991), p. 481; Cioffi, *Freud* (1998), pp. 293–94; Webster, *Why* (1996), pp. 289–90; there is also a line included from a comment by Danielle Knafo, "What You See Is Not Always What You Get: Voyeurism and the Primal Scene in Art." www.plexus.org/newobs/112/knafo.html (12/2007).
15. Obholzer, *Wolf Man* (1982/1980), quotes from pp. 25, 30, 32, 33, 31, 34, respectively.
16. Obholzer, *Wolf Man* (1982/1980), quotes from pp. 30, 35, 36, 43, respectively; Freud, "History" (1972/1918), p. 188n.18.
17. Freud quoted in Ginzburg, *Clues* (1989), pp. 151, 152; Macmillan, *Freud* (1997/1991), pp. 482, 647; Freud, "History" (1972/1918), pp. 180, 182n.12.
18. Freud, "History" (1972/1918), pp. 163–72; Obholzer, *Wolf Man* (1982/1980), quotes from pp. 36–37, 145, 147, 176, 37, 29–30, respectively. In his turn, the Wolf Man had asked if this play with his penis must *necessarily* have had such consequences, or "is it already a sign of sickness that something like that has consequences?" And: "Perhaps it also happened to other little boys and had no effect, I don't know." "So you see, that sort of thing happens, it's no reason for someone to turn into a neurotic. It had no consequences."
19. Ginzburg, *Clues* (1989), p. 151; Macmillan, *Freud* (1997/1991), pp. 482–84, 647, italics

in quote from p. 483 in the original; Fish, "Withholding" (1986); Freud, "History" (1972/1918), p. 180.
20. Foulkes, *Children's* (1999), p. 83, in general: pp. 56–84; Freud, "History" (1972/1918), p. 179. See also Esterson, *Seductive* (1993), pp. 69–70, the sources involved can be found there, p. 70n.27, pp. 71–76; Freud, "History" (1972/1918), p. 188n.18.
21. Ginzburg, *Clues* (1989), pp. 146–55, a chapter entitled "Freud, the Wolf Man, and the Werewolves."
22. Sperry, "Impact" (1993), see, for example, pp. 878, 879, 881; Hartmann, "Dreams" (1991); Cartwright, "Dreams" (1991); see also Zimbardo and Leippe, *Psychology* (1991), pp. 92, 173, 187, 256–57.
23. Lakoff, "How" (1993); Blackmore, *Consciousness* (2003), pp. 338–53, quote p. 347.
24. Hartmann, "Outline" (1996); Hobson, *Dreaming* (2002); Blackmore, *Consciousness* (2003), p. 342; Revonsuo, "Reinterpretation" (2000); Revonsuo and Valli, "Dreaming" (2000); Maquet et al., "Functional" (1997); Feldman, *From* (2008), pp. 78–82. See also Kahn, Krippner, and Combs, "Dreaming" (2000).
25. See Merritt, Stickgold, Pace-Schott, Williams, and Hobson, "Emotion" (1994); Foulkes, *Children's* (1999); also Stickgold's website, home.earthlink.net/~sleeplab/stickgold.html (11/1999). Furthermore, Tedlock, "New Anthropology" (1991); Montangero et al., "Remembering" (1996); Kramer, "Nightmare" (1991); Bonato et al., "Bizarreness" (1991); Cuddy and Belicki, "Nightmare Frequency" (1992); D. Barrett, "Committee" (1993); Kahn and Hobson, "Self-organization" (1993); D. Stewart and Koulack, "Function" (1993).
26. The Domhoff lecture at *YouTube* UcTv, www.youtube.com/watch?v=e6qhwdTzilg (10/2009); and, discovermagazine.com/2002/mar/breakdialogue (10/2009). See also Domhoff, *Scientific* (2002). McNally, *Remembering* (2003), pp. 105–13.
27. McNally, *Remembering* (2003), pp. 186–228; Ladwig et al., "Psychophysiological" (2002), p. 242; Volkan, *Bloodlines* (1997), or "Traumatized" (2000).
28. McNally, *Remembering* (2003), p. 217.
29. McNally, *Remembering* (2003), pp. 105–13.
30. Sherman, "Evolutionary" (2001); Holmes, "Evidence" (1990); Loftus and Ketcham, *Myth* (1994); Whetstone and Cross, "Control" (1998); LeDoux, *Emotional* (1996); Wegner, *White* (1994). See Tyson and Tyson, *Psychoanalytic* (1990), pp. 327, 336; for example, Perry, "Memories" (1999).
31. Wegner and Erber, "Hyperaccessibility" (1992), quote from p. 911; Kunda, *Social* (1999), quotes from pp. 299 and 300; McNally, *Remembering* (2003), p. 75.
32. *Dioses*, written and directed by Josué Méndez, premiere 2008 (Peru), 91 minutes; photography by Mario Bassino.
33. See: www.diosesthemovie.com/ (10/2009).
34. Pagel, Kwiatkowski, and Boyles, "Dream" (1999); Rock, *Mind* (2004), pp. 146–47.
35. McNally, *Remembering* (2003), pp. 189–90, 197–98.
36. McNally, *Remembering* (2003), pp. 183–84, quote from p. 275.

## Chapter 6

1. Apart from viewing the DVD (in Holland produced by *AFilm*), in summarizing the plot of this film, I profited from the *IMDb* user reviews, www.imdb.com/title/tt0338013/usercomments/ (01/2011); a long piece by Kelley Ross, 2004, at www.friesian.com/sunshine.htm (01/2011); Rob Gonsalves for *eFilmCritic*, at efilmcritic.com/review.php?movie=8888&reviewer=416 (01/2011); Cynthia Fuchs, *PopMatters*, at popmatters.com/film/reviews/e/eternal-sunshine-of-the-spotless-mind.shtml (01/2011). Published sources include Klawans, "Speak" (2004); Grau, "*Eternal*" (2006); Cardullo, "Falling" (2007); Edwards, "White" (2008); Meyer, "Reflections" (2008); Reeve, "Two" (2009); Simmons, "Memory" (2009); Silvey, "Not" and at http://www.britannica.com/bps/additionalcontent/18/37292340/Not-Your-Average-Love-Story-FILM-TECHNIQUES-IN-ETERNAL-SUNSHINE-OF-THE-SPOTLESS-MIND-# (2009).
2. Klawans, "Speak" (2004); Reeve, "Two" (2009), especially pp. 18–19.

3. As annotated in Edwards, "White" (2008), p. 119: John Bartlett, *Bartlett's Familiar Quotations: A Collection of Passages, Phrases, and Proverbs Traced to Their Sources in Ancient and Modern Literature,* ed. Justin Kaplan (Boston: Little Brown & Co, 2002, orig. 1855).

4. Meyer, "Reflections" (2008), p. 79; Simmons, "Memory" (2009), p. 114.

5. Silvey, "Not" (2009), p. 140; Edwards, "White" (2008), p. 120.

6. A graduate and faculty member of the New York University Psychoanalytic Institute at NYU Medical Center, Herbert Stein practices psychiatry in New York, and has been the editor of the *PANY Bulletin* for over ten years. He writes a column on psychoanalysis and film for each issue. Stein, "Memory" (2005); see also the *International Psychoanalysis* website, internationalpsychoanalysis.net/2010/09/14/memory-repression-and-transference-in-eternal-sunshine-of-the-spotless-mind/ (01/2011).

7. Reeve, "Two" (2009), pp. 22–23, 29.

8. See drdeborahserani.blogspot.com/2006/09/eternal-sunshine-of-spotless-mind.html (01/2011), referring to an article in *Science* 313, no. 5790 (August 25, 2006), pp 1141–44.

9. Edwards, "White" (2008).

10. On lucid dreaming, see Blackmore, *Consciousness* (2003), pp. 349–53.

11. Cardullo, "Falling" (2007), p. 301.

12. Baars, "Theatre" (1997), pp. 294–99; see also Stevens and Zador, "Neural" (1997); Blagrove, "Scripts" (1992), and "Dreams" (1992); Harré and Gillett, *Discursive* (1994), pp. 38–42; Damasio, *Feeling* (1999); McCrone, "Wild" (1997); Thomas, "Stimulus" (1997); also R.D. Ellis, *Questioning* (1995); Barrett, "Committee" (1993); Cartwright and Lamberg, *Crisis* (1992); Hobson, *Dreaming* (2002); and Paul Taylor at www.nous.org.uk/ (01/2011). Technically, memory erasure may be possible in the coming decades. Scientists at State University of New York at Downstate Center have discovered a molecular mechanism called "protein kinase M zeta" that maintains memories in the brain through persistent strengthening of synaptic connections between neurons. By inhibiting the molecule in *mice,* scientists were able to erase a memory that had been stored for one day, or even one month. The researchers say they can erase long-term memories, much as you might erase a computer disk. This research may be a breakthrough treatment for acute trauma, post-traumatic stress disorder, and chronic pain, just to name a few. And this discovery may unlock the mystery to Alzheimer's Disease and other memory loss disorders. Freud, of course, had no idea about this.

13. For this discussion I used interviews and reviews found at: //www.imdb.com/title/tt1365451/ (07/2011); noticias.universia.cl/entrevistas/noticia/ 2010/09/22/485980/matias-lira-es-necesa (07/2011); www.variety.com/review/VE1117944457/ (07/2011).

14. See, for example, Rumelhart's synthesis in his "Architecture" (1989); McCrone, "Wild" (1997), p. 30; Damasio, *Feeling* (1999), p. 154; Pinker, *How* (1997); and Deacon, *Symbolic* (1997).

15. LeDoux, *Emotional* (1996); Frijda's *The Emotions* (1986).

16. This paragraph is partly based on Nancy Eisenberg's overview article "Emotion" (2000); also Damasio, *Descartes'* (1994), and *Feeling* (1999), pp. 50–53, also pp. 340–42, notes 9 and 10. De Waal, *Ape* (2001), pp. 16 and 365; Thagard and Barnes, "Emotional" (1996); Thagard and Kunda, "Making" (1997); Thagard and Millgram, "Inference" (1997); Thagard and Verbeurgt, "Coherence" (1997); Kunda, *Social* (1999), pp. 262–63; Ben-Ze'ev, "Subtlety" (2001). For the record it must be noted that Damasio later distinguished more strongly between emotions and feelings; Damasio, *Looking* (2003). See also Cosmides and Tooby, "Evolutionary" (2000).

17. McCrone, "Wild" (1997), p. 29; also Churchland, "Neurobiology" (1997); Dennett and Kinsbourne, "Time" (1997).

18. For example, Bermudez, *Paradox* (1998). Several researchers have gathered powerful and appealing evidence from neuroscience, psychology, and philosophy that refutes Lacan's psychoanalysis. Much of this paragraph was paraphrased from LeDoux, *Emotional* (1996), p. 193; and from the central argument of Damasio, *Feeling* (1999). See also McCrone, "Wild" (1997).

19. LeDoux, *Emotional* (1996), p. 204; S.E. Taylor, "Asymmetrical" (1991), p. 67; Levine, "Reconstructing" (1997), pp. 167, 174–75; Kayzer, ed., *Schitterend* (1993), pp. 16–45; Rosenzweig et al., *Biological* (1996), pp. 123–24; Atkinson et al., *Hilgard's* (1996), pp. 62–63, 351–53, 371–72, 522–23, 536, 540; Churchland, "Neurobiology" (1997); also Vroon, *Tranen* (1989), pp.

52–55, 151–53. In short, the "I" comes *after* self-consciousness. Thus, language is not *prior* to, or constitutive of, self-consciousness — as Lacan thought.
  20. Unless otherwise indicated, all information about GWT comes from Baars's work, published in a series of papers and two books: *Cognitive Theory* (1988), and *Theater* (1997), as well as "Metaphors" (1998), "Thoroughly" (1994/2007), "Contrastive" (1997), and "Theatre" (1997).
  21. Reeve, "Two" (2009).
  22. See the philosophy blog, *The Information Philosopher,* www.informationphilosopher.com/solutions/scientists/baars/ (03/2011).

## Chapter 7

  1. Interesting sources are, again, Wikipedia "*Speak* (film)," at en.wikipedia.org/wiki/Speak_(film) (03/2011), as well as Wikipedia "*Speak* (novel)," at en.wikipedia.org/wiki/Speak_(novel) (03/2011); and some of the *IMDb* user comments at www.imdb.com/title/tt0378793/usercomments (03/2011). I like to privilege one comment in particular: by "aimless-46 from Kentucky." Two other texts that were useful include Rashmi Rajshekhar, theviews paper.net/movie-review-speak-2004/ (03/2011); and the only reviewer listed at *Rotten Tomatoes* for this film, Chris Parry, efilmcritic.com/review.php?movie=8551&reviewer=1 (03/2011). There is also a blog-comment at www.bukisa.com/articles/177282_movie-review-speak-2004 (03/2011).
  2. Useful were reviews and interviews published at cineconmcfly.com.ar/2008/10/cosas-insignificantes-producida-por.html (05/2011; interview); miradadeulises.com/2009/05/cosas-insignificantes-objetos-y-sentimientos-bien-guardados/ (05/2011; Julio Chico); movie-on.blogspot.com/2010/10/cosas-insignificantes-insignificant.html (05/2011); jccubeirojc.blogspot.com/2010/09/cosas-insignificantes.html (05/2011; Juan Carlos Cubeiro); beyondrace.com/reviews/movies/1358-cosas-insignificantes (05/2011; Andoni Elias Nava); www.jornada.unam.mx/2009/04/17/index.php?section=espectaculos&article=a (05/2011); www.artshub.com.au/au/news-article/reviews/film-tv-radio/cosas-insignificantes-insignificant-things-spanish-film-festival-2009-1 (05/2011; Zoe Wolfendale).
  3. G.A. Taylor, *Castration* (2000). This is not just a short detour, because also in Mary Weismantel's book *Cholas and Pishtacos* (2001), pp. 15, 222–30, examples are presented of Amerindian pishtaco or fat sucker stories about removing the scrotum, not the penis. However, Weismantel, probably uninformed of this problem, believes that in the Andes the people meant "castration" to be castration of the penis and not of the testes. She continues arguing that in the Andes the penis is a condensed symbol of reproductive potency and of social fatherhood in general. From p. 227: "Thus the story of the pishtaco who castrates an Indian involves two different masculinities. The destructive virility of the killer is enhanced when he emasculates another man, who is rendered symbolically female. This is white masculinity in action — even when the pishtaco himself is an indigenous man. The bloody wound of the Indian, however, can signify in a different register. This loss represents more than just one man's humiliation: it stands for the community's collective loss of children, and so of a part of the future — a social death larger and more final than the immediate bodily destruction of the individual." But what, if the penis had no "white" role in the Andes at all? What if the castrating pishtaco — if he can be identified — did not cut off penises? What if the Andeans played out castration games meaning the scrotum? Weismantel recognizes part of the problem. The pishtaco liked an Amerindian, she concludes. "He finds the reproductive organs of women as desirable as those of men: the same knife that removes the testes also rips open women's wombs." The pishtaco worked like anyone involved in Andean animal sacrifice. "Male domestic animals are routinely castrated to control reproduction and to fatten them for later consumption; during butchering, the testes of intact males are removed and eaten as a delicacy." The fetuses of female llamas were used for medicinal and divination purposes.
  4. A quote from www.edge.org/3rd_culture/lakoff/lakoff_p1.html (10/2008); Lakoff and Turner, *More* (1989), p. xi; Lakoff, "Metaphor" (1995). See also cogweb.ucla.edu/CogSci/Lakoff.html (10/2008).
  5. Lakoff, *Women* (1987), p. 303; Lakoff and Johnson, "Afterword, 2003" in *Metaphors*

(2003/1980), pp. 243–76; Lakoff, "Metaphor" (1995). See also cogweb.ucla.edu/CogSci/Lakoff.html (10/2008). See also Johnson, *Body* (1987); Feldman, *From* (2006).
  6. Lakoff, "Metaphor" (1995); and a quote from www.edge.org/3rd_culture/lakoff/lakoff_p1.html (10/2008). See also cogweb.ucla.edu/CogSci/Lakoff.html (10/2008). See also Johnson, *Body* (1987); Feldman, *From* (2006).
  7. Lakoff, *Political* (2008), pp. 232, 232, and *Women* (1987), p. 303; Feldman, *From* (2006).
  8. Examples found in Feldman, *From* (2008), pp. 200–201, originally from a PhD thesis by Joseph Grady (1997), also pp. 8, 272–73, quote from p. 201; Lakoff, *Women* (1987), pp. xiv, xv, xvi, and *Political* (2008), p. 245; Lakoff and Turner, *More* (1989), p. xi; Lakoff and Johnson, *Metaphors* (2003/1980), pp. 254–64, especially pp. 247, 255. See also the article by Borensztajn, Zuidema, and Bod, "Children's Grammars" (2009). Thought and language are neural systems and they do not work by formal symbol manipulation — meaningless symbols put together in sequence to form a sentence, which in turn is put together with other sentences to form a language. Consequently, where Noam Chomsky suggested many years ago that language has nothing to do with meaning or communication, less so with embodiment, Lakoff and Feldman argue the opposite.
  9. Tyson and Tyson, *Psychoanalytic* (1990), p. 324; Cottom, "Work" (1999), pp. 65–74; Lakoff, "How" (1993), see also his *Women* (1987); Brottman, "Some" (2008); Volkan, *Bloodlines* (1997), or "Traumatized" (2000).
  10. Maturana and Varela, *Tree* (1992/1984), p. 241; Varela, Thompson, and Rosch, *Embodied* (1991), p. 9; Noë, *Action* (2004), p. 1; Krueger, "Enacting" (2009), pp. 100–104; Lakoff, "Metaphors" (2001).
  11. Lea Winerman of the APA's *Monitor on Psychology*, "The Mind's Mirror," at www.apa.org/monitor/oct05/mirror.html (10/2008).
  12. On mirror neurons: Rizzolatti and Craighero, "Mirror-Neuron System" (2004); Rizzolatti and Sinigaglia, *Mirrors* (2008); Iacoboni, *Mirroring* (2008); WGBH Boston, PBS, *Nova scienceNow*, January 25, 2005, transcript at www.pbs.org/wgbh/nova/sciencenow/3204/01.html, under "transcript" (10/2008); Wikipedia gives good information at en.wikipedia.org/wiki/Mirror_neurons (10/2008), as does the APA's *Monitor on Psychology* at www.apa.org/monitor/oct05/mirror.html (10/2008). De Waal, *Ape* (2001), pp. 23–24; Lakoff, *Political* (2008), pp. 251–52.
  13. Iacoboni, *Mirroring* (2008); Fadiga et al., "Motor" (1995); Wicker et al., "Both" (2003); Gallese et al., "Unifying" (2004), and "Empathy" (2006); Keysers et al., "Touching" (2004); Keysers and Gazzola, "Towards" (2006); WGBH Boston, PBS, *Nova scienceNow*, January 25, 2005, transcript at www.pbs.org/wgbh/nova/sciencenow/3204/01.html, under "transcript" (10/2008); Wikipedia at en.wikipedia.org/wiki/Mirror_neurons (10/2008), Apa's *Monitor on Psychology* at www.apa.org/monitor/oct05/mirror.html (10/2008). Mentioned is *Journal of Neurophysiology* 73, no. 6 (1995): 2.608–2.611.
  14. On Grounding: Barsalou, "Grounded"(2008); also Gibbs, *Embodiment* (2006).
  15. afilmodyssey.wordpress.com/2010/06/15/review-speak-2004/ (03/2011).
  16. Buss, *Evolutionary Psychology* (1999), pp. 278–311, 345–69, especially pp. 352–56.
  17. Buss, *Evolutionary Psychology* (1999), pp. 278–311, 345–69; and the main psychology introductory textbook by Atkinson et al., *Hilgard's* (1996), pp. 397–404.
  18. Although this sounds like the theory of the phallus, it had nothing to do with some Oedipus Complex and development by repressions, less so with any phallus. Buss, *Evolutionary Psychology* (1999), pp. 352–56; Cummins, "Social" (1998); Lakoff and Turner, *More* (1989), pp. 221–23.
  19. Harris, *Nurture* (1999/1998), pp. 38–40, 45–51; Plomin and Daniels, "Why" (1987).
  20. Harris, "Why" (2007).
  21. Harris, "Why" (2007), also *Nurture Assumption* (1998).
  22. Also taken from Harris, "Why" (2007).
  23. Harris, *Nurture* (1998), pp. 57–58, 60, 62, 64; Rovee-Collier, "Capacity" (1993).
  24. Harris, "Why" (2007).
  25. Perhaps, this view is even older than James. Eighteenth-century Scottish philosopher David Hume (1711–76) wrote in his *Treatise of Human Nature* (1739) that the self was "nothing

but a bundle or collection of different perceptions, which succeed each other with an inconceivable rapidity, and are in a perpetual flux and movement." Perhaps Hume might have come to this insight after reading the work of his French forerunner Pierre Bayle (1647–1706). See Ginzburg, *No Island* (2000), pp. 65–66; James, *Principles* (1890), p. 294.
26. Harris, *Nurture* (1998), p. 56.
27. Mullen argues that her theory can easily do without the context provided by evolutionary psychology, although evolution may indeed have been at its roots. Harris, "Why" (2007), and *No Two Alike* (2006), pp. 143–240; and Mullen's review in *Metapsychology Online Reviews* 10, no. 10 (March 8, 2006).
28. Harris, "Why" (2007).
29. Harris, "Why" (2007).
30. Harris, "Why" (2007).
31. Lakoff and Johnson, *Metaphors* (2003/1980), pp. 14–21.

## Chapter 8

1. For good plot summaries see: Wikipedia, en.wikipedia.org/wiki/Black_Swan_ (film) (04/2011); and Ebert, rogerebert.suntimes.com/apps/pbcs.dll/article?AID=/20101201/REVIEWS/101209994/1023 (04/2011).
2. Gottschall, *Storytelling* (2012), for example pp. 95–103.
3. Gazzaniga, *Who's* (2011), pp. 75–103, quotes from 82, 83, 86 and 102.
4. Reed, *Psychology* (1988/1972); Arzy et al., "Induction" (2006).
5. Sabbadini, "Introduction" (2003), pp. 4–5.
6. Dufresne, *Tales* (2000), pp. 14 (Letter to Ferenczi), 15 and 16 (quotes from *Beyond the Pleasure Principle*), 16 (Letter to the Princess), 23 (quoting Marcuse, and Deleuze and Guattari), 24, 45–50, 51, 59 (quotes from Freud), 52–60.
7. Dufresne, *Tales* (2000), pp. 17–19, 28–34, 39, 41, 35 (quote to D. Burston, *The Legacy of Erich Fromm*, [Cambridge, 1991], p. 199). Furthermore, see Freud, "Uncanny" (1955/1925), pp. 219–20, 251–52, p. 232 note 1 reads about (and italics are added) the "*psychological truth* of the situation in which the young man, fixated upon his father by his castration complex [...]"; Royle, *Uncanny* (2003), pp. 6–12; R.M. Young, "Psychoanalytic" (1984), p. 93; Cixous, "Fiction" (1976/1972), p. 525; Kofman, *Freud* (1991/1974) p. 121; and, Freud's letters to Ferenczi in Falzeder and Brabant, eds., *Correspondence* (1996), pp. 354 and 363.
8. As is the case with most of his concepts, the Freudian "Uncanny" is based on misdiagnosis and bad reading. Freud, "Uncanny" (1955/1919), pp. 218, 219–26, translator's note; Dufresne, *Tales* (2000), for example, pp. 13–144, especially pp. 43–65, quotes from pp. 43–45. A long quote from Daniel Sander's *Wörterbuch des Deutschen Sprache* (1860) can be found on pp. 222–24, and from Grimm's dictionary (1877) on pp. 225–26. A more accurate framing of Hoffmann's "Uncanny" presents us with a conflict between warm Romanticism and cold Enlightenment. For Freud's reading of Hoffman and other readings of Hoffman, see Freud, "Uncanny" (1955/1925), the introduction of the Sand-Man in pp. 226–31, quote from note 1 on p. 230; E.T.A. Hoffmann, "The Sandman," in *Tales of Hoffmann*, trans. and ed. R.J. Hollingdale (Harmondsworth: Penguin, 1982); Brantly, "Thermographic" (1982); Tatar, "E.T.A. Hoffmann's" (1980); Cottom, "Work" (1999); and a text written by Inge Stephan in Beutin et al., *Deutsche Literaturgeschichte* (1994), pp. 194–96. Hoffmann used the word unheimlich six times in his tale. Nathanael remembered the Sandman as "*den unheimlichen Spuk,*" that "uncanny specter." Klara labeled Coppelius's activities with Nathanael's father as "*Das unheimliche Treiben mit Deinem Vater.*" "These uncanny dealings with your father." And she spoke of the dark powers in his mind, "*jene unheimliche Macht,*" "that uncanny power." Spotting Olimpia, also Nathanael felt a little frightened at first, "*wurde ganz unheimlich,*" "he felt quite uncanny." Although he changed his mind, he did realize that the others, cold prosaic people, would find her spooky ("*Wohl mag euch, ihr kalten prosaischen Menschen, Olimpia unheimlich sein.*"). And the author agreed that Olimpia was indeed rather uncanny ("*Uns ist diese Olimpia ganz unheimlich geworden.*"). Is this reason to look at Hoffmann as a precursor to Freud? And Freud as a belated

Hoffmannesque theorist? See Fletcher, "Freud" (2002), p. 125; and on the background of all this, see Munck, *Enlightenment* (2000). His Romanticism blinded Freud from a historicist look at art. He missed Hoffmann's humor and his satire to ridicule the activities from the new emerging Structuralist-Romantic Order to merge or reconcile with the Enlightenment universe. Freud took the horror seriously.

9. For example, Pinker, *Better* (2011), pp. 32–33.

10. Discussion of the film at *IMDb:* www.imdb.com/title/tt0159097/usercomments?start=0 (01/2011); Wikipedia has a good summary at en.wikipedia.org/wiki/The_Virgin_Suicides_(film) (01/2011). For reviews: Jeffrey M. Anderson for *CineMatical,* blog.moviefone.com/2007/05/21/retro-cinema-the-virgin-suicides/ (01/2011); Roger Ebert at rogerebert.suntimes.com/apps/pbcs.dll/article?AID=/20000505/REVIEWS/5050305/1023 (01/2011); Todd R. Ramlow for *PopMatters,* at www.popmatters.com/film/reviews/v/virgin-suicides.shtml (01/2011); Graham Fuller's review in *Sight & Sound* of April 2000, at www.bfi.org.uk/sightandsound/feature/26/ (01/2011); A.O. Scott, *New York Times,* at; movies.nytimes.com/movie/ (01/2011); Stephanie Zacharek (film) and Jeff Stark (DVD) both at *Salon.com,* www.salon.com/entertainment/movies/dvd/review/2001/01/23/virgin_suicides (01/2011), and www.salon.com/entertainment/movies/review/2000/04/21/suicides/index.html (01/2011); and blogger Carram at *InfoBarrel,* at www.infobarrel.com/The_Virgin_Suicides:_A_review_and_a_look_into_the_minds_of_troubled_teens (01/2011).

11. Crucial is an article by Bree Hoskin, "Playground" (2007). Interviews with Coppola at: *FilmCritic.com,* www.filmcritic.com/features/2000/04/virgin-tendencies-sofia-coppola-takes-on-filmmaking/ (01/2011); one with Jenny Cooney Carrillo for *Urban CineFile* at www.urbancinefile.com.au/home/view.asp?a=3912&Section=Interviews (01/2011); and another one by Rob Blackwelder for *SPLICEDwire* at www.splicedwire.com/00features/scoppola.html (01/2011).

12. Fuller, *Sight & Sound,* at www.bfi.org.uk/sightandsound/feature/26/ (01/2011).

13. Fuller, *Sight & Sound,* at www.bfi.org.uk/sightandsound/feature/26/ (01/2011).

14. Hoskin, "Playground" (2007), pp. 218–9.

15. Hoskin, "Playground" (2007), p. 218.

16. Zacharek at *Salon.com,* www.salon.com/2000/04/21/suicides (01/2011).

17. Ebert, at rogerebert.suntimes.com/apps/pbcs.dll/article?AID=/20000505/REVIEWS/5050305/1023 (01/2011); Coppola interview with *FilmCritic.com,* www.filmcritic.com/features/2000/04/virgin-tendencies-sofia-coppola-takes-on-filmmaking/ (01/2011).

18. Hoskin, "Playground" (2007), p. 219.

19. Ramlow, *PopMatters,* at www.popmatters.com/film/reviews/v/virgin-suicides.shtml (01/2011).

20. Fuller, *Sight & Sound,* at www.bfi.org.uk/sightandsound/feature/26/ (01/2011).

21. Fuller, *Sight & Sound,* at www.bfi.org.uk/sightandsound/feature/26/ (01/2011); Cooney Carrillo for *Urban CineFile* at www.urbancinefile.com.au/home/view.asp?a=3912&Section=Interviews (01/2011).

22. Fuller, *Sight & Sound,* at www.bfi.org.uk/sightandsound/feature/26/ (01/2011); Ramlow, *PopMatters,* at www.popmatters.com/film/reviews/v/virgin-suicides.shtml (01/2011).

23. Zacharek, *Salon.com,* www.salon.com/2000/04/21/suicides (01/2011).

24. Hoskin, "Playground" (2007), p. 216.

25. References for this paragraph and the next include: Cole, *Cultural* (1996), p. 58; Atkinson et al., *Hilgard's* (1996), pp. 289–90; Nishida, "Cognitive" (1999), p. 755; Lakoff, *Political* (2008), pp. 24, 38, 59; Feldman, *From* (2008), pp. 78–82; Bartlett's book is called *Remembering* (Cambridge, 1932). The price to be paid of course is distortion if the schema used to encode it does not fit well. Research over the past decades has confirmed Bartlett's suggestion.

26. Lakoff, *Political* (2008), pp. 24, 38, 59.

27. For anyone not at home in Schema Theory, most useful may be the college note by Sharon Alayne Widmayer, "Schema Theory: An Introduction," at chd.gse.gmn.edu/immersion/knowledgebase/strategies/cognitivism/SchemaTheory.htm (07/2003). She mentions some interesting examples and some links that can easily be followed.

28. Thomas, "Stimulus" (1997); R.D. Ellis, *Questioning* (1995); Harré and Gillett, *Discursive*

(1994), pp. 38–49, 67, 77; Allot, "Objective" (1991); Singh-Manoux and Finkenauer, "Cultural" (2001).
29. Pasupathi, "Social" (2001), quotes from pp. 651, 652.
30. Swaab, *Wij zijn* (2010), pp. 35–44; Rosenzweig, et al. *Biological* (1996), pp. 227–228 and G-18.
31. Sacks in Kayzer, ed., *Schitterend* (1993), p. 21; Harré and Gillett, *Discursive* (1994), pp. 45–77, 80–83; S.E. Taylor, "Asymetrical" (1991), p. 71; Sperry, "Impact" (1993), pp. 879–80; S.S. Jones, "Interview with Susan Greenfield," at www.merlin.com.au/brain_proj (1997) (04/98). The Theory of the World (ToW) is not an "objective" vision of reality; it is restricted to individual lived experiences within the context in which the person lives. Because each human being develops a series of ToWs according to sensory inputs, memory information of past experiences, emotions, and personal history, including all kinds of present and past interpretations, contextualized and developed within well-defined ecological boundaries, the ToW is loaded with records of the expected *next* moment. This predictive, private, internal process, which is individually unique yet socially appropriate, cannot rule out fiction and fictitious experiences during the computation of all existing information.
32. Hogg and Vaughan, *Social* (1995), p. 48; Atkinson et al., *Hilgard's* (1996), pp. 288–92, 594–96; S. Fiske, "Thinking" (1992).
33. Cole, *Cultural* (1996), pp. 117–20, 125; Hogg and Vaughan, *Social* (1995), pp. 56–60; D'Andrade, *Development* (1995).
34. McNally, *Remembering* (2003), p. 40.
35. McNally, *Remembering* (2003).
36. Cole, *Cultural* (1996), pp. 117–20, 125 (quote from p. 117); Hogg and Vaughan, *Social* (1995), pp. 56–60; also Schacter, *Searching* (1996); D'Andrade, *Development* (1995).
37. Thomas, "Stimulus" (1997); R.D. Ellis, *Questioning* (1995); Harré and Gillett, *Discursive* (1994), pp. 38–49, 67, 77; Allot, "Objective" (1991); Singh-Manoux and Finkenauer, "Cultural" (2001).

## Afterword

1. Borrowed from abcnews.go.com/Entertainment/WolfFiles/story?id=440961&page=1 (04/2007).
2. Gerrig, *Experiencing* (1993), pp. 3, 5, 7, 10–24, 26, 28–29.
3. Onfray, *Anti Freud* (2011), pp. 377ff; Freud saw these resemblances himself and wrote about it with consent.
4. Israëls, *Weense kwakzalver* (1999), pp. 59–130, quote p. 61; also Paul, "Psychoanalytic" (1987); for an article that tried to understand Freud's errors, see Elms, "Sigmund Freud" (2003).
5. Israëls, *Weense kwakzalver* (1999), pp. 59–130.
6. On the popular vision of *Guernica* as anti-war icon: en.wikipedia.org/wiki/Guernica_ (painting) (08/2008); and the *Treasures of the World* website at www.pbs.org/treasuresoftheworld/a_nav/guernica_nav/main_guerfrm.html (08/2008); this and the following paragraphs.
7. Ginzburg, *Schwert* (1999), pp. 73–75, and "Sword" (2001), pp. 128–40, 158–61, 165.
8. See previous note for references in: Ginzburg, *Schwert* (1999), and "Sword" (2001).
9. See note 7 for references in: Ginzburg, *Schwert* (1999), and "Sword" (2001).
10. As always, Wikipedia proved helpful. This is retrieved from en.wikipedia.org/wiki/Seinfeld (09/2007), and the transcript by Dan Coogan from www.seinology.com/scripts/script-118.shtm (06/2007), also at www.cooganphoto.com, posted originally on "The News Guys (Mike's) Site." www.geocities.com/tnguym.
11. George's Worlds Theory is similar but not identical to the Many Worlds Theory popular in quantum physics, which states that all possible quantum universes can exist simultaneously. It solves the Schrodinger cat problem by stating that the universe splits at each quantum juncture, and hence the cat is alive in one universe and dead in another. In other words, everything that can happen, does happen (just in separate worlds). Every possibility plays itself out in one

universe or another. See the entry by *OneBadAsp*, October 20, 2006, at www.urbandictionary.com/define.php?term=worlds+theory (10/2009).
   12. Lugones, "Playfulness" (1987).
   13. Dennett, *Freedom* (2003).
   14. Webster, "Cult" (1996).

# Bibliography

Abbott, H.P. "Narrating Conversion in an Age of Darwinian Gradualism." *Storyworlds: A Journal of Narrative Studies* 2 (2010): 1–18.
Allot, R. "Objective Morality." www.percep.demon.co.uk/morality.htm (10/2007). Republished from *Journal of Social and Biological Structures* 14, no. 4 (1991): 455–71.
Altschule, M. *Origins of Concepts in Human Behavior: Social and Cultural Factors.* New York: Wiley, 1977.
Andersen, S.M., L.A. Spielman, and J.A. Bargh. "Future-Event Schemas and Certainty About the Future: Automaticity in Depressives' Future-Event Predictions." *Journal of Personality and Social Psychology* 63 (1992): 711–23.
Anderson, J.D. *The Reality of Illusion: An Ecological Approach to Cognitive Film Theory.* Carbondale: Southern Illinois University Press, 1996.
Anderson, J.D., and B.F. Anderson, eds. *Moving Image Theory: Ecological Considerations.* Carbondale: Southern Illinois University Press, 2005.
\_\_\_\_\_. *Narration and Spectatorship in Moving Images.* Newcastle: Cambridge Scholars Publishers, 2007.
Apps, L., and A. Gow. *Male Witches in Early Modern Europe.* Manchester: Manchester University Press, 2003.
Armstrong, R. "*Oedipus* as Evidence: The Theatrical Background to Freud's Oedipus Complex." *Psyart: A Hyperlink Journal for the Psychological Study of the Arts.* web.clas.ufl.edu/ipsa/journal/articles/psyart1999/oedipus/armstr01.htm (1998; 10/2007).
Arzy, S., M. Seeck, S. Ortigue, L. Spinelli, and O. Blanke. "Induction of an Illusory Shadow Person." *Nature* 287, no. 443 (2006), at www.nature.com/nature/journal/v443/n7109/full/443287a.html (03/2011).
Atkinson, R.L., R.C. Atkinson, E.E. Smith, D.J. Bem, and S. Nolen-Hoeksema. *Hilgard's Introduction to Psychology.* 12th ed. Forthworth: Harcourt Brace College Publishers, 1996.
Atmanspacher, H. "Complexity and Meaning as a Bridge across the Cartesian Cut." *Journal of Consciousness Studies* 1, no. 2 (1994): 168–81.
Austin, J.L. *How to Do Things with Words: The William James Lectures Delivered at Harvard University in 1955.* Cambridge: Clarendon, 1962.
Baars, B.J. *A Cognitive Theory of Consciousness.* Cambridge: Cambridge University Press, 1988.
\_\_\_\_\_. "Contrastive Phenomenology: A Thorough Empirical Approach to Consciousness." In Block et al., *The Nature of Consciousness: Philosophical Debates,* 187–201.
\_\_\_\_\_. "In the Theatre of Consciousness: Global Workspace Theory, A Rigorous Scientific Theory of Consciousness." *Journal of Consciousness Studies* 4, no. 4 (1997): 292–309.

———. *In the Theater of Consciousness: The Workspace of the Mind.* New York: Oxford University Press, 1997.
———. "Metaphors of Consciousness and Attention in the Brain." *Trends in Neurosciences* 21, no. 2 (1998): 58–62. www.phil.vt.edu/ASSC/baars/(1997).
———. "A Thoroughly Empirical Approach to Consciousness: Contrastive Analysis." psyche.cs.monash.edu.au/vl/psyche-1-06-baars.html (1994; 10/2007).
Balderston, D., and F. Masiello, eds. *Approaches to Teaching Puig's Kiss of the Spider Woman.* New York: Modern Language Association of America, 2007.
Barrett, D. "The 'Committee of Sleep': A Study of Dream Incubation for Problem Solving." *Dreaming: Journal of the Association for the Study of Dreams* 3, no. 2 (1993): 115–23.
———. "Flying Dreams and Lucidity: An Empirical Study of Their Relationship." *Dreaming: Journal of the Association for the Study of Dreams* 1, no. 2 (1991): 129–34.
———. "Just How Lucid Are Lucid Dreams?" *Dreaming: Journal of the Association for the Study of Dreams* 2, no. 4 (1992): 221–28.
Barsalou, L. "Grounded Cognition." *Annual Review of Psychology* 59 (2008): 617–45.
Bartlett, R. *The Making of Europe: Conquest, Colonization and Cultural Change, 950–1350.* Princeton, NJ: Princeton University Press, 1993.
Bauer, P.J. "What Do Infants Recall of Their Lives? Memory for Specific Events by One- to Two-Year-Olds." *American Psychologist* 51, no. 1 (1996): 29–41.
Bem, S.L. "Gender Schema Theory: A Cognitive Account of Sex Typing." *Psychological Review* 88 (1981): 354–64.
———. *The Lenses of Gender: Transforming the Debate on Sexual Inequality.* New Haven, CT: Yale University Press, 1993.
Bénesteau, J. *Mensonges freudiens: Histoire d'une désinformation séculaire.* Sprimont: P. Mardaga, 2002.
Ben-Ze'ev, A. "The Subtlety of Emotions." *Psycoloquy* 12, no. 7 (2001). psycprints.ecs.soton.ac.uk/archive/00000136/ (10/2007).
Bergstrom, J., ed. *Endless Night. Cinema and Psychoanalysis, Parallel Histories.* Berkeley: University of California Press, 1999.
Bermudez, J.L. *The Paradox of Self-Consciousness.* Cambridge, MA: MIT Press, 1998.
Beutin, W. et al. *Deutsche Literaturgeschichte: Von den Anfängen bis zur Gegenwart.* Stuttgart: J.B. Metzler, 1994.
Billig, M. "The Dialogic Unconscious: Psychoanalysis, Discursive Psychology and the Nature of Repression." *British Journal of Social Psychology* 36 (1997): 139–59.
———. "Freud and Dora: Repressing an Oppressed Identity." *Theory, Culture & Society* 14, no. 3 (1997): 29–55. Used is its offprint on www.massey.ac.nz/~Alock/virtual/dora4abs.htm (1997; 10/2007).
Blackmore, S. *Consciousness: An Introduction.* London: Hodder and Stoughton, 2003.
Blagrove, M. "Dreams as a Reflection of Our Waking Concerns and Abilities: A Critique of the Problem-Solving Paradigm in Dream Research." *Dreaming: Journal of the Association for the Study of Dreams* 2, no. 4 (1992): 205–20.
———. "Scripts and the Structuralist Analysis of Dreams." *Dreaming: Journal of the Association for the Study of Dreams* 2, no. 1 (1992): 23–37.
Block, N., O. Flanagan, and G. Güzeldere, eds. *The Nature of Consciousness: Philosophical Debates.* Cambridge, MA: MIT Press, 1997.
Bonanno, G.A. "Loss, Trauma, and Human Resilience: Have We Underestimated the Human Capacity to Thrive After Extremely Aversive Events?" *American Psychologist* 59, no. 1 (2004): 20–28.
———. *The Other Side of Sadness: What the New Science of Bereavement Tells Us About Life After Loss.* New York: Basic Books, 2009.
Bonanno, G.A., A. Holen, D. Keltner, and M.J. Horowitz. "When Avoiding Unpleasant Emotions Might Not Be Such a Bad Thing: Verbal-Autonomic Response Dissociation and Midlife Conjugal Bereavement." *Journal of Personality and Social Psychology* 69, no 5 (1995): 975–89.
Bonato, R.A., A.R. Moffitt, R.F. Hoffmann, M.A. Cuddy, and F.L. Wimmer. "Bizarreness in

Dreams and Nightmares." *Dreaming: Journal of the Association for the Study of Dreams* 1, no. 1 (1991): 53–61.
Bond, M.H., and P.B Smith. "Cross-Cultural Social and Organizational Psychology." *Annual Review of Psychology* 47 (1996): 205–35.
Borch-Jacobsen, M. "How to Predict the Past: From Trauma to Repression." *History of Psychiatry* 11 (1996): 15–35.
———. *Lacan. The Absolute Master*. Stanford, CA: Stanford University Press, 1991.
———. "Little Brother, Little Sister." *London Review of Books* 23, no 10 (2001). www.lrb.co.uk/v23/n10 /print/borc01_html (06/2008).
———. "The Oedipus Problem in Freud and Lacan." *Critical Inquiry* 20, no. 2 (1994): 267–82.
———. *Remembering Anna O.: A Century of Mystification*. New York: Routledge, 1996.
Borch-Jacobsen, M., J. Cottraux, D. Pleux, J. van Rillaer, et al., *Libro negro del psicoanálisis. Vivir, pensar y estar mejor sin Freud*. Buenos Aires: Editorial Sudamericana, 2007 (orig. 2005).
Borch-Jacobsen, M., and S. Shamdasani. *Le dossier Freud: Enquête sur l'histoire de la psychanalyse*. Paris: Les Empêcheurs de penser en rond, 2006.
Bordwell, D. "Contemporary Film Studies and the Vicissitudes of Grand Theory." In *Post-Theory: Reconstructing Film Studies*, edited by D. Bordwell and N. Carroll, 3–36. Madison: University of Wisconsin Press, 1996.
———. *Making Meaning: Inference and Rhetoric in the Interpretation of Cinema*. Cambridge, MA: Harvard University Press, 1989.
———. "The Part-Time Cognitivist: A View from Film Studies." *Projections* 4, no. 2 (2010): 1–18.
Bordwell, D., and N. Carroll, eds. *Post-Theory: Reconstructing Film Studies*. Madison: University of Wisconsin Press, 1996.
Bordwell, D., and K. Thompson. *Film Art: An Introduction*. 8th ed. New York: McGraw-Hill, 2008.
Borensztajn, G., W. Zuidema, and R. Bod. "Children's Grammars Grow More Abstract with Age: Evidence from an Automatic Procedure for Identifying the Productive Units of Language." *Topics in Cognitive Science* 1 (2009): 175–88.
Borkowski, J.G., S.L. Ramey, and M. Bristol-Power, eds. *Parenting and the Child's World: Influences on Academic, Intellectual, and Social-Emotional Development*. Mahwah, NJ: Lawrence Erlbaum Associates Publishers, 2002.
Bourdieu, P. *Outline of a Theory of Practice*. Cambridge: Cambridge University Press, 1977 (orig. 1972).
Brantly, S. "A Thermographic Reading of E.T.A. Hoffmann's *Der Sandmann*." *German Quarterly* 55, no. 3 (1982): 324–35.
Braudy, L., and M. Cohen, eds. *Film Theory and Criticism: Introductory Readings*. Oxford: Oxford University Press, 1999.
Brenneis, D. "Talk and Transformation." *Man ns* 22, no. 3 (1987): 499–510.
Brent, J. *Charles Sanders Peirce: A Life*. Bloomington: Indiana University Press, 1993.
Brewer, M.B., J.G. Weber, and B. Carini. "Person Memory in Intergroup Contexts: Categorization Versus Individuation." *Journal of Personality and Social Psychology* 69, no. 1 (1995): 29–40.
Brewin, C.B. "Theoretical Foundations of Cognitive-Behavior Therapy for Anxiety and Depression." *Annual Review of Psychology* 47 (1996): 33–57.
Bricmont, J., and A. Sokal. "Defense of a Modest Scientific Realism." Paper Bielefel-Zif Conference on "Welt and Wissen/ Monde et Savoir/ World and Knowledge." Bielefeld, June 18, 2001.
———. "Science and the Sociology of Science: Beyond War and Peace." In *The One Culture*, edited by J.A. Labinger and H.M. Collins, 27–47. Chicago: University of Chicago Press, 2001.
Britton, R. *Sex, Death, and the Superego: Experiences in Psychoanalysis*. New York: Karnac, 2003.
Brody, G., ed. *Sibling Relationships: Their Causes and Consequences*. Norwood: Ablex Publishing Corporation, 1996.
Brottman, M. "Some Thoughts on Dream Aesthetics." *Image [&] Narrative: Online Magazine of the Visual Narrative* 23 (2008). www.imageandnarrative.be/Timeandphotography/brottman. html (11/2008).

Brown, B.B., N. Mounts, S.D. Lamborn, and L. Steinberg. "Parenting Practices and Peer Group Affiliation in Adolescence." *Child Development* 64 (1993): 467–82.
Bruer, J.T. *The Myth of the First Three Years: A New Understanding of Early Brain Development and Lifelong Learning.* New York: Free Press, 1999.
Bucci, W. *Psychoanalysis and Cognitive Science: A Multiple Code Theory.* New York: Guilford Press, 1997.
Buekens, F. *Jacques Lacan: Proefvlucht in het luchtledige.* Voorburg: Acco, 2006.
Buller, D.J. *Adapting Minds. Evolutionary Psychology and the Persistent Quest for Human Nature.* Cambridge, MA: MIT Press, 2006.
_____. "DeFreuding Evolutionary Psychology: Adaptation and Human Motivation." In *Where Biology Meets Psychology: Philosophical Essays,* edited by V.G. Hardcastle, 99–114. Cambridge, MA: MIT Press, 1999. cogprints.soton.ac.uk/abc/phil/199806032 (12/1998).
Burkhart, L.M. *The Slippery Earth: Nahua-Christian Moral Dialogue in Sixteenth-Century Mexico.* Tucson: University of Arizona Press, 1989.
Buss, D.M. *Evolutionary Psychology: The New Science of the Mind.* Boston: Allyn and Bacon, 1999.
Butler, J. "Doing Justice to Someone: Sex Reassignment and Allegories of Transsexuality." *GLQ: A Journal of Lesbian and Gay Studies* 7, no. 4 (2001): 621–36.
_____. *Undoing Gender.* New York: Routledge, 2004.
Cardullo, B. "Falling In and Out of Love, Again." *Hudson Review* 60, no. 2 (2007): 299–307.
Carrier, J.G. "Occidentalism: The World Turned Upside-Down." *American Ethnologist* 19, no. 2 (1992): 195–232.
Cartwright, R. "Dreams That Work: The Relation of Dream Incorporation to Adaptation to Stressful Events." *Dreaming: Journal of the Association for the Study of Dreams* 1, no. 1 (1991): 3–10.
Cartwright, R., and L. Lamberg. *Crisis Dreaming: Using Your Dreams to Solve Your Problems.* New York: HarperCollins, 1992.
Carus, C.G. *Psyche: Zur Entwicklungsgeschichte der Seele.* Stuttgart: C.P. Scheitlin, 1851 (orig. 1846).
Catalán-Morseby, E. "Vampires in *The Twilight Saga:* The Reinvention and Humanization of the Vampire Myth." MA thesis, Växjö University, 2010.
Churchland, P.S. "Can Neurobiology Teach Us Anything About Consciousness?" In Block et al., *The Nature of Consciousness: Philosophical Debates,* 127–40.
Cioffi, F. *Freud and the Question of Pseudoscience.* Chicago: Open Court, 1998.
Cixous, H. "Fiction and Its Phantoms: A Reading of Freud's *Das Unheimliche* (The 'Uncanny')." *New Literary Journal* 7, no. 3 (1976): 525–48; orig. 1972.
Clark, S. *Thinking with Demons: The Idea of Witchcraft in Early Modern Europe.* Oxford: Clarendon Press, 1997.
Cole, M. *Cultural Psychology. A Once and Future Discipline.* Cambridge: Belknap Press of Harvard University Press, 1996.
Cole, M., S.R. Cole, and C. Lightfoot. *The Development of Children.* New York: Worth Publishers, 2001.
Cole, M., Y. Engeström, and O. Vasquez, eds. *Mind, Culture, and Activity.* Seminal Papers from the Laboratory of Comparative Human Cognition. Cambridge: Cambridge University Press, 1997.
Collins, W. A., E.E. Maccoby, L. Steinberg, E. M. Hetherington, and M. H. Bornstein. "Contemporary Research on Parenting: The Case for Nature *and* Nurture." *American Psychologist* 55 (2000): 218–32.
Connerton, P. *How Societies Remember.* Cambridge: Cambridge University Press, 1989.
Corner, J., and J. Hawthorn, eds. *Communication Studies: An Introductory Reader.* London: Arnold, 1980.
Cosmides, L., and J. Tooby. "Evolutionary Psychology and the Emotions." Url. : www.psych.ucsb.edu/research/cep/emotion. html (2000; 10/2007). Also published in M. Lewis and J. M. Haviland-Jones, eds. *Handbook of Emotions.* 2d ed. London: Guilford Press, 2000.
Cottom, D. "The Work of Art in the Age of Mechanical Digestion." *Representations* 66 (1999): 52–74.

Crews, F., and His Critics. *The Memory Wars. Freud's Legacy in Dispute.* New York: A New York Review Book, 1995.
Crombag, H.F.M., and H.L.G.J. Merckelbach. *Hervonden herinneringen en andere misverstanden.* Amsterdam: Uitgeverij Contact, 1996.
——. "De meervoudige persoonlijkheidsstoornis: Kritische kanttekeningen ii." *De Psycholoog* 32 (1997): 247–50.
Crombag, H.F.M., and P.J. van Koppen. "Verdringen als sociaal verschijnsel." *De Psycholoog* 29 (1994): 409–15.
Cuddy, M.A., and K. Belicki. "Nightmare Frequency and Related Sleep Disturbance as Indicators of a History of Sexual Abuse." *Dreaming: Journal of the Association for the Study of Dreams* 2, no. 1 (1992): 15–22.
Cummins, D.D. "Social Norms and Other Minds: The Evolutionary Roots of Higher Cognition." In *The Evolution of Mind,* edited by C. Cummins and C. Allen, 30–50. New York: Oxford University Press, 1998.
Cummins, D.D., and C. Allen, eds. *The Evolution of Mind.* New York: Oxford University Press, 1998.
Currie, G. *Image and Mind. Film, Philosophy, and Cognitive Science.* Cambridge: Cambridge University Press, 1995.
Damasio, A.R. *Descartes' Error: Emotion, Reason, and the Human Brain.* New York: G.P. Putnam's Sons, 1994.
——. *The Feeling of What Happens: Body and Emotion in the Making of Consciousness.* New York: Harcourt, Inc., 1999.
——. *Looking for Spinoza: Joy, Sorrow, and the Feeling Brain.* New York: Harcourt Brace & Company, 2003.
D'Andrade, R. *The Development of Cognitive Anthropology.* New York: Cambridge University Press, 1995.
Darnton, R. *The Great Cat Massacre and Other Episodes in French Cultural History.* New York: Basic Books, 1984.
——. *Mesmerism and the End of the Enlightenment in France.* Cambridge, MA: Harvard University Press, 1968.
——. *Mesmerisme en het einde van de Verlichting in Frankrijk.* Amsterdam: Bert Bakker, 1988 (orig. 1968).
Davies, J. "Imagining Intergenerationality: Representation and Rhetoric in the Pedophile Movie." *GLQ: A Journal of Lesbian and Gay Studies* 13, no. 2–3 (2007): 369–85.
Davis, D.A. "Freud's Unwritten Case: The Patient 'E.'" *Psychoanalytic Psychology* 7 (1990): 185–209.
Deacon, T.W. *The Symbolic Species. The Co-Evolution of Language and the Brain.* New York: MIT Press, 1997.
Decker, H.S. *Freud, Dora and Vienna 1900.* New York: Maxwell Macmillan International, 1991.
Deleuze, G. *Cinema 2. The Time-Image.* Minneapolis: University of Minnesota Press, 1989 (orig. 1985).
Deleuze, G., and F. Guattari. *Anti-Oedipus: Capitalism and Schizophrenia.* London: Athlone Press, 1983 (orig. 1972).
——. *A Thousand Plateaus: Capitalism and Schizophrenia.* Minneapolis: University of Minnesota Press, 1987 (orig. 1980).
Demick, J., K. Bursik, and R. DiBiasen, eds. *Parental Development.* Hillsdale, NJ; L. Erlbaum, 1993.
Demos, J. P. *Entertaining Satan: Witchcraft and the Culture of Early New England.* New York: Oxford University Press, 1982.
Dennett, D.C. *Consciousness Explained.* Boston: Little, Brown and Company, 1991.
——. *Darwin's Dangerous Idea: Evolution and the Meanings of Life.* New York: Penguin Books, 1995.
——. *Freedom Evolves.* New York: Viking, 2003
Dennett, D.C., and M. Kinsbourne. "Time and the Observer: The Where and When of Con-

sciousness in the Brain." In Block et al., *The Nature of Consciousness: Philosophical Debates*, 141–74.
Dennison, S., and L. Shaw, eds. *Latin American Cinema. Essays on Modernity, Gender and Nationhood.* Jefferson, NC: McFarland, 2005.
Derrida, J. *Specters of Marx: The State of the Debt, the Work of Mourning, and the New International.* New York: Routledge, 1994 (orig. 1993).
De Swaan, A. "Dyscivilization, Mass Extermination and the State." *Theory, Culture & Society* 18, no. 2–3 (2001): 265–76.
De Vos, L. "To See or Not to See: The Ambiguity of Medusa in Relation to Mulisch's *The Procedure*." *Image [&] Narrative* 5 (2003). www.imageandnarrative.be/uncanny/ (05/2008).
De Waal, F. *The Ape and the Sushi Master: Cultural Reflections by a Primatologist.* London: Penguin, 2001.
Diamond, M. "Sex and Gender Are Different: Sexual Identity and Gender Identity Are Different." *Clinical Child Psychology and Psychiatry* 7 (2002): 320–34.
Dolar, M. "'I Shall Be with You on Your Wedding-Night': Lacan and the Uncanny." *October* 58 (1991): 5–23.
Domhoff, G.W. *The Scientific Study of Dreams: Neural Networks, Cognitive Development, and Content Analysis.* Washington, DC: American Psychological Association, 2003.
Dooley, B. *Morandi's Last Prophecy and the End of Renaissance Politics.* Princeton, NJ: Princeton University Press, 2002.
Doorman, M. *De romantische orde.* Amsterdam: Bert Bakker, 2004.
Doreian, P., and T. Fararo, eds. *The Problem of Solidarity: Theories and Models.* Amsterdam: Gordon and Breach Publishers, 1998.
Drux, R. *E.T.A. Hoffmann, Der Sandmann: Erläuterungen und Dokumente.* Stuttgart: P. Reclam, 1994.
Dufresne, T. *Killing Freud: Twentieth-Century Culture and the Death of Psychoanalysis.* New York: Continuum, 2003.
———. *Tales from the Freudian Crypt: The Death Drive in Text and Context.* Stanford, CA: Stanford University Press, 2000.
Eakin, P.J. *How Our Lives Become Stories: Making Selves.* Ithaca, NY: Cornell University Press, 1999.
———. "Living Autobiographically." *Biography* 28, no. 1 (2005): 1–14.
———. *Living Autobiographically: How We Create Identity in Narrative.* Ithaca, NY: Cornell University Press, 2008.
Edinger, D. *Bertha Pappenheim: Freud's Anna O.* Highland Park, IL: Congregation Solel, 1968.
———. *Bertha Pappenheim, Leben und Schriften.* Frankfurt am Main: Ner-Tamid-Verlag, 1963.
Edman, J.L., and V.A. Kameoka. "Cultural Differences in Illness Schemas: An Analysis of Filipino and American Illness Attributions." *Journal of Cross-Cultural Psychology* 28, no. 3 (1997): 252–65.
Edwards, K. "White Spaces and Blank Pages: *Eternal Sunshine of the Spotless Mind*." *Screen Education* 51 (2008): 119–24.
Eisenberg, N. "Emotion, Regulation, and Moral Development." *Annual Review of Psychology* 51 (2000): 665–97.
Ellenberger, H.F. *The Discovery of the Unconscious: The History and Evolution of Dynamic Psychiatry.* London: Basic Books, 1970.
———. "The Story of 'Anna O': A Critical Review with New Data." *Journal of the History of the Behavioral Sciences* 8, no. 3 (1972): 267–79.
Elliott, D. *Fallen Bodies: Pollution, Sexuality and Demonology in the Middle Ages.* Philadelphia: University of Pennsylvania Press, 1999.
Ellis, J.M. "Clara, Nathanael, and the Narrator: Interpreting Hoffmann's *Der Sandmann*." *German Quarterly* 54, no. 1 (1981): 1–18.
Ellis, R.D. *Questioning Consciousness. The Interplay of Imagery, Cognition and Emotion in the Human Brain.* Philadelphia: J. Benjamins, 1995.
Elms, A.C. "Sigmund Freud, Psychohistorian." *Annual of Psychoanalysis* 31 (2003): 65–78.
Entralgo, L. *La curación por la palabra en la antigüedad clásica.* Madrid: Revista de Occidente, 1958.

Epstein, S. "Integration of the Cognitive and the Psychodynamic Unconscious." *American Psychologist* 49 (1994): 709–24.

Erikson, E.H. *Identity: Youth and Crisis*. New York: W.W. Norton & Co., 1994 (orig. 1968).

———. *Observations on the Yurok: Childhood and World Image*. Berkeley: University of California Press, 1943.

Erwin, E. *A Final Accounting: Philosophical and Empirical Issues in Freudian Psychology*. Cambridge, MA: MIT Press, 1996.

Erwin, E., and H. Siegel. "Is Confirmation Differential?" *British Journal for the Philosophy of Science* 40 (1989): 105–19.

Esterson, A. *Seductive Mirage: An Exploration of the Work of Sigmund Freud*. Chicago: Open Court, 1993.

Evans, D. *An Introductory Dictionary of Lacanian Psychoanalysis*. London: Routledge, 1996.

Eysenck, H.J. *Decline and Fall of the Freudian Empire*. Harmondsworth: Viking, 1986 (orig. 1985).

Fadiga, L., L. Fogassi, G. Pavesi, and G. Rizzolatti. "Motor Facilitation During Action Observation: A Magnetic Stimulation Study." *Journal of Neurophysiology* 73, no 6 (1995): 2608–11.

Falzeder, E., and E. Brabant, eds. *The Correspondence of Sigmund Freud and Sándor Ferenczi. Volume 2, 1914–1919*. London: Harvard University Press, 1996.

Fan, V. "The Unanswered Question of *Forrest Gump*." *Screen* 49, no. 4 (2008): 450–61.

Feldman, J.A. *From Molecule to Metaphor. A Neural Theory of Language*. Cambridge, MA: MIT Press, 2006.

Ferro-Luzzi, G.E. "The Female Lingam: Interchangeable Symbols and Paradoxical Associations of Hindu Gods and Goddesses." *Current Anthropology* 21, no. 1 (1980): 45–68.

Fish, S. "Withholding the Missing Portion: Power, Meaning and Persuasion in Freud's 'The Wolf Man.'" *Times Literary Supplement* (August 29, 1986): 935–38.

Fiske, J. *Introduction to Communication Studies*. London: Routledge, 1982.

Fiske, S.T., "Social Cognition and Social Perception." *Annual Review of Psychology* 44 (1993): 155–94.

———. "Thinking Is for Doing: Portraits of Social Cognition from Daguerreotype to Laserphoto." *Journal of Personality and Social Psychology* 63, no. 6 (1992): 877–89.

Fiske, S.T., and S.E. Taylor. *Social Cognition*. 2d ed. New York: McGraw-Hill, 1991.

Fletcher, J. "Freud, Hoffmann and the Death-Work." *Angelaki: Journal of the Theoretical Humanities* 7, no. 2 (2002): 125–41.

Foucault, M. *Les mots et les choses: Une archéologie des sciences humaines*. Paris: Gallimard, 1966.

———. *De woorden en de dingen: Een archeologie van de menswetenschappen*. Baarn: Ambo, 1966.

Foulkes, D. *Children's Dreaming and the Development of Consciousness*. Cambridge, MA: Harvard University Press, 1999.

Fowkes, K.A. *Giving Up the Ghost: Spirits, Ghosts, and Angels in Mainstream Comedy Films*. Detroit: Wayne State University Press, 1998.

Freeland, C. "Cognitive Science and Film Theory." Paper for the American Society for Aesthetics, Santa Fe, NM, 1997. www.class.uh.edu/COGSCI/CogSciFilmTheory.html (06/2001).

Freud, S. "Beyond the Pleasure Principle." In *The Standard Edition of the Complete Psychological Works of Sigmund Freud*, vol. 18, edited by James Strachey, 1–64. London: Hogarth Press and the Institute of Psycho-Analysis, 1955 (orig. 1920–22).

———. "Civilization and Its Discontents." In *The Standard Edition of the Complete Psychological Works of Sigmund Freud*, vol. 21, edited by J. Strachey, 59–145. London: Hogarth Press and the Institute of Psycho-Analysis, 1989 (orig. 1927–31).

———. *Drei Abhandlungen zur Sexualtheorie*. Leipzig: Internationaler Psychoanalytischer Verlag, 1904.

———. "From the History of an Infantile Neurosis." In *The Standard Edition of the Complete Psychological Works of Sigmund Freud*, vol. 17, edited by James Strachey, 7–122. London: Hogarth Press and the Institute of Psycho-Analysis, 1955 (orig. 1918); also in *The Wolf Man and Sigmund Freud*, edited by M. Gardiner, 153–262. London: Hogarth Press and the Institute of Psycho-Analysis, 1972.

———. *The Interpretation of Dreams.* New York: Gramercy Books, 1996 (orig. 1900).
———. "On Narcissism: An Introduction." In *The Standard Edition of the Complete Psychological Works of Sigmund Freud,* vol. 14, edited by J. Strachey, 67–102. London: Hogarth Press and the Institute of Psycho-Analysis, 1981 (orig. 1914–16).
———. *Sexuality and the Psychology of Love.* New York: Collier Books, 1963.
———. "Three Essays on Sexuality." In *The Standard Edition of the Complete Psychological Works of Sigmund Freud,* vol. 7, edited by J. Strachey, 125–245. London: Hogarth Press and the Institute of Psycho-Analysis, 1949 (orig. 1901–05).
———. *Totem and Taboo: Resemblances Between the Psychic Lives of Savages and Neurotics.* Harmondsworth: Penguin Books, 1938 (orig. 1912–13).
———. *Ueber Coca.* Vienna: M. Perles, 1885.
———. "Ueber die Allgemeinwirkung des Cocains." *Zeitschrift für Therapie* 3, no. 7 (1885): 49–51.
———. "The 'Uncanny.'" In *The Standard Edition of the Complete Psychological Works of Sigmund Freud,* vol. 17, edited by James Strachey, 217–256. London: Hogarth Press and the Institute of Psycho-Analysis, 1955 (orig. 1917–19).
———. "Zeitgemässes über Krieg und Tod." *Imago* 4 (1915): 1–21, translated in 1915 and reprinted as "Thoughts for the Times on War and Death." In *The Standard Edition of the Complete Psychological Works of Sigmund Freud,* vol. 14, edited by J. Strachey, 275–301. London: Hogarth Press and the Institute of Psycho-Analysis, 1981 (orig. 1914–16).
Freud, S., and W.C. Bullitt. *Thomas Woodrow Wilson, 28th President of the United States: A Psychological Study.* Boston: Houghton Mifflin, 1966.
Frijda, N.H. *De emoties: Een overzicht van onderzoek en theorie.* Amsterdam: Bert Bakker, 1988.
———. *The Emotions.* Cambridge and Paris: Cambridge University Press and Editions de la maison des sciences de l'homme, 1986.
Fromm, M.G. "The Other in Dreams." *Journal of Applied Psychoanalytic Studies* 2, no. 3 (2000): 287–98.
Funder, D. "Personality." *Annual Review of Psychology* 52 (2001): 197–221.
Gackenbach, J. "Frameworks for Understanding Lucid Dreaming: A Review." *Dreaming: Journal of the Association for the Study of Dreams* 1, no. 2 (1991): 109–28.
Gallagher, C., and S. Greenblatt. *Practicing New Historicism.* Chicago: University of Chicago Press, 2000.
Gallese, V. et al. "Empathy and the Somatotopic Auditory Mirror System in Humans." *Current Biology* 16 (2006): 1824–29.
———. "A Unifying View of the Basis of Social Cognition." *Trend in Cognitive Science* 8 (2004): 396–403.
Gampel, Y. "Reflections on the Prevalence of the Uncanny in Social Violence." In *Cultures under Siege: Collective Violence and Trauma,* edited by A.C.G.M. Robben and M.M. Suárez-Orozco, 48–69. Cambridge: Cambridge University Press, 2000.
Garber, M. *Vice Versa: Bisexuality and the Eroticism of Everyday Life.* New York: Simon & Schuster, 1995.
García Márquez, G. *De kolonel krijgt nooit post.* Amsterdam: Meulenhoff, 1973. Translated by B. van der Pol. Originally published as *El coronel no tiene quién le escriba* (Barcelona: Bruguera, 1961).
———. *No One Writes to the Colonel, and Other Stories.* New York: Harper & Row, 1968. Translated by J. S. Bernstein. Originally published as *El coronel no tiene quién le escriba* (Barcelona: Bruguera, 1961).
———. *Of Love and Other Demons.* New York: Penguin Books, 1995. Translated by Edith Grossman. Originally published as *Del amor y tros demonios* (Buenos Aires: Editorial Sudamericana, 1994).
Gardiner, M., ed. *The Wolf Man and Sigmund Freud.* London: Hogarth Press and the Institute of Psycho-Analysis, 1972.
Gay, P. *Freud voor historici.* Amsterdam: Wereldbibliotheek, 1987 (orig. 1985).
Gazzaniga, M.S. *The Social Brain. Discovering the Network of Minds.* New York: Basic Books, 1985.

———. *Who's in Charge? Free Will and the Science of the Brain*, New York: HarperCollins, 2011.
———, ed. *The Cognitive Neurosciences*. Cambridge, MA: MIT Press, 1995.
Gedo, J.E. "The Enduring Scientific Contributions of Sigmund Freud." *Annual of Psychoanalysis* 29 (2001): 105–15.
Gelder, K., and J. Jacobs. *Uncanny Australia: Sacredness and Identity in a Postcolonial Nation*. Melbourne: Melbourne University Press, 1998.
Gelfand, M.J., H.C. Triandis, and D.K-S. Chan. "Individualism Versus Collectivism or Versus Authoritarianism?" *European Journal of Social Psychology* 26 (1996): 397–410.
Gerrig, R.J. *Experiencing Narrative Worlds: On the Psychological Activities of Reading*. Boulder, CO: Westview Press, 1998 (orig. 1993).
Gibbs, R.W. *Embodiment and Cognitive Science*. Cambridge: Cambridge University Press, 2005.
Giddens, A. *The Constitution of Society: Outline of a Theory of Structuration*. Oxford: Polity Press, 1984.
Gilbert, D. *Stumbling on Happiness*. New York: A.A. Knopf, 2006.
Ginzburg, C. *Clues, Myths, and the Historical Method*. Baltimore: Johns Hopkins University Press, 1989 (orig. 1986).
———. *Ecstasies. Deciphering the Witches' Sabbath*. New York: Pantheon Books, 1990 (orig. 1989).
———. "Family Resemblances and Family Trees: Two Cognitive Metaphors." *Critical Inquiry* 30 (2004): 537–56.
———. *I Benandanti*. Turin: G. Einaudi, 1966.
———. *Myths, Emblems, Clues*. London: Vintage, 1990 (orig. 1986).
———. *The Night Battles*. Baltimore: Johns Hopkins University Press, 1983 (orig. 1966).
———. *No Island Is an Island: Four Glances at English Literature in a World Perspective*. New York: Columbia University Press, 2000.
———. *Das Schwert und die Glühbirne: Eine neue Lektüre von Picassos* Guernica. Frankfurt am Main: Suhrkamp, 1999.
———. "The Sword and the Lightbulb: A Reading of *Guernica*." In *Disturbing Remains: Memory, History and Crisis in the Twentieth Century*, edited by M.S. Roth and C.G. Salas, 111–77. Los Angeles: Getty Research Institute, 2001.
Gitlin, T. *The Whole World Is Watching: Mass Media in the Making and Unmaking of the New Left*. Berkeley: University of California Press, 1980.
Goffman, E. *Frame Analysis: An Essay on the Organization of Experience*. Cambridge, MA: Harvard University Press, 1974.
———. *The Presentation of Self in Everyday Life*. Garden City, NY: Doubleday, 1959.
Goldschmidt, W. "A Perspective on Anthropology." *American Anthropologist* 102, no. 4 (2001): 789–807.
Goldstein, J. et al. "Normal Sexual Dimorphism of the Adult Human Brain Assessed by In Vivo Magnetic Resonance Imaging." *Cerebral Cortex* 11, no. 6 (2001): 490–97.
Gómez, L. *An Introduction to Object Relations*. New York: New York University Press, 1997.
Göncü, A., ed. *Children's Engagement in the World: Sociocultural Perspectives*. New York: Cambridge University Press, 1999.
Gordon, J.A., and R. Hen. "Genetic Approaches to the Study of Anxiety." *Annual Review of Neuroscience* 27 (2007): 193–222.
Gorton, K. *Theorising Desire: From Freud to Feminism to Film*. Basingstoke: Palgrave Macmillan, 2008.
Gottschall, J. *The Storytelling Animal: How Stories Make Us Human*, Boston, NJ: Houghton Mifflin Harcourt, 2012.
Grafton, A. *Cardano's Cosmos: The Worlds and Works of a Renaissance Astrologer*. Cambridge, MA: Harvard University Press, 1999.
Grau, C. "*Eternal Sunshine of the Spotless Mind* and the Morality of Memory." *Journal of Aesthetics and Art Criticism* 64, no. 1 (2006): 119–33.
———, ed. *Eternal Sunshine of the Spotless Mind*. London: Taylor & Francis, 2009.
Greenwald, A.G., and M.R. Banaji. "Implicit Social Cognition: Attitudes, Self-Esteem, and Stereotypes." *Psychological Review* 102, no. 1 (1995): 4–27.

Grodal, T. *Moving Pictures. A New Theory of Film Genres, Feelings, and Cognition.* Oxford: Clarendon Press, 1997.
Grossman, J. "The Trouble with Carol: The Costs of Feeling Good in Todd Haynes's *[Safe]* and the American Cultural Landscape." *Other Voices* 2, no. 3 (2005). www.othervoices.org/2.3/jgrossman (01/2011).
Gur, R. et al. "Sex Differences in Temporo-Limbic and Frontal Brain Volumes of Healthy Adults." *Cerebral Cortex* 12 (2002): 998–1003.
Hagin, B. "Examples in Theory: Interpassive Illustrations and Celluloid Fetishism." *Cinema Journal* 48, no 1 (2008): 3–26.
Haier, R. et al. "The Neuroanatomy of General Intelligence: Sex Matters." *Neuroimage* 25, no. 1 (2005): 320–27.
Halari, R. et al. "Comparable fMRI Activity with Differential Behavioural Performance on Mental Rotation and Overt Verbal Fluency Tasks in Healthy Men and Women." *Experimental Brain Research* 169 (2006): 1–14.
Hale, J. *The Civilization of Europe in the Renaissance.* New York: Atheneum, 1993.
Hall, S. "Cultural Identity and Cinematic Representation." *Framework* 36 (1989): 68–81.
―――. "Encoding and Decoding in the Television Discourse." Occasional Paper No. 7. Birmingham, 1973.
―――. "Encoding/Decoding." In *Culture, Media, Language: Working Papers in Cultural Studies, 1972–79,* edited by S. Hall, D. Hobson, A. Low, and P. Willis, 128–38. London: Routledge in association with the Centre for Contemporary Cultural Studies, University of Birmingham, 1980.
Hall, S., D. Hobson, A. Low, and P. Willis, eds. *Culture, Media, Language: Working Papers in Cultural Studies, 1972–79.* London: Routledge in association with the Centre for Contemporary Cultural Studies, University of Birmingham, 1980.
Halpern, L. *Dreams on Film. The Cinematic Struggle Between Art and Science.* Jefferson, NC: McFarland, 2003.
Hardcastle, V.G., ed. *Where Biology Meets Psychology: Philosophical Essays.* Cambridge, MA: MIT Press, 1999.
Hardt, M., and A. Negri. *Empire.* Cambridge, MA: Harvard University Press, 2000.
Harkness, S., and C. Super, ed. *Parents' Cultural Belief Systems: Their Origins, Expressions, and Consequences.* New York: Guilford Press, 1996.
Harré, R., and G. Gillett. *The Discursive Mind.* Thousand Oaks, CA: Sage Publications, 1994.
Harris, J.R. *No Two Alike: Human Nature and Human Individuality.* New York: W.W. Norton & Co., 2006.
―――. *The Nurture Assumption. Why Children Turn Out the Way They Do.* New York: Touchstone, 1999 (orig. 1998).
―――. "Socialization, Personality Development, and the Child's Environments: Comment on Vandell." *Developmental Psychology* 36, no. 6 (2000): 711–23.
―――. "Where Is the Child's Environment? A Group Socialization Theory of Development." *Psychological Review* 102, no. 3 (1995): 458–89.
―――. "Why Home Doesn't Matter." *Prospect Magazine* 134 (2007). www.prospect-magazine.co.uk/article_details.php?id=9275 (06/2007).
Hartmann, E. "Dreams That Work or Dreams That Poison? What Does Dreaming Do? An Editorial Essay." *Dreaming: Journal of the Association for the Study of Dreams* 1, no. 1 (1991): 23–25.
―――. "Outline for a Theory on the Nature and Functioning of Dreaming." *Dreaming: Journal of the Association for the Study of Dreams* 6, no. 2 (1996): 147–70.
Haslam, R. "'A Race Bashed in the Face': Imagining Ireland as a Damaged Child." *Jouvert: A Journal of Postcolonial Studies* 4, no. 1 (1999). social.chass.ncsu.edu/jouvert/v4i1/hasla.htm. (10/2007).
Hatfield, E., and R.L. Rapson. *Love and Sex: Cross-Cultural Perspectives.* Boston: Allyn and Bacon, 1996.
Healy, D. *The Creation of Psychopharmacology.* Cambridge, MA: Harvard University Press, 2002.

Heerden, J. van. "Een psychologie voor leken. Waarom de psychoanalyse zo populair is." *Intermediair* 32, no. 52 (1996): 26–29.
Henningsen, G. *The Witches' Advocate: Basque Witchcraft and the Spanish Inquisition (1609–1614)*. Reno: University of Nevada Press, 1980.
Herman, D. "Editor's Column. The Scope and Aims of Storyworlds." *Storyworlds: A Journal of Narrative Studies* 1 (2009): vii–x.
Herman, E. "How Children Turn Out and How Psychology Turns Them Out." *History of Psychology* 4, no. 3 (2001): 297–316.
Hilton, J.L., and W. von Hippel. "Stereotypes." *Annual Review of Psychology* 47 (1996): 237–71.
Hines, M. *Brain Gender*. Oxford: Oxford University Press, 2004.
———. "Sex Differences in Response to Children's Toys in Non-Human Primates (Cercopithecus Aethiops Sabaeus)." *Evolution and Human Behavior* 23 (2002): 467–79.
Hirschmüller, A. *Physiologie und Psychoanalyse in Leben und Werk Josef Breuers*. Bern: H. Huber, 1978.
Hobson, J.A. *Dreaming: An Introduction to the Science of Sleep*. New York: Oxford University Press, 2002.
Hobson, J.A., E. Pace-Schott, and R. Stickgold. "Dreaming and the Brain: Toward a Cognitive Neuroscience of Conscious States." *Behavioral & Brain Sciences* 23, no. 6 (2000): 793–842.
Hoenisch, S.M. "The Myth of Psychoanalysis: Wittgenstein Contra Freud." www.criticism.com/md/tech.htm (1996; 08/1998; 10/2007).
Hoffman, L.W. "The Influence of the Family Environment on Personality: Accounting for Sibling Differences." *Psychological Bulletin* 110, no. 2 (1991): 187–203.
Hofstadter, D.R., and D.C. Dennett. *The Mind's I: Fantasies and Reflections on Self and Soul*. Toronto: Bantam Books, 1981.
Hogg, M.A., and G.M. Vaughan. *Social Psychology: An Introduction*. New York: Prentice Hall, 1995.
Hollan, D. "Suffering and the Work of Culture: A Case of Magical Poisoning in Toraja." *American Ethnologist* 21, no. 1 (1994): 74–87.
Hollander, N.C. *Love in a Time of Hate: Liberation Psychology in Latin America*. New Brunswick, NJ: Rutgers University Press, 1997.
Holmes, D. "The Evidence for Repression: An Examination of Sixty Years of Research." In *Repression and Dissociation*, edited by J.L. Singer, 85–102. Chicago: University of Chicago Press, 1990.
Hoskins, B. "Playground Love: Landscape and Longing in Sofia Coppola's *The Virgin Suicides*." *Literature Film Quarterly* 35, no. 3 (2007): 214–21.
Hrdy, S.B. *Mother Nature: A History of Mothers, Infants, and Natural Selection*. New York: Pantheon Books, 1999.
Hughes, F.P. *Children, Play and Development*. Boston: Allyn and Bacon, 1995 (orig. 1991).
Humphrey, N. "The Private World of Consciousness." *New Scientist* (January 8, 1994): 23–25. www.newscientist.com/nsplus/insight/big3/conscious (10/1997).
Hunt, L. *The Family Romance of the French Revolution*. Berkeley: University of California Press, 1992.
———, ed. *The New Cultural History: Essays (Studies on the History of Society and Culture)*. Berkeley: University of California Press, 1989.
Hyde, J. "The Gender Similarities Hypothesis." *American Psychologist* 60, no. 6 (2005): 581–92.
Hyde, J. et al. "Gender Differences in Mathematics Performance: A Meta-Analysis." *Psychological Bulletin* 107 (1990): 139–55.
Iacoboni, M. *Mirroring People: The New Science of How We Connect with Others*. New York: Farrar, Straus and Giroux, 2008.
Illich, I. *In the Vineyard of the Text: A Commentary to Hugh's Didascalicon*. Chicago: University of Chicago Press, 1993.
Israëls, H. "Freuds Phantasien über Leonardo da Vinci." *Luzifer-Amor: Zeitschrift für Geschichte der Psychoanalyse* 10 (1992): 8–41.

———. *Het geval Freud: Scheppingsverhalen.* Amsterdam: Bert Bakker, 1993.
———. "Een pathologische Leugenaar: Had Freud niet wat voorzichtiger kunnen liegen?" *Intermediair* 32, no. 52 (1996): 21–24.
———. *De Weense kwakzalver: Honderd jaar Freud en de freudianen.* Amsterdam: Bert Bakker, 1999.
Israëls, H., and M. Schatzman. "The Seduction Theory." *History of Psychiatry* 4 (1993): 23–59.
Ivey, G. "Sex in the Mourning: Oedipal Love and Loss in *The Door in the Floor* (2004)." *International Journal of Psychoanalysis* 87 (2006): 871–79.
James, W. *The Principles of Psychology.* New York: H. Holt & Co., 1890.
Jankowiak, W.R., and E.F. Fischer. "A Cross-Cultural Perspective on Romantic Love." *Ethnology* 31 (1992): 149–55.
Johnson, M. *The Body in the Mind: The Bodily Basis of Meaning, Imagination, and Reason.* Chicago: University of Chicago Press, 1987.
Johnson, M.K., and C.L. Raye. "Cognitive and Brain Mechanisms of False Memories and Beliefs." In *Memory, Brain, and Belief,* edited by D.L. Schacter and E. Scarry, 35–86. Cambridge: Harvard University Press, 2000.
Joiner, T.E., Jr., et al. "Perceived Burdensomeness and Suicidality: Two Studies on the Suicide Notes of Those Attempting and Those Completing Suicide." *Suicide and Life-Threatening Behavior* 21, no. 5 (2002): 531–45.
Jones, J.B. "The Time of Interpretation: Psychoanalysis and the Past." *PostModern Culture* 14, no. 3 (2004). muse.jhu.edu/journals/pmc/v014/14.3jones. html (10/2007).
Jordan, J.S., ed. *Modeling Consciousness across the Disciplines.* New York: University Press of America, 1999.
Kahn, D., and J.A. Hobson. "Self-Organization Theory of Dreaming." *Dreaming: Journal of the Association for the Study of Dreams* 3, no. 3 (1993): 151–78.
Kahn, D., S. Krippner, and A. Combs. "Dreaming and the Self-Organizing Brain." *Journal of Consciousness Studies* 7, no. 7 (2000): 4–11.
Kaplan, E.A., ed. *Psychoanalysis and Cinema.* New York: Routledge, 1990.
Kaplan, R. "O Anna: Being Bertha Pappenheim — Historiography and Biography." *Australasian Psychiatry* 12, no. 1 (2004): 62–68.
Kashima, Y., U. Kim, M.J. Gelfand, S. Yamaguchi, S.-C. Choi, and M. Yuki. "Culture, Gender, and Self: A Perspective from Individualism-Collectivism Research." *Journal of Personality and Social Psychology* 69, no. 5 (1995): 925–37.
Kayzer, W., ed. *Een schitterend ongeluk. Wim Kayzer ontmoet Oliver Sacks, Stephen Jay Gould, Stephen Toulmin, Daniel C. Dennett, Rupert Sheldrake en Freeman Dyson.* Amsterdam: Contact, 1993.
Kessel, F.S., P.M. Cole, and D.L. Johnson, eds. *Self and Consciousness. Multiple Perspectives.* Hillsdale, NJ: L. Erlbaum, 1992.
Keysers, C., and V. Gazzola. "Towards a Unifying Neural Theory of Social Cognition." *Progress in Brain Research* 156 (2006): 379–401.
Keysers, C., B. Wicker, V. Gazzola, J.-L. Anton, L. Fogassi, and V. Gallese. "A Touching Sight: SII/PV Activation During the Observation and Experience of Touch." *Neuron* 42 (2004): 335–46.
Kieckhefer, R. *Magic in the Middle Ages.* Cambridge: Cambridge University Press, 1989.
———. "The Specific Rationality of Medieval Magic." *American Historical Review* 99, no. 3 (1994): 813–36.
Kimura, D. "Sex, Sexual Orientation and Sex Hormones Influence Human Cognitive Function." *Current Opinion in Neurobiology* 6 (1996): 259–63.
Kirchoff, B.K. "Consciousness, Communities and the Brain: Toward an Ontology of Being." Paper Tucson iii 1997. Published in *Modeling Consciousness Across the Disciplines,* edited by J.S. Jordan, 243–68. New York: University Press of America, 1999.
Klawans, S. "Speak, Memory." *The Nation,* April 12, 2004, 32–36.
Klein, M. *Narrative of a Child Analysis: The Conduct of the Psychoanalysis of Children as Seen in the Treatment of a Ten-Year-Old Boy.* New York: Basic Books, 1961.
———. *The Psycho-Analysis of Children.* London: L. & Virginia Woolf at the Hogarth Press and the Institute of Psycho-Analysis, 1932.

Klein, S.B., and J. Loftus. "The Nature of Self-Referent Encoding: The Contributions of Elaborative and Organizational Processes." *Journal of Personality and Social Psychology* 55, no. 1 (1988): 5–11.
Klein, S.B., J. Loftus, and H.A. Burton. "Two Self-Reference Effects: The Importance of Distinguishing Between Self-Descriptiveness Judgments and Autobiographical Retrieval in Self-Referent Encoding." *Journal of Personality and Social Psychology* 56 (1989): 853–65.
Kleinpenning, G., and L. Hagendoorn. "Contextual Aspects of Ethnic Stereotypes and Interethnic Evaluations." *European Journal of Social Psychology* 21 (1991): 331–48.
Kofman, S. *Freud and Fiction*. Oxford: Polity Press, 1991 (orig. 1974).
Kowalik, J.A. "Attachment, Patriarchal Anxiety, and Paradigm Selection in German Literary Criticism." *German Quarterly* 77, no. 1 (2004): 1–8.
Kramer, M. "Dream Translation: A Nonassociative Method for Understanding the Dream." *Dreaming: Journal of the Association for the Study of Dreams* 1, no. 2 (1991): 147–59.
———. "The Nightmare: A Failure in Dream Function." *Dreaming: Journal of the Association for the Study of Dreams* 1, no. 4 (1991): 277–85.
Krueger, J.W. "Enacting Musical Experience." *Journal of Consciousness Studies* 16, no. 2–3 (2009): 98–123.
Kunda, Z. "Motivated Inference: Self-Serving Generation and Evaluation of Causal Theories." *Journal of Personality and Social Psychology* 53, no. 4 (1987): 636–47.
———. *Social Cognition: Making Sense of People*. Cambridge, MA: MIT Press, 1999.
Kunda, Z., and P. Thagard. "Forming Impressions from Stereotypes, Traits, and Behaviors: A Parallel-Constraint-Satisfaction Theory." *Psychological Review* 103, no. 2 (1996): 284–308.
LaBerge, S. *Lucid Dreaming*. New York: J.P. Tarcher, 1985.
LaBerge, S., L. Levitan, and W.C. Dement. "Lucid Dreaming: Physiological Correlates of Consciousness During REM Sleep." *Journal of Mind and Behavior* 7 (1986): 251–58.
LaBerge, S., and H. Rheingold. *Exploring the World of Lucid Dreaming*. New York: Ballantine Books, 1990.
Lacan, J. *Écrits: A Selection*. New York: W.W. Norton, 1977.
———. *Speech and Language in Psychoanalysis*. Baltimore: Johns Hopkins University Press, 1968.
Ladwig, K.H. et. al. "Psychophysiological Correlates of Peritraumatic Dissociative Responses in Survivors of Life-Threatening Cardiac Events." *Psychopathology* 35 (2002): 241–48.
Laird, R.D., K.Y. Jordan, K.A. Dodge, G.S. Pettit, and J.E. Bates. "Peer Rejection in Childhood, Involvement with Antisocial Peers in Early Adolescence, and the Development of Externalizing Problems." *Development and Psychopathology* 13 (2001): 337–54.
Lakoff, G. "The Contemporary Theory of Metaphor." In *Metaphor and Thought*, edited by A. Ortony, 202–51. 2d ed. Cambridge: Cambridge University Press, 1993.
———. "How Metaphor Structures Dreams: The Theory of Conceptual Metaphor Applied to Dream Analysis." *Dreaming: Journal of the Association for the Study of Dreams* 3, no. 2 (1993): 77–98.
———. "Metaphor, Morality, and Politics, Or, Why Conservatives Have Left Liberals in the Dust." www.wwcd.org/issues/Lakoff.html (1995; 03/2009).
———. "Metaphors of Terror." *University of Chicago Press News*. www.press.uchicago.edu/News/911lakoff.html (10/2008).
———. *The Political Mind: Why You Can't Understand 21st-Century Politics with an 18th-Century Brain*. New York: Viking, 2008.
———. *Women, Fire, and Dangerous Things: What Categories Reveal about the Mind*. Chicago: University of Chicago Press, 1987.
Lakoff, G., and M. Johnson. *Metaphors We Live By*. Chicago: University of Chicago Press, 2003 (orig. 1980).
Lakoff, G., and M. Turner. *More than Cool Reason. A Field Guide to Poetic Metaphor*. Chicago: University of Chicago Press, 1989.
Lakoff, R.T., and J.C. Coyne. *Father Knows Best: The Use and Abuse of Power in Freud's Case of Dora*. New York: Teachers College Press, 1993.
Lane, J.D., and D.M. Wegner. "The Cognitive Consequences of Secrecy." *Journal of Personality and Social Psychology* 69 (1995): 237–53.

Layton, R. *An Introduction to Theory in Anthropology.* Cambridge: Cambridge University Press, 1997.
Leary, M.R. "Motivational and Emotional Aspects of the Self." *Annual Review of Psychology* 58 (2007): 317–44.
Lebeau, V. *Psychoanalysis and Cinema: The Play of Shadows.* New York: Wallflower, 2001.
LeDoux, J. "Emotion, Memory, and the Brain." Special issue, *Scientific American,* 1997, 68–75.
_____. *The Emotional Brain: The Mysterious Underpinnings of Emotional Life.* New York: Simon and Schuster, 1996.
Lerner, R.M., ed. *Handbook of Child Psychology.* Vol. 1, *Theoretical Models of Human Development.* New York: Wiley, 1998.
Levine, L.J. "Reconstructing Memory for Emotions." *Journal of Experimental Psychology: General* 126, no. 2 (1997): 165–77.
Libet, B. *Mind Time. The Temporal Factor in Consciousness.* Cambridge, MA: Harvard University Press, 2004.
Lidov, D. *Elements of Semiotics.* Oxford: St. Martin's Press, 1999.
Lilienfeld, S.O., S.J. Lynn, J. Ruscio, and B.L. Beyerstein. *50 Great Myths of Popular Psychology: Shattering Widespread Misconceptions About Human Behavior.* Chichester: Wiley-Blackwell, 2010.
Littlewood, R. "Science, Shamanism and Hermeneutics: Recent Writing on Psychoanalysis." *Anthropology Today* 5, no. 1 (1989): 5–11.
Llinás, R.R., and U. Ribary. "Coherent 40-Hz Oscillation Characterizes Dream State in Humans." *Proceedings of the National Academy of Sciences* 90 (1993): 2078–81.
Loewenberg, P. "The Psychohistorical Origins of the Nazi Youth Cohort." *American Historical Review* 76 (1971): 1457–1502.
Loftus, E.F. "Creating False Memories." *Scientific American* 277, no. 3 (1997): 50–55.
_____. *Eyewitness Testimony.* Cambridge, MA: Harvard University Press, 1996 (orig. 1979).
_____. "Remembering Dangerously; Recovered Memory." *Skeptical Inquirer* 19, no. 2 (1995). www.csicop.org/si/9503/memory.htm (10/1998; 10/2007).
Loftus, E.F., and K. Ketcham. *The Myth of Repressed Memory: False Memories and Allegations of Sexual Abuse.* New York: St. Martin's Press, 1994.
Lugones, M. "Playfulness, 'World'-Travelling, and Loving Perception," *Hypatia* 2:2 (1987): 3–19.
Maccoby, E.E. "Parenting and Its Effects on Children: On Reading and Misreading Behavior Genetics." *Annual Review of Psychology* 51 (2000): 1–27."
_____. The Role of Parents in the Socialization of Children: A Historical Overview." *Developmental Psychology* 28 (1992): 1006–17.
Maccoby, E.E., and C.N. Jacklin. *The Psychology of Sex Differences.* Stanford, CA: Stanford University Press, 1974.
Macmillan, M. *Freud Evaluated: The Completed Arc.* Cambridge, MA: MIT Press, 1997 (orig. 1991).
Mahowald, M.W., S.R. Woods, and C.H. Schenck. "Sleeping Dreams, Waking Hallucinations, and the Central Nervous System." *Dreaming: Journal of the Association for the Study of Dreams* 8, no. 2 (1998): 89–102.
Malcolm, J. *Psychoanalysis. The Impossible Profession.* London: Maresfield, 1988.
Manlove, C.T. "Visual 'Drive' and Cinematic Narrative: Reading Gaze Theory in Lacan, Hitchcock, and Mulvey." *Cinema Journal* 46, no. 3 (2007): 83–108.
Maquet, P., C. Degueldre, G. Delfiore, J. Aerts, J-M. Péters, A. Luxen, and G. Franck. "Functional Neuroanatomy of Human Slow Wave Sleep." *Journal of Neuroscience* 17, no. 8 (1997): 2807–12.
Mar, R.A., and K. Oatley. "The Function of Fiction Is the Abstraction and Simulation of Social Experience." *Perspectives on Psychological Science* 3, no. 3 (2008): 173–92.
Marcuse, M., ed. *Handwörterbuch der Sexualwissenschaft; Enzyklopädie der natur- und kulturwissenschaftlichen Sexualkunde des Menschen.* Bonn: Marcus & Webers Verlag, 1923.
Markus, H.R. "Self-Schemata and Processing Information About the Self." *Journal of Personality and Social Psychology* 35, no. 2 (1977): 63–78.

Markus, H.R., and S. Kitayama. "Culture and the Self: Implications for Cognition, Emotion, and Motivation." *Psychological Review* 98, no. 2 (1991): 224–53.
Markus, H.R., and P. Nurius. "Possible Selves." *American Psychologist* 41 (1986): 954–69.
Martin, C.L., and R.A. Fabes. "The Stability and Consequences of Young Children's Same-Sex Peer Interactions." *Developmental Psychology* 37, no. 3 (2001): 431–46.
Martin, J.J. *Myths of Renaissance Individualism*. Houndmills: Palgrave Macmillan, 2004.
Martin-Jones, D. *Deleuze, Cinema and National Identity: Narrative Time in National Contexts*. Edinburgh: Edinburgh University Press, 2006.
Masschelein, A. "A Homeless Concept: Shapes of the Uncanny in Twentieth-Century Theory and Culture." *Image [&] Narrative: Online Magazine of the Visual Narrative* 5 (2003). www.imageandnarrative.be/uncanny/uncanny.htm (11/2003; 10/2007).
Masson, J.M. *The Assault on Truth. Freud's Suppression of the Seduction Theory*. New York: Farrar, Straus and Giroux, 1984.
\_\_\_\_\_, ed. *The Complete Letters of Sigmund Freud to Wilhelm Fliess, 1887–1904*. Cambridge, MA: Belknap Press of Harvard University Press, 1985.
Matsumoto, D. *Culture and Psychology: People Around the World*. 2d ed. Belmont, CA: Wadsworth Thomson Learning, 2000.
Maturana, H.R., and F.J. Varela. *The Tree of Knowledge: The Biological Roots of Human Understanding*. 3d ed. Boston: Shambhala, 1992 (orig. 1984).
Mazlish, B. "A Triptych: Freud's *The Interpretation of Dreams,* Rider Haggard's *She,* and Bulwer-Lytton's *The Coming Race.*" *Comparative Studies in Society and History* 35 (1993): 726–45.
McConaghy, M.J. "Gender Permanence and the Genital Basis of Gender: Stages in the Development of Constancy of Gender Identity." *Child Development* 50 (1979): 1223–26.
McCrone, J. "A Bifold Model of Freewill." *Journal of Consciousness Studies* 6, no. 8–9 (1999): 241–59.
\_\_\_\_\_. "Wild Minds." *New Scientist* 2112 (1997): 26–30.
McGowan, T. "Looking for the Gaze: Lacanian Film Theory and Its Vicissitudes." *Cinema Journal* 42, no. 3 (2003): 27–47.
\_\_\_\_\_. *The Real Gaze: Film Theory After Lacan*. New York: State University of New York Press, 2007.
McHugh, P.R. "Witches, Multiple Personalities, and Other Psychiatric Artifacts." *Nature Medicine* 1 (1995): 110–14.
McIntosh, J. "Cognition and Power." Paper for the Society for Literature & Science, Pittsburgh Meetings, 1997.
McNally, R.J. *Remembering Trauma*. Cambridge, MA: Belknap Press of Harvard University Press, 2003.
Meadow, P.W. *The New Psychoanalysis*. Lanham, MD: Rowman & Littlefield, 2003.
Merckelbach, H. "Het probleem Freud. De psychoanalyse heeft geen toekomst." *Intermediair* 32, no. 52 (1996): 40.
Merritt, J.M., R. Stickgold, E. Pace-Schott, J. Williams, and J.A. Hobson. "Emotion Profiles in the Dreams of Men and Women." *Consciousness and Cognition* 3, no. 1 (1994): 46–60.
Merry, S.E. *Colonizing Hawai'i: The Cultural Power of the Law*. Princeton, NJ: Princeton University Press, 2000.
Meyer, M.J. "Reflections on Comic Reconciliations: Ethics, Memory, and Anxious Happy Endings." *Journal of Aesthetics and Art Criticism* 66, no. 1 (2008): 77–87.
Meyers, J. "The Making of John Huston's *Freud: The Secret Passion.*" *Kenyon Review IJLCA* 33, no. 1 (2011): 178–99.
Miall, D.S., and D. Kuiken. "Foregrounding, Defamiliarization, and Affect: Response to Literary Stories." *Poetics* 22 (1994): 389–407.
Micale, M.S. *Approaching Hysteria: Disease and Interpretation*. Princeton, NJ: Princeton University Press, 1995.
Miller, G.F. *The Mating Mind. How Sexual Choice Shaped Human Nature*. New York: Doubleday, 2000.
Miller, J.G. "Culture and the Development of Everyday Social Explanation." *Journal of Personality and Social Psychology* 46 (1984): 961–78.

Mills, Ch.W. *The Racial Contract,* Ithaca, NY: Cornell University Press, 1997.
Mischel, W., and Y. Shoda. "A Cognitive-Affective System Theory of Personality: Reconceptualizing Situations, Dispositions, Dynamics, and Invariance in Personality Structure." *Psychological Review* 102, no. 2 (1995): 246–68.
Mitchell, J. *Mad Men and Medusas: Reclaiming Hysteria and the Effects of Sibling Relationships on the Human Condition.* Harmondsworth: Basic Books, 2000.
Montangero, J., P. Pasche, and P. Willequet. "Remembering and Communicating the Dream Experience: What Does a Complementary Morning Report Add to the Night Report?" *Dreaming: Journal of the Association for the Study of Dreams* 6, no. 2 (1996): 131–45.
Moore, R.I. *La formación de una sociedad represora: Poder y disidencia en la Europa occidental, 950–1250.* Barcelona: Editorial Crítica, 1989.
———. *The Formation of a Persecuting Society: Power and Deviance in Western Europe, 950–1250.* Oxford: B. Blackwell, 1987.
Moshman, D. "Identity as a Theory of Oneself." *The Genetic Epistemologist: Journal of the Jean Piaget Society* 26, no. 3 (1998): 1–9.
Muir, E. *The Culture Wars of the Late Renaissance: Skeptics, Libertines, and Opera.* Cambridge, MA: Harvard University Press, 2007.
Mulvey, L. "Visual Pleasure and Narrative Cinema." *Screen* 16, no. 3 (1975): 6–18. Reprinted in *Film Theory and Criticism: Introductory Readings,* edited by L. Braudy and M. Cohen, 833–844. Oxford: Oxford University Press, 1999.
Munck, T. *The Enlightenment: A Comparative Social History 1721–1794.* London: Arnold, 2000.
Nath, L., and R. Simon. "Gender and Emotion in the United States: Do Men and Women Differ in Self-Reports of Feelings and Expressive Behavior?" *American Journal of Sociology* 109 (2004): 1137–76.
Nelson, D.M. *A Finger in the Wound: Body Politics in Quincentennial Guatemala.* Berkeley: University of California Press, 1999.
Newberg, A., E.G. d'Aquili, and V. Rause. *Why God Won't Go Away: Brain Science and the Biology of Belief.* New York: Ballantine Books, 2001.
Nicholson, N. "Evolutionary Psychology: Toward a New View of Human Nature and Organizational Society." *Human Relations* 50, no. 9 (1997): 1053–78.
Nicolopoulou, A. "Play, Cognitive Development, and the Social World: Piaget, Vygotsky, and Beyond." *Human Development* 36 (1993): 1–23.
Nisbett, R.E., and L. Ross. *Human Inference: Strategies and Shortcomings of Social Judgment.* Englewood Cliffs, NJ: Prentice Hall, 1980.
Nishida, H. "A Cognitive Approach to Intercultural Communication Based on Schema Theory." *International Journal of Intercultural Relations* 23, no. 5 (1999): 753–77.
Noë, A. *Action in Perception.* Cambridge, MA: MIT Press, 2004.
Noll, R. *The Aryan Christ: The Secret Life of Carl Jung.* New York: Random House, 1997.
———. *The Jung Cult: Origins of a Charismatic Movement.* Princeton, NJ: Princeton University Press, 1994.
Oatley, K., R.A. Mar, and M. Djikic. "The Mind's Flight Simulator." *The Psychologist* 21, no. 12 (2008): 1030–32.
———. "The Psychology of Fiction: Present and Future." In *Cognition Literary Studies,* edited by I. Jaén and J. Simon. Austin: University of Texas Press, 2012.
Obeyesekere, G. *The Work of Culture: Symbolic Transformation in Psychoanalysis and Anthropology.* Chicago: University of Chicago Press, 1990.
Obholzer, K. *The Wolf Man Sixty Years Later: Conversations with Freud's Controversial Patient.* New York: Continuum, 1982 (orig. 1980).
Ochs, E., and L. Capps. "Narrating the Self." *Annual Review of Anthropology* 25 (1996): 19–43.
Ogden, T. *Subjects of Analysis.* Northvale, NJ: J. Aronson, 1994.
Ojemann, G., and C. Mateer. "Human Language Cortex: Localization of Memory, Syntax, and Sequential Motor-Phoneme Identification Systems." *Science* 205 (1979): 1401–3.
Oldridge, D. *Strange Histories: The Trial of the Pig, the Walking Dead, and Other Matters of Fact from the Medieval and Renaissance Worlds.* London: Routledge, 2005.

———, ed. *The Witchcraft Reader.* London: Routledge, 2002.
Onfray, M. Anti Freud. *Die Psychoanalyse wird entzaubert,* München: Knaus, 2011 (orig. 2010).
———. *Le crépuscule d'une idole. L'affabulation freudienne.* Paris: Grasset, 2010.
Ortony, A., ed. *Metaphor and Thought.* 2d ed. Cambridge: Cambridge University Press, 1993.
Ostow, M. "The Interpretation of Apocalyptic Dreams." *Dreaming: Journal of the Association for the Study of Dreams* 2, no. 1 (1992): 1–14.
Ouweneel, A. *The Flight of the Shepherd: Microhistory and the Psychology of Cultural Resilience in Bourbon Central Mexico.* Amsterdam: Aksant, 2005.
———. *Terug naar Macondo: Het spook van* Honderd jaar eenzaamheid *en het inheemse innerlijk van de mesties.* Amsterdam: Rozenberg Publishers, 2007.
Pagel, J.F., C. Kwiatkowski, and K.E. Broyles. "Dream Use in Film Making." *Dreaming: Journal of the Association for the Study of Dreams* 9, no. 4 (1999): 247–56.
Parel, A.J. *The Machiavellian Cosmos.* New Haven, CT: Yale University Press, 1992.
Pasupathi, M. "The Social Construction of the Personal Past and Its Implications for Adult Development." *Psychological Bulletin* 127, no. 5 (2001): 651–72.
Pateman, C. *The Sexual Contract,* Stanford, CA: Stanford University Press, 1988.
Paul, R.A. "Psychoanalytic Anthropology." *Annual Review of Anthropology* 18 (1989): 177–202.
Peirce, C.S. *Philosophical Writings of Peirce.* Edited by J. Buchler. New York: Dover Publications, 1955 (orig. 1940).
Pennebaker, J.W. "Putting Stress into Words: Health, Linguistic, and Therapeutic Implications." *Behaviour Research and Therapy* 31 (1993): 539–48.
Penrose, R. *Shadows of the Mind. A Search for the Missing Science of Consciousness.* Oxford: Oxford University Press, 1994.
Perring, C. "A Forlorn Hope: Psychoanalysis in Search of Scientific Respectability." *Psyche: An Interdisciplinary Journal of Research on Consciousness* 4, no. 11 (1998). psyche.cs.monash.edu.au/v4/psyche-4-11-perring.html (10/2007).
Perry, B.D. "Memories of Fear: How the Brain Stores and Retrieves Physiologic States, Feelings, Behaviors and Thoughts from Traumatic Events." *Child Trauma Academy.* www.childtrauma.org/ctamaterials/memories.asp (09/1999; 10/2007).
Persinger, M.A. *Neuropsychological Bases of God Beliefs.* New York: Praeger, 1987.
Persson, P. *Understanding Cinema: A Psychological Theory of Moving Imagery.* Cambridge: Cambridge University Press, 2003.
Pettigrew, T.F. "Intergroup Contact Theory." *Annual Review of Psychology* 49 (1998): 65–85.
Petty, R.E., D.T. Wegener, and L.R. Fabrigar. "Attitudes and Attitude Change." *Annual Review of Psychology* 48 (1997): 609–47.
Phillips, A., *On Flirtation.* Cambridge, MA: Harvard University Press, 1994.
Pickering, J. "The Self Is a Semiotic Process." *Journal of Consciousness Studies* 6, no. 4 (1999): 31–47.
Pillemer, D.B. *Momentous Events, Vivid Memories: How Unforgettable Moments Help Us Understand the Meaning of Our Lives.* Cambridge, MA: Harvard University Press, 1998.
Pinker, S. *The Better Angels of Our Nature. Why Violence Has Declined,* New York: Viking, 2011.
———. *How the Mind Works.* New York: W.W. Norton, 1997.
Pisters, P. *Opereren in de werkelijkheid: Politieke cinema en de vrije indirecte rede.* Oratie. Amsterdam: Amsterdam University Press, 2005.
Plomin, R., K. Asbury, and J. Dunn. "Why Are Children in the Same Family So Different? Nonshared Environment a Decade Later." *Canadian Journal of Psychiatry* 46 (2001): 225–33.
Plomin, R., and D. Daniels. "Why Are Children in the Same Family So Different from One Another?" *Behavioral and Brain Sciences* 10 (1987): 1–60.
Plomin, R., B. Manke, and A. Pike. "Siblings, Behavioral Genetics, and Competence." In *Sibling Relationships: Their Causes and Consequences,* edited by G. Brody, 75–104. Norwood: Ablex Publishing Corporation, 1996.
Plotkin, M.B. *Freud in the Pampas: The Emergence and Development of a Psychoanalytic Culture in Argentina.* Stanford, CA: Stanford University Press, 2001.
Pomata, G. *Contracting a Cure: Patients, Healers, and the Law in Early Modern Bologna.* Baltimore: Johns Hopkins University Press, 1998 (orig. 1994).

Pope, H.G., and J.I. Hudson. "Can Memories of Childhood Sexual Abuse Be Repressed?" *Psychological Medicine* 25 (1995): 121–6.
Posner, M.I., ed. *Foundations of Cognitive Science*. Cambridge, MA: MIT Press, 1989.
Potter, S. "Dangerous Spaces: Safe." *Camera Obscura* 19, no. 3 57 (2004): 124–54.
Praz, M. *The Romantic Agony*. Oxford: Oxford University Press, 1970 (orig. 1933).
Prosser, J. *Second Skins. The Body Narratives of Transsexuality*. New York: Columbia University Press, 1998.
Ratner, C. "Agency and Culture." *Journal for the Theory of Social Behavior* 30 (2000): 413–34.
Reddy, W.M. "Against Constructionism: The Historical Ethnography of Emotions." *Current Anthropology* 38, no. 3 (1997): 327–40, 346–51.
———. *The Navigation of Feeling: A Framework for the History of Emotions*. Cambridge: Cambridge University Press, 2001.
Reed, G.F. *The Psychology of Anomalous Experience: A Cognitive Approach*. Buffalo: Prometheus Books, 1988 (orig. 1972).
Reeve, C.D.C. "Two Blue Ruins: Love and Memory in *Eternal Sunshine of the Spotless Mind*." In *Eternal Sunshine of the Spotless Mind*, edited by C. Grau, 15–30. London: Taylor & Francis, 2009.
Reid, R. "UnSafe at Any Distance: Todd Haynes' Visual Culture of Health and Risk: For Steven Shaviro." *Film Quarterly* 51, no. 3 (1998): 32–44.
Revonsuo, A. "The Reinterpretation of Dreams: An Evolutionary Hypothesis of the Function of Dreaming." *Behavioral and Brain Sciences* 23 (2000): 793–1121.
Revonsuo, A., and K. Valli. "Dreaming and Consciousness: Testing the Threat Simulation Theory of the Function of Dreaming." *Psyche: An Interdisciplinary Journal of Research on Consciousness* 6, no. 8 (2000). psyche.cs.monash.edu.au/v6/psyche-6-08-revonsuo.html (10/2007).
Rhee, E., J.S. Uleman, H.K. Lee, and R.J. Roman. "Spontaneous Self-Descriptions and Ethnic Identities in Individualistic and Collectivistic Cultures." *Journal of Personality and Social Psychology* 69, no. 1 (1995): 142–52.
Riccio, D.C., V.C. Rabinowitz, and S. Axelrod. "Memory: When Less Is More." *American Psychologist* 49, no. 11 (1994): 917–26.
Richards, R.J. *The Tragic Sense of Life: Ernst Haeckel and the Struggle Over Evolutionary Thought*. Chicago: University of Chicago Press, 2008.
Rizzolatti, G., and L. Craighero. "The Mirror-Neuron System." *Annual Review of Neuroscience* 27 (2004): 169–92.
Rizzolatti, G., and C. Sinigaglia. *Mirrors in the Brain: How Our Minds Share Actions and Emotions*. New York: Oxford University Press, 2008.
Roach, M. *Bonk: The Curious Coupling of Science and Sex*. New York: W.W. Norton, 2008.
Roazen, P. *The Trauma of Freud. Controversies in Psychoanalysis*. New Brunswick, NJ: Transaction Publishers, 2002.
Robinson, P. *Freud and His Critics*. Berkeley, CA: University of California Press, 1993.
Rock, A. *The Mind at Night: The New Science of How and Why We Dream*. New York: Basic Books, 2004.
Róheim, G. "Freud and Anthropology: Freud's 80th Birthday." *Man* 36, no. 97–98 (1936): 76–78.
Rosario, V.A. "The Biology of Gender and the Construction of Sex?" *GLQ: A Journal of Lesbian and Gay Studies* 10, no. 2 (2004): 280–87.
Rosenzweig, M.R., A.L. Leiman, and S.M. Breedlove. *Biological Psychology*. Sunderland, MA: Sinauer Associates, 1996.
Roth, M.S., and C.G. Salas, eds. *Disturbing Remains: Memory, History and Crisis in the Twentieth Century*. Los Angeles: Getty Research Institute, 2001.
Roudinesco, E. *Jacques Lacan and Co.: A History of Psychoanalysis in France, 1925–1985*. London: Free Association, 1990 (orig. 1986).
———. *Why Psychoanalysis?* New York: Columbia University Press, 2001 (orig. 1999).
Roustang, F. *The Lacanian Delusion*. Oxford: Oxford University Press, 1990 (orig. 1986).
Routledge, C., J. Arndt, C. Sedikides, and T. Wildschut. "A Blast from the Past: The Terror

Management Function of Nostalgia." *Journal of Experimental Social Psychology* 44 (2008): 132–40.
Routledge, R.B., P.S. Mani, A.R. Pence, and M.L. Hoskins. "Exploring the Role of Family and Peers in Adolescent Self-Representation: Toward a Dialectical Perspective." *Child & Youth Care Forum* 30, no. 1 (2001): 35–54.
Rovee-Collier, C. "The Capacity for Long-Term Memory in Infancy." *Current Directions in Psychological Science* 2 (1993): 130–35.
Rowe, D.C. *The Limits of Family Influence: Genes, Experience, and Behavior.* New York: Guilford Press, 1994.
Royle, N. *The Uncanny.* Manchester: Manchester University Press, 2003.
Rubin, H. *Self-Made Men: Identity and Embodiment Among Transsexual Men.* Nashville, TN: Vanderbilt University Press, 2003.
Ruggiero, G. *Binding Passions: Tales of Magic, Marriage, and Power at the End of the Renaissance.* Oxford: Oxford University Press, 1993.
———. *Machiavelli in Love: Sex, Self, and Society in the Italian Renaissance.* Baltimore: Johns Hopkins University Press, 2007.
Rumelhart, D.E. "The Architecture of Mind: A Connectionist Approach." In *Foundations of Cognitive Science,* edited by M.I. Posner, 133–59. Cambridge, MA: MIT Press, 1989.
Russell, J.A. "Culture and the Categorization of Emotions." *Psychological Bulletin* 110, no. 3 (1991): 426–50.
Sabbadini, A. "Introduction." In *The Couch and the Silver Screen: Psychoanalytic Reflections on European Cinema,* edited by A. Sabbadini, 1–15. New York: Bruner-Routledge, 2003.
Sabbadini, A., ed. *The Couch and the Silver Screen: Psychoanalytic Reflections on European Cinema.* New York: Bruner-Routledge, 2003.
Said, E.W. *Freud and the Non-European.* London: Verso, 2003.
Schacter, D.L. *Searching for Memory: The Brain, the Mind, and the Past.* New York: Basic Books, 1996.
Schacter, D.L., and E. Scarry, eds. *Memory, Brain, and Belief.* Cambridge, MA: Harvard University Press, 2000.
Schacter, D.L., and E. Tulving. *Memory Systems.* Cambridge, MA: MIT Press, 1994.
Scheufele, D.A. "Framing as a Theory of Media Effects." *Journal of Communication* 49 (1999): 103–22.
Scheufele, D.A., and D. Tewksbury. "Framing, Agenda Setting, and Priming: The Evolution of Three Media Effects Models." *Journal of Communication* 57 (2007): 9–20.
Schorske, C.E. *Fin-de-siècle Vienna: Politics and Culture.* New York: Vintage Books, 1981.
Schutte, A.J. *Aspiring Saints: Pretense of Holiness, Inquisition, and Gender in the Republic of Venice, 1618–1750.* Baltimore: Johns Hopkins University Press, 2001.
Sebeok, T.A. *Signs: An Introduction to Semiotics.* Toronto: University of Toronto Press, 1994.
Sedikides, C., and C.A. Anderson. "Causal Perceptions of Intertrait Relations: The Glue That Holds Person Types Together." *Personality and Social Psychology Bulletin* 20 (1994): 294–302.
Shank, G. "Abductive Multiloging: Semiotic Perspectives of Navigating the Net." *Arachnet Electronic Journal of Virtual Culture.* ftp.byrd.mu.wvnet.edu/pub/ejvc/SHANK.V1N1 (1993) and www.ibiblio.org/pub/academic/communications/papers/ejvc/SHANK.V1N1 (10/2007).
———, and D.J. Cunningham. "Modeling the Six Modes of Peircean Abduction for Educational Purposes." Paper, Maics, 1996. www.cs.indiana.edu/event/maics96/Proceedings/shank.html (10/2007).
Sherman, J.A. "Evolutionary Origin of Bipolar Disorder." *Psycoloquy* 12, no. 28 (2001). psycprints.ecs.soton.ac.uk/archive/00000157 (10/2007).
Shohat, E., and R. Stam. *Unthinking Eurocentrism: Multiculturalism and the Media.* London: Routledge, 1994.
Shore, B. *Culture in Mind: Cognition, Culture, and the Problem of Meaning.* New York: Oxford University Press, 1996.
Shorter, E. *A History of Psychiatry: From the Era of the Asylum to the Age of Prozac.* New York: John Wiley & Sons, 1996.

Shotter, J. "Social Accountability and the Social Construction of 'You.'" In *Texts of Identity,* edited by J. Shotter and K.J. Gergen, 133–51. London: Sage Publications, 1989.
Shotter, J., and K.J. Gergen, eds. *Texts of Identity.* London: Sage Publications, 1989.
Shweder, R.A. "The Surprise of Ethnography." *Ethos* 25, no. 2 (1997): 152–63.
Shweder, R.A., and M.A. Sullivan. "Cultural Psychology: Who Needs It?" *Annual Review of Psychology* 44 (1993): 497–523.
Silvey, V. "Not Your Average Love Story: Film Techniques in *Eternal Sunshine of the Spotless Mind.*" *Screen Education* 53 (2009): 139–44.
Simmons, G. "Memory and Reality in *Eternal Sunshine of the Spotless Mind.*" *Screen Education* 55 (2009): 113–18.
Simon, B. "Self and Group in Modern Society: Ten Theses on the Individual Self and the Collective Self." In Spears et al., *The Social Psychology of Stereotyping and Group Life,* 318–35.
Simon, B., G. Pantaleo, and A. Mummendey. "Unique Individual or Interchangeable Group Member? The Accentuation of Intra-Group Differences Versus Similarities as an Indicator of the Individual Self Versus the Collective Self." *Journal of Personality and Social Psychology* 69, no. 1 (1995): 106–19.
Simpkins, S. *Critical Semiotics, Semiotic Review of Books: Cyberinstitute Cyber Course.* www.chass.utoronto.ca/epc/srb/cyber/simout.html (1998; 10/2007).
Singer, J.L., ed. *Repression and Dissociation.* Chicago: University of Chicago Press, 1990.
Singer, M. "Signs of the Self: An Exploration in Semiotic Anthropology." *American Anthropologist* 82, no. 3 (1980): 485–507.
Singh-Manoux, A., and C. Finkenauer. "Cultural Variations in Social Sharing of Emotions: An Intercultural Perspective." *Journal of Cross-Cultural Psychology* 32, no. 6 (2001): 647–61.
Sinha, M. *Colonial Masculinity: The "Manly Englishman" and the "Effeminate Bengali" in the Late Nineteenth Century.* Manchester: Manchester University Press, 1995.
Slater, D. "Geopolitical Imaginations Across the North-South Divide: Issues of Difference, Development and Power." *Political Geography* 16, no. 8 (1997): 631–53.
Smith, P.B., and M.H. Bond. *Social Psychology Across Cultures.* 2d ed. London: Prentice Hall Europe, 1993.
Sokal, A., and J. Brincmont. *Intellectual Impostures: Postmodern Philosophers' Abuse of Science.* London: Profile Books, 1998 (orig. 1997).
Solomon, J. *The Signs of Our Time: The Secret Meanings of Everyday Life.* New York: J.P. Tarcher, 1988.
Sorbille, M. "Argentine Military Terrorism (1976–1983): Insatiable Desire, Disappearances, and Eruption of the Traumatic Gaze-Real in Alejandro Agresti's Film *Buenos Aires Viceversa* (1996)." *Cultural Critique* 68, no. 2 (2008): 86–128.
Sorensen, K. *Media, Memory, and Human Rights in Chile.* New York: Palgrave Macmillan, 2009.
Sovik, L. "We Are Family: Whiteness in the Brazilian Media." *Journal of Latin American Cultural Studies* 13, no. 3 (2004): 315–25.
Spears, R., P.J. Oakes, N. Ellemers, and S.A. Haslam, eds. *The Social Psychology of Stereotyping and Group Life.* Oxford: B. Blackwell, 1997.
Spelke, E. "Sex Differences in Intrinsic Aptitude for Mathematics and Science?" *American Psychologist* 60 (2005): 950–58.
Sperry, R.W. "The Impact and Promise of the Cognitive Revolution." *American Psychologist* 48, no. 8 (1993): 878–85.
Spinoza, B. *The Chief Works of Benedict de Spinoza.* New York: Dover, 1955.
Spivak, Gayatri Chakravorty. *A Critique of Postcolonial Reason: Toward a History of the Vanishing Present.* Cambridge, MA: Harvard University Press (1999).
Squire, L.R., B. Knowlton, and G. Musen. "Memory, Hippocampus, and Brain Systems." In *The Cognitive Neurosciences,* edited by M.S. Gazzaniga, 825–38. Cambridge, MA: MIT Press (1995).
———. "The Structure and Organization of Memory." *Annual Review of Psychology* 44 (1993): 453–95.
Stam, R. *Film Theory: An Introduction.* Malden: Blackwell, 2000.

———. *Literature Through Film: Realism, Magic, and the Art of Adaptation*. Oxford: Blackwell Publishers, 2005.
Stam, R., and A. Raengo, eds. *Literature and Film: A Guide to the Theory and Practice of Film Adaptation*. Oxford: Blackwell, 2005.
Stearns, P.N., and C.Z. Stearns. "Emotionology: Clarifying the History of Emotions and Emotional Standards." *American Historical Review* 90 (1985): 813–36.
Steedly, M.M. "The Importance of Proper Names: Language and 'National' Identity in Colonial Karoland." *American Ethnologist* 23, no. 3 (1996): 447–75.
Stein, H.H. "Memory, Repression and Transference in *Eternal Sunshine of the Spotless Mind*." *Bulletin of the PANY* 43, no. 1 (2005): 15–20.
Steiner, D., and M. Nauser, eds. *Human Ecology: Fragments of Anti-Fragmentary Views of the World*. London: Routledge, 1993.
Stephens, W. *Demon Lovers: Witchcraft, Sex, and the Crisis of Belief*. Chicago: University of Chicago Press, 2002.
Stevens, C.F., and A. Zador. "Neural Coding: The Enigma of the Brain." www.sloan.salk.edu/~zador (1997).
Stewart, D.W., and D. Koulack. "The Function of Dreams in Adaptation to Stress Over Time." *Dreaming: Journal of the Association for the Study of Dreams* 3, no. 4 (1993): 259–68.
Stewart, L., A. Sebastiani, G. Delgado, and G. López. "Consequences of Sexual Abuse of Adolescents." *Reproductive Health Matters* 4, no. 7 (1996): 129–34.
Strawson, G. "The Self." *Journal of Consciousness Studies* 4, no. 5–6 (1997): 405–28.
Street, B. *Literacy in Theory and Practice*. Cambridge: Cambridge University Press, 1984.
Stroud, S.R. "Simulation, Subjective Knowledge, and the Cognitive Value of Literary Narrative." *Journal of Aesthetic Education* 42, no. 3 (2008): 19–41.
Sulloway, F.J. *Freud, Biologist of Mind: Beyond the Psychoanalyst Legend*. New York: Basic Books, 1979.
Sumbadze, N. *The Social Web: Friendship of Adult Men and Women*. Leiden: DSWO Press, 1999.
Summers, A. *The Arrogance of Power: The Secret World of Richard Nixon*. New York: Viking, 2000.
Super, C.M., and S. Harkness. "The Developmental Niche: A Conceptualization at the Interface of Child and Culture." *International Journal of Behavioral Development* 9 (1986): 545–69.
Swaab, D. *Wij zijn ons brein: Van baarmoeder tot Alzheimer*. Amsterdam: Contact, 2010.
Tan, E.S. *Emotion and the Structure of Narrative Film: Film as an Emotion Machine*. Mahwah, NJ: Erlbaum, 1996.
Tatar, M.M. "E.T.A. Hoffmann's *Der Sandmann*: Reflection and Romantic Irony." *Modern Language Notes* 95, no. 3 (1980): 585–608.
Taylor, G.A. *Castration: An Abbreviated History of Western Manhood*. New York: Routledge, 2000.
Taylor, J. *The Race for Consciousness*. Cambridge, MA: MIT Press, 1999.
Taylor, S.E. "Asymmetrical Effects of Positive and Negative Events: The Mobilization-Minimization Hypothesis." *Psychological Bulletin* 110, no. 1 (1991): 67–85.
Taylor, S.E., and S.C. Thompson. "Stalking the Elusive 'Vividness' Effect." *Psychological Review* 89 (1982): 155–81.
Tedlock, B. "The New Anthropology of Dreaming." *Dreaming: Journal of the Association for the Study of Dreams* 1, no. 2 (1991): 161–78.
Thagard, P., and A. Barnes. "Emotional Decisions." *Proceedings of the Eighteenth Annual Conference of the Cognitive Science Society*, 1996, 426–29.
Thagard, P., and Z. Kunda. "Making Sense of People: Coherence Mechanisms." In *Connectionist Models of Social Reasoning and Social Behavior*, edited by S.J. Read and L.C. Miller, 3–26. London: Psychology Press, 1998.
Thagard, P., and E. Millgram. "Inference to the Best Plan: A Coherence Theory of Decision." cogsci.uwaterloo.ca/Articles/Pages/Inference.Plan.html (1997; 10/2007).
Thagard, P., and K. Verbeurgt. "Coherence as Constraint Satisfaction." cogsci.uwaterloo.ca/Articles/Pages/Cohere.Constrain.html (1997; 10/2007).
Thomas, N.J. "A Stimulus to the Imagination." *Psyche: An Interdisciplinary Journal of Research*

on Consciousness 3, no. 4 (1997). psyche.cs. monash.edu.au/v3/psyche-3-04-thomas.html (10/2007).
Thornton, E.M. *Freud and Cocaine: The Freudian Fallacy.* Garden City, NY: Dial Press, 1983.
Thurston, R.W. "The World, the Flesh and the Devil." *History Today* 56, no. 11 (2006): 51–57.
_____. *Witch, Wicce, Mother Goose: The Rise and Fall of the Witch Hunts in Europe and North America.* Harlow: Longman, 2001.
Tice, D.M. "Self-Concept Change and Self-Presentation: The Looking Glass Self Is Also a Magnifying Glass." *Journal of Personality and Social Psychology* 63 (1992): 435–51.
Tilly, C. *Coercion, Capital, and European States, A.D. 990–1990.* Oxford: B. Blackwell, 1990.
Todd, J.M. "The Veiled Woman in Freud's 'Das Unheimliche.'" *Signs: Journal of Women in Culture and Society* 2, no. 3 (1986): 519–28.
Trafimow, D., E.S. Silverman, R.M.-T. Fan, and J.S.F. Law. "The Effects of Language and Priming on the Relative Accessibility of the Private Self and the Collective Self." *Journal of Cross-Cultural Psychology* 28, no. 1 (1997): 107–23.
Triandis, H.C. *Culture and Social Behavior.* New York: McGraw-Hill, 1994.
_____. *Individualism and Collectivism.* Boulder, CO: Westview Press, 1995.
Triantafyllou, M., and G. Triantafyllou. "An Efficient Swimming Machine." *Scientific American* 272, no. 3 (1995): 64–70.
Tyson, P., and R.L. Tyson. *Psychoanalytic Theories of Development: An Integration.* New Haven, CT: Yale University Press, 1990.
Umiltà, C. *Attention and Performance xv: Conscious and Nonconscious Information Processing.* Cambridge, MA: MIT Press, 1994.
Varela, F.J., E. Thompson, and E. Rosch. *The Embodied Mind: Cognitive Science and Human Experience.* Cambridge, MA: MIT Press, 1991.
Vasudevan, R., ed. *Making Meaning in Indian Cinema.* Delhi: Oxford University Press, 2000.
Volkan, V.D. *Bloodlines: From Ethnic Pride to Ethnic Terrorism.* New York: Farrar, Straus and Giroux, 1997.
_____. "Traumatized Societies and Psychological Care: Expanding the Concept of Preventive Medicine." *Mind and Human Interaction* 11 (2000): 177–94.
Vroon, P. *Tranen van de krokodil: Over de te snelle evolutie van onze hersenen.* Baarn: Boom, 1989.
_____. *Wolfsklem: De evolutie van het menselijk gedrag.* Baarn: Boom, 1992.
Waddington, I. *The Medical Profession in the Industrial Revolution.* Dublin: Gill and Macmillan, 1984.
_____. *Power and Control in the Doctor-Patient Relationship. A Developmental Approach.* Leicester: University of Leicester Press, 1978.
Wagenaar, W.A., P.J. van Koppen, and H.F.M. Crombag. *Anchored Narratives: The Psychology of Criminal Evidence.* Hemel Hempstead. Harvester Wheatsheaf, 1993.
Webster, R. *Freud.* London: Weidenfeld & Nicholson, 2003.
_____. *Why Freud Was Wrong: Sin, Science and Psychoanalysis.* Rev. ed. London: HarperCollins, 1996.
Wegner, D.M. *The Illusion of Conscious Will.* Cambridge, MA: MIT Press, 2002.
_____. *White Bears and Other Unwanted Thoughts: Suppression, Obsession and the Psychology of Mental Control.* 2d ed. New York: Guilford Press, 1994.
Wegner, D.M., and R. Erber. "The Hyperaccessibility of Suppressed Thoughts." *Journal of Personality and Social Psychology* 63, no. 6 (1992): 903–12.
Weismantel, M. *Cholas and Pishtacos: Stories of Race and Sex in the Andes.* Durham, NC: Duke University Press, 2001.
Werbner, P. "The Limits of Cultural Hybridity: On Ritual Monsters, Poetic Licence and Contested Postcolonial Purifications." *Journal of the Royal Anthropological Institute* 7, no. 1 (2001): 133–52.
Whetstone, T., and M.D. Cross. "Control of Conscious Contents in Directed Forgetting and Thought Suppression." *Psyche: An Interdisciplinary Journal of Research on Consciousness* 4, no. 16 (1998). psyche.cs.monash.edu.au/v4/psyche-4-16-whetstone.html (10/2007).
Whyte, L.L. *The Unconscious Before Freud.* London: Basic Books, 1960.

Wicker, B., C. Keysers, J. Plailly, J.-P. Royet, V. Gallese, and G. Rizzolatti. "Both of Us Disgusted in My Insula: The Common Neural Basis of Seeing and Feeling Disgust." *Neuron* 40, no. 3 (2003): 655–64.
Wilcocks, R. *Mousetraps and the Moon. The Strange Ride of Sigmund Freud and the Early Years of Psychoanalysis*. Lanham, MD: Lexington Books, 2000.
Wilson, D.S. *Darwin's Cathedral: Evolution, Religion, and the Nature of Society*. Chicago: University of Chicago Press, 2002.
Wilson, E.O. *On Human Nature*. Cambridge: Harvard University Press, 1978.
Yairi, E., and N.G. Ambrose. *Early Childhood Stuttering for Clinicians by Clinicians*. Austin, TX: PRO-ED, 2005.
Yamada, A.M., and T.M. Singelis. "Biculturalism and Self-Construal." *International Journal of Intercultural Relations* 23, no. 5 (1999): 697–709.
Young, R.M. "Psychoanalytic Criticism: Has It Got Beyond a Joke?" *Paragraph* 4 (1984): 87–114.
Yzerbyt, V., S. Rocher, and G. Schadron. "Stereotypes as Explanations: A Subjective Essentialistic View of Group Perception." In Spears et al., *The Social Psychology of Stereotyping and Group Life*, 20–50.
Zeddies, T.J. "More Than Just Words: A Hermeneutic View of Language in Psychoanalysis." *Psychoanalytic Psychology* 19, no. 1 (2002): 3–23.
Zimbardo, P.G., and M.R. Leippe. *The Psychology of Attitude Change and Social Influence*. Philadelphia: Temple University Press, 1991.
Žižek, S. *How to Read Lacan*. New York: W.W. Norton & Co., 2007.
———. *In Defense of Lost Causes*. London: Verso, 2008.
Zunshine, L. *Why We Read Fiction: Theory of Mind and the Novel*. Columbus: Ohio State University Press, 2006.

# Index

Adler, Alfred 204
adolescence 101, 167, 190, 210–212, 215
Afanasyev, Alexander N. 140
aggression 53, 66, 96, 111, 121, 130, 131, 137, 138, 189, 191, 204, 252
AIDS 5, 80, 85, 102, 129, 133; and Louis Hay, *The AIDS Book: Creating a Positive Approach* (1988) 85
*The AIDS Book: Creating a Positive Approach* (1988) 85
Amerindian 147, 180, 247n14, 255n3
amnesia (forgetting) 128, 131, 133, 137, 144–145, 149, 154
Anderson, Barbara 27; *Narration and Spectatorship in Moving Images* (2007) 27
Anderson, Joseph 27; *Narration and Spectatorship in Moving Images* (2007) 27
Anderson, Laurie Halse 176; *Speak* (1999) 176, 185
androcentrism 13, 58, 65–69, 71–73, 77, 84–85, 93, 95, 99, 118, 236
Angarano, Michael 177
anthropology 3-4, 9, 25, 26, 48, 242n14, 247n22, 252n7
anxiety (non–Freudian) 8, 28, 38, 60, 74, 78, 84, 91–93, 95, 98, 102, 129, 132, 142, 209, 211, 221; generalized fear 95, 102; *see also* fear
*The Ape and the Sushi Master* (2001) 186
Araki, Gregg 5, 126–127, 129, 130, 132, 251–252n2
archetype (Jung) 70
Arenas, Eusebio 165
Aronofsky, Darren 5, 198

Artaud, Antonin 165–167
*The Aryan Christ* (1997) 70
astrology 27, 120–121, 238
Austin, J.L. 111; *How to Do Things with Words* (1962) 111
autobiography 93–95, 145, 170–173, 203, 220–221, 228

Baars, Bernard 170–173, 182; and Global Workspace Theory 170–171, 182, 255n20
Barsalou, Lawrence 188; and Theory of Grounded Cognition 188
Bartlett, Frederick C. 217, 258n25
*Bartlett's Familiar Quotations* (1855) 157, 254n3
Bataille, Georges 232–233; "Soleil pourri" (1929, poem) 232–233
Beauvoir, Simone de 58
Bem, Sandra Lipsitz 58, 72
*benandanti* (good-doers) 62–63, 73, 77, 139–140
Berkeley, Xander 82
Bernheim, Hippolyte 45
Bertuccelli, Valeria 105
Best, Eve 32
*Beyond the Pleasure Principle* (1920, *Jenseits des Lustprinzips*) 130–131, 202–204
biology 5, 12, 13, 18, 37, 40, 46, 47, 58, 67, 70, 79, 91, 93, 106, 112, 116, 124, 163, 164, 167, 177, 186, 189, 193, 203; biological essentialism 58
bisexuality 5, 42, 47, 103, 109–110, 113, 116, 123–124
Bismuth, Pierre 152

285

*Black Swan* (2010) 5, 99, 101, 197–201, 205, 219–220, 223–225, 236
Blackmore, Susan 141; *Consciousness* (2003) 141
Bonham Carter, Helena 29
Borch-Jacobsen, Mikkel 24, 39–40, 88–89, 115–118; *Le Dossier Freud: Enquête sur l'histoire de la psychanalyse* (2006) 24, 40; *Lacan: The Absolute Master* (1991) 24; *Remembering Anna O: A Century of Mystification* (1996) 24; and Sonu Shamdasani 24, 40
Bordwell, David 27; *Making Meaning* (1989) 27
Braga, Alice 55
brain: children's 7, 48, 144; circuits (processes, workings) 78, 115, 141–142, 146, 164, 167–172, 164, 182, 185, 186, 193, 200–206, 218, 221–223; 205; mapping 37, 152; mobilization (longterm) 170; mobilization (short-term) 170; modules 193–194; scanning 50; and *tabula rasa* (blank slate) 158, 162; and unconscious 13; *see also* metaphor; thinking; thought
*Breaking Dawn I* (2011) 73, 77
*Breaking Dawn II* (2012) 73, 77
Breuer, Josef 35–37, 39–43, 45, 64, 119
Britton, Ronald 26; *Sex, Death, and the Superego* (2003) 26
Brody, Adam 97
Buñuel, Luis 202
Burke, Robert John 177
Burston, Daniel 204
Buss, David M. 188–189; *Evolutionary Psychology* (1999) 188
Butler, Judith 5, 111–113, 118–119, 124; *Undoing Gender* (2004) 111, 113

Cardano, Girolamo 120
Cárdenas, Anahí de 147
Cardullo, Bert 163
Carrey, Jim 151, 153
Carrillo, Jenny Cooney 215
Cartesian *see* Descartes, René
Cartwright, Rosalind 140
Cassel, Vincent 199
caul, being born with the 139–140
Charcot, Jean-Marie 45–46, 119
*Chloe* (2009) 5, 121–124, 205, 236
*Cholas and Pishtacos* (2001) 25
Christianity (Christendom) 6, 13, 23, 54, 58–65, 67, 70, 71, 75, 121, 233
Chronic Fatigue Syndrome 91
"Civilization and Its Discontents" (1930) 69

*Civilization of Europe in the Renaissance* (1993) 61
cocaine *see* psychoanalysis
Cody, Diablo 5, 96–99
cognition: and behavior therapy 96, 102; and cognitive revolution 25, 28; Cognitive Schema Theory 217, 224, 233; *see also* psychology
Cognitive Evolutionary Order 6, 15, 72, 73, 77, 94, 96, 205, 225, 233, 238
(Cognitive) Schema Theory 15, 217, 224, 225, 233
Cole, Michael 223–224
Conceptual Metaphor Theory 71, 140, 181–188, 190, 192, 195–196, 218–219, 225
*Consciousness* (2003) 141
consciousness 5, 9, 13, 36, 47, 95, 141, 163–164, 167, 170–173, 199; consciousness studies 5, 163
Cook, A.J. 208
Coppola, Francis Ford 204
Coppola, Sofia 5, 205–216, 221, 222, 225
Corbet, Brady 125, 126
*Cosas insignificantes* (2008) 5, 179–181, 183, 188, 194, 196, 209, 223
cosmology (worldview) 59, 63, 65, 68, 77, 121, 185, 218, 236
Covert, Colin 33
cranioscopy 38
cue 9–10, 150, 198, 222–223; as memory device 223
Cultural Studies 1, 4–5, 119
culture as conglomeration of schemas and conceptual metaphors 192
Cummins, Denise 189
Currie, Gregory 27; *Image and Mind* (1995) 27

Damasio, Antonio 93–94, 168, 254n16; *Descartes' Error* (1994) 93, 94; *The Feeling of What Happens* (1999) 94
*Dangerous Liaisons* (book, 1782) 16
*Dangerous Liaisons* (film, 1988) 16
Darín, Ricardo 104
Darwin, Charles 4, 18–20, 37; *see also* Cognitive Evolutionary Order
*The Decalogue* (1989) 11
depression 26–27, 88, 102, 134, 140, 176, 191, 208
Descartes, René 93, 172; and the Cartesian Cut 93–96, 172; and the Cartesian Theater 172; *cogito ergo sum* 93
*Descartes' Error* (1994) 93, 94
*The Desperate Housewives* (ABC) 226
Devil 13, 56–57, 59–66, 71, 74–77, 98,

139; Baal 53; Evil 6, 13, 55, 59, 61–62, 71, 74, 96, 98, 196, 198; (Evil) Within 13, 53, 62, 64–66, 130, 201, 204; Lucifer 55; Satan 13, 55, 71, 97–98; *see also* psychoanalysis
DeVito, Danny 208, 214
de Waal, Frans 186; *The Ape and the Sushi Master* (2001) 186
*Diagnostic and Statistical Manual of Mental Disorders (DSM)* 24–25, 140
Diamond, Milton 113
dictionary 19, 91–93, 102, 173, 204–205, 242n19, 257n8
*Dioses* (2008) 5, 146–148
Dollfuss, Engelbert 21
Domhoff, G. William 143
dominance hierarchy *see* status
Doorman, Maarten 14–17, 242n12; *see also* order
"Der Doppelgänger" (1914) 203
*Le Dossier Freud: Enquête sur l'histoire de la psychanalyse* (2006) 24, 40
double (doppelgänger) 197–205; *see also* psychoanalysis
*Dracula* (1897) 74
*Drama* (2010) 5, 165–167, 172–174, 223
dream: and bizarreness 142–143, 164; and children 139; and films 5, 131, 149; lucid 163–164, 169; nightmare 131, 142, 144–145; psychology of dreaming 62–63, 138–144, 164, 173, 184, 219–220, 251n11; and REM sleep 141; and Romanticism 22; and symbols 9, 22, 164–165; and trauma 146; and witchcraft 62; *see also* psychoanalysis
"dream book" 44-45, 204
Dufresne, Todd 22, 24; *Killing Freud* (2003) 22; *Tales from the Freudian Crypt* (2000) 24
Dunst, Kirsten 157, 207

Eakin, Paul John 93–95
Ebert, Roger 33, 55, 82, 86, 126, 132, 133, 212
*Eclipse* (2010) 73
Edelstein, David 33–34
Edwards, Kim 158, 162
effeminate 13, 74
Effio, Maricielo 146
Efrón, Inés 104, 108
Egoyan, Atom 5, 121
Eitzen, Dirk 77–79
electroencephalogram (EEG) 37
Ellison, Chase 126
"Eloisa to Abelard" (1717) 158

embodiment 5, 93, 113, 182–183, 186–188, 195–196
emotion (psychology) 2–3, 9, 11, 15, 17, 19, 25, 27, 58, 90, 94–96, 132, 140–142, 145, 150, 167–170, 172, 181–186, 187, 189, 198, 200, 218–220, 222, 227, 242n19, 254n16, 259n31; and decisionmaking 145–146, 168; and social sharing 219
*Emotion and the Structure of Narrative Film* (1996) 27
*The Emotional Brain* (1996) 95
encoding 2, 140, 141, 146, 149, 164, 167, 217–223, 227
Enlightenment *see* Functionalist-Enlightened Order
Erikson, Erik 42, 243n27, 251n11
Erwin, Edward 24, 119–120; *A Final Accounting* (1996) 24, 119
*Eternal Sunshine of the Spotless Mind* (2004) 5, 152–158, 161–167, 170–174, 179, 181, 188, 209, 223
Eugenides, Jeffrey 206, 212, 214, 216; *The Virgin Suicides* (1993) 206, 216
evolution *see* Cognitive Evolutionary Order; Darwin, Charles
evolutionary psychology *see* psychology
*Evolutionary Psychology* (1999) 188
exorcism (exorcist paradigm) 4, 5, 13–14, 23, 28, 38, 39, 43, 45, 52–56, 59, 60, 62, 75, 77, 79, 89, 118, 132, 154, 201, 238

Fadiga, Luciano 187; *see also* mirror neurons
fascism 21, 68, 231–232, 233
fear (psychology of) 6, 8, 28, 60, 65, 77–79, 93, 95–96, 102, 141–142, 167, 173, 202; fear of castration *see* psychoanalysis
*The Feeling of What Happens* (1999) 94
Feldman, Jerome 184
femininity 59, 63, 64, 86, 87, 117, 118, 137, 138, 217
feminism 5, 17n, 39, 42, 58, 68, 73, 88, 111, 112, 235
Ferenczi, Sándor 203
Film Studies 1, 3–4, 9, 27, 88, 202, 239
*A Final Accounting* (1996) 24, 119
Firth, Colin 29, 33, 35
Fiske, Susan 222
Fleischl-Marxow, Ernst von 37
Fliess, Wilhelm 36, 38, 40–42, 44, 47–48, 51, 56–57, 90, 92, 109, 124, 202
folk psychology *see* psychology
Folley, Caitlyn 176
Fontaine, Anne 121
40-Hz 164, 168
Foulkes, David 138–139

Fox, Megan  96, 99
Frazer, James George  247n22
Frears, Stephen  16–17
Freud, Sigmund: *Beyond the Pleasure Principle* (1920, *Jenseits des Lustprinzips*) 130–131, 202–204; "Civilization and Its Discontents" (1930) 69; "dream book" 44-45, 204; "From the History of an Infantile Neurosis" (1918) 133; *The Interpretation of Dreams* (1900) 21, 44, 50, 66, 68, 93, 119; *Studien über Hysterie* (1895, with Breuer) 36; *Three Essays on the Theory of Sexuality* (1905) 47; *Totem and Taboo* (1912–13) 68–69, 190; "Das Unheimliche" (1919, "The Uncanny") 202; *see also* psychoanalysis
*Freud Evaluated* (1991) 24
Freudian Edifice  3-5, 8, 11, 28, 32, 33, 35, 50, 56, 99, 118, 131, 198, 217, 230, 237, 238
Freudian Excuse (Trope)  3–5, 8, 11, 28, 32, 33, 35, 50, 56, 99, 103, 121, 123–124, 127, 130–132, 133, 149, 152, 164, 174, 181, 199, 202, 209, 214, 227, 230, 233, 238, 239
Friedman, Peter  85
Frijda, Nico  167
"From the History of an Infantile Neurosis" (1918)  133
Fuller, Graham  206–208, 214–216
functional magnetic resonance imaging (*f*MRI)  37
Functionalist-Enlightened Order  15–17, 26, 32, 46, 65, 72, 225, 237, 242n12, 257–258n8

Gaitán, Paulina  179
Galilei, Galileo  37
Gall, Franz Joseph  38–39, 245n11
Gallese, Vittorio  187; *see also* mirror neurons
Gambon, Michael  31
Garber, Marjorie  109–110; *Vice Versa* (1995) 109
Gastini, Marta  52
gender: identity 13, 17n, 70, 72, 108–113, 116–117, 124, 229; othering of women 13–14, 71, 75; performance 5, 111–113, 221, 233; polarization 58, 108; transgender 5, 112, 236
gene (genetic; behavioral)  49–51, 96, 101, 108, 109–110, 112, 134, 158, 167, 189, 190–195, 201, 224
Gerrig, Richard  2
*Het geval Freud* (1993; *The Freud Case*) 24
Ginzburg, Carlo  62, 73, 139–140, 230–233; "The Sword and the Lightbulb" (2001), also published as *Das Schwert und die Glühbirne* (1999) 230–233
Gjurinovic, Sergio  147
Glenn, Scott  209
Goethe, Johann Wolfgang von  17–18, 19, 20, 47; *Iphigenie auf Tauris* (1779) 19
Goffman, Erving 111, 113; *The Presentation of Self in Everyday Life* (1959) 111
Gómez, Carmelo  180
Gondry, Michel  5, 152–164, 173, 179
Gonsalves, Rob  154
Gordon-Levitt, Joseph  126
Gorton, Kristyn  87–91, 95; *Theorising Desire* (2008) 87
Gottschall, Jonathan  8, 121, 198; *The Storytelling Animal* (2012) 8
gradualist narrative  18–19, 28
Grodal, Torben  27; *Moving Pictures* (1997) 27
*Guernica* (1937, painting)  230, 231–233

Haeckel, Ernst  46–48, 70-71, 109, 116–117, 137, 203, 246n25; and ontogeny 47, 68, 70, 138, 203; phylogeny 47, 68, 70, 109, 137, 138, 203
Håfström, Mikael  4, 53–54, 78
Haggard, H. Rider  21, 74, 117; *Heart of the World* (1896) 21; *She* (1887) 21, 74
Hale, John  61; *Civilization of Europe in the Renaissance* (1993) 61
Hall, Hanna R.  208
hallucination  5, 36, 39, 96–103, 199–201, 205, 236
Hampton, Christopher  16
Hansen, Carl  40
Hardwicke, Catherine  75
Harris, Judith R.  49, 117–118, 190–196, 257n27; *No Two Alike* (2006) 117, 190–196; *The Nurture Assumption* (1998) 49, 118
Hartmann, Ernest  140
Hartnett, Josh  211
Haslam, Richard  25
Hauer, Rutger  54
Hay, Louis: *The AIDS Book: Creating a Positive Approach* (1988) 85
Hayman, Leslie  208
Haynes, Todd  5, 81–87, 91, 101–102, 126; and *Superstar* (1988) 87
*Heart of the World* (1896)  21
Heim, Scott  126, 133; *Mysterious Skin* (1995) 126
Herman, David  10
Hershey, Barbara  198

heterosexuality 38, 72, 85, 113, 116–117, 228
Heyman, Mark 198
Hinds, Ciarán 54
Hirsh, Hallee 175
history 3–4, 9, 13, 14, 25, 33, 58, 61, 71, 118, 120, 167, 189, 201, 216, 222–223, 232
Hitchcock, Alfred 202
Hitler, Adolf 32
Hobson, J. Allan 141
Hoenisch, Steven 89
Hollywood 51, 74, 87, 215
homeostasis 94–95
homosexuality 47, 61, 70–71, 75, 113, 116–117, 119, 124, 134, 138, 228–229, 248n24
Hooper, Tom 4, 31, 33
Hopkins, Anthony 52
Hornaday, Ann 33, 127, 132
Hoskin, Bree 210
"How Metaphor Structures Dreams" (1993) 184;
*How to Do Things with Words* (1962) 111
Hrdy, Sarah 48; *Mother Nature* (1999) 48
Hyde, Janet 111
hyperventilation 38, 95
hypnosis 35, 36, 40, 43, 45, 127
hysteria *see* psychoanalysis

Iacoboni, Marco 187; *see also* mirror neurons
identity 16, 72, 86, 94, 96, 112, 149, 158, 198, 218, 224–225, 233, 236; as theory of oneself 224
*Image and Mind* (1995) 27
incest 69, 116, 148
*Inland Empire* (2006) 165
interpreter: "group interpreter" 205–206, 208–214, 216, 219; left hemisphere 6, 156, 198–201, 205, 219, 222, 224, 237
*The Interpretation of Dreams* (1900) 21, 44, 50, 66, 68, 93, 119
intersexuality 105–106, 108, 112–113
*Interview with the Vampire* (film, 1994) 75
*Interview with the Vampire* (novel, 1976) 74
*Iphigenie auf Tauris* (1779) 19
Israëls, Han 24, 229; *The Freud Case*) 24; *Het geval Freud* (1993; *De Weense kwakzalver* (1999; *The Viennese Quack*) 24

James, William 111, 193, 228, 256n25; *The Principles of Psychology* (1890) 193, 228
Janet, Pierre 20, 40, 45
*Jennifer's Body* (2009) 5, 96–101, 198, 205, 236
Jones, Toby 54
Jordan, Neil 75

Jung, Carl Gustav 70, 143, 203
*The Jung Cult* (1994) 70

Kaufman, Charlie 5, 152, 159–160, 162, 164, 173
Kazan, Elia 86
Kieslowski, Krysztof 11
*The Killer Inside Me* (2000) 3, 8, 11, 28, 35, 50
*Killing Freud* (2003) 22
*The King's Speech* (2010) 4, 31–35, 43, 50–51
Kish, Kimberly 177
Klawans, Stuart 155
Klinefelter's Syndrome 105
Koch, Robert 46
Krafft-Ebing, Richard Freiherr von 36
Kramer, Heinrich (Institoris) 57, 63–66; *see also* Malleus Maleficarum or *The Hammer of Witches*
Kramer, Milton 142
Kristeva, Julia 26–27
Kunda, Ziva 146, 168
Kunis, Mila 197
Kuras, Ellen 153
Kusama, Karyn 5, 96

Lacan, Jacques 3, 4, 24, 27, 68, 88, 113, 164, 202, 244n34, 254n18, 254–255n19
*Lacan: The Absolute Master* (1991) 24
Lachman, Edward 210
Lakoff, George 71, 181–190, 195, 218; and Conceptual Metaphor Theory 71, 140, 181–188, 190, 192, 195–196, 218–219, 225; "How Metaphor Structures Dreams" (1993) 184; and Nurturant Parent Model 71–72; and Strict Father Model 71–72, 73, 76–77; *Women, Fire, and Dangerous Things* (1987) 182; *see also* metaphor (conceptual)
Lamarck, Jean-Baptiste Pierre Antoine de Monet, Chevalier de 20, 46, 48, 70, 109, 116, 137
Lane, Anthony 34
LaSalle, Mick 126
Lautner, Taylor 73
LeDoux, Joseph 95, 167 168; *The Emotional Brain* (1996) 95
LeGros, James 80
Lehrer, Jonah 35, 50–51
Leonardo da Vinci 228–230
Leopardi, Chauncey 82
Licon, Jeffrey 127
Lidz, Theodore 144–145
Lim, Dennis 127, 133

Lira, Matías 5, 165–166
literary sciences (studies) 1, 3, 4, 9, 162, 163; literary criticism 14
Lively, Eric 175
Lugones, María 235–236
Luján, Fernando 180
lycanthropy 74
Lyles, Leslie 177
Lynch, David 164; *Inland Empire* (2006) 165; *Mulholland Dr.* (2001) 164

Machiavelli, Niccolò 120–121; *Il Principe* (*The Prince*, 1513–32) 120
*The Machiavellian Cosmos* (1992) 120
Macmillan, Malcolm 24, 49, 138; *Freud Evaluated* (1991) 24
magnetic resonance imaging (MRI) 37
*Making Meaning* (1989) 27
Malcolm, Janet 24, 42; *Psychoanalysis* (1988) 24
*Malleus Maleficarum* or *The Hammer of Witches* see Kramer, Heinrich (Institoris)
Mandel, David 234
Mar, Raymond 3, 10
Martínez, Andrea 5, 179
masculinity 58–59, 62, 64, 107, 110, 117–118, 216
masturbation *see* sex
McCrone, John 142
McGowan, Todd 27; *The Real Gaze* (2007) 27
McGregor-Stewart, Kate 85
McLaughlin, John 198
McManus, Jaime 165
McNally, Richard 143–146, 150, 223; *Remembering Trauma* (2003) 143, 223
medication 25, 88, 90, 101–103, 143, 152, 202
memory 1, 3, 6, 9, 16, 94, 131, 141–150, 152, 154, 163–164, 166–174, 188, 198, 206, 210, 217–225, 227–228, 242n19, 254n12, 259n31
Memory Wars 24, 228
Méndez, Josué 5, 146–149
mental models
Merritt, Jane 142
Mesmer, Franz Anton 45–46
metaphor: "Impotence Is Blindness" 184–185; "Knowing Is Seeing" 183–185; physically present in the brain 184; "Testicles Are Eyes" 184, 185; theater 170–171; *see also* Baars, Bernard; Lakoff, George
metarepresentation 14, 113, 230, 238
Meyer, Michael 157
Meyer, Stephenie 73

Millais, John Everett 208; *Ophelia* (1852, painting) 208
Miller, Arthur 72
mind-reading 1, 14, 76, 237, 238
mirror neurons 1, 185–188, 220, 227, 236
misogyny 59, 65
Mitchell, Juliet 88–89
Mondello, Bob 34
Money, John 110–112
Moore, Julianne 80, 121
Mori, Barbara 180
Morris, Wesley 126
*Mother Nature* (1999) 48
*Moving Pictures* (1997) 27
*Mulholland Dr.* (2001) 164
Mussolini, Benito 21
*Mysterious Skin* (1995) 126
*Mysterious Skin* (2004) 5, 126-133, 144, 145, 149, 188, 223

*Narration and Spectatorship in Moving Images* (2007) 27
narrative: and anchoring 12–14; and master- or metanarratives 4, 13, 60, 79, 239; and narrative world 2, 10, 14, 23, 59, 81, 93, 227, 236; transported into 2, 23, 31, 79, 81, 100, 227, 236
nature versus nurture 3, 49–50, 118, 139; *see also* Harris, Judith
Neeson, Liam 121
neurobiology 93–95, 170, 193, 201; *see also* brain
neurology 25, 37, 93–94, 162, 186–187, 201, 222; *see also* brain
neurons 48, 50, 142, 164, 167, 171, 172, 184–188, 219, 221–224, 227, 236; *see also* brain
neuropsychology 3; *see also* brain
neuroscience 6, 12, 25, 28, 48, 115, 141, 152, 163, 186–187, 198, 238; *see also* brain
neurotransmitter 167, 189, 221; *see also* brain
New Age 85, 88
Newton, Isaac 17–18, 20, 46
Nishida, Hiroko 217
*No Two Alike* (2006) 117, 190–196
Nóbile, Luciano 107
Noë, Alva 185
Noll, Richard 70; *The Aryan Christ* (1997) 70; *The Jung Cult* (1994) 70
Norman, Susan 81
Núñez, Rafael 181
*The Nurture Assumption* (1998) 49, 118

Oatley, Keith, 1, 3, 10–11

Obholzer, Karin 136–138
O'Donoghue, Colin 52
Oedipus Complex *see* psychoanalysis
*Oedipus Rex* (ca. 425 B.C.) 66
O'Hehir, Andrew 34, 55
*On Flirtation* (1994) 26
Onfray, Michel 21, 24, 227
ontogeny *see* Haeckel, Ernst
*Ophelia* (1852, painting) 208
orgasm 51, 203, 221, 233

Pagel, James 149
Palacios, Germán 106
Paré, Michael 212
Parel, Anthony 120–121; *The Machiavellian Cosmos* (1992) 120
Pasteur, Louis 46
Pasupathi, Monisha 220
Pattinson, Robert 73
peer 48–49, 89, 108, 118, 133, 147, 188, 190, 192–195
Pelleritti, Carolina 107
performance 2, 3, 5, 9, 10, 16, 46, 68, 94, 97, 111–112, 132, 152, 165–168, 176, 200, 202, 221, 227, 233; *see also* stage
Perkins, Elizabeth 176
personality 11, 15, 16, 23, 36, 38, 67, 70, 90, 190–191, 193–195, 219, 224, 229
Petroni, Michael 53–54
Phillips, Adam 26–27; *On Flirtation* (1994) 26
phrenology 38–39
phylogeny *see* Haeckel, Ernst
Picasso, Pablo 230–233; *Guernica* (1937, painting) 230, 231–233
Pillar, Megan 177
Pinker, Steven 167
Pinochet, Augusto 166
Piroyanski, Martín 105
Pitt, Brad 74
politics 4, 6, 17*n*, 20–21, 26, 71, 72, 121, 225, 230–231; conservative 20, 68, 71; progressive 20, 71, 72; reactionary 26
Pope, Alexander 158; "Eloisa to Abelard" (1717) 158
popular psychology *see* psychology
Portman, Natalie 197
Potter, Susan 81–86
*The Presentation of Self in Everyday Life* (1959) 111
Princess Marie Bonaparte of Greece and Denmark 51, 101, 203
*Il Principe* (*The Prince*, 1513–32) 120
*The Principles of Psychology* (1890) 193, 228
Prosser, Jay 112; *Second Skins* (1998) 112

pseudo-science 8, 24, 39
psychoanalysis: *abreaction* 131, 202; anal personality 71; Anna O. (Bertha Pappenheim) 24, 36, 39–40, 43, 53, 136 245*n*6; attachment 160, 191, 193; bisexuality 5, 42, 47, 103, 109–110, 113, 116, 123, 124; castration (anxiety) 114, 117, 118, 127, 135–138, 185; catharsis 19, 43, 45, 50, 233; and cocaine 24, 37, 43, 100, 118, 202; coitus 38, 40, 46, 70, 135, 137, 203; and collective unconscious 69–70; compulsion to repeat 127, 129, 130–134, 201, 203, 232; and cure 26, 37, 39, 40–49, 70, 73, 89, 90, 101, 113, 118–120, 129, 132, 134, 136, 138, 144, 152, 162, 203; the Deep 4, 11, 16, 18, 22, 23, 27, 28, 35, 39, 50, 79, 96, 102, 119, 160, 165, 196, 202, 225, 227; and delusion of grandeur 37, 118; and the demon inside 56; Dora (Ida Bauer) 39, 42–43, 49, 53, 87; dream 5, 9, 21, 23, 44, 66–68, 101, 130–132, 134–140, 143, 164, 204; drive (Eros, Death Thanatos) 17, 64, 94, 116, 130–131, 133, 189, 202–204, 205, 233–233, 238; Emma Eckstein 41–42, 43, 56; and essentialism 68, 79; Frau Emmy von N. 35, 43; and fraud 24, 37; the (Freudian) father 67–69, 71, 95, 114–118, 124, 136–138, 229; and haunting un/subconscious 28, 39, 56, 69, 71, 79, 85, 88, 101, 114, 126, 131–132, 144–145, 164, 202, 227, 237, 251*n*11; hysteric (hysteria) 4, 5, 19–23, 35–48, 51–57, 86–91, 95, 101–102, 113, 119, 128, 132, 144, 242*n*19; libido 47, 109–110, 114–115, 131, 137; masturbation 38, 40, 42, 44, 47, 70, 109, 137–138, 148, 199–200, 203; Oedipus (Complex) 3, 13, 21, 23, 42, 66–68, 87–89, 109–111, 113–118, 124, 130, 133, 136–139, 228, 238, 256*n*18; penis envy 114, 117, 118; the phallus 69, 116, 117, 181, 185; phase of 21, 24, 35–36; Pleasure Principle 115, 130–311, 202–204; primal scene (*Urszene*) 135–137; and progress 88–89, 91, 101; regression 3, 69; repression 3, 5, 7–9, 19, 20, 23, 26, 35, 39, 41–42, 47, 50–51, 53, 66–70, 87–91, 101–103, 109, 114 115, 117, 129–131, 136–150, 156, 158–166, 170–178, 196, 202, 214, 218, 227–228; return of the repressed 130, 202, 214; subconscious 5, 18, 28, 43, 50, 66, 88, 101, 109, 131, 132, 165, 166, 171, 238; SuperEgo (Ego Ideal) 71, 95, 117, 118; and talking 41, 70, 89, 90, 101, 120, 129, 131, 132, 152, 170, 220–221; "technique" 38, 43, 45, 53, 56,

57, 64, 66, 165–166, 174, 228; transference 89, 90, 130, 159, 161–162, 174; and trauma 23, 28, 34, 41, 43, 48, 50, 51, 53, 70, 89, 119, 126–136, 141–150, 152, 158, 165, 166, 196, 199, 214, 223, 228, 254n12; tribal 68; uncanny (*unheimlich*) 5–6, 202–205, 257n7, 257n8; the Wolf Man (Sergei Pankejeff) 43, 113, 133–143, 252n18

*Psychoanalysis* (1988) 24

psychology: cognitive 1, 12, 25, 28, 102, 149, 152, 162, 174; developmental 49, 94, 192; evolutionary 3, 188, 193, 225; popular (folk) 3–9, 12–14, 23, 26, 28, 33, 48, 66, 69, 77, 92, 124, 132, 152, 158, 174, 191, 217, 233, 237–238; *see also* emotion

*The Psychology of Anomalous Experience* (1992) 201

psychomythology 3–5, 9, 12–14, 50, 66–67, 75, 92, 93, 102, 131, 158, 163, 191, 233, 238; *see also* brain

Puenzo, Lucía 5, 105–108, 116, 124

queer 5, 81, 112; New Queer Cinema 81, 126; *see also* sex

Rajskub, Mary Lynn 125
Ramlow, Todd 214–216
Rank, Otto 203; "Der Doppelgänger" (1914) 203
*The Real Gaze* (2007) 27
Reed, Graham 201; *The Psychology of Anomalous Experience* (1992) 201
Reeve, C.D.C. 155, 162, 171
Reimer, David 110–112
relationship system (RELS) 194
*Remembering Anna O: A Century of Mystification* (1996) 24
*Remembering Trauma* (2003) 143, 223
Revonsuo, Antti 141
Rice, Anne 74–75
*The Rite* (2011) 4, 53–63, 77–79, 236
Rizzolatti, Giacomo 186–187; *see also* mirror neurons
Robinson, Paul 25–26
Rolley, Tyranna 176
Roman Catholic Church 19, 54–55, 59, 61, 79
Romanticism (Romantic mind) *see* Structuralist-Romantic Order
*Romeo and Juliet* 166n7
Rosario, Vernon 112–113
Roseboro, Tony 177
Rosenberg, Melissa 4, 73
Roudinesco, Elisabeth 88

Rovee-Collier, Carolyn 192
Rubin, Henry 112; *Self-Made Men* (2003) 112
Ruffalo, Mark 157
Ruggiero, Guido 64, 67
Ruiz, Diego 165
Rush, Geoffrey 29, 33
Ryder, Winona 198

Saba, Edgar 147
Sabbadini, Andrea 25, 202
Sacks, Oliver 222
*[SAFE]* (1995) 5, 81–91, 96, 100–102, 129, 188, 205, 236
Sage, Bill 126
Salas, Allín 108
Schager, Nick 34
Schelling, Friedrich 204
schema(ta) (mental) 2, 8, 10, 11, 14, 79, 127, 140–141, 171, 181, 192, 198, 217–224, 227, 235, 237, 242n7, 258n25, 258n27; (Cognitive) Schema Theory 15, 217, 224, 225, 233
schizophrenia 101, 200–202, 205
Schorr, Collier 81, 85–86
Scott, A.O. 132–133
Scrotum, Fall of the 181, 255n3; versus Rise of the Penis (Phallus) 181
*Second Skins* (1998) 112
Seidler, David 31
*Seinfeld* (sitcom) 233–235
self 15, 17, 20, 81, 94, 95, 167–171, 194, 195
self-esteem 76, 195
*Self-Made Men* (2003) 112
sensory inputs (sight, smell, sound, taste, touch) 141–142, 144, 164, 167–169, 172, 182, 184, 187, 221
*Sex, Death, and the Superego* (2003) 26
Seyfried, Amanda 96, 121
Shamdasani, Sonu 24, 40
Sharzer, Jessica 5, 176, 190
*She* (1887) 21, 74
Shue, Elisabeth 126
Siko, Allison 177
Silvey, Vivien 158
Simmons, Gary 158
Simmons, Johnny 97
simulation(s) 1–4, 8, 10–13, 28, 40, 51, 79, 102, 124, 173–174, 188, 196, 198, 224, 227, 238, 242n7
Simulation Theory 1, 3, 188
socialization 49, 190, 194, 196
socialization system (SOCS) 194–196, 223
"Soleil pourri" (1929, poem) 232–233

Sophocles 66–68, 228; *Oedipus Rex* (ca. 425 B.C.) 66
Spall, Timothy 32
*Speak* (2004) 5, 175–179, 181, 185, 186, 187–190, 194–196, 223, 236
Spielrein, Sabina 204
*Splendor in the Grass* (1961) 86
Sprenger, James 64
stage (theater, schema) 3, 10, 16, 40, 68, 93, 106, 165–166, 170–172, 182, 192–194, 199, 205, 224, 233, 235, 237; setting 104, 139, 191–192, 219
status system (STATS) 16, 194–196; dominance hierarchy 188–189
Stein, Herbert H. 158–162, 164, 166, 254n6
Stekel, Wilhelm 204
Stevens, Dana 99
Stevens, Nettie 109
Stevenson, Robert Louis 204; *The Strange Case of Dr. Jekyll and Mr. Hyde* (1866) 204
Stewart, Kristen 73, 75, 175, 176
Stickgold, Robert 142
Stoker, Bram 74; *Dracula* (1897) 74
storytelling 10, 12, 18, 95, 179, 220; storytelling animal 8, 198; and storyworlds 10, 54, 79, 100, 211, 237
*The Storytelling Animal* (2012) 8
*The Strange Case of Dr. Jekyll and Mr. Hyde* (1866) 204
stress 9, 17, 95–96, 101–102, 131, 140–141, 146, 149, 201, 205, 223, 224
Structuralist-Romantic Order 3–6, 14–17, 20–23, 26, 28, 32, 46–47, 69–72, 77, 81, 88, 93, 117, 124, 203–205, 219, 221, 225, 230, 232–233, 237, 242n12, 257–258n8
*Studien über Hysterie* (1895, with Breuer) 36
Sundance Film Institute 149
*Superstar* (1988) 87
Svevo, Italo (Ettore Schmitz) 162
Swain, Chelse 208
Sweeney, D.B. 177
"The Sword and the Lightbulb" (2001), also published as *Das Schwert und die Glühbirne* (1999) 230–233
Sybersma, Paul 209
Symbolism (art movement) 22, 203

*Tales from the Freudian Crypt* (2000) 24
Tan, Ed 27; *Emotion and the Structure of Narrative Film* (1996) 27
Taylor, Gary 181
Taylor, Shelley 170
testosterone 109–110, 189

Thagard, Paul 168
*Theorising Desire* (2008) 87
Theory of Grounded Cognition 188
Theory of the World 221, 259n31
Thieriot, Max 122
thinking 2, 6, 8, 13, 15, 19, 22, 27, 28, 78, 93, 140, 145, 149, 166–167, 181, 185, 188, 218, 222, 228, 237
Thompson, Jim 8
thought 5, 8, 50, 78, 142, 146, 150, 163–164, 167, 169, 181–183, 185–186, 218–221, 223; social 185, 220–221, 223; suppression 150
*Three Essays on the Theory of Sexuality* (1905) 47
*Totem and Taboo* (1912–13) 68–69, 190
Trachtenberg, Michelle 127
transsexual 112–113
trauma (psychological) 9, 141, 143–146, 149–150, 223, 228
trope 3, 8, 12, 28, 48, 50, 108, 233; childhood trauma 9, 28, 34, 48, 50, 51, 130–133, 143, 152, 199, 214; *see also* Freudian Excuse
Truffaut, François 202
Turner, Kathleen 208
Turner, Mark 181
*Twilight* (2008) 73, 75, 76, 236
*The Twilight Saga: New Moon* (2009) 4, 73–76

uncanny *see* psychoanalysis
*Undoing Gender* (2004) 111, 113
"Das Unheimliche" (1919, "The Uncanny") 202
Urrejola, Isidora 165

vampire 73–79, 98, 236
van der Hart, Onno 144
van der Kolk, Bessel 144, 145
*Vice Versa* (1995) 109
*The Virgin Suicides* (1993) 206, 216
*The Virgin Suicides* (1999) 5, 96, 205–223, 224, 236
Vognar, Chris 34
Volkan, Vamik 144

warrior (culture) 58–60, 62, 72, 180, 232
Webster, George 126
Webster, Richard 24–26, 27, 39, 71, 239, 242n19; *Why Freud Was Wrong* (1996) 24, 71
*De Weense kwakzalver* (1999; *The Viennese Quack*) 24
Wegner, Daniel 146

Weismantel, Mary  25, 250*n*8, 252*n*7, 255*n*3; *Cholas and Pishtacos* (2001) 25
Weitz, Chris  4, 75
werewolves  4, 73–76, 79, 140
*Why Freud Was Wrong* (1996)  24, 71
*Why We Read Fiction* (2006)  14
Wilkinson, Tom  151
Wilson, Edmund Beecher  109
Wilson, Erin C.  121
Winslet, Kate  151, 153
Winterbottom, Michael  8
witchcraft  4, 56–59, 62–65, 71, 74
Witches' Sabbath  57, 62, 63, 139
*Wolf* (1994)  74
*The Wolf Man* (film, 1941)  74
*Women, Fire, and Dangerous Things* (1987)  182

Wood, Elijah  156
Wood, Natalie  86
Woods, James  208
World War I  28, 29, 36, 115, 130, 203, 204, 233
World War II  25, 33, 144, 227, 231
worldview *see* cosmology

*XXY* (2007)  5, 103, 105–107, 116, 124, 188, 236

Zacharek, Stephanie  127, 132, 211, 216
Zahn, Steve  175
Zunshine, Lisa  14; *Why We Read Fiction* (2006) 14

www.ingramcontent.com/pod-product-compliance
Lightning Source LLC
Chambersburg PA
CBHW051210300426
44116CB00006B/511